MONT

Persian Letters

MONTESQUIEU

Persian Letters

With Related Texts

Translated, with Introduction and Notes, by
Raymond N. MacKenzie

Hackett Publishing Company, Inc.
Indianapolis/Cambridge

Printed in the United States of America

17 16 15 14 1 2 3 4 5 6 7

For further information, please address
Hackett Publishing Company, Inc.
P.O. Box 44937
Indianapolis, Indiana 46244-0937

www.hackettpublishing.com

Interior and cover design by Elizabeth L. Wilson
Composition by Aptara, Inc.

Library of Congress Cataloging-in-Publication Data

Montesquieu, Charles de Secondat, baron de, 1689–1755.
[Lettres persanes. English]
The Persian Letters, with related texts / Montesquieu ; translated, with introduction and notes, by Raymond N. MacKenzie.
pages cm
Includes bibliographical references.
ISBN 978-1-62466-180-8 (pbk.) — ISBN 978-1-62466-181-5 (cloth)
I. MacKenzie, Raymond N., editor of compilation. II. Title.
PQ2011.L5E57 2014
843'.5—dc23 2014006398

The paper used in this publication meets the minimum requirements of American National Standard for Information Sciences—Permanence of Paper for Printed Library Materials, ANSI Z39.48–1984.

∞

CONTENTS

INTRODUCTION

The period we call the Enlightenment in Europe—roughly spanning the eighteenth century—constituted a vast, wide-ranging reversal of much that had been assumed, believed, and taught for many centuries. By the end of the century, ideas that had been radical, even heretical before became commonplace, and most of those ideas remain fundamental to our worldview today. For example, by the end of the century it was no longer necessary to argue that our universe is rationally ordered and fundamentally understandable, that there is a knowable structure and pattern to the universe. European intellectuals largely turned their back on many Christian dogmas, such as the doctrine of original sin and the fundamental weakness of human reason and virtue. Instead, by the end of the period, most saw human history in terms of progress and continual improvement, the story of gradual progress toward a better understanding of all things. There was every reason to believe this progress would continue as human reason and science become ever more improved: the more we know, the better our lives and societies will be. Toward the end of the century, Immanuel Kant articulated the rallying cry, declaring that the motto of Enlightenment is "*sapere aude*," dare to know: "have courage," Kant urged, "to make use of your own understanding!"[1]

Knowledge, in this sense of the word, required daring, courage to resist the many threats against free inquiry, and Montesquieu's *Persian Letters* (1721) was one of the most daring, even scandalous, of its day.[2] The book both reflected and gave new impetus to many of the themes, ideas, and attitudes that came to characterize the Enlightenment. That great movement in eighteenth-century Europe, like Montesquieu's book, prided itself on its questioning spirit, its refusal to accept the conventional, received wisdom on virtually any topic, from modes of governing to religious toleration. Montesquieu's *Persian Letters* not only recognizes

1. Immanuel Kant, "An Answer to the Question, 'What is Enlightenment?'" [1784], in Mary J. Gregor, trans. and ed., *Immanuel Kant: Practical Philosophy* (Cambridge U Press, 1996), p. 17. The Latin phrase, *sapere aude*, comes from Horace's *Epodes* (1.2, 40).

2. And it would remain scandalous long after too, eventually being put on the Church's Index of Forbidden Books.

but welcomes new and multiple perspectives, and is very comfortable in suggesting that some of our long-revered "truths" are really only culturally specific conventions, and, even more importantly, that some of those conventions actually work to conceal the truths we seek, actually blind us to what is right in front of us. Contemporary readers must have found the experience thrilling, as the book sold wildly, and imitators sprang up almost at once. It would be an exaggeration to say that any one book inaugurated the Enlightenment, but the *Persian Letters* can certainly be said to have captured the spirit of the era, and to have given it a shape and a direction that later writers and thinkers would pursue throughout the century. The book set the agenda for a century of thinking and reading and arguing, a period that would issue in two great revolutions, each in their different ways trying to put the growing belief in human perfectibility—or at least human improvement—into the concrete form of new kinds of states with new modes of governing. And Montesquieu's work—his later *The Spirit of the Laws* (1748) especially, but also the early, rougher, more satiric *Persian Letters*—would make very significant contributions to the new political thought.

Charles-Louis de Secondat, Baron de la Brède and de Montesquieu was born in the family's chateau outside Bordeaux on January 18, 1689.[3] His family was aristocratic on both his mother's and father's sides, and Charles-Louis was born in the family's La Brède chateau, a moated, fourteenth-century gothic castle that is a tourist site today. But his father wanted his son to remember that the poor were his brothers, so he arranged for a local beggar to be the boy's godfather; that responsible attitude toward class distinction would help form the personality of the boy, as well as his independent, adult outlook on life.

In 1700, he was sent to the Collège of the Oratorians in Juilly, near Paris, one of the premier schools in the country (still operating today, and still run by the Oratorians). The Oratorians, unlike the Jesuits in many ways, ran a progressive, relatively liberal-minded school, though one still steeped in the study of Latin; but boys at Juilly also studied history, mathematics, and music—a far wider range of subjects than was typical of the era's schools.[4] The most famous Oratorian

3. The best biography of Montesquieu in English remains Robert Shackleton's *Montesquieu: A Critical Biography* (Oxford U Press, 1961). A briefer treatment is in Peter V. Conroy, *Montesquieu Revisited* (NY: Twayne, 1992).

4. The Oratorians had previously been humbled for their progressivism in 1678; they were forced to abjure their "errors" in teaching the new philosophy of Descartes.

was the philosopher Nicolas Malebranche (1638–1715), for whom Montesquieu retained a fondness even after he had moved beyond Malebranche's Descartes-inspired views.[5] Montesquieu—or, as he would still have been known during his school days, Secondat, the son of the Baron de la Brède—received an education that helped shape his wide range of interests and his many intellectual strengths. And considering that the works of the great Malebranche were banned in France (for their Cartesian materialism), his education also taught him one supremely practical lesson: that the establishment's decrees and the Church's condemnations need not be accepted uncritically.

He came back home and studied law in Bordeaux from 1705 to 1708, and then did further study in Paris until 1713. A mentor during his early years in Paris was an Oratorian priest, Pierre-Nicolas Desmolets, a learned man who introduced Montesquieu to new circles and to new ways of thinking, and who encouraged a scholarly tendency in the young man. But upon the sudden death of his father in 1713, Montesquieu returned to Bordeaux, inheriting the title of Baron de la Brède as well as the family estates. It was an appropriate time to begin thinking of settling down, and he soon married Jeanne de Lartigue. Relatively little is known about her, except that she was from a recently ennobled family and was a Protestant, and remained so until her death; marriages between Catholics and Protestants were not exactly rare, but this one does suggest a certain broadmindedness in both parties—or, perhaps, a relative indifference to the stricter demands of religion.[6] Soon after the marriage, in 1716, his uncle died, and he now inherited the title of Baron de Montesquieu—the name he had already begun to call himself. The additional inheritance was considerable, but perhaps the most significant inheritance lay in the young man taking over his uncle's role as *président à mortier* for the Bordeaux *parlement*.

The dozen or so *parlements* in early eighteenth-century France were regional bodies that had been designed for a certain degree of self-

---

See Henry Philips, *Church and Culture in Seventeenth-Century France* (Cambridge U Press, 1997). As for the Jesuits, Montesquieu, like many progressives, looked upon their conservatism with suspicion: in one of his notebooks, he wrote, "One thing I cannot reconcile with the enlightenment of this age is the Jesuits' authority" (*My Thoughts*, trans. Henry C. Clark [Indianapolis: Liberty Fund, 2012], p. 217).

5. Descartes' tendency (which Malebranche continued) to refer to the body as the "machine"—as opposed to the mind or spirit—comes up a number of times in the *Persian Letters*, sometimes satirically (see, for example, Letter 145).

6. Montesquieu's great-grandfather, Jacob de Secondat, was in fact a Protestant, though his children converted to Catholicism.

governance, though their powers had been increasingly restricted under the absolutist monarch, Louis XIV. For instance, they originally had the power to object to a decree of the King, but after 1673, they were required to first validate the decree and only then issue an objection—effectively rendering their objections impotent. In this respect the French *parlements* were very different from the English Parliament, which came to be seen, for Montesquieu and many other French thinkers in the era, as the very model of an enlightened political structure. The French *parlements* had judicial work, not legislative, for their primary business; they often chafed at this, and acted as if they were something closer to the English institution. Montesquieu's inherited office of *président à mortier* (the name derives from the mortar-board style of hat that was worn) would give him first-hand experience with judicial business—in fact he served as judge for criminal cases—but working with the *parlement* also gave him experience with a political structure in urgent need of reform. And the death of Louis XIV in 1715 gave him, and many others throughout France, hope that such reforms could finally come.

The year 1716 saw Montesquieu elected to the Académie of Bordeaux.[7] If the office in the Bordeaux *parlement* introduced him to political and administrative realities, the Académie gave him formal entry into the intellectual life of the city. This Académie was a recently formed formal group dedicated to scientific, scholarly, and intellectual pursuits—and the very fact that such groups were forming in provincial cities suggests a great deal about the atmosphere of early eighteenth-century France, and the widespread excitement that was in the air about new ideas and new discoveries. There were over thirty such academies by mid-century, guaranteeing that scientific and cultural advances would be disseminated and discussed throughout France, not just in the capital. Montesquieu was immediately active in the Académie, contributing a paper on religion in ancient Rome in his first year, and being selected to act as the group's director the following year. Most papers discussed were scientific ones, and Montesquieu took a strong interest in them; like many enthusiasts of his era, he owned microscopes and conducted experiments, keeping careful records of all his investigations. While he could only qualify as an amateur in science, the experience no doubt strengthened a tendency within him for empirical research and for what we might call a more scientific approach to human society and psychology, an approach

7. The Académie Nationale des Sciences, Belles-Lettres et Arts de Bordeaux was founded in 1712 and continues to thrive today.

based on observation and questioning rather than simply mastering what the authorities had said.

During this period of his life, as he came into his own as a titled landowner, a husband, and an active, involved citizen and legislator, he began work on his first major literary effort, the project that would eventually be the *Persian Letters*. He brought the finished manuscript to Paris in 1721 and showed it to his old friend Desmolets, who excitedly proclaimed that the book would sell like hotcakes.[8] And it did, spawning imitations almost immediately and continuing to do so throughout the century. Before the book's publication, few would have predicted such a work from this particular young man, who would have been seen as solid, responsible, and more than a little scholarly—but not at all the type likely to produce a major, culturally important book like this one. Where did the book come from?

There had already been a number of works in which fictitious foreign travelers commented on what they saw in letters, so Montesquieu did not originate the idea; he had a number of previous models before him. But these previous works are rarely read today for, as one scholar of his sources put it, Montesquieu took up these earlier books "as a ready tool, but, with superior talent, he knew how to intensify them in suggestive expression, and how to deepen them out in thought."[9] One of the most important of these was Marana's *Letters of a Turkish Spy* (1684),[10] which employed a fictional Arab named Mahmut who wrote back home describing what he saw in France, an amalgamation of political satire, society gossip, and interpolated tales of varying lengths. It has the merits of wit and pace, but does not venture into much intellectual depth. The book was reprinted a number of times, and Shackleton points out (p. 32) that Montesquieu owned a copy of the 1717 edition—and 1717 was the year Montesquieu probably began work on his *Persian Letters*; so the influence of Marana is quite direct. But while Marana and his imitators provided a fictional

8. Desmolets is reported to have said, "*çela sera vendu comme du pain*"—this will sell like bread. Quoted in Shackleton, *Montesquieu*, p. 27.

9. G. L. Van Roosbroeck, *Persian Letters before Montesquieu* [1936], rpt. NY: Burt Franklin, 1972, p. 84. This study remains a good, brief overview of the various books that can claim to anticipate Montesquieu's *Persian Letters*.

10. Giovanni Paola Marana (1642–1693) was a political exile from Genoa who came to reside in Paris. The original Italian title of his book was *L'Esploratore turco*. It was almost immediately translated into English and French, and was often reprinted in the eighteenth century. In England, Daniel Defoe published a "continuation" of the *Turkish Spy* in 1718.

outsider's view of French politics and society, they did not provide much in the way of description or insight concerning Turkey or any of the "oriental" societies.

For those insights, Montesquieu turned to the accounts of travelers who had visited those places, and among those, two in particular were most important to him: the first was Jean Chardin's ten-volume *Travels* (1711),[11] and the second was Jean-Baptiste Tavernier's *Six Voyages* (1676).[12] Montesquieu consulted many other sources, but Chardin and Tavernier gave him the greater part of the details he used in *Persian Letters*. Other important sources for him included the 1647 translation of the Koran into French by André Du Ryer, which was the basis for much of Montesquieu's understanding of Islam—and indeed, it functioned in just that way for much of Western Europe.[13] A more indirect source—perhaps less a source and more an indirect inspiration—was the 1704 publication of Antoine Galland's *Arabian Nights*.[14] These tales created an eroticized, sensual "orient" of sultans and harems, genies and magic, and something of that stream of images and atmospheres found its way into Montesquieu's book as well.

Two events outside of books had an impact on him too. The first was his meeting a Chinese traveler in France. One of his Juilly schoolmates, Nicolas Fréret, introduced him to Arcadio Huang, a Chinese convert to Christianity who was working on a Chinese-French dictionary for

11. Jean Chardin (1643–1713) spent a number of years traveling in Persia and India. When he returned home, he found a France hostile to his Protestant roots, and so he moved to England, where he was celebrated and even knighted by Charles II. He ended his life there, as Sir John Chardin.

12. Jean-Baptiste Tavernier (1605–1689) was a renowned explorer and jewel merchant, selling what is known as the Great Blue Diamond (which Tavernier probably acquired in India) to King Louis XIV for an enormous sum. Louis took a great interest in him, urging him to publish an account of his travels; his book remains an important resource for scholars today. He was famous in his lifetime, and he continued to travel, dying ultimately in Moscow.

13. On the European impact of Du Ryer, see Alastair Hamilton and Francis Richard, *André Du Ryer and Oriental Studies in Seventeenth-Century France* (Oxford U Press, 2004).

14. Galland's translation, titled *Les mille et une nuits*, came out in a twelve-volume series between 1704 and 1717. Scholars have long been skeptical about the origins of a number of the key stories—whether they were translations at all or entirely fabricated by Galland. A good collection of essays on the topic is Sari Makdisi and Felicity Nussbaum, eds., *The "Arabian Nights" in Historical Context: Between East and West* (Oxford U Press, 2008).

Louis XIV.[15] This meeting must have given him the idea of trying to see how France would look through the eyes of a foreigner. And another influence was the 1715 visit of a Persian ambassador to Paris. Mohammed Reza Beg had with him a lavish entourage, and this together with his exotic clothing and manners made him a fascinating topic to the French of the era—so much so that at least one novel was quickly written to capitalize on the gossip about him.[16] So Montesquieu's reading as well as his life experiences all contributed to the literary project he began at the family chateau of La Brède sometime around 1717.

The book that was ultimately called *Persian Letters*, then, was not created *ex nihilo*, but was, like so many literary masterpieces, a combining, shaping, and arranging of existing forms and themes into a new whole. But what kind of whole was it? The early eighteenth century, especially in France, was a highly genre-conscious age; the rigorous rules of neoclassicism, with their insistence on genre purity, were not to be fully relaxed for another century. But precisely because the age was so genre-conscious, writers could and did create playful mixes of styles and types, and could expect their audience to see and appreciate the wit in doing so. Nicolas Boileau-Despréaux's mock-heroic poem *Le Lutrin* (1674–1683), for example, derived much of its comedy from the mismatch in lofty style and mundane subject matter; and the English poet Alexander Pope's *Rape of the Lock* (1712) had an enormous success with the same approach. Far down the hierarchy of literary merit was the new vogue for realistic prose fiction, which eventually settled into what we still call—though it is hardly new anymore—the novel.

Looking back on the *Persian Letters* three decades later, Montesquieu makes it sound as though writing a novel was not what he had had in mind, but that seeing the book that way is as good an approach as any:

> Nothing has given readers more pleasure in the *Persian Letters* than to have found—without expecting it—a kind of novel in them. One can see a beginning, a middle, and an end; the various characters are linked by a chain. The longer they stay in Europe, the customs of this part of the world come to seem less marvelous and less bizarre to them; and they are either more or less struck by the bizarre and the marvelous according to the differences in their personalities.

---

15. Huang's story is told by Jonathan Spence, *The Question of Hu* (NY: Knopf, 1988), and his importance is discussed by Linda Barnes in *Needles, Herbs, Gods, and Ghosts: China, Healing, and the West to 1848* (Harvard U Press, 2005).

16. The novel was titled *Amanzolide* (1716), written by M. d'Hostelfort, and quickly translated into English and German.

> Meanwhile, disorder continues to grow in the Asiatic seraglio, in proportion to the length of Usbek's absence—that is, as the fury increases, the love decreases.

The passage makes it sound as if the letters forming a "kind of novel" was as much a surprise to him as it was to readers, and perhaps it was. But rather than insisting on the novel category, it may be best to say that *Persian Letters* has novelistic *qualities*, and that these have an important role to play in the book, but that something other than the novelistic—something other than a tightly constructed plot, and characterization, and setting—is what powers the book. The power of the book is in its ideas, in its intellectual content, and in the sheer diversity of topics that it addresses, far too many for anything like a conventional novel to be able to contain: finance, religion, statecraft, the role of women, the origins of societies, even population history . . . Perhaps a good categorization for *Persian Letters* is what Northrop Frye called the "anatomy," a compendious work whose aim is "dissection or analysis"[17]—and in this sense, Montesquieu's novel might be viewed as a sort of anatomy of Regency France. The plot concerning Usbek and his harem provides not so much a linking "chain" as Montesquieu put it, but rather is one of numerous threads that hold together all these topics, all these reflections and all these modes from the comic and satiric to the tragic.

A little later in the 1754 "Reflections," he notes that the novel form—fluid as that form still was in the early eighteenth century—cannot contain much digression, but a collection of letters by definition ought to be varied in its topics and tones. However, in the original "Introduction" for the 1721 edition, Montesquieu—who published the book anonymously in Amsterdam, thus avoiding any issues with French censorship—presents himself as merely an editor, not the author of the letters, and goes to some lengths to convince us that the book is not fictional at all:

> The Persians who wrote these letters lodged with me; we spent our time together. They saw me as belonging to another world, and as a result they hid nothing from me. Indeed, men who are transplanted from so very far away could no longer have any secrets. They showed me most of their letters, and I copied them. I even intercepted some of the ones that they tried to keep hidden from me, because they were so mortifying to Persian vanity and jealousy.
>
> I have therefore only played the role of translator; all my efforts have been spent adapting the work to our tastes.

17. Northrop Frye, *Anatomy of Criticism* (Princeton U Press, 1957; rpt. 1973), p. 311.

Such pretenses, the author claiming to be an editor or translator, were quite common with early novels, and it is difficult to say how seriously the ordinary reader would have taken these earnest assurances. Montesquieu's friend, the priest Pierre-Nicolas Desmolets, wrote about this issue in a memoir, arguing that novel readers are able to "both recognize and ignore narrative conventions."[18] Desmolets—like Montesquieu, and like most novel readers even today—expected the novel to contain a mix of fact ("*histoire*," he called it) and fiction. And he gave readers credit for being able to discriminate between the two.

However, Montesquieu was like the majority of writers and critics of his era in believing firmly in the moral effect of literature, and likewise of its potential to do moral harm. He articulated this fear in his notebooks:

> Reading novels is dangerous, no doubt. What isn't? Would that one had only to reform the bad effects of reading novels! But to command an always sensitive being not to have sensations; to want to ban the passions without even allowing them to be rectified; to propose perfection to an age that is worse every day; to revolt against mere weakness in the midst of so much wickedness—I am really afraid that such a lofty morality may become merely speculative, and that in showing us from such a distance what we ought to be, it will leave us as we are.[19]

The passage is interesting for the assumptions it makes about novels. First, they seem to arouse our passions, though they are also capable of "rectifying" them. And second, these novels seem to provide us a view of life the way it really is, not the way it ideally ought to be. And third, this realism seems to be the path toward real moral teaching and learning. In *Persian Letters*, Rica goes to a library where he hears about many recent literary productions, and the novel that is *not* realistic—the kind of prose fiction we call the romance—is derided. Such books "wreak havoc on both the language of reason and that of the heart. They spend their time seeking out nature, but miss it every time" (Letter 137). The word "nature" in the period refers not to the external world but to the way things are, the essence of things, the truth about things; to "seek nature" is to try to depict things in such a way as to get at their essential

18. Thomas DiPiero, *Dangerous Truths and Criminal Passions: The Evolution of the French Novel, 1569–1791* (Stanford U Press, 1992), p. 259. Desmolets made his points about novels and readers in his *Continuation des Mémoires de littérature et d'histoire* (1728).

19. Montesquieu, *My Thoughts*, pp. 413–14.

truth. And a book only manages to achieve the goal of "nature" by hewing to realistic language and an adherence to reason.

Whether one believed that Usbek and Rica and the others were real or not, the key attraction the book offered was a chance for French readers to see themselves from an entirely new point of view. This had been done before, as we saw above, but never with such wit and such insight, and never accompanied by such a probing intellect. Seeing ourselves from an outsider's perspective, or at least from some new, unexpected and unconventional perspective, became a hallmark of enlightenment literature, though the keynote had been struck in the late sixteenth century by Montaigne. In a widely read and quoted essay, "Of Cannibals," he compares Native Americans' mores and ethics to those of Europeans, concluding that the Europeans may call them barbarians, but "we surpass them in every kind of barbarity."[20] Montaigne's essay is an early version of the perspectival shift, but it was left to Montesquieu to fully explore the possibilities of this method. The great English masterpiece in the genre is Swift's 1726 satire, *Gulliver's Travels* (though whether Swift had been influenced by Montesquieu's work is not clear).[21] This delight in the play of perspectives is typical of an age that was anxious to progress, to move beyond accepted beliefs and attitudes, an age that was impatient to denounce the fervent beliefs of the past as mere superstition, and to substitute empirical research and testing for the word of long-revered authorities. Shifting perspectives can of course make for comedy—when, for instance, a foreign visitor fails to understand the use of some common European household object, or fails to appreciate the depth of some idea. In cases like these, the perspective makes the outsider into the butt of the joke. But the method has subtler and more powerful possibilities, as Montesquieu was to show. When the foreign observer, apparently innocently, mentions some critical religious dogma, the comedy is suddenly more disturbing. In this passage, Rica (Letter 24) moves from discussing the all-powerful French king to the Pope, saying:

---

20. Michel de Montaigne, "Of Cannibals," in *The Complete Essays of Montaigne*, trans. Donald M. Frame (Stanford U Press, 1958), p. 156. Montaigne's interest in the subject had been piqued by meeting three visiting Native Americans in Rouen in 1562—as Montesquieu's was by meeting the Chinese Huang.

21. For an extended discussion of the two works and the interplay between them, see Frederick M. Keener, *The Chain of Becoming: The Philosophical Tale, the Novel, and a Neglected Realism of the Enlightenment: Swift, Montesquieu, Voltaire, Johnson, and Austen* (NY: Columbia U Press, 1983), especially pp. 127–93.

> there is another magician even more powerful . . . , one who has just as much power over the king's mind as the king does over those of his subjects. This magician is called the Pope: he can make people believe that three are but one, that the bread one eats is not bread, and that the wine one drinks is not wine, and a thousand other things of that nature.

These casual references that fail to appreciate the doctrine of the Trinity and the Catholic belief in transubstantiation might make the reader smile at Rica's naiveté, but that smile quickly turns into the suspicion that perhaps there is more than one way of looking at such things. Montesquieu's use of the Persian observer lets him indirectly suggest things that few would have dared put into print in a more direct manner.

A related and important aspect of Montesquieu's method is a broader kind of destabilizing. A shifting perspective makes what had been entirely "natural" and hence beyond questioning—for instance, the French model of kingship—suddenly appear narrow, the product of a limited point of view. And if that model of kingship, for example, suddenly seems to align quite closely with a vaguely understood model of oriental despotism—the conclusions are there to be drawn. In a recent study on the subject, Sylvie Romanowski argues that the foreign observers in Enlightenment literature function not just to destabilize—not just to disturb and disrupt our sense of what we believe and value—but ultimately to help us find what really is "natural," what the universal laws of human nature really are.[22] Her point is that Montesquieu's critique is more reformist than radical; many of the things we call truths may turn out to be relative—that is, relative to a culture, true for a Persian but not for a Parisian—but even after allowing for such surprises, there are, ultimately, real truths, and humankind can presumably gain access to them. The way to those truths, though, is no longer through faith in authority, but through empirical, rational, questioning method. The *Persian Letters* involve the reader in a manner that exemplifies the method: the reader copes with multiple and sometimes disorienting perspectives, and the result is a fresh outlook, and a new skepticism regarding one's own inherited point of view.

The book is, naturally, deeply embedded in its historical moment, and the modern reader needs to become familiar with certain aspects of early eighteenth-century France in order to appreciate fully what Montesquieu is doing. The footnotes in the present translation are meant to help in this regard, but two issues need more extensive explanation at

22. Sylvie Romanowski, *Through Strangers' Eyes: Fictional Foreigners in Old Regime France* (West Lafayette, IN: Purdue U Press, 2005).

this point: the religious situation in the period, and the recent economic upheavals that France had undergone.

France was of course a Catholic country, but that should not imply that the population was perfectly unified in their faith. To begin with, there were Protestants in the country—such as Montesquieu's wife—despite the greatest of efforts to drive them out. The relationship between Catholic and Protestant in France was a fraught one, as it remained in most European countries. Louis XIV had gone on a quest for a religious unity, one to be achieved by force if necessary. In 1685 he had revoked the Edict of Nantes, which had for nearly a century more or less guaranteed French Protestants, or Huguenots as they were known, a considerable degree of freedom and considerable civil rights. The Edict, originally promulgated by Henri IV in 1598, was now rendered null, and Huguenots, under threat of losing their homes, their possessions, and perhaps even their lives, fled the country by the hundreds of thousands, the refugees spilling into England, the Netherlands, and even America. Montesquieu has his character Usbek comment, implicitly but quite clearly, on this French disaster by comparing it to a misguided Persian initiative to expel the Armenians. That plan was abandoned before it could be put into practice, and Rica notes that "Expelling the Armenians would have meant the immediate loss of all the business men and almost all the skilled workers in the kingdom" (Letter 85). He concludes that perhaps having more than one religion might actually benefit a state, for "all religions teach precepts that are useful to society." This spirit of not only tolerating but welcoming religious diversity would not have found favor in the France of Louis XIV.

Upon the death of Louis (September 1, 1715), the heir to the throne was a boy of five, so rule passed to a regent, a caretaker until the boy came of age, and that was to be his uncle, Philippe, Duc d'Orléans. The dying king had sought to limit the regent's power in his will, but Orléans convoked the *parlement* of Paris—that little-used, rarely consulted body—and traded them greater powers in return for overturning certain provisions of the king's will, and the *parlement* lost no time in agreeing. The new Regent made it clear that he intended greater toleration for Protestants, one of the first instances of a general thaw that the country would experience now that the Sun King, the great symbol of royal absolutism, had passed away. Some of course stood to lose by such changes, and some feared that Orléans himself was a man of questionable character and morals. But whatever he had been in the past, he quickly showed that he intended to take his new role with perfect seriousness, and the atmosphere of the Regency period (1715–1723) was buoyant and optimistic.[23] This is the period and the atmosphere in which the *Persian Letters* was written, and the period in which Usbek and Rica are in France. It is hard to imagine Montesquieu having written it under the reign of Louis XIV, especially during the last decade or two of his life, when the national atmosphere was somber, even dour, reflecting the obsessions of the aging monarch.

But if French Protestants could begin to feel some relief with the Regency, there remained a serious controversy within French Catholicism involving Jansenism, another contemporary issue that crops up repeatedly in the *Persian Letters*. Jansenism takes its name from the Dutch theologian, Cornelius Jansen (1585–1638); Jansen's interpretation of the key ideas in St. Augustine's writings on grace and free will found a number of enthusiastic adherents in France, and by the middle of the seventeenth century they constituted something of a movement within Catholicism. Jansenism was introduced into France by Jean du Vergier de Hauranne, Abbé of Saint-Cyran (1581–1643), a monk who had been friends with Cornelius Jansen. Hauranne was director of the convent of Port-Royal, which had two locations: Port-Royal des Champs was in the countryside southwest of Paris, and a new branch had opened in 1625 in Paris itself. The name Port-Royal became synonymous with Jansenism, for it was the base for Jansenist thinking, scholarship, and writing; schools sprung up, especially around Port-Royal des Champs, offering an excellent education: the great poet and playwright Jean Racine, for example, was a student at Port-Royal. And its most brilliant champion was Blaise Pascal. Some of the century's finest minds were formed by Jansenism.

The Jansenist movement was not simply an educational or scholarly one though. Jansen, and one of his major French exponents, Pasquier Quesnel (1634–1719), emphasized the radical corruption of the human person since the Fall, to the point where the person is powerless to do anything to effect his salvation; moreover, God has predestined all of

23. Orléans was, like Montesquieu, something of a polymath, interested in nearly every subject, from chemistry to literature. There are a number of biographies available in English, one of the best being Christine Pevitt, *Philippe, Duc D'Orléans: Regent of France* (NY: Atlantic Monthly Press, 1997). One of many surprising traits in Orléans' character is the fact that he enjoyed drawing and produced a superb set of twenty-eight illustrations for a translation of Longus' pastoral poem, *Daphnis and Chloe* in 1718. The significance of the poem for the era is traced by James Munro, "*Daphnis and Chloe* in the Eighteenth Century," in Keith Aspley, ed., *Myth and Legend in French Literature: Essays in Honor of A. J. Steele* (NY: Legenda, 1982), pp. 117–36.

us either to salvation or to perdition, and nothing we do in this life can alter our fate. Such a position might disturb some contemporaries as smacking of Calvinism, as indeed it does—but it is a set of doctrines that derive from St. Augustine, one of the very greatest of all Catholic theologians. The Jansenists in no way saw themselves as a sect, and in no way wanted to break away from the Church; they saw themselves as faithful Catholics—perhaps even the most faithful to the Church's longstanding vision of the human person, grace, and the will.[24]

The dominant priestly order in France was the Jesuits, and they were greatly disturbed by what they saw in Jansenism; they called upon the King and even the Pope to put down what they saw as heresy. They also, no doubt, were motivated by some professional anxiety, for they were the primary educators in the country, and their spirituality was the dominant one. At their urging, Pope Innocent X officially condemned a set of five key theses of Jansen's in 1653, but this did not end the Jansenist movement. Strife between Jesuits and Jansenists continued to simmer, and eventually the king, Louis XIV, asked the next Pope, Clement, to issue a definitive condemnation of Jansenist beliefs as heresies. Louis was driven to unify his nation under one religion, a drive that resulted, as we have seen, in the disastrous revocation of the Edict of Nantes, and his campaign against the Jansenists arguably was equally ill advised; he had already ordered Port-Royal to be burned to the ground, and now he wanted a definitive Papal document to close the matter once and for all. The result was the Pope's "constitution" titled *Unigenitus*,[25] issued in September 1713. *Unigenitus* condemned 101 propositions from Quesnel's writings (which were all associated with Jansen and Jansenism). This should have been the end of the matter, but in fact the Jansenists had attracted a great deal of sympathy, and in the new atmosphere of the Regency, following the death of Louis, that sympathy could be even more openly expressed. The Regent—whose daughter was a Jansenist—made it plain immediately that he would be more tolerant. But the

24. The best modern treatment of the issues involved in Jansenist theology is Leszek Kolakowski, *God Owes Us Nothing: A Brief Remark on Pascal's Religion and on the Spirit of Jansenism* (U of Chicago Press, 1995). Kolakowski argues that Church teachings were in fact in accord with these Augustinian beliefs until the seventeenth century, when a set of internal and external factors began to move it in the direction of a theology based more directly on the idea of justice and less on the inscrutable ways of God.

25. An "apostolic constitution" is the highest level of Papal decree, and as such the most binding. The second highest is the encyclical. The title comes from the document's opening sentence, "Unigenitus Dei Filius," the only begotten Son of God.

controversy had reached such a fever pitch that he imposed a moratorium in 1717 on all publications regarding *Unigenitus*, thus trying to tone down the war that was being waged in the press, and forbade further discussion on the matter.

One could sympathize with the Jansenists for reasons having nothing to do with theology. The Papal decree struck many as unwarranted meddling in the internal affairs of France—even though that decree had been sought by the King himself. Thus, by a strange logic, Jansenism could be equated with patriotism, and with an endorsement of the longstanding "Gallic liberties," the tradition holding that Rome's authority over French Catholicism was contingent upon French consent. Moreover, since the Papal decree was associated with Louis XIV, one could feel some common cause with the Jansenists on anti-absolutist grounds: *Unigenitus* could be seen as tyrannical on Rome's part or on Louis' part, or both. The Jansenists were increasingly seen as republicans, even insurrectionists, and in the new Regency atmosphere such an alignment was a positive. Thus, the *parlements*, which were charged with officially ratifying *Unigenitus*, often refused to do so. In Bordeaux, the *parlement* under Montesquieu's uncle refused to ratify one of the principal clauses in the document. As Robert Shackleton points out, for a short period of time "there was a real possibility of an alliance between the Jansenists . . . and the nascent movement of the *philosophes*."[26] He goes on to note that such an alliance could not have endured, as the *philosophes* were at best skeptical about religion if not outright scornful of it. But for a time, the Jansenists were not at all a party of fanatics, as the Jesuits and their other enemies had always depicted them—and they are presented quite sympathetically in the *Persian Letters*.

A second topic that comes up repeatedly in Montesquieu's novel involves the economy and some recent attempts to invigorate it. By the death of Louis XIV, the country's economy was in dire shape. Taxes were high and getting higher, and the country was deeply in debt. The recent exodus of Protestants—many of whom were skilled professionals who contributed a great deal to the economy—had hurt as well. The wars Louis had waged had been expensive, and massive debts remained,

26. Robert Shackleton, "Jansenism and the Enlightenment" [1967], in *Essays on Montesquieu and on the Enlightenment*, ed. David Gilson and Martin Smith (Oxford: The Voltaire Foundation, 1988), p. 300. A more recent and more thorough treatment of the political role played by Jansenism is Brian E. Strayer, *Suffering Saints: Jansenists and Convulsionnaires in France, 1640–1799* (Eastbourne, UK: Sussex Academic Press, 2008).

resulting in even more state borrowing. The world of high finance was complex and shadowy, then as now, and credit brokers made enormous fortunes helping heads of state balance their budgets. In France, the king had borrowed heavily from the nobility, whose wealth was in their vast estates, and the brokers tended to arrange very lucrative deals for the lenders; thus, the aristocracy grew richer, while paying little if any tax. Most of the tax burden fell on the agrarian sector—which was the prime engine of the country's economy—and on the peasants working the land. But two decades of terrible weather and bad crops had reduced their possibilities of paying as much as the government had hoped. And this was the situation that Orléans inherited when he took up the post of Regent in 1715.

He had no shortage of people offering advice, among them Montesquieu himself, who wrote in 1715 an essay on the state's debts.[27] Montesquieu—who retained a lifelong interest in economics—proposed a plan to address the problem by a complex system of repudiating the debt via a shared levy paid by all who owned government stock. No new taxes would need to be raised, and, as Judith Shklar put it, "the main point of the project was that the burden of repudiation [would] be distributed proportionately in such a way that every bondholder would remain in exactly the same position relative to all the others as before. There was to be no relative deprivation at all, and therefore no real injury."[28] The proposal, whatever its merits might have turned out to be had it been put into practice, in any case shows us Montesquieu thinking in terms not only of finance but also of justice, and of social impact. Much of the economic material in the *Persian Letters* reveals that kind of thinking as well.

But the Regent turned to a very different adviser, one who is an important figure in the *Persian Letters*: John Law, whose story is one of the most dramatic in an era filled with dramatic stories.[29] Born in 1671,

27. *Mémoire sur les dettes de l'État* was addressed to the Regent, though there is no evidence it was ever read by him.

28. Judith N. Shklar, *Montesquieu* (Oxford U Press, 1987), p. 18.

29. Among the numerous studies of Law, one of the most thorough and careful is Antoin E. Murphy's *John Law: Economic Theorist and Policy-maker* (Oxford U Press, 1997). Among the many briefer treatments of Law's ideas, two which connect him directly with modern economics are the discussions in Joseph T. Salerno, *Money, Sound and Unsound* (Auburn, AL: Von Mises Institute, 2010) and Philip Coggan, *Paper Promises: Debt, Money, and the New World Order* (NY: Public Affairs, 2012). Coggan, like many other modern economists, sees Law as having been ahead of his time.

he was a Scot, the son of a banking family, who turned away from the family business and toward more exciting pursuits, notably gambling and, ultimately, dueling. In London, he killed a man in a duel and was arrested for murder; his death sentence for murder was commuted to a lesser sentence for manslaughter, but he escaped from prison and fled to the Continent. While drifting from country to country in Europe, and at times earning a living by gambling, he began thinking seriously about large-scale economic issues, publishing an influential book in 1705, *Money and Trade Considered*. His great desire was to found a bank, based on the Bank of England, which would allow him to put his most dramatic scheme into practice: shifting a national economy from a gold and silver money system to a paper one. Law could show a winning personality when needed, and during the 1690s he had met Orléans, and made a favorable impression on him. Since that time, Law's ideas had begun to percolate in French political circles, and when Orléans became Regent in 1715, it was not long before he called on the Scotsman for assistance with straightening out the nation's finances, and Law presented the outlines of what came to be called his "system." In hindsight, one wonders how a nomadic gambler and escaped criminal could rise to the level that John Law did in France, and the answer lies, in part, with the fact that the Regent simply wanted to believe in him. As Colin Jones puts it:

> Building up wealth and prosperity at home without the need for international military involvement which was hugely expensive and socially divisive was a siren's song which Orléans, whose room for financial manoeuvre was dangerously thin, found increasingly seductive.[30]

Law was persuasive, especially to people who wanted to be persuaded. And he could play upon national pride as well by pointing out that England had a national bank, and France should have nothing less.

Orléans could not agree to the national bank scheme immediately, but in 1716, he authorized Law to set up a private bank, whose capital was to come from a public stock offering; the bank was authorized to issue its own notes. Early large-scale depositors included the Regent himself and other well-known, influential people, thus enhancing Law's credibility with the public. The bank was so successful that the Regent allowed Law to turn it into a national bank, and his Banque Générale was to be known henceforth as the Banque Royale—thus fulfilling one important step in

---

30. Colin Jones, *The Great Nation: France from Louis XV to Napoleon* (London: Allen Lane, 2002), p. 64.

Law's grand economic plan. Soon, the Regent put him in charge of the nation's tax collections as well, and by 1719 he was given sole authority to coin and issue money. In the meantime, Law was busy on another front, establishing the Company of the West (*la Compagnie d'Occident*), which consolidated the nation's colonial holdings into a company, and then sold stock in it to the public. At first, sales were moderate, but, as we read in *Persian Letters*, before long there was a public frenzy for the stock, and a widespread belief, almost a delirium, that this was the road to wealth. The company took on the national debt, issuing over a billion *livres* in paper notes. Buyers took on debt in order to purchase stock. Fortunes were made overnight, as Montesquieu's Rica observes:

> All those who were wealthy six months ago are now in poverty, and those who could not afford bread are now gorging themselves on riches. Never have the two extremes come so close together. The foreigner has flipped the state inside out the way a tailor does a coat: what used to be hidden inside is now on the outside, and what used to be outside is now inside. What unhoped-for fortunes, unbelievable even to those who have made them! God has never before brought people up so high from nothingness. How many valets today are being served by their erstwhile comrades—and perhaps tomorrow by the men who used to be their masters! (Letter 138)

The frenzy inflated the price of the stock, and inevitably there was a collapse when it became apparent that the real value of the company—as opposed to its notional stock value—was almost zero; the few colonists who populated Louisiana and Mississippi were not finding vast reserves of resources, and were not shipping vast amounts of valuable materials back to France. In fact they were often dying in an inhospitable wilderness. The crash finally came in 1720, amid a series of desperate maneuverings by Law and the Regent to stave off the inevitable, and the stock owners were left holding worthless paper. Once the most celebrated and one of the wealthiest men in France, Law was now in disgrace, and was dismissed from his posts. He took up his wanderings again, turning back to his old way of living—gambling—and died in poverty in Venice in 1729.

Montesquieu was drafting the *Persian Letters* between 1717 and 1721, and these national controversies—involving the Jansenists and the Pope's *Unigenitus* document on the one hand, and the rise and fall of John Law and his "system" on the other—helped give his novel a sense of immediacy for its first readers, and helped guarantee the book's huge success. But perhaps more importantly, these controversies also stimulated Montesquieu's evolving thoughts on politics, economics, religion, and society, and the novel gave him a forum for putting those thoughts into play. Calling *Persian Letters* a satire is correct in more ways than one: the word derives from the Latin *satura*, meaning a medley or mixed bag, and Montesquieu's novel is certainly that; the form allows him to touch upon almost any topic of interest.

One major topic is of course the very idea of foreignness—how contemplating the foreigner as stranger helps us see our own strangeness. The opening sequence of the book establishes a certain exoticism. The modern French or Western reader had to become acclimated to the Muslim names for months, and puzzle over references to places and topics from an unfamiliar religious history. But beyond all this was the sheer titillation provided by the appearance of eunuchs, seraglios, open polygamy, despotic rule, and all the paraphernalia of a sensual, violent East. This is the essence of what Edward Said taught us to call *Orientalism*: the West arrogates to itself the representation of the East, and in doing so constructs a kind of "Other" characterized by a set of negative traits, with values often inverted from European ones.[31] To the extent that Montesquieu's novel titillates—and there is little doubt that this is at least one of the book's effects for a Western reader, perhaps especially a Western male reader—to that extent, *Persian Letters* is complicit in the construction of such an Other. But this is only one aspect of the book, and arguably a rather minor one, because the novel is much smarter than that: it is interested in root concepts like foreignness itself, not just in presenting the foreign. It wants the foreigner to cause us to reflect on ourselves. Julia Kristeva sees the Enlightenment as a time when such self-reflection was quite central to the main stream of thought. As she puts it, during the Enlightenment,

> the image of the "good savage" that had already been coined by the Renaissance underwent a metamorphosis. What comes into view is a *foreigner*, as odd as he is subtle, and who is none other than the alter ego of national man, one who reveals the latter's personal inadequacies at the same time as he points to the defects in mores and institutions. Beginning with Montesquieu's *Persian Letters* . . . philosophical fiction became peopled with foreigners who invited the reader to make a twofold journey. . . . The *foreigner* then becomes the figure onto which the penetrating, ironical mind of the philosopher is delegated—his double, his mask.[32]

---

31. Edward W. Said, *Orientalism* [1978] (NY: Vintage, rpt. 1994). In this extremely influential study, Said had little to say about the image of the Orient in the European Enlightenment, concentrating instead on the nineteenth and twentieth centuries; he does not discuss *Persian Letters*.

32. Julia Kristeva, *Strangers to Ourselves*, trans. Leon S. Roudiez (NY: Columbia U Press, 1991), pp. 133–34.

This literary device—present in so many major texts from the era, including *Persian Letters*, *Gulliver's Travels*, Voltaire's tales, *Candide* and *Zadig*, Goldsmith's *Citizen of the World*, not to mention the host of imitators each inspired—was of tremendous value in what we now see as the larger project of the Enlightenment, that unceasing questioning, that endless quest for a fresh perspective, a new point of view, some way to move forward without simply repeating the mistakes of the past.

The contemporary fascination with the foreign—not the philosophical kind of fascination, but rather the sheer gawking kind—is satirized at a number of points in the novel, especially in Rica's letter:

> The people of Paris are curious to the point of extravagance. When I first arrived, people stared at me as if I had dropped down out of the sky: old men, young men, women, children, everybody wanted to have a look at me. When I went out, everyone rushed to the windows to see me; when I went to the Tuileries, a group of people soon formed a circle around me; even women formed a kind of rainbow around me, with their many-colored fashions. When I went to the theater, I saw a hundred pairs of opera glasses trained upon me. In short, no man has ever been as observed as I was. I smile sometimes when I hear people who have never traveled any farther than their own rooms saying to each other, "He does look quite Persian." (Letter 30)

And the height of cultural insularity comes at the end of the letter, when a Frenchman gazes at him and says "Monsieur is a Persian? What a strange thing! How can one be a Persian?"

The primary function of Montesquieu's imaginary Persians is, then, not to present some cultural exotica but instead to use cultural difference to help the Western reader see things in a new, clearer, better light. The realm of politics is, arguably, the most important of the many traversed in the novel. And politics, in Europe, remained a matter of monarchy—not yet whether monarchies should exist, a question that would be raised thunderously in the next generation, but more simply what kind of monarchy is best. This was a tender subject, to say the least. One of Montesquieu's immediate forbears in political fiction, the archbishop Fénelon, found his brilliant ecclesiastical career cut short after writing his ersatz ancient-Greek romance, *Télémaque* (1699), in which he hazarded the surprisingly controversial thesis that the law should be above the king and not vice-versa. Such was the state of probing political fiction under Louis XIV. But Montesquieu was writing in the new, clearer air of the Regency, and could be considerably bolder. In a sense, he visits the same topics that Fénelon had, especially by making his readers consider the concept of despotism.

The word "despot" had begun to come into wide use during the late seventeenth century, not surprisingly, during the period when Louis XIV was most fully establishing his absolutist rule; it appears in the 1694 dictionary of the Académie Française in the adjective form "*despotique*," and was defined as "absolute, arbitrary."[33] But the word comes from the Greek, where it originally referred not to a form of government but to a father's or patriarch's rule over his slaves and/or his family. To be called a "despot" in that ancient sense was evidently not suggestive of undue tyranny, but rather of a quite natural, perhaps even benign, kind of power over others. But as the term came into use in Enlightenment France, it had an oriental overtone. Thus, a dictionary from 1771 defined despotism as a:

> form of government in which the sovereign is absolute master, with limitless authority and arbitrary power, having no other law but his will. This is the government of Turkey, of the Mogul, of Japan, Persia, and almost all of Asia. The principle, the character and the evils incurred by despotism have been well enough elaborated by the best of our writers.[34]

We observe how even as late as 1771—with the Revolution only 18 years away—despotism is defined in such a way as to distance it, to insist that it is "oriental" and not at all a French thing. However, in the 1721 *Persian Letters*, despotism is never far from our view, and it is always implicitly being ascribed to the European system.

In this regard, Usbek's Letter 102 deserves careful study. Montesquieu lets his fictional character come perilously close to very plain speaking:

> Most governments in Europe are monarchies, or at least they are called that; I am not sure I have ever seen a pure monarchy, and in any case pure monarchies are never able to stay that way for long. The pure monarchy is a turbulent state that always degenerates into either despotism or a republic. Power can never be equally shared between people and prince; the equilibrium is too delicate to maintain, and the power has to diminish on one side and grow on the other. But the advantage usually lies on the side of the prince, who commands the army. (Letter 102)

---

33. The 1694 *Dictionnaire de L'Académie française* is available online at http://artfl-project.uchicago.edu. Montesquieu has some satiric points to make about this dictionary in Letter 73 of *Persian Letters*.

34. The definition is from the Trévoux dictionary of 1771, which is a descendant of the Furetière dictionary mentioned in Letter 73. It is quoted here from Alain Grosrichard, *The Sultan's Court: European Fantasies of the East*, trans. Liz Heron (London: Verso, 1998), p. 4. Grosrichard's book was originally published in French in 1979—just about the same time as Said's *Orientalism*, and it addresses similar topics from a different, more psychoanalytical angle.

Usbek pulls back as the letter proceeds, insisting that real absolute power is only wielded by Persian and eastern monarchs—but the point had been made, and anyone who lived in early eighteenth-century France could not fail to see it. And the concluding encomium could not fail to raise a smile in the thoughtful reader:

> The kings of France are so far from taking the lives of their subjects, as our sultans do, that on the contrary, wherever they go, they bring pardons for all criminals with them. It is sufficient for a man to look upon the august face of his prince to cease being unworthy of life. These monarchs are like the sun, bringing warmth and life everywhere.

The allusion to the favorite title of Louis XIV, the Sun King, strikes the perfect ironic note here.

Usbek continues his ruminations on monarchy for the next few letters, and he returns to this and similar topics from time to time throughout his stay in France. And we know that he has fled Persia in part because of having dared to speak the truth at the sultan's court:

> I have frequented the court since my earliest youth, yet I can swear that my heart has not been corrupted by it. In fact, I formed a grand plan for myself: I would dare to be virtuous. When I first saw vice, I fled from it, but I later returned and approached it, in order to unmask it. I carried truth with me to the very steps of the throne, speaking a language there that was unknown until then. (Letter 8)

He is motivated by genuine curiosity about the West and about the world in general outside Persia, but Letter 8 suggests that there is an even more insistent reason for his travels—one of the very few times he makes reference to this. Usbek is a complex character, though his letters can lull us sometimes into seeing him as merely a passive observer. And the most complicating factor in his character is that he is on the one hand a curious, sensitive, introspective man, almost a paradigm of the Enlightenment man in the process of educating himself—but he is on the other hand the very image of the despot when it comes to his seraglio at home in Ispahan. Judith Shklar puts the point as bluntly as possible when she says he is almost entirely unable to see himself: "What he believes and what he does never meet. Thus he can say with complete conviction that all that religion demands is that one be a good son and father, obey the rules of one's society, and be kind to everyone, and never notice that he is none of these things" (p. 34).

This blindness in Usbek is, however, a brilliant stroke on Montesquieu's part. For one thing, are we not all like Usbek in exactly this respect, seeing the wrong everywhere else but not in ourselves?

But secondly, and more subtly, the connection between the domestic despot, the lord of the seraglio, and the political one is slowly but powerfully drawn. Thus, Alain Grosrichard's superb analysis of this connection argues that it is the very essence of Montesquieu's project with his novel:

> The disorder which increases in the seraglio . . . is the very image of the degradation of absolute power into despotic power, when the too-loved monarch is no longer there. This is perhaps the purpose of the secret chain which links historical analysis with the fiction of a novel in the *Persian Letters*, and gives the work's conclusion its true meaning. Fiction has the last word: it is fiction which can spill out over the present historical conjuncture, which at this point [that is, the France of 1720] is nothing more than the corruption of monarchical morals and the vacancy of power. (p. 29)

The seraglio sequences, and all the details about sex and eunuchs, are not at all titillation, not at all mere exoticism, but are woven into the novel with serious purpose.

Since Grosrichard, a number of scholars have gone even further in exploring Montesquieu's implicit analogy between the despotism of the private harem and the despotism of the public monarchy. Mary Shanley and Peter Stillman, for example, examine the "family" aspect of the two despotisms, noting the irony that it is only when Usbek has gone and the despotic authority has been removed that the wives are able to form a certain degree of community.[35] E. J. Hundert sees the harem revolt as the moment when the wives finally enter into true selfhood, whereas the same moment undoes Usbek's identity as patriarch and master. He reads the book as an allegory of the eighteenth-century conception of the self as a kind of costumed performance that everyone had to play, and the tragic end of Roxane and the Ispahan seraglio leads the Western reader "to an uneasy examination of the potential 'Oriental' within himself."[36]

Whether in the seraglio or in the French Regency society that Rica and Usbek contemplate, the novel puts a remarkable emphasis on women throughout, and this aspect has likewise attracted a great deal of modern scholarly attention. Many modern readers have begun to

35. Mary Shanley and Peter Stillman, "Political and Marital Despotism: Montesquieu's *Persian Letters*," in Jean Bethke Elshtain, *The Family in Political Thought* (Amherst: U of Massachusetts Press, 1982), pp. 67–79.

36. E. J. Hundert, "Sexual Politics and the Allegory of Identity in Montesquieu's *Persian Letters*," *The Eighteenth Century* 31.2 (Summer 1990), pp. 110.

see Montesquieu as something of an early feminist. The remarkable Letter 141—in which Rica relates the tale told by a female sage named Zuléma, concerning a paradise for women—is one of the key passages for such an interpretation. It is a kind of revenge tale, but one with a great deal of humor, and one that results in the undoing of a male "despot"; perhaps just as striking is its frank treatment of women's sexual desire, a desire that is shown as natural and blameless. Rica's Letter 38, about the degrees of freedom granted to women in different societies, is likewise an important part of the whole picture. That such topics arise from the pen of Rica rather than Usbek helps in suggesting the enormous differences between the two men, and we begin to see that Rica is by far the more open, less troubled and conflicted of the two. Of course the major difference is that Rica has not left a seraglio behind; he is not molded, as Usbek has been, by the experience of being a master or despot for a set of wives. A modern Montesquieu scholar, Pauline Kra, points out that the word *rica* in Latin referred to the veil worn by women during religious sacrifices; she explores some of the social and literary symbolism of the veil, the harem revolt beginning with the removal of the veil, and she suggests that perhaps Montesquieu names his character Rica as a kind of identification with the women's revolt.[37] And all this gains yet another layer of sophistication and complexity when we recall that the tale of Zuléma about the vengeful wife Anaïs is told in a letter (141) to Usbek, from Rica.[38] In this letter, is Rica somehow trying to goad his friend? And what should we make of the fact that Rica says he has altered the tale to appeal to a Parisian lady? Questions such as these remind us that the book is, after all, a novel, not simply a straightforward satire or social analysis. The motives of the various speakers at the various moments in the plot all matter, often just as much as what they are saying.

It is of some interest that two of the most successful imitations of *Persian Letters*—imitations in the best sense, that is, in the sense of having been inspired by the earlier work, and not in the sense of being mere copies—were novels by women. Both Françoise de Graffigny's *Letters of a Peruvian Woman* (*Lettres d'une Péruvienne*, 1747) and Elizabeth Hamilton's *Translations of the Letters of a Hindoo Rajah* (1796) show that

37. Pauline Kra, "The Name Rica and the Veil in Montesquieu's *Lettres Persanes*," *Studi Francesi* 42.1 (1998), 78–79.

38. A good discussion of these complexities is in Mary McAlpin, "Between Men for All Eternity: Feminocentrism in Montesquieu's *Lettres Persanes*," *Eighteenth-Century Life* 24.1 (2000), pp. 45–61.

their authors had read *Persian Letters* carefully and well.[39] Madame de Graffigny's novel was a runaway best seller in its day, and was itself copied and imitated. It uses the same format of letters from what a French reader would have considered an exotic and almost fabulous source, and it asks the reader implicitly to reflect less on the strangeness of the Peruvians and more on the moral and political shortcomings of the Europeans. Elizabeth Hamilton, born in Ireland and raised in Scotland, grew up with a brother, Charles, who became an "orientalist," a student of Eastern cultures, and who went on to translate some Islamic texts. After her brother's death, she embodied a satire on contemporary Britain in a set of letters by imaginary Indians, and her book too found many readers, going through five editions. Both de Graffigny and Hamilton are concerned with the status and role of women, and both are concerned, like Montesquieu, with questions of justice and right rule, especially ruling in absentia from great distances—as the Spanish did with Peru, the English with India, and Usbek with his Ispahan seraglio. That *Persian Letters* could be so inspiring to women writers suggests something crucial about Montesquieu's novel—its spirit of free, even radical inquiry. Nothing is taboo, and certainly not inherited prejudices about sex roles. Free, unfettered inquiry must—simply must—lead to a better, more just world.

Since Montesquieu's greatest fame came with his later book of political philosophy, *The Spirit of the Laws* (*De l'esprit des lois*, 1748), there has been a perhaps natural temptation to take this earlier work as an anticipation of the later one. *Persian Letters* does lend itself to such a reading. But this tends to minimize or even ignore altogether the sheer artfulness of Montesquieu's novel, with its subtleties of character and event, its juxtapositions of writers and recipients, its interweaving of the topics discussed with the evolution of the two main characters. For many first-time readers, the sudden tragedies at the book's conclusion come as a shock, seeming out of place with the often light-hearted and

39. Madame de Graffigny's *Letters of a Peruvian Woman* is available in an English translation by Jonathan Mallinson (Oxford U Press, 2009). There is a growing body of critical commentary on the book; a good introduction is Charlotte Daniels, *Subverting the Family Romance: Women Writers, Kinship Structures, and the Early French Novel* (Lewisburg, PA: Bucknell U Press, 2000). Elizabeth Hamilton's novel is likewise available (Peterbourough, Ontario: Broadview, 1999), and is attracting renewed scholarly interest. See, for example, Julie Straight, "Promoting Liberty through Universal Benevolence in Hamilton's *Translations of the Letters of a Hindoo Rajah*," *Eighteenth-Century Fiction* 25.3 (2013), pp. 589–614, and Kathryn Freeman, *British Women Writers and the Asiatic Society of Bengal, 1785–1835* (Farnham, Surrey: Ashgate, 2015).

wide ranging speculations in so many of the letters. But on a second reading, we see that the tragedy has been simmering beneath the surface almost from the beginning—from Usbek's need to escape Persia, and from the first letters from the seraglio depicting the abjection of the wives and eunuchs imprisoned there, and the hierarchy of often cruel command in place there—white eunuchs, black eunuchs, wives, children, slaves. . . . Reminding ourselves that *Persian Letters* is a novel first and foremost helps us appreciate many details that can otherwise be missed—such as, to mention one major example, the fact that Rica's letter 141 about the women's paradise and the deposed despotic husband actually comes after Roxane's suicide letter (161). The suicide letter is not received until later, but it was written earlier. Thus, as with any good novel, the details matter.

One important recent reading of *Persian Letters* that both explicates its large political themes and treats it seriously as a novel is by Srinivas Aravamudan. He concludes that the book is indeed a tragic one, but the tragedy is not just in the story of Usbek and his wives. We follow Usbek's thought processes as he comes to terms with a foreign world and culture, as he opens up his mind to many new ways of thinking and ways of living, and as he considers the great topic of justice from one angle after another, we may feel that we are watching a man in the process of intellectual blossoming. But Aravamudan argues that the overall pattern of the book, sadly, undoes all that:

> Small successes of analogical reasoning are followed by the catastrophic failure of the harem. The dream of an alternative mode of understanding fails even as local pseudoethnographic insights remain valuable. The thought-experiment unravels, showing the desirability but also the difficulty of thinking transculturally.[40]

Thinking transculturally is indeed what *Persian Letters* sets out to perform—or to dramatize—or to critique. One of the great dreams of the Enlightenment is that of cosmopolitanism, of a world that progresses beyond nations and nationalities, freeing us from our suspicions and hatreds of the other nations and tribes. The great tide of progress, the eighteenth-century philosophers believed, was slowly but surely taking us to such a destination. The citizen of the future would not be French or German or English but a citizen of the world. Immanuel Kant articulated the ideal most stirringly in a number of essays, including

40. Srinivas Aravamudan, *Enlightenment Orientalism: Resisting the Rise of the Novel* (U of Chicago Press, 2012), p. 94.

his "Idea for a Universal History with a Cosmopolitan Purpose" (1784) and his "Toward Perpetual Peace" (1795); as those titles indicate, Kant, and many others in the era, believed that true justice and lasting peace would only be possible when the divisiveness that is the inevitable effect of a world broken into nation states was finally overcome. Of course, later historical events were to dash the hopes that a new, post-nationalist era was coming soon.[41] But this ideal of Kant and many of the Enlightenment philosophers continues to resonate today in the work of poststructuralist thinkers such as Kristeva and Derrida, to name only two.[42] Montesquieu is the first to have tried to imagine it concretely. The infection at the root, though, as Montesquieu sees it, is not the nation as such but rather the complex of issues summed up by the term despotism—and indeed it was Montesquieu who coined that particular form of the word, *despotisme*, being the first to see it clearly as a condition that poisons everything.

Persian Letters, then, is one of the model texts of the Enlightenment, ranging over all its favored topics, from human nature and the origins of society as in the great fable of the Troglodytes (Letters 11–14) to the nature and role of religious belief and on to the largest topics of justice and morality and even human identity. The originality of Montesquieu's thinking did not end with this 1721 publication, of course, for he continued to write, but without ever repeating himself. His next important work was *Considerations on the Causes of the Greatness of the Romans and Their Decline* (*Considérations sur les causes de la grandeur des Romains et de leur décadence*, 1734), a book that predates Gibbon's masterpiece on the same subject, and one that is arguably more republican and more hostile to monarchy than the later *Spirit of the Laws*.[43] Here, Montesquieu sees a connection between life in a republic and the growth and maintenance of personal virtue, a connection many eighteenth-century

---

41. For a full discussion, see Pauline Kleingeld, *Kant and Cosmopolitanism: The Philosophical Ideal of World Citizenship* (Cambridge U Press, 2011).

42. See, for instance, Kristeva; "Could cosmopolitanism as moral imperative be the secular form of that bond bringing together families, languages, and states that religion claimed to be?" (*Strangers to Ourselves*, p. 173). See also the later work of Jacques Derrida, especially *Politics of Friendship* (*Politiques de l'amitié*, 1994; translated version by George Collins, London: Verso, 1997) and *Rogues: Two Essays on Reason* (*Voyous*, 2003; translated version by Pascale-Anne Brault and Michael Naas, Stanford U Press, 2005).

43. See David Lowenthal's Introduction to his translation, *Considerations on the Causes of the Greatness of the Romans and Their Decline* (Hackett, 1999), especially pp. 17–20.

thinkers saw as well, in the belief that political freedom would have profound moral effects on a populace; likewise, a populace living under despotism is one likely to be slavish in their personal lives as well. Most would agree that Montesquieu's real masterpiece, his greatest contribution to Western culture and political life, was his *Spirit of the Laws*. In that large, complex work, the problem of despotism, of political power corrupting those who wield it, underlies everything, and the solution Montesquieu develops—the famous concept of a "separation of powers" within a state—has become central to political thought ever since, and especially since the American Revolution.

A fuller discussion of Montesquieu's later books is not possible here, but giving them at least a mention helps to suggest the sheer diversity of Montesquieu's interests and works. *Persian Letters*, a work that contains within itself a great deal of diversity as well, is in many respects predictive of the later Montesquieu, but it surely deserves full attention as a masterpiece of its own, and a masterpiece of its century.

ACKNOWLEDGMENTS

I wish to express my gratitude to my research assistant, Mary Jane O'Brien, who was a great help to me. The superb bibliography at the end of this book is her work.

I am also very grateful to Henry C. Clark, who gave the translation a very careful and very helpful reading. Any weaknesses that remain are of course my own responsibility. Professor Clark has put all English-speaking Montesquieu readers in his debt with his recent translation of Montesquieu's notebooks titled *My Thoughts* (Indianapolis: Liberty Fund, 2012).

THE CALENDAR OF THE *PERSIAN LETTERS*

Montesquieu sought to add some flavor of authenticity to his fictional Persians by dating their letters according to the Islamic year, and to do this he turned to his chief sources, Tavernier and Chardin (both discussed above, pp. xii). Some inconsistencies crept in, chiefly having to do with the difference between a solar year and a lunar one; another major inconsistency, but one which Western readers must be grateful for, is that Montesquieu maintained the Western designation of years. Thus, Usbek sets out in 1711, and the final letter is dated 1720. Robert S. Shackleton's analysis of the issue has become the definitive one.[44] As Shackleton explains it, Montesquieu saw the Islamic year as a solar one beginning in March. The months and their Western equivalents are as follows:

Maharram	March
Saphar	April
Rebiab I	May
Rebiab II	June
Gemmadi I	July
Gemmadi II	August
Rhegeb	September
Chahban	October
Rhamazan	November
Chalval	December
Zilcadé	January
Zilhagé	February

Shackleton notes that Montesquieu tried to be as accurate as he could be about the time it took to travel from one place to another—again, using Chardin and Tavernier as his sources. Thus, it took Usbek over a year—399 days—to get from Ispahan to Paris.

44. Robert S. Shackleton, "The Moslem Chronology of the *Lettres Persanes*" [1954], in *Essays on Montesquieu and on the Enlightenment*, ed. David Gilson and Martin Smith (Oxford: The Voltaire Foundation, 1988), pp. 73–83.

Shackleton also notes that there are some dating errors within *Persian Letters*: for example, there is Letter 24, which is dated 1712 but refers to the Papal Constitution *Unigenitus*—and *Unigenitus* was not issued until September 1713. These errors suggest that the whole scheme of Islamic months and dates may have been something of a last-minute idea for Montesquieu.

THE TEXT OF THE *PERSIAN LETTERS*

Montesquieu's *Persian Letters* (*Lettres Persanes*) was first published anonymously in Amsterdam in 1721, in a two-volume format; anonymity was quite typical of books published in the era, especially those that could conceivably offend the powerful or run afoul of censorship laws. But in the case of *Persian Letters*, there was an additional layer of protection: the publisher is listed on the title page as Pierre Marteau, an entirely fictional name (*marteau* is the French word for hammer), and the place is given as Cologne. Many books in the seventeenth and eighteenth centuries are ascribed to Marteau in Cologne; its nonexistence would have been an open secret. Jacques Desbordes, the real publisher, was a French Protestant who had fled the country after the revocation of the Edict of Nantes; his family had roots in Bordeaux, and this may be the reason Montesquieu brought the book to him.

The *Persian Letters* was a major success, and a second edition was called for in that same year, also published by Marteau, and again in two volumes. Montesquieu did some tinkering with this edition, removing thirteen of the original letters, and adding three new ones. The omitted letters were 1, 5, 10, 16, 25, 32, 41, 42, 43, 47, 65, 70, and 71. The newly added letters were 111, 124, and 145. But he made no further changes to the ensuing editions—of which there were many—until 1754. He prefaced this new edition with the short "Some Reflections on the *Persian Letters*." This edition included all 150 of the original letters, and an added section at the end of volume two titled *Supplément*. Here, Montesquieu placed the three new ones from the second edition along with eight new ones. In 1758, after his death, a new edition was printed that took the eleven new letters and placed them in their proper order within the text. This 1758 edition is the one that is most often read today, and the current translation is based on it.

The new letters, when inserted into the sequence within the 1758 edition, were as follows: 15, 22, 77, 91, 144, 157, and 160. Montesquieu also made some changes to the text of several letters in the 1754 edition; the notes in the present translation point out some of the major alterations.

The definitive French critical edition of *Persian Letters* is edited by Edgar Mass, and is volume 1 of a new *Oeuvres complètes de Montesquieu*

(Oxford: Voltaire Foundation, 2004). For this translation, I have also consulted three excellent editions of *Lettres Persanes* that preceded the Edgar Mass one: those by Paul Vernière (Paris: Garnier, 1960), Antoine Adam (Geneva: Droz, 1965), and Jean Starobinski (1973; rpt. Paris: Folio, 2000).

Persian Letters

Some Reflections on the *Persian Letters*[1]

Nothing has given readers more pleasure in the *Persian Letters* than to have found—without expecting it—a kind of novel in them.[2] One can see a beginning, a middle, and an end; the various characters are linked by a chain. The longer they stay in Europe, the customs of this part of the world come to seem less marvelous and less bizarre to them; and they are either more or less struck by the bizarre and the marvelous according to the differences in their personalities. Meanwhile, disorder continues to grow in the Asiatic seraglio, in proportion to the length of Usbek's absence—that is, as the fury increases, the love decreases.

Furthermore, novels like this usually are successful because the characters are describing the experiences they are currently having, which makes their feelings more vivid than any kind of pure narrative could do. And this is one of the reasons for the success of a number of charming works that have appeared since the *Persian Letters.*[3]

Finally, in ordinary novels, digressions can only be permitted when they form in themselves a new and separate novel. One should not mix in philosophical elements, because the characters were not brought in to speculate, and having them do so would mar the design and the nature of the work. But in letters, where the actors are not freely chosen, and where the subjects they write about are not dependent upon any pre-formed design or plan, the author has the advantage of being able to fuse philosophy, politics, and morality

1. The "Reflections" were first printed in the 1754 edition. Montesquieu was anxious to answer the charges of impiety that a Jansenist priest, Jean-Baptiste Gaultier, had brought against him in a pamphlet titled *Lettres persanes convaincues d'impiété* [*Persian Letters* guilty of impiety], 1751. Gaultier had written a similar attack on Voltaire in the preceding year, and one on the English poet Alexander Pope in 1746. He was not a trivial adversary.

2. Montesquieu uses the word *roman*, which I have translated here as "novel." The word had a number of possible uses though, and can sometimes be better translated as "romance," and sometimes simply as "story," and I have varied my translation of *roman* according to how Montesquieu seems to be using it in each instance.

3. In the draft version of these reflections, Montesquieu referred to the epistolary form as "one of the causes of the success of *Pamela* and the *Letters of a Peruvian Woman* (charming works that have appeared since)" [*My Thoughts*, p. 627]. *Pamela* is the hugely popular English epistolary novel by Samuel Richardson (1740), and *Lettres Péruviennes*, by Madame de Graffigny (1747), was a direct imitation of Montesquieu's book.

with the novel, connecting it all with a secret and, in some sense, unknown chain.[4]

The *Persian Letters* had such a tremendous success when they were published that the booksellers tried everything they could to generate sequels. They would tug on the sleeves of anyone passing by, saying, "Monsieur, write me some Persian letters."

But considering everything I have just said, it is clear that the book is not suited to any kind of sequel, and even less to any combination with letters written by someone else, no matter how ingenious they might be.[5]

There are a few aspects of the book that some have found too daring. But I would beg those readers to consider the nature of this work. The Persians, who of course play such a major role in the book, find themselves suddenly transported to Europe, or in other words, to a different world. It was necessary to portray them as being, for a while, both ignorant and full of prejudices. The author was intent then on representing the beginnings and the progress of their thoughts. Their first reflections would necessarily be strange ones: it seemed that all the author had to do was ensure that this strangeness would be compatible with intelligence. All that was needed was to depict their feelings and their reactions to everything that struck them as extraordinary. Far from intending to reflect on any principle of our religion, the author never even suspected he was being imprudent. The characters reacted with surprise and amazement, but the author's intention was in no way to suggest some kind of questioning, much less some kind of critique. When they spoke about our religion, these Persians could not seem to be more informed than they were when they spoke about our fashions and our customs. And if they sometimes found our beliefs bizarre, that bizarreness is always put within the context of their perfect ignorance of all the ways in which our beliefs and our other truths are interrelated.

This justification is presented out of love for these great truths, to say nothing of the author's respect for humankind in general: he has had no intention of wounding anyone's sensitivities. I beg the reader therefore

4. Many scholars have pondered what this "secret chain" might be. A good summary of several interpretations is provided in Theodore Braun's "*La Chaine Secrète*: A Decade of Interpretations," *French Studies* 42:3 (1988), pp. 278–91.

5. This is probably a reference to Poullain de Saint-Foix's *Lettres d'une Turque à Paris, écrites à sa sœur* [Letters from a Turk in Paris to His Sister] (1730), which had been printed sometimes together with Montesquieu's book—without, of course, his permission.

always to regard these aspects of the book as reflecting the surprise of men who must inevitably have been surprised by what they saw, or else as paradoxical remarks written by men who were not really in a position to be making them. I beg the reader to pay attention to the continual contrast to be found between things that are real and the singular, naïve, or bizarre manner in which they are perceived. Certainly, the nature and the design of the *Persian Letters* are so clear that the only people who can misunderstand them are those who are determined to do so.

Persian Letters: Introduction[6]

I will add no dedicatory epistle here, and I will not ask for anyone's protection for this book. If it is good, people will read it, and if it is bad, I do not especially want it to be read.

I have selected these first letters to gauge the public taste. I have a great many others in my keeping, which I may publish later.

But this is conditional upon my remaining unknown; for the moment my name becomes known, I will be silent. A woman of my acquaintance walks perfectly well, but when people are looking at her, she develops a limp.[7] The faults in the book are enough, without adding to them a possible critique of my person. If people knew who I am, they would say: "His book does not suit his character. He ought to spend his time on better things; this is not worthy of a serious man." Critics never miss a chance to make comments like this, simply because it takes no effort to come up with them.

The Persians who wrote these letters lodged with me; we spent our time together. They saw me as belonging to another world, and as a result they hid nothing from me. Indeed, men who are transplanted from so very far away could no longer have any secrets. They showed me most of their letters, and I copied them. I even intercepted some of the ones that they tried to keep hidden from me, because they were so mortifying to Persian vanity and jealousy.

I have therefore only played the role of translator; all my efforts have been spent adapting the work to our tastes. I have spared the reader as much of the Asiatic style as I possibly could, and have spared him an infinite number of sublime expressions which would have bored him (in the loftiest possible way).

But this is not all I have done for the reader. I have abbreviated those lengthy compliments that the Asiatics like even more than we do; and I have eliminated an infinite number of trivial details, the kind of thing

6. This Introduction, which originally prefaced the 1721 edition, should be compared with the 1754 "Reflections." Here, Montesquieu maintains a pretense—which probably fooled no one—that the letters were real. Such pretenses were common with novels in the early eighteenth century. A good discussion of the two prefaces and their importance is in Frederick M. Keener, *The Chain of Becoming: The Philosophical Tale, the Novel, and a Neglected Realism of the Enlightenment* (NY: Columbia U Press, 1983), especially pp. 131–50.

7. This has traditionally been taken as a reference to Montesquieu's wife, Jeanne de Lartigue.

that scarcely withstands being brought into the light of day, and that should be allowed to die away privately between two friends.

If others who have given us collections of letters had done the same, they would have seen their works shrink down to nothing.

One thing has struck me repeatedly, and that is to observe these Persians often as well informed about our French customs and manners as I am myself, right down to the finest of details, taking note of things that, I am quite sure, have entirely escaped many Germans who have traveled in France. I attribute this to the long period of time they stayed here—not to mention the fact that it is easier for an Asiatic to learn about the customs of the French in one year than it would be for a Frenchman to learn about theirs in four, because the one group is as communicative as the other is reserved.

Tradition permits every translator, and even the most barbarous of commentators, to adorn the opening of his version or his commentary with a panegyric upon the original, praising its usefulness, its merit, and its excellence. I have not done this, and the reasons should be quite obvious. One of the best is that such a eulogy would be very boring, and it would be put in a place that is already the most boring—that is, a preface.

Letter 1

Usbek to his friend Rustan
At Ispahan

We only spent one day at Qum. After we had made our devotions at the tomb of the virgin who bore twelve prophets, we resumed our journey; and yesterday, the twenty-fifth day since our departure from Ispahan, we arrived at Tabriz.

Rica and I may be the first among the Persians with so great a thirst for knowledge that we have been led to get up and leave our native land, turning our backs on all the pleasures of a tranquil life in order to travel abroad and, with much labor, seek out wisdom.

The kingdom we were born into is a flourishing one; but even so, we never allowed ourselves to believe that its borders were also the borders of our knowledge, or that the Eastern sun was the only one that could enlighten us.

Send me word of what they are saying about our journey back home, and do not simply flatter me: I assume there will be very few who approve. Address your letter to me at Erzerum, where I will stop a while. Farewell, my dear Rustan. And you may always be certain that whatever part of the world I am in, you have a most faithful friend.

From Tabriz, the 15th of the moon of Saphar, 1711

Letter 2

Usbek to his Chief Black Eunuch
At the seraglio in Ispahan

You are the faithful guardian of the most beautiful women in Persia. I have entrusted to you what are the dearest things in the world to me: I have placed in your hands the keys to the fateful doors, which are to be opened to no one but me. As long as you are watching over this priceless storehouse, my heart can rest in a sense of complete security. You stand guard over it during the silence of the night as well as during the tumult of the day. Your tireless care will serve to support virtue when she stumbles. Should the women you watch over desire to stray from the path of duty, you will be there to cut off all hope. You are the scourge of vice, and the pillar of fidelity.

You command them, and you also obey them; you blindly carry out every one of their wishes, and at the same time you force them to follow the laws of the seraglio: you take pride in performing the meanest service for them: you submit utterly to their legitimate demands, with fear and respect: you serve them like the slave of their slaves. But when the power returns to you, you will rule over them as their master in my stead whenever you fear any relaxation of the laws regarding decency and modesty.

Contemplate every day the nothingness out of which I have raised you up, when you were the lowest of my slaves, in order to place you in this position and to entrust the joys of my heart to you. Keep yourself in a state of profound abasement when you are near those who share my love; but at the same time, be sure they remain aware of their complete dependence upon me. Procure any and every little pleasure they ask for, so long as the request is an innocent one: stave off all their anxieties; amuse them with music, with dance, with delicious drinks; persuade them to assemble as a group often. If they want to go out into the countryside, you may escort them: but if any man dares to present himself before them, act at once, and put him to the sword. Exhort the women to cleanliness, for a clean body is the image of a clean soul; and speak to them from time to time about me. I yearn to see them again in that lovely setting that they make lovelier. Farewell.

From Tabriz, the 18th of the moon of Saphar, 1711

Letter 3

Zachi to Usbek
At Tabriz

We ordered the chief eunuch to take us out to the countryside; he will tell you that we encountered no accident. When we had to cross the river and step out of our litters, we followed custom and got into boxes; two slaves carried each of us on their shoulders, and we avoided anyone's gaze.

How have I managed to go on living, my dear Usbek, in your seraglio in Ispahan—in this place where I am reminded of our past pleasures every moment, where my desire for you grows more violent all the time? I wander from apartment to apartment seeking you always, but finding you never, encountering instead only some cruel reminder of my past happiness. Sometimes I see myself back in that spot where, for the first time in my life, I received you into my arms; sometimes, in the place where you settled that famous quarrel among your wives: each of us thought herself superior in beauty to all the others; we presented ourselves to you, after having exhausted our imaginations on every possibility of jewelry and finery, and you saw, with pleasure, the results of all our art, delighted at the lengths to which we had gone to please you. But soon, you made all those borrowed charms give way to more natural ones; you wiped away all our labor, and ordered us to remove all those ornaments, as they had grown tiresome to you; we now had to present ourselves to you in all the simplicity of nature. I had no interest in modesty; my only aim was glory. O, fortunate Usbek! How many delights were now spread out before your eyes! We watched you take your time, letting your gaze wander slowly from one enchantment to another: you were uncertain, and took a long time deciding. Every new charm you saw received its tribute: we were all covered with your kisses, and your curiosity carried you into the most secret places: you had us pass before you in a thousand different poses; always there were new commands, and always new obedience to them. I admit it to you, Usbek: there was a motive stronger than mere ambition in my desire to please you. I could see myself slowly becoming the mistress of your heart: you took me, then quit me; you returned, and I knew how to retain you. The victory was everything to me, and despair for my rivals. It was as if we two were alone in the world; out of all that surrounded us, nothing was worthy of our attention. May Heaven grant that my rivals witnessed all those marks of love I received from you! And if they had witnessed my bliss, they would have seen the great difference between my love and theirs; they would have seen that, though they might have been able to compete with me in charms, they could never compete in sensibility . . .

But where am I now? Where has this vain story led me? It is misery not to be loved, but it is an offense to be loved no longer. You leave us, Usbek, to go wandering in barbarian lands. Why? Do you count it as nothing to be loved? Alas, you do not even know what it is you are losing. I sigh, and no one hears me; my tears fall, and you do not take pleasure in the sight. Love, it seems, is alive and breathing here in the seraglio, but you do not feel it, and you distance yourself from it! Oh, my dear Usbek, if only you knew how to be happy!

From the seraglio at Fatmé, the 21st of the moon of Maharram, 1711

Letter 4

Zéphis to Usbek
At Erzerum

This black monster is determined to drive me to despair. He has forced me to give up my slave Zélide, the Zélide who serves me with so much affection, and whose expert touch ornaments and beautifies me so well. He isn't satisfied at having forced such a sorrowful separation between us; he wants it to be a dishonorable one as well. The traitor is determined to view my confidence in her as criminal; and because he is bored standing outside my door, where I typically send him to wait, he dares to imagine that he has heard or seen certain things, things I cannot even imagine. Oh, I am so unhappy! Neither my quiet, retired life nor my virtue are enough to make me safe from his outrageous suspicions: a vile slave has dared to attack me in the place I live, within your heart and love, and I must defend myself. No, I have too much self-respect to condescend to answer his accusations: I need no greater guarantee of my conduct than yourself, than the love you have for me and the love I have for you—and, I must add, my dear Usbek, no greater guarantee than my tears.

From the seraglio at Fatmé, the 29th of the moon of Maharram, 1711

Letter 5

Rustan to Usbek
At Erzerum

You are the subject of every conversation in Ispahan; everybody talks of nothing but your departure. Some attribute it to a strange whim on your part, and others to some unhappiness: your friends are the only ones who defend you, and they don't persuade anyone. No one can understand how you could possibly leave your wives, your family, your friends, your native land, to go wandering in lands unknown to the Persians. Rica's mother is inconsolable; she keeps asking for her son, and saying that you have taken him away from her. As for me, my dear Usbek, I am naturally inclined to approve everything you do—but I really cannot pardon you for your absence, and no matter how many reasons for it you might give me, my heart cannot accept them. Farewell. Love me always.

From Ispahan, the 28th of the moon of Rebiab I, 1711

Letter 6

Usbek to his friend Nessir
At Ispahan

After one day's journey from Erivan, we passed the border of Persia and entered into the lands that pay their fealty to the Turks. And twelve days after that, we arrived in Erzerum, where we will sojourn some three or four months.

I must admit to you, Nessir, that I felt a secret sorrow when I saw Persia receding from view and found myself in the homeland of the perfidious Osmanlis. The farther I go into this profane land, the more profaned I feel myself.[8]

8. The reference here is to the early schism in Islam between Sunni and Shia. For the Sunnis, the direct line of succession led from Mohammed through his father-in-law Abu Bekr, down to Osman—hence the phrase, "the perfidious Osmanlis." The Persians were Shia, and in their view the direct line of succession led from Mohammed's son-in-law, Hali or Ali.

My homeland, my family, my friends—all are present in my heart: I feel my tenderness for them reawakened, and a certain anxiety has begun to trouble me, making me feel that I have taken on too great an enterprise for my own peace.

But what chiefly pains me is the thought of my wives. Whenever I think of them, I am overwhelmed with heartache.

It is not so much that I love them, Nessir: no, in that regard I find myself in a state of non-feeling, a state of no desire at all. In that plentiful seraglio of mine, such abundant love ended up destroying love altogether; but out of that very coldness of mine springs a secret jealousy that torments me. I see in my mind's eye a large group of women left practically to themselves, with only cowardly nonentities to guard them and report to me. I would scarcely feel secure, even if my slaves were all faithful: and what will happen if they are not? Imagine the sorrowful reports I will be receiving as I travel far off in those distant lands! This is an evil that none of my friends can remedy: this is a region of secret woes into which they may not enter: and if they could, what could they do? And would I not prefer, a thousand times over, some hidden, secret impunity to a public, open punishment? My dear Nessir, I confide all my anxieties to you: it is the only consolation that remains to me, in this present state of mine.

From Erzerum, the 10th of the moon of Rebiab II, 1711

Letter 7

Fatmé to Usbek
At Erzerum

It is now two months since you parted, my dear Usbek, though I can scarcely believe it, I have fallen into such a despondency. I walk through the seraglio as if you were there; I cannot help believing you still are. What fate do you wish for a woman who loves you so—who is so used to holding you in her arms—who never cared for anything beyond giving you more and more proofs of her tenderness—a woman free by birth, but a slave by the intensity of her love?

When I married you, I had never yet laid eyes on a man: you are still the only one I have been permitted to see—for I do not count those hideous eunuchs; the least of their imperfections is the fact that they are not even men. When I compare the beauty of your face with the deformities of theirs, I cannot help but count myself fortunate. My imagination cannot begin to create anything nearly as beautiful as you, with all the enchanting charms of your person. I swear to you, Usbek, that when and if I were permitted to leave this place, where I am confined due to my condition—when and if I were permitted to leave behind all the guards that surround me—when and if I were allowed to make my choice from among all the men living in this, the capital of all nations—Usbek, I swear to you, I would choose only you.

Do not think that your absence has led me to neglect the beauty you love so much. Even though I must not be seen by anyone, and the adornments that I make to my appearance cannot add to your happiness, I nevertheless strive to maintain the habit of pleasing: I never go to bed at night without first perfuming myself with the most delicious of scents. In bed, I think about the wonderful times when you were within my arms; a flattering dream seduces me, showing me the object of my love; my imagination leads me on until I am lost in desires, just as it buoys me with hopes. I sometimes imagine that you will return to us soon, tired of this wearisome journeying, and the nights pass away in thoughts such as these, in thoughts that are not quite dreams, not quite waking: I turn and seek you by my side, but it seems you have slipped away from me; and finally the fire of love that devours me burns away all these enchantments, and returns me to myself. And at that point I find myself so excited . . . You may not believe it, Usbek, but it is impossible to live in a state like this, with the fire roaring through my veins. If only I could express to you what I feel so intensely! But how is it that I can feel something so strongly and be unable to express it? In moments like these, Usbek, I would trade the throne of the world for a single one of your kisses. Oh, how miserable is it for a woman to feel such violent desires, while she is deprived of the one man who could satisfy them; how miserable for a woman to be left all to herself with nothing to distract her, to be forced to live in continual sighs, and in the fury of an unsatisfied passion; how miserable, how far from happiness, to be unable even to serve as a means to some other person's felicity—a worthless ornament in the seraglio, kept under guard there for the sake of honor, not for the pleasure of her spouse!

How cruel you are, you men! It charms you, our having desires that we cannot satisfy: you treat us like unfeeling creatures, but you would be unhappy enough if we really were; you believe that our long suppressed passions will be instantly rekindled at the sight of you. But it takes effort to make oneself loved; it is much easier to profit from our starved desire than it is to make us love you for your merits.

Farewell, my dear Usbek, farewell. Depend upon it, I live only to adore you. My soul is filled with you; and your absence, far from allowing me to forget you, would only arouse my love more and more—if it were possible for it to become even more violent than it is.

From the seraglio at Ispahan, the 12th of the moon of Rebiab I, 1711

Letter 8

Usbek to his friend Rustan
At Ispahan

Your letter reached me at Erzerum, where I remain for now. I did fear that my departure would give rise to a great deal of talk, but this does not bother me. Which would you have me follow, Rustan, my own counsel, or that of my enemies?

I have frequented the court since my earliest youth, yet I can swear that my heart has not been corrupted by it. In fact, I formed a grand plan for myself: I would dare to be virtuous. When I first saw vice, I fled from it, but I later returned and approached it, in order to unmask it. I carried truth with me to the very steps of the throne, speaking a language there that was unknown until then. I gave the lie to flattery, shocking both the idolaters and their idol.

But when I saw that my sincerity only made me enemies; when I saw that it attracted the jealousy of the ministers but not the favor of the prince; when, in that corrupt court, I was able to sustain my integrity only by a weak virtue—then I resolved to leave the place behind. I feigned a great love for the sciences, and by dint of feigning it, it eventually became real. I no longer mixed in any worldly affairs, but retired instead to my house in the country. But even this had its problems: I remained exposed to the malice of my enemies, and had abandoned all the means I might have used to shield myself from it. A few confidential warnings made me look more seriously at my situation: I resolved to exile myself from my country, and my retreat from the court provided me a plausible pretext: I went to the king, and told him of my desire to instruct myself in the sciences of the West, implying that he might profit from my journey. This found favor in his eyes and I departed, depriving my enemies of a victim.

And there you have it, Rustan, the real motive behind this trip of mine. Let Ispahan gossip; defend me only to those who love me. Let my enemies make all the clever interpretations they wish; I am only too fortunate in that they can harm me no more than that.

People speak about me now, but perhaps I will be forgotten, and my friends . . . No, Rustan, I will not finish that unhappy thought: no, I will always be dear to my friends; I depend upon their faithfulness, as I do upon yours.

From Erzerum, the 20th of the moon of Gemmadi II, 1711

Letter 9

The Chief Eunuch to Ibbi
At Erzerum

You follow your long-time master in his journeys; you pass through provinces and kingdoms, and the difficulties scarcely bother you at all; every moment you see something new, and everything you see is diverting, helping the time pass by without your even noticing it.

But it is not the same with me, shut up here in a frightful prison, always surrounded by the same objects and eaten up with the same problems. I groan under the weight of all these cares and of all the anxieties of fifty years; in the course of this long life of mine, I cannot say that I have had even one day of serenity, no, not even one tranquil moment.

When my first master formed the cruel scheme of having me guard his wives, he employed endless seductive arguments and a thousand threats to convince me to give up my manhood, to separate myself forever from myself; worn out from serving in harsher conditions, I considered that sacrificing my passions would lead me to peace and to fortune. Fool that I was! My anxious mind saw only the benefits, not the loss; I expected to be delivered from the attacks of love by an inability to satisfy it. But alas, only the effects of passion were extinguished in me, not their cause; and far from being relieved from passion, I found myself surrounded by objects that endlessly aroused it. I entered the seraglio, where everything I saw made me regret what I had lost; I was aroused every moment, as a thousand charms revealed themselves to my gaze, only to make me miserable. And to make my pains even worse, I always had a happy man in my sight. During that difficult time, I never escorted a woman to my master's bed, never undressed one without returning to my room with rage in my heart and hideous despair in my soul.

And that is how I passed my miserable youth. I had no one I could confide in. Overwhelmed with both ennui and heartache, I had no choice but to swallow them. And those women—in the past I would have been tempted to look on them with eyes of desire, but now I could only look at them with severity: if they divined the truth, I would be lost, for they would have taken full advantage of my feelings.

I remember once, when I was putting a woman into her bath, I felt myself so overcome that I lost my reason altogether and dared to put my hand in a forbidden place. I thought then that this would be the last day of my life, but I was lucky enough to escape death by horrendous torture. The beauty who had become the confidant of my weakness, however, sold her silence dearly: I lost all authority over her, and she went on to force me to agree to a thousand things, each one of which could have cost me my life.

But finally the fires of youth have burned down; I am old now, and in that regard at least I have found some tranquility: I look on women with indifference, and now I give to them all the contempt and torment that they have given to me. I often pause and remember that I was born to command them, and I become a man again the moment I do command them. I hate them, now that I can observe them coolly, now that my reason shows me all their weaknesses. Even though I guard them for another, the joy of making myself obeyed gives me a secret pleasure; when I deprive them of everything, it feels as if I am doing it for myself, and I always experience an indirect satisfaction. In the seraglio, I am in my own little empire, and my ambition—the only passion left to me—feels somewhat satisfied. I observe with pleasure how everything here revolves around me, and how necessary I am. And I am happy to be the object of hatred for all these women, for it confirms my position. They certainly deserve to hate me: I make it a point to stand in the way of even their most innocent pleasures; I make of myself an impenetrable barrier. They dream up their little schemes and projects, and I put an end to them. I use refusal like a weapon; I bristle with scruples and difficulties; I speak of nothing but duty, virtue, chastity, modesty. I drive them to despair, speaking to them endlessly about the weaknesses of their sex, and about the master's authority, and then I complain about having to be so severe; I try to make it appear as if my only motivations are their own self-interest and my profound attachment to them.

It is not as if I don't suffer any number of disagreeable moments, or as if these vindictive women aren't seeking every day for some means to avenge themselves on me. Their reprisals are terrible. There is a kind of ebb and flow between us of empire and submission: they constantly make me carry out the most humiliating tasks, showing an unexampled level of contempt for me; and despite my age, they make me get up ten times during the night for the merest whims. I am overwhelmed by their endless orders, commands, tasks, caprices; it is as if they take turns keeping me moving to fulfill their endless train of whims, and they often enjoy multiplying my tasks. They confide in me, but their confidences are falsehoods: sometimes they will come to say that a man has been seen outside the walls, or that they have heard some sound, or even that one of them is going to be receiving a letter. All this gives me trouble, and they laugh at my trouble; they delight in watching me torment myself. Sometimes they will have me stand behind their door and keep watch night and day. They know so well how to counterfeit illness, fainting spells, and frights; they can always come up with some pretext for bringing me to the desired point. Such occasions require only blind obedience and limitless deference from me, for if a man in my position were to refuse—unheard of!—or even to hesitate, they would have the right to punish me. I would much rather die, my dear Ibbi, than descend to that humiliation.

That is not all: I am never sure whether I am in favor with my master, for I have all these enemies who are so close to his heart, enemies who would love nothing more than my destruction. They have these fifteen-minute periods alone with him when my voice is not heard, these periods when he refuses them nothing, these periods when I am always in the wrong. I escort irritated women to my master's bed: do you suppose that she will labor there for me, that my side of the story will prevail? I have everything to fear from their tears, their sighs, their embraces, their very pleasures, for in that place, they are triumphant. Their charms become frightening things to me; their present services can efface all of my past services in a moment, and there is no way to reason with a master who is no longer himself.

How many times have I gone to bed in favor, and awakened in disgrace? That day when I was whipped so shamefully all through the seraglio, what had been my crime? I left a woman in the arms of my master, and the moment she saw him enflamed with desire, she burst into a torrent of tears; she complained, and she managed her complaints so skillfully that they grew in proportion to the love she was arousing. How could I stand up for myself at such a critical moment? I was lost, lost when I least expected it, the victim of an amorous negotiation, a treaty composed of sighs. There you have it, dear Ibbi: this is the cruel state in which I have always lived.

How lucky you are! All you have to be concerned about is Usbek. It is easy for you to please him, and to keep yourself in his favor until the end of your days.

From the seraglio at Ispahan, the last of the moon of Saphar, 1711

Letter 10

Mirza to his friend Usbek
At Erzerum

You were the only one who could console me for the absence of Rica, and Rica is the only one who could console me for yours. We miss you, Usbek; you were the very heart of our group. It takes real violence to rupture the bonds that heart and mind have formed!

We debate a great deal here; our debates normally center on morality. Yesterday somebody posed the question, are men rendered more happy by pleasure and the senses, or by the practice of virtue? I have often heard you say that men are born to be virtuous, and that justice is for us as native and natural as existence itself. Would you please explain what you meant by that?

I spoke with the mullahs about it, but they exasperated me with their endless quotations from the Koran—for I do not speak to them as a true believer, but rather as a man, as a citizen, and the head of a household. Farewell.

From Ispahan, the last day of the moon of Saphar, 1711

Letter 11

Usbek to Mirza
At Ispahan

So, you renounce your own judgment in order to give mine a try; you consult me, believing me capable of instructing you. My dear Mirza, the only thing I cherish more than the good opinion you have developed of me is your friendship, from which that good opinion arises.

To carry out the task you ask of me, I think it best not to employ highly abstract arguments. There are certain truths that one conveys not so much by persuasion, but by making one feel them, and such are the truths of morality. Perhaps this little story will have a greater impact on you than subtle philosophizing.

Once upon a time in Arabia, there was a small tribe known as the Troglodytes, the descendants of the ancient Troglodytes who, if we can believe the historians, were more like beasts than men. But these later Troglodytes were not so deformed, were not shaggy like bears, did not hiss at all, and had two eyes: but still they were so wicked and ferocious that there was no principle of equity among them, nor of justice either.

They had a king of foreign origin who, in order to cure them of their natural wickedness, treated them with great severity. But they conspired against him, killed him, and wiped out the entire royal family.

The coup having succeeded, they all assembled to choose a new government, and after much debate and disagreement they created magistrates. But the magistrates had barely been elected before the Troglodytes found them intolerable, so they wiped them out too.

Having liberated themselves from this new yoke, the people now consulted only their own natural savagery. They agreed that from now on, they would no longer obey anyone, and that each one would concern himself solely with his own interests, considering no one else's.

This unanimous resolution delighted them in the extreme. They said, "Why should I go on working myself to death for people I care nothing about? From now on, I will think only of myself. I will live a happy life: what do I care if others do or not? I will take care to procure everything for my own needs, and provided I have that, I don't care in the slightest if all the other Troglodytes are sunk in poverty."

It was planting season, and each one said, "I will only work my own field, so as to grow just the wheat that I need for myself. Anything more would be useless to me; I will not trouble myself for anything useless."

Now, the farming lands in this little kingdom were not all the same: some were arid and mountainous, while others were low-lying and watered from many different streams. This particular year turned out to be a very dry one, so that the elevated lands could grow nothing, while the lower ones were very fertile. Thus, almost all the mountain people were dying from hunger, for all the others coldly refused to share their harvests with them.

The next year was very rainy, so that the upland fields were hugely productive, while the lowlands were sunk under water. Half the people again were suffering from famine, but they found the others just as harsh and inflexible as they had been themselves.

One of the foremost inhabitants had a very beautiful wife; his neighbor became infatuated with her, and carried her off. A great quarrel ensued, and after a great many insults and blows, they all agreed to submit the case to a Troglodyte who, during the days of the republic, had been a person of some repute. They all went to him, and began to explain their side of the argument to him. But this man said, "What do I care if this woman belongs to you, or to you? I have my field to work; I am not going to spend my time settling your quarrels and seeing to your business while I neglect my own. Please, leave me in peace, and do not come to me with your problems any more." With that, he left them, and went back to working his land. The abductor, who was the stronger man, swore that he would die before he would give the woman back; and the other, pained by the injustice of his neighbor and the indifference of the judge, headed back to his home in a state of desperation. On the way, he encountered a young, beautiful woman who was returning from the well. He liked her very much, and he liked her all the more when he learned that she was the wife of the man they had asked to be judge, and who had cared so little about him and his happiness. He abducted the woman, and took her back to his house.

There was another man who owned a large and fertile field, which he cultivated with great care: two of his neighbors joined together and chased him out of his house, taking over his field. They united to fend off anyone who would try to take it back from them, and in fact they held the place for several months this way. But one of them, growing irritated with having to share something that he could have all to himself, killed the other, becoming sole master of the field. His empire did not last long: two other Troglodytes came and attacked him; he was not strong enough to withstand them, and he was slaughtered.

Another Troglodyte, nearly naked, saw some wool for sale; he asked the price, and the merchant said to himself, "Ordinarily, I would only expect to get enough money for the wool to buy two measures of grain; but I am going to offer it for four times that price, enough for me to buy eight measures." The man had no choice but to pay the exorbitant price. "I am quite pleased now," said the merchant, "and now I need to buy some grain." The man who had bought the wool replied, "What did you say? You need some grain? I have some I can sell you, but the price may surprise you a bit: grain, you see, is quite dear now, with famine raging everywhere. But give me back my money, and I will give you exactly one measure of grain. I will not budge from this price even if you die of starvation."

At the same time, a cruel plague was ravaging the area. A skilled doctor arrived from a neighboring country and provided such effective remedies that everyone who consulted him recovered. When the disease subsided, he went to each of those he had treated and asked for his payment, but he heard nothing but refusals. He returned to his country, worn out after so long a journey. But soon afterward, he heard that the disease had sprung to life again, and was raging even more fiercely in that ungrateful country. This time, the Troglodytes came to him without waiting for him to travel to them. "Go away, you unjust people," he said to them; "you have a poison within your souls far more lethal than the disease you want to be cured of. You do not deserve a place upon the earth, because you have no humanity, and because the basic rules of justice are entirely unknown to you. I would fear offending the gods who are punishing you if I let myself get in the way of their righteous wrath."

From Erzerum, the 3rd of the moon of Gemmadi II, 1711

Letter 12

Usbek to the same
At Ispahan

So you see, my dear Mirza, how the Troglodytes were destroyed by their own wickedness, victims of their own injustices. Out of the entire nation, only two families remained. Now, there were two men in the country who stood out: they were both possessed of basic humanity; they understood the concept of justice; they both loved virtue. The honesty of their hearts drew them together, as did the corruption of all those around them. They observed the general desolation, and felt nothing but pity: and pity became yet another bond between them. They labored with solicitude for each other, working for the common good; their only disagreements were of that gentle, tender kind that naturally arise between friends, and they lived in a distant area of the country, far from those compatriots who were unworthy of their presence. Theirs was a happy, tranquil life; the earth seemed to produce food for them by itself, being cultivated by such virtuous hands.

They loved their wives, who in turn cherished them. Their great aim was to raise their children in the path of virtue. They constantly told them stories about their compatriots, putting that unhappy example before their eyes. Above all, they stressed that one's self-interest is always contained within the common interest, and that to separate those two was to take a step toward ruin; they taught also that virtue need cost us nothing, that we must not regard virtue as a painful burden; finally, they taught that to do justice for one is to do good for all.

In time they enjoyed the consolation of virtuous fathers, which is to have children who resemble them. The young race who grew up before their eyes made happy marriages and thrived; their numbers grew, without straining their union of hearts. Virtue, far from being weakened and diluted in the multitude, grew stronger from the growing number of examples.

How can one describe the happiness of these Troglodytes? A people so just must be beloved by the gods. They learned to fear the gods from the moment they opened their eyes, and those aspects that nature had left too rough were smoothed and softened by religion.

They instituted feast days in honor of the gods. The young girls festooned themselves with flowers, and the young boys celebrated with dances to rustic music; the banquets that followed combined joy with frugality. Pure, naïve nature was expressed in these gatherings. Here they learned how to give their hearts, and how to receive the love of others; here virgin modesty surprised itself with sudden avowals, which in turn were ratified by their fathers; and here loving mothers enjoyed the vision of sweet, faithful unions to come.

They went to the temple to ask favors of their gods—not for riches or an onerous overabundance, for such things were beneath these happy Troglodytes, who knew only to wish for the good of their fellows. No, they came to the foot of the altars to pray only for health for their fathers, for union among their brothers, for the tenderness of their wives and the love and obedience of their children. Girls came bearing the tender sacrifice of their hearts, and asked no grace beyond that of being able to render some Troglodyte a happy man.

At night, when the flocks had left the meadows, and the wearied oxen brought back from the plow, they all assembled. During their frugal meal, they sang of the injustices of the first Troglodytes and of all the evils that had befallen them, of the rebirth of virtue with a new people, and of their felicity. They celebrated the greatness of the gods, the way they favored those who prayed to them, and were wrathful toward those who did not fear them. They went on to describe the delights of the rural life, and the happiness that comes from living in innocence. Soon, they went off to sleep, undisturbed by cares and anxieties.

Nature furnished them with what they wanted as well as what they needed. In this fortunate country, greed was unknown; when they gave each other presents, the giver always considered himself to have been the gainer. The Troglodyte people saw themselves as one single family: their flocks were always getting mixed up together, and the only labor they tended to spare themselves was the bother of separating them.

From Erzerum, the 6th of the moon of Gemmadi II, 1711

Letter 13

Usbek to the same

I cannot say enough about the Troglodytes' virtue. One day, one of them said: "My father has to work in his field tomorrow. I will get up two hours ahead of him, and when he gets to the field, he will find the work is already done."

Another one said to himself, "I believe my sister is attracted to a young Troglodyte related to us. I must speak to my father, and convince him to arrange the marriage."

Another was told that thieves had made off with his entire herd. "I am very upset," he said, "because there was a pure white heifer in the herd that I had hoped to offer to the gods."

Another was overheard saying, "I must go to the temple to give thanks to the gods, because my brother who is so beloved by my father, and whom I cherish so highly, has recovered his health."

Again, "My field borders one of my father's, and the workers in that area are exposed every day to the hot sun. I must plant a couple of trees along the border so that the poor men can have some shade to rest in."

One day when a number of Troglodytes were assembled, an old man spoke about a young one who, he suspected, was involved in some criminal doings, and he reproached him. The young Troglodytes assembled there said, "We do not believe he has committed this crime, but if he has, may he be the last in his family to die!"

A Troglodyte was told that some strangers had robbed his house and carried off all his belongings. He replied, "Well, if they had not been unjust people, I would have wished for them to be blessed with a longer use of my things than I have had."

All their prosperity was observed by others, and not without envy. The neighboring peoples assembled and under a trumped-up pretext, determined to invade and steal away all their flocks. As soon as this resolution became known, the Troglodytes sent ambassadors to meet them on their way, speaking to them thus:

"What have the Troglodytes done to you? Have they abducted your wives, stolen your beasts, ravaged your countrysides? No: we are a just people, and we fear the gods. What, therefore, do you want from us? Do you want wool to make your clothes? Do you want milk from our cattle, or the fruits of our farms? Lay down your arms, come among us, and we will give you all of that. But we swear by all that is most holy, that if you enter our lands as enemies, we will regard you as a wicked people, and we will treat you like savage beasts."

The message was received with contempt; the savage peoples invaded the lands of the Troglodytes, thinking the Troglodytes' innocence was their only defense.

But in fact they had given a great deal of thought to defense. They had put their wives and children in a safe place far from the borders. It was their enemies' wickedness and not their numbers that shocked them. They felt a new ardor burning within their hearts: one hoped to die for his father, another for his wife and children, this one for his brothers, that one for his friends, and all for the Troglodyte people. When one man died, another swiftly took his place, for there was now another death to avenge, in addition to the common cause.

Such was the combat between wickedness and virtue. That cowardly race, who went to war only for the spoils, felt no shame in fleeing; and they surrendered to the virtue of the Troglodytes, even though they were not touched by it.

From Erzerum, the 9th of the moon of Gemmadi II, 1711

Letter 14

Usbek to the same

As their numbers continued to grow, the Troglodytes considered that it was time for them to choose a king. They decided to confer the crown on the most just man, and all eyes turned to a particular old man venerable both for his great age and his long-standing virtue. He had not wanted to attend the meeting, though; he remained shut up in his house, consumed with grief.

When deputies were sent to inform him that he had been chosen, he said: "God forbid that I should do such a wrong to the Troglodytes, as to allow them to think there is no one more just than me. You offer me the crown, and if you truly insist, I will have to accept it. But rest assured that I will die of sorrow at having seen the Troglodytes, once free, now reducing themselves to subjects." As he said this, tears ran down his face. "Oh, why have I lived to see so miserable a day?" Then he spoke in a more severe tone: "Now I see what it is, Troglodytes: your virtue is beginning to weigh upon you. In your current state, having no ruler, you must be virtuous despite yourselves; otherwise, you could not survive, and you would fall back into the state of your ancestors. But now this yoke seems too demanding to you: you would rather submit yourselves to a prince, and accept laws from him that would be less rigid and demanding than your own morality. You know that under such laws you can satisfy your ambitions, acquire riches, and languish in sordid pleasures, and that so long as you avoid overt and extreme crimes, you will be able to forget about virtue." He paused a moment, the tears running even more freely down his face. "And what do you expect me to do? How can I bring myself to command anything to a Troglodyte? Do you want him to perform a virtuous act on my command—the Troglodyte who would do exactly that without me, simply by following the bent of his nature? Oh Troglodytes, I am at the end of my days, the blood is cooling in my veins, and I will soon meet again with your sacred ancestors. Why do you ask me to pain them so? Why do you want to make me tell them that I have left you weighted under a yoke other than that of virtue?"

From Erzerum, the 10th of the moon of Gemmadi II, 1711

Letter 15

The Chief Eunuch to Jaron, the Black Eunuch
At Erzerum

I pray that heaven will bring you back to these lands, and preserve you from all danger.

Although I have never really known that attachment that people call friendship, and have remained entirely within myself, you have, nevertheless, made me feel that in fact I have a heart. While I have been like bronze when it comes to all the slaves living under my command, I observed your growth from childhood with pleasure.

The time came when my master cast his gaze upon you. Nature had scarcely begun to speak within you, when steel separated you from that nature. I will never reveal whether I felt pity for you, or whether I felt pleased to see you being raised to the same status as me. I dried your tears and soothed you when you cried. It seemed to me that you were undergoing a new birth, leaving behind a servitude where you must always obey and entering upon one in which you would always command. I took charge of your education. Severity, always inseparable from instruction, long hid from you just how dear you were to me. But you were dear: and now I can tell you that I loved you as a father loves his son, if the words father and son can be used by people with our fate.

You are about to traverse countries inhabited by Christians, people who have never believed. It will be impossible for you to remain pure there. How can the Prophet keep you in his view when you are lost among millions of his enemies? I hope that my master will make the pilgrimage to Mecca upon his return: you will all purify yourselves again there, in the land of the angels.

From the seraglio at Ispahan, the 10th
of the moon of Gemmadi II, 1711

Letter 16

Usbek to Mullah Mohammed Ali,
Guardian of the Three Tombs
At Qum

Why do you live in the tombs, divine mullah? You were made to dwell among the stars. No doubt you conceal yourself there in order not to obscure the sun: for you are unspotted, unlike that star; but like that star, you cover yourself with clouds.

Your knowledge is like an abyss, deeper than the ocean; your mind is more penetrating than Zufagar, Ali's double-pointed sword. You know what takes place among the nine choirs of the celestial powers; you read your Koran on the breast of our divine Prophet, and when you find some passage obscure, he sends a swift-winged angel with rapid wings from the throne to reveal the secret meaning to you.

I too could, with your help, have intimate correspondence with the seraphim, for after all, O thirteenth imam, are you not the very point where heaven and earth converge, the point of communication between the abyss and the empyrean?

I find myself among profane people. Allow me to purify myself with you; allow me to turn my face toward the sacred places where you dwell; distinguish me from the wicked ones as the white thread is distinguished at dawn from the black.[9] Grant me your counsel, and care for my soul: intoxicate it with the spirit of the prophets, nourish it with the knowledge of paradise, and allow me to lay its wounds at your feet. Please address your holy letters to me at Erzerum, where I shall remain for some months.

From Erzerum, the 11th of the moon of Gemmadi II, 1711

Letter 17

Usbek to the same

I cannot contain my impatience, divine mullah; I cannot wait for your sublime response. I am experiencing doubts, and I must resolve them; I think my reason is leading me astray: bring me back to the true path—enlighten me, O source of light—strike down, with your divine pen,

9. The expression comes from the Koran, Sura 2, verse 187.

the difficulties that I am about to express to you. Take pity on me, and make me blush at the question I am about to raise.

Why does our great lawgiver forbid us the flesh of the pig, and all those other foods that he calls unclean? Why does he forbid us to touch a dead body? And why does he have us wash our bodies endlessly in order to purify our souls? It seems to me that these things in themselves are neither pure nor impure: I can find no quality inherent in them that would render them one or the other. Mud appears filthy to us because it offends our sight, or one of the other senses, but in itself it is neither more nor less dirty than gold or diamonds. The idea that contacting a dead body is polluting comes from the natural repugnance that we feel. If the bodies of those who do not wash did not offend our sense of smell or our eyesight, how would we know that they were impure?

The senses then, divine mullah, must be the sole judges of whether a thing is pure or impure. Objects do not affect all men in the same manner, though: what is agreeable to one is disgusting to others. Therefore, the testimony of the senses cannot establish rules for us, unless we are to conclude that each may, according to his own imagination, distinguish for himself what is pure from what is not.

And, sacred mullah, would that not overthrow the distinctions that our divine prophet has set up, along with the fundamental points of the law written by the hands of the angels?

From Erzerum, the 20th of the moon of Gemmadi II, 1711

Letter 18

Mohammed Ali, Servant of the Prophet, to Usbek
At Erzerum

You continue to ask the questions that were asked of our holy prophet a thousand times. Why do you not read in the Traditions of the Doctors?[10] Why not betake yourself to the pure fountainhead of all intelligence? You would find all your doubts resolved there.

---

10. The *Traditions of the Doctors* refers to the *Hadith*, or collections of commentary on Mohammed's sayings and the text of the Koran. These began to be collected and compiled in the generation after Mohammed himself.

Unhappy man! You have always been distracted by the things of the earth, and have failed to keep your gaze fixed on those of heaven; you revere the mullah's condition, but you do not dare to embrace it or follow it!

Profane man! You will never enter into the secrets of the Eternal, for your light is only an abysmal shadow; and all the reasonings of your mind are like the dust kicked up by your feet, when the sun is at its height in the torrid month of Chahban.

Thus, the very zenith of your mind is lower than the nadir of the lowest of the imams.[11] Your futile philosophy is as the lightning that foretells the coming of the storm and of darkness; you stand in the midst of the tempest, wandering here and there like the winds.

Your doubts and questions are easy to resolve; all that is necessary is to recount the story of what happened one day to our holy prophet, when tempted by the Christians and harassed by the Jews, he confounded them all.

The Jew Abdias Ibesalon asked him why God had forbidden men from eating the flesh of pigs. Mohammed responded, "it is not unreasonable, for the animal is impure, and I will convince you of it." He molded the figure of a man out of mud, and threw it down on the ground, crying, "Get up!" Immediately a man arose, saying, "I am Japhet, son of Noah." The holy prophet asked him, "Did you have these same white hairs at the time of your death?" "No," he replied; "but when you called to me, I thought the day of judgment had come, and I was so frightened that my hair turned white on the spot."

God's envoy then said, "Tell me now the whole story of Noah and the ark." Japhet obeyed, and detailed exactly what had happened in the first months, and then he continued:

"We shoveled the excrement from all the animals onto one side of the ark, which made the boat list to one side, putting the fear of death into all of us, and especially our wives, who lamented vigorously. Our father Noah asked God for advice, and was told to take the elephant and make him turn his head toward the side that was dipping downward. The great beast expelled so much excrement that a pig was born from out of it." Now can you still wonder, Usbek, why it is that we abstain from eating pork, or why we consider the pig an unclean animal?

"Furthermore, the pig wallowed in the excrement so much that he raised a foul stench throughout the ark, which caused him to sneeze. From his nose there sprang a rat, who ran off gnawing everything he saw. Noah found this so intolerable that he consulted God a second

11. *This word is in more common use among Turks than among Persians* [Montesquieu's note].

time, and he was told to strike the lion on its forehead; this caused the lion to sneeze, and from his nose there sprang a cat." Do you still fail to see why these animals are unclean? How does it seem to you?

Therefore, when you fail to see the reason why certain things are impure, it is because you are ignorant of what has taken place among God, the angels, and men. You do not know the history of eternity; you have not read the books that were written in heaven; what has been revealed to you is no more than a tiny part of the great library of the divine. And even those of us who have approached much closer to heaven remain in obscurity and darkness. Farewell. May Mohammed be in your heart.

From Qum, the last of the moon of Chahban, 1711

Letter 19

Usbek to his friend Rustan
At Ispahan

We stayed only a week at Tocat, and after thirty-five days' journey, we have arrived in Smyrna.

Between Tocat and Smyrna, we did not pass a single city worth mentioning. I was shocked to see the weakness of the Osmanli empire. The sick body is sustained not by a gentle, temperate regime but by violent remedies, which only weaken and diminish it continually.

The Pashas, who hold their positions only by means of payoffs, enter a province broke, and ravage it like a conquered country. A shameless militia answers only to its own whims. Forts and towns are torn down and deserted, whole countrysides desolated, both agriculture and commerce entirely abandoned.

Impunity is the watchword for this harsh regime; Christians who farm the land and Jews who collect the taxes are subject to a thousand violent attacks.

Ownership of land is uncertain, and as a result the desire to cultivate it is minimal; there is no title, no possession that can stand up to the caprices of the authorities.

These barbarians have abandoned all the arts, even including the military arts. While the nations of Europe continue to advance in refinement, these remain sunk in their ancient ignorance; they take notice of new war machines and devices only after they have been used against them a thousand times.

They have no naval experience, and are clumsy in seagoing maneuvers. It is said that a handful of Christians, issuing forth from a rock, have put the Ottomans into a sweat and shaken their empire.[12]

Inept at commerce themselves, they barely tolerate the hard-working and enterprising Europeans who have come into the country to carry it out themselves; they believe they are doing the foreigners a favor by permitting them to come and enrich them.

Out of the entire vast extent that I have traversed in this country, only Smyrna strikes me as a rich and powerful city: and it is the Europeans who have made it so. If it were left up to the Turks, it would resemble all the others.

And there you have, my dear Rustan, my considered estimate of this empire, which will be the scene of some conqueror's triumph within two hundred years.

From Smyrna, the 2nd of the moon of Rhamazan, 1711

Letter 20

Usbek to Zachi, His Wife
At the seraglio in Ispahan

You have offended me, Zachi; I sense movements beginning within my heart that you should fear, even though my distance from you allows you the time to change your behavior and to soften the violent jealousy you have aroused in me.

I have learned that you were found alone with Nadir, the white eunuch, who will pay with his head for his infidelity and perfidy. How could you let yourself forget that you are forbidden to allow a white eunuch in your room, when you have black ones designated to serve you? It is in vain for you to tell me that eunuchs are not men, and that your virtue keeps you above any thoughts that might make you see in them even an imperfect resemblance to men. That is not enough, either

12. *This is evidently a reference to the knights of Malta* [Montesquieu's note]. The Knights of Malta, a Catholic military order, were active as early as the twelfth century; their greatest military exploits were against the Turks in the sixteenth century, and they were legendary for being effective fighters despite their small numbers.

for you or for me—for you, because you have done something that is forbidden by the laws of the seraglio; and for me, because you sully my honor in exposing yourself to the gaze of others. But to the gaze only? Perhaps more, perhaps exposing yourself to the designs of a traitor who would pollute you with his crimes, and then pollute you even further with his regret, with the despair of his impotence.

Perhaps you will reply that you have always been faithful to me. Well, did you have any choice? How could you have outwitted the vigilance of the black eunuchs, who are shocked at the life you choose to lead? How could you have broken all those locks on all those doors that keep you enclosed from the world? You brag of your virtue, but it is not a free virtue; and perhaps your impure desires have already stripped you, a thousand times over, of the merit of that fidelity you boast about.

I hope that you have not done all that I suspect you have; that this villain has not put his sacrilegious hands upon you; that you have refused to lay open to his eyes the delights that belong to his master; that, covered by your clothing, you have kept that feeble barrier between him and you; that he himself, struck by a sense of holy respect, has lowered his eyes before you; and that, his bravery evaporating at once, he trembled at the thought of the punishments to come to him. But even if all that is true, it is still a fact that you have done something that is contrary to your duty. And if you have violated your duty in that way without satisfying your unruly inclinations, to what lengths might you go to satisfy them? What would you do if you could leave that sacred place—which in your eyes is a prison, while for your companions it is a safe haven, an escape from the world's vice, a sacred temple in which your sex transcends its weakness and indeed finds itself invincible, despite all its natural disadvantages? What would you do if, left to yourself, you had only your love for me as a defense—that love which is so grievously injured—and your duty, which you have so shamefully betrayed? Oh, how holy are the ways of your country, which snatch you away from the attacks of vile slaves! You should give me thanks for the confinement in which I make you live, for it is only in that way that you deserve to live at all.

You say you cannot tolerate the head eunuch, because he is always watching what you do, and because he gives you wise advice. His ugliness, you say, is so terrible that you cannot bear to look upon him. As if these sorts of posts called for the most beautiful of objects! What really bothers you is not having the white eunuch in his place, the man who dishonors you.

But what in fact has your chief slave done to you? He has told you that your familiarity with the young Zélide is not proper: this is why you hate him.

I should be a severe judge, Zachi; I am only a spouse, seeking some way to find you innocent. The love I have for Roxane, my newest bride, has not reduced the tenderness I should feel for you, who are no less beautiful than she. I share my love between you; and Roxane has no other advantage than what virtue can add to beauty.

From Smyrna, the 12th of the moon of Zilcadé, 1711

Letter 21

Usbek to the Chief White Eunuch

You ought to tremble upon opening this letter; or rather, you should have trembled when you permitted the perfidy of Nadir. You who, even in your cold and listless old age, cannot lift your eyes to the fearful objects of my love without crime—you, to whom it is never permitted to set your sacrilegious foot through the door of that terrible place that keeps them from all men's gaze—you, who are responsible for their behavior, nonetheless allow them to do what you are not rash enough to do: do you not see that the lightning is about to strike them, and you?

And what are you but vile instruments that I can smash on a whim, creatures that exist only to obey, who live in this world subject entirely to my laws, and who will die when I give the command—you, who draw breath only because my happiness, my love, even my jealousy sometimes have need of you and your lowness—and finally you, who have no part to play in this life but that of submission, no other will but mine, no other hope but my happiness?

I know that some of my wives are impatient with the austere laws of duty, and that the continual presence of a black eunuch annoys them; I know they are weary of those hideous sights that are only there to keep bringing them back to their husband: yes, I know all this. But you, who were the cause of this disorder, you will be punished in a way calculated to strike fear into all those who would dare abuse my trust.

I swear by all the prophets in heaven, and by Ali, the greatest of them all, that if you deviate from your duty henceforth I will regard your life exactly the way I regard those of insects that I crush beneath my feet.

From Smyrna, the 12th of the moon of Zilcadé, 1711

Letter 22

Jaron to the Chief Eunuch

The farther Usbek travels away from the seraglio, the more his thoughts turn to his consecrated wives: he sighs, he sheds tears; his sorrows turn to bitterness, and his suspicions increase. He wants to increase the number of their guardians. He is going to send me back, along with all the blacks who came along with him. He no longer fears for himself, but for what is a thousand times dearer to him than himself.

So I am coming to live under your laws, and to share your cares. Good God! How many things are required for one man to be made happy!

Nature seems to have formed women for dependence, and then loosed them from that dependence; disorder and conflict arise between the sexes because they each claim similar rights. But we have entered into a new kind of harmony: we have sown hatred between women and us eunuchs, and love between men and women.

My face will turn severe. I will cast only somber glances. Joy will flee forever from my lips. My exterior will appear all tranquility, while my heart will be unquiet. My griefs will show long before the wrinkles of age come upon me.

I would have liked to follow my master in his travels to the West, but my will belongs to him. He wants me to guard his wives: I will guard them, and faithfully. I know how I must comport myself among that sex in whom vanity must be permitted, for otherwise it turns into arrogance, and that sex that is more easily destroyed than humbled. I prostrate myself before you.

From Smyrna, the 12th of the moon of Zilcadé, 1711

Letter 23

Usbek to his friend Ibben
At Smyrna

We arrived at Livorno after forty days at sea. It is a new city, and a testimony to the genius of the dukes of Tuscany, who have made the most flourishing city in Italy out of a swampy village.

Women enjoy a great deal of freedom here; they can observe men through certain windows called *jalousies*, and they can go out any day accompanied by some elderly women. They wear only one veil.[13] Their brothers-in-law, their uncles, their nephews all can see them, and their husbands rarely object.

It is a great spectacle for a Mohammedan, seeing his first Christian city. I am not referring to the things that strike one immediately, such as the difference in architecture, in manners and clothing: rather, in the smallest details, I sense that there is something singular here, though I cannot put it into words.

Tomorrow we leave for Marseille; our stay will not be long. Rica's plan, which is also mine, is to travel as rapidly as we can to Paris, which is the seat of the European empire. Travelers always seek out the big cities, for they are a kind of nation common to all foreigners. Farewell. Remember that I will love you always.

From Livorno, the 12th of the moon of Saphar, 1712

Letter 24

Rica to Ibben
At Smyrna

We have been in Paris for a month, and we have been in constant motion. There is so much to be done to get settled, to find the people you are supposed to meet, and acquire all the necessities of life at the same time.

Paris is as large as Ispahan. The houses here are so tall that you would think they were all inhabited by astrologers. As you might imagine, a city built up so high, with six or seven houses piled atop one another, is very populous, and indeed when everyone is out on the streets at the same time, there is enormous confusion.

You may not believe it, but in the month that I have been here, I have not seen anyone actually walking. No one in the world is so addicted to their vehicles as the French: they roll along, they fly. The slower carriages of Asia, the deliberate pace of our camels—these would give the

13. *The Persians wear four* [Montesquieu's note].

Frenchman a fit. As for myself, I am not of that sort, and I often go out for a walk without quickening my pace. But before long I am cursing like a Christian, for even if I did not mind the carriages spattering me with mud from head to toe, what I cannot pardon is the constant elbowing and jostling: one man comes up from behind me and passes, knocking me half-way around, while another coming from the other direction knocks me back to my original position, and before I have gone a hundred paces I am as bruised as if I had come ten leagues.

Do not expect me to speak to you in depth now about the habits and customs of the Europeans: I have only the vaguest idea of them myself at this point, and I have scarcely had time to do more than be astonished.

The French king is the most powerful prince in Europe. Unlike his neighbor, the king of Spain, he owns no gold mines, but he is much richer because he draws his wealth from the vanity of his subjects, which is more inexhaustible than any mine. He has been known to undertake large-scale wars with no other means than the sale of titles of honor—and in a stunning display of human pride, his troops are paid, his towns defended, and his navies fully equipped.

Moreover, this king is a great magician: he exercises his empire over the very minds of his subjects; he can even make them think the way he does. For example, if he has only a million écus[14] in his treasury but he needs two million, he simply persuades the populace that one écu is worth two, and they believe him. If he finds a war difficult to sustain and he has run out of money, he puts the idea into their heads that pieces of paper are money, and they are all immediately convinced of it. He goes so far as to have them believe that he can cure all sorts of diseases simply by touching the patient, so great is the power he has over people's minds.

But do not let what I have said about the king surprise you, for there is another magician even more powerful than him, one who has just as much power over the king's mind as the king does over those of his subjects. This magician is called the Pope: he can make people believe that three are but one, that the bread one eats is not bread, and that the wine one drinks is not wine, and a thousand other things of that nature.

And in order to keep the king on tenterhooks, so that he does not lose the habit of belief, the Pope sometimes gives him certain articles of

14. The *écu* is an obsolete currency; its value was approximately six *livres* or francs.

faith to exercise him. Two years ago he sent him a major one called the *Constitution*, along with great threats to the king and his subjects if they failed to believe the items contained within it.[15] He succeeded with the king, who believed immediately, providing an example for the populace; but some of the latter revolted, saying they refused to believe what was written in that document. Women were the driving force behind this revolt, which divided the court, the whole kingdom, and every family. This constitution forbade them from reading the book that Christians believe was delivered to them from heaven; it is, essentially, their Koran. All the women, indignant over this insult to their sex, rose up against this constitution, and they managed to get the men to join their side; the men in this case wanted no special privilege.[16] It must be admitted, though, that the mufti reasoned not badly in this case; indeed, he must have been instructed by the great Ali in the principles of our own holy law: for, since women are of a creation inferior to our own, and since our prophets tell us they will not enter into paradise, why should they be allowed to meddle with a book whose only goal is to teach the path to paradise?

I have heard talk of near-miraculous things attributed to this king, and I am sure you will be hesitant to credit them.

They say that, while he was waging war against his neighbors, who had leagued against him, he had an enormous number of invisible enemies surrounding him in his own kingdom. They also say that he has tried to find them for thirty years now, but that, despite the indefatigable help of certain dervishes who have his complete trust, he has been unable to find a single one.[17] They live with him; they are at his court, in his capital, among his troops, within the law courts—and yet they say that he will have the misfortune of going to his deathbed without having

---

15. In September of 1713, Pope Clement XI issued the document ("constitution") *Unigenitus*, which condemned 101 propositions associated with Jansenism. (Montesquieu is guilty of anachronism in putting a reference to it in a letter dated 1712.) Apart from the theological issues involved, whether to accept the Papal document or to see it as interfering with the French church—which had long insisted on its own "liberties" in such matters—became a lengthy and often bitter debate. The Regent finally ordered all sides to keep silent on the topic in 1717. See the Introduction for further discussion.

16. *Unigenitus* did condemn a proposition that everyone, including women, should read the Bible.

17. The "dervishes" trusted by the king are the Jesuits, and the invisible enemies are the Jansenists. See the Introduction for further discussion.

discovered them. One might say that they exist in general, but not in particular: as if they formed a body, but a body with no members. Evidently heaven wants to punish this prince for not having been moderate enough in his treatment of his conquered enemies, and so he is given these invisible ones, whose genius and fate are superior to his own.

I will continue to write you, and I will be telling you some things very different from the Persian character and genius. Certainly, the same earth supports both peoples, but the men in the country where I am, and those in the place where you are, are two very different sorts of men.

From Paris, the 4th of the moon of Rebiab II, 1712

Letter 25

Usbek to Ibben
At Smyrna

I have received a letter from your nephew Rhédi; he tells me that he is leaving Smyrna, being desirous of seeing Italy, and that his sole reason for traveling is to instruct himself, so as to become more worthy of you. I congratulate you on having a nephew who someday will be the consolation of your old age.

Rica is writing you a long letter; he tells me that he has included a great deal of detail about this land we are in. His lively mind guarantees that he grasps everything quickly; but as for me, a much more deliberate thinker, I am not quite ready to tell you anything yet.

You are the subject of our warmest conversations; we cannot say enough about the fine welcome you gave us in Smyrna, and the many services that your friendship continues to do us. My generous Ibben, may you find everywhere friends as grateful and as faithful as us!

May I see you again soon, and enjoy again those happy days that flow past so sweetly when two friends are together! Farewell.

From Paris, the 4th of the moon of Rebiab II, 1712

Letter 26

Usbek to Roxane
At the seraglio in Ispahan

How fortunate you are, Roxane, to be in the sweet land of Persia, and not in these poisonous climes where both modesty and virtue are unknown! How fortunate you are! You live in my seraglio as in the very abode of innocence, safe from every possible kind of assault; you find yourself in a joyous state, the state of being unable to lapse. No man has ever sullied you with his lascivious gaze; even your father-in-law, in the freedom of festival time, has never seen your lovely mouth: you have never lacked for a sacred veil to keep it hidden. Fortunate Roxane! When you have been out in the countryside, you have always had eunuchs walking before you, ready to deal out death to any bold fool who failed to run from the sight of you. And I too—the man to whom heaven gave you, to form his happiness—what troubles I had to face in order to make myself master of that great treasure that you defended so faithfully! What sorrow it was for me, during those first days of our marriage, not to be able to see you! And then, what impatience when I did see you! But still you did not satisfy my yearning; you worsened it instead by your obstinate refusals and your frightened modesty: you confused me with all those other men from whom you are constantly hiding yourself. Do you remember that day when I lost you, hidden among your slaves, who betrayed me by hiding you from me? And do you remember that other day when, seeing that your tears were not strong enough to deter me, you deployed your mother's authority to arrest the fury of my love? Do you remember too, when all your resources failed you, what method your courage suggested to you? You snatched up a dagger, and threatened to sacrifice the husband who loved you if he persisted in demanding that which you cherished even more than you cherished him. Two months it went on, this combat between love and virtue. You clung to your chaste scruples too long, and you did not surrender, even when you had been vanquished. You defended your doomed virginity to the last possible moment, and you regarded me as an enemy who was inflicting an outrage upon you, not as a spouse who loved you. It was more than three months before you could bring yourself to look at me without blushing; your embarrassment seemed to reproach me for the advantage I had taken. And I was not to enjoy a tranquil possession, either: you hid from me every charm, every grace that you could, so that, being intoxicated with the greatest of your favors, I was unable to obtain the least of them.

If you had been raised in this country, though, you would not have been so anxious. The women here have lost all restraint. They come into the company of men with their faces uncovered, as if they are actively looking for their own downfall. They go out looking for men, and they go to see them in the mosques, on promenades, and even receive them in their own homes; they are entirely unfamiliar with the services of eunuchs. Thus, instead of that noble simplicity, that attractive modesty that characterizes you, one encounters a harsh impudence, which is impossible to get used to.

Yes, Roxane, if you were here, you would feel outrage at the hideous dishonor into which your sex has fallen: you would flee this abominable land, and you would sigh for that sweet haven where you found innocence, where you were sure of yourself, where no danger could make you tremble, and where you could love me without fear of ever losing that love you owe me.

When you strengthen the beauty of your skin by even more beautiful colors; when you perfume your entire body with the most precious of essences; when you dress in your finest garments; when you seek to distinguish yourself from your companions by the grace of your dancing or the sweetness of your singing; when you compete gracefully with them in charm, sweetness, and cheerfulness—I cannot imagine that you have any other goal in life but to please me. And when I see you blushing modestly, when your gaze meets mine, and when you insinuate yourself into my heart with tender, flattering words—then, Roxane, I cannot doubt your love.

But what to think of these European women? Their art in cosmetics, the ornaments with which they adorn themselves, the lengths to which they go in caring for their bodies, and that continual desire to please that obsesses them, are simply so many stains on their virtue, and so many insults to their husbands.

It is not, Roxane, that I believe that they actually go as far as their conduct would lead one to believe, that they would take their dissoluteness to the horrible extreme of violating their conjugal fidelity—a thought that makes one tremble. There are precious few of them who are abandoned enough for that. They all carry a certain image of virtue in their hearts, inscribed there at birth, weakened by their education but not entirely effaced. Certainly, they can relax some of the external duties that modesty demands, but when it comes to that final step, nature itself revolts. And so it is that when we lock you up so carefully and have you guarded by so many slaves, when we restrain your desires and keep them from going astray, it is not that we fear that ultimate infidelity, but we know that purity cannot be too cautious, and that the slightest stain on it will corrupt it.

I feel sorry for you, Roxane. Having maintained your chastity so well for so long, you deserve a spouse who would never leave you, and who could keep those desires quelled, desires that now can only be mastered by your virtue.

From Paris, the 7th of the moon of Rhegeb, 1712

Letter 27

Usbek to Nessir
At Ispahan

We are in Paris now, that proud rival of the City of the Sun.[18]

When I left Smyrna, I asked my friend Ibben to pass a box on to you, containing some gifts, and you will receive this letter by the same method. Though I am some five or six hundred leagues distant from him, I send him my news and I receive his just as easily as if he were in Ispahan and I were in Qum. I send my letters via Marseille, whence ships are departing continually for Smyrna; from there, he sends those addressed to Persia via the Armenian caravans that leave daily for Ispahan.

Rica is in perfect health: his strong constitution, his youth, and his natural gaiety make him equal to any challenge.

But as for me, I am not well. I feel beaten down in body and spirit; I cannot help but indulge in reflections that grow sadder by the day. My health is weakening, and it makes me turn toward my native land, making the land I am in even more foreign to me.

But, my dear Nessir, I beg you, make sure my wives do not know the state I am in. If they love me, I want to spare them tears; if they do not love me, I do not want to encourage their boldness.

If my eunuchs think I am in danger, if they can hope their cowardly compliance might go unpunished, they would soon cease to turn a deaf ear to the insidious words of that sex that can make the very stones hear and lifeless things move.

Farewell, Nessir. It gives me pleasure to be able to confide in you.

From Paris, the 5th of the moon of Chahban 1712

18. *Ispahan* [Montesquieu's note].

Letter 28

Rica to * * *

Yesterday I saw the most extraordinary thing—though it is an everyday occurrence in Paris.

All the people get together toward the end of the day and go to a kind of spectacle which I have heard them call a play. It takes place on a kind of platform in a place they call the theater. On either side, you can see little recessed nooks they call boxes, and inside them are men and women acting out mute scenes, somewhat like the ones we know in Persia.

In this section, we see a woman afflicted by love, expressing her longing; another woman, this one more animated, is devouring her lover with her eyes, who returns her hungry gaze. All the different passions are depicted on the various faces and expressed with an eloquence that, though mute, is quite intense. In this place, the actresses appear only from the waist up, and they typically have a kind of muff for concealing their hands and arms. Further down below them stand a group of people who make fun of the people up above, while the latter laugh at those who stand below.

But there are certain people who seem to have to work harder than everyone else; they seem to have been chosen for the task due to their youth, which allows them to sustain the labor. They are obliged to be everywhere at all times; they move about via passageways that only they know about, moving with stunning agility from level to level—they are up, down, below, in all the boxes. They plunge from one level to another, it would seem. You lose sight of them for a moment, but then they reappear, often quitting one scene to go and play a role in another. There are even some on crutches who nonetheless miraculously get around as readily as the others. Eventually, everyone ends up in rooms where they perform a particular kind of play, which begins with bows, and proceeds to embraces: they say that the slightest acquaintance gives one man the right to practically smother another. Evidently the locale itself inspires such tender feelings. And in fact they say that the princesses who reign there are not at all cruel, and that apart from the two or three hours a day when they are downright savage, the rest of the time they are most accommodating, and quickly recover from their impassioned states.

Everything I have just told you applies also to another sort of place, one that they call the opera—except that people speak in the one place, and sing in the other. One of my friends took me the other day into a box where one of the main actresses was changing her costume. We got along so well together that the following morning, I received this letter from her:

> Monsieur,
>
> I am the unhappiest woman in the world; I have always been the most virtuous actress at the opera. Seven or eight months ago I was in the room where you met me yesterday, and as I was dressing for my role as a priestess of Diana, a young *abbé* came in, and with no respect whatever for my white dress, my veil and my headband, he ravished me of my innocence.[19] When I vehemently explained the nature of the sacrifice I had made for him, he laughed and told me he found me profane enough. But now I am with child and so big that I can no longer go on stage, for I am, when it comes to honor, a person of unbelievable delicacy, and I have always maintained that it is easier for a well-born young woman to lose her virtue than her sense of modesty. Considering that delicacy of mine, you can believe that that young *abbé* would never have succeeded if he had not promised to marry me—which made everything so legitimate that I thought it acceptable to bypass the ordinary formalities and go directly to the point. But since his infidelity has dishonored me, I no longer wish to live here at the opera where, just between you and me, I am scarcely given enough to live on, and now that I am beginning to get older and starting to lose some of my charms, my pay, though it remains the same, somehow seems to buy less all the time. I heard from one of the men in your retinue that the opportunities for a good dancer in your country are unlimited, and that if I were in Ispahan, my fortune would be quickly made. If you were to take me under your protection and take me along with you back to that country, you would have the advantage of having done a good turn to a girl who, in both her virtue and her conduct, would never show herself unworthy of your kindness. Yours truly, . . .

From Paris, the 2nd of the moon of Chalval, 1712

19. An *abbé* was a cleric; the term can have varied meanings, but in this context it is a young man who has taken priestly vows in order to have a profession (as opposed to one who does so in answer to a deeply felt vocation), but does not have any specified priestly duties. If we believe the literature of the era, such *abbés* were numerous enough, and were often quite a bit like this one, less than perfectly moral men.

Letter 29

Rica to Ibben
At Smyrna

The Pope is the chief of the Christians. He is an old idol that they worship out of habit. In other days, he was as powerful as many of the princes, for he deposed them as readily as our magnificent sultans deposed the kings of Irimetia[20] and Georgia. But no one fears him any more. He is said to be the heir to one of the first Christians, who was called Saint Peter, and it was certainly a rich inheritance, for the Pope has immense treasures and a great country under his domination.

The bishops are men of law subordinate to him, and by his authority they have two very different functions. When they meet in assembly, they make articles of faith, as he does. But when they are on their own, they have really only one function, and that is to excuse people from following the laws. For, as you may know, the Christian religion involves an infinite number of demanding, difficult practices, and since they have decided that it is less easy to follow all the rules than it is to have bishops who excuse you from following them, they have followed the latter practice in the interests of public convenience. So, for example, if one does not want to observe Ramadan, or does not want to be subject to the requirements that marriage entails, or wishes to break one's vows, or wishes to marry in a way that is against the legal prohibitions, or even simply wants to get out of an oath—one simply goes to the bishop, or to the Pope, who immediately grants a dispensation.

The bishops do not create the articles of faith on their own. There is an infinite number of theologians, dervishes for the most part, who raise thousands of new religious questions themselves. They are allowed to debate among themselves for a long while, and this battle goes on until a decision comes along to put an end to it.

And this is why I can assure you that no countries have had as many civil wars as those in the realm of Christ.

Those who put forward a new proposition are at first called heretics. Each heresy has a name, which becomes a rallying cry for its adherents. But no one need be a heretic unless he really wants to be, for all one has to do is split the issue into two parts and make up some complicated

---

20. Montesquieu erroneously calls Imiretia *Irimette*. Both Imiretia and Georgia were kingdoms in the Caucasus that paid tribute to Persia in the era.

distinction for one's accusers, whether intelligible or not, and this will render the heretic white as snow, and he may go on and call himself orthodox.

All this applies to France and Germany, but I have heard that in Spain and Portugal there are certain dervishes who have no sense of humor, and who will burn a man as readily as a heap of straw. When one falls into the hands of men like that, one is fortunate if one has always prayed to God with little pieces of wood between one's fingers, worn two scraps of cloth attached to two ribbons, and gone at some time or another to a place they call Galicia.[21] Otherwise, the poor devil is in a real fix. When he swears like a pagan that he is orthodox, they might not agree with his definition of the term, and burn him as a heretic; he cannot use the expedient of submitting distinctions, because they will have him reduced to ashes before he even gets the words out of his mouth.

Other judges presume that an accused man is innocent, but these always assume he is guilty. In doubtful cases, they tend to err on the side of severity, because they believe that men are basically wicked. But at the same time they have such a high opinion of people that they seem to think they are incapable of lying, and therefore they admit testimony from deadly enemies, immoral women, and people who make their living by criminal means. When they pass sentence, they give a little compliment to those who appear wearing a sulphur-colored garment,[22] saying they are terribly sorry to see them so poorly dressed, that the judges themselves are really decent people who detest bloodshed, and feel terrible about having to condemn them. But, as a consolation, they will confiscate all the condemned's property for themselves.

Happy are the lands inhabited by the children of the prophets! Such sad spectacles are unknown there.[23] The holy faith brought down to us by the angels needs only the truth to defend itself; it certainly does not need to stoop to this kind of violence to sustain itself.

From Paris, the 4th of the moon of Chalval, 1712

---

21. The little pieces of wood are the rosary, the two scraps of cloth the scapular, and going to Galicia is making the pilgrimage to Saint James of Compostella (in the province of Galicia in Spain).

22. The condemned appeared wearing reddish garments, suggestive of the hellfire into which they presumably were headed.

23. *The Persians are the most tolerant of all Muslims* [Montesquieu's note].

Letter 30

Rica to the same
At Smyrna

The people of Paris are curious to the point of extravagance. When I first arrived, people stared at me as if I had dropped out of the sky: old men, young men, women, children, everybody wanted to have a look at me. When I went out, everyone rushed to the windows to see me; when I went to the Tuileries, a group of people soon formed a circle around me; even women formed a kind of rainbow around me, with their many-colored fashions. When I went to the theater, I saw a hundred pairs of opera glasses trained upon me. In short, no man has ever been as observed as I was. I smile sometimes when I hear people who have never traveled any farther than their own rooms saying to each other, "He does look quite Persian." And another extraordinary thing: I found pictures of myself put up everywhere; I saw myself multiplied in all the shops, on every mantelpiece—as if they were afraid of not seeing enough of me.

So much honor eventually becomes a burden. I do not think of myself as an especially curious or rare man, and while I have a reasonably good opinion of myself, I would never have imagined that I could disturb the repose of a great city where no one knew me at all. It all made me resolve to quit dressing in my Persian clothing, and to wear what the Europeans do, in order to learn whether there would still be something all that fascinating in my appearance. The experiment gave me a clearer sense of my real value. Free of all my foreign ornament, I found that people took me more nearly for what I am really worth. I would have been justified in complaining about my tailor, though, for he had made me lose in a moment all that public attention and esteem, for I dropped at once into the most terrible state of being a nobody. I could stay for an hour among a group of people without anyone paying me any attention or giving me the opportunity to speak. But if by chance someone informed the group that I was a Persian, I would soon hear a kind of muttering: "Oh, really? Monsieur is a Persian? What a strange thing! How can one be a Persian?"

From Paris, the 6th of the moon of Chalval, 1712

Letter 31

Rhédi to Usbek
At Paris

I am currently in Venice, my dear Usbek. A person could have seen all the cities of the world and still be surprised upon arriving in Venice: it will always be a surprise to see a city with its towers and mosques rising up out of the water, and to find a huge population in a place where there really ought to be nothing but fish.

But this profane city lacks the single most precious treasure in the world: fresh water. It is impossible to accomplish a single lawful ablution here. Our holy prophet sees the place as an abomination, and he looks down upon it from the heavenly heights with fury.

Apart from that, dear Usbek, I would find it charming to live in this city where I am continually learning—about the secrets of business, the affairs of princes, the forms of the government. And I am not neglecting European superstitions either. I am applying myself to medicine, physics, and astronomy. I am studying the arts. In short, I am finally emerging from the clouds that covered my eyes in the land of my birth.

From Venice, the 16th of the moon of Chalval, 1712

Letter 32

Rica to * * *

I recently visited a place that houses some three hundred people under quite poor conditions. I was done quickly, for the church and the buildings do not bear much examination. Those living there were cheerful enough, and I saw a number of them playing cards or other games that were not so familiar to me. As I was leaving, one of them was leaving too, and when he heard me asking directions to the Marais, the most remote sector of Paris, he said to me, "I am going that way; I will show you the route. Follow me." He led me most expertly, helping me thread my way through difficult spots and adroitly keeping me out of danger from passing vehicles and coaches. Our journey was nearly finished when curiosity got the better of me: "My good friend," I said, "may I know who you are?" He said, "I am blind, Monsieur." I exclaimed, "Blind? How can that be? And why did you not ask that man who was playing cards with you to conduct us here?" He replied, "He is blind too. Three hundred blind people have been housed there for some four hundred years now.[24] But now I must leave you: this is the street you were looking for, and I must join the crowd and go into that church where, I can assure you, I will be more trouble to the others than they will be to me."

From Paris, the 17th of the moon of Chalval, 1712

Letter 33

Usbek to Rhédi
At Venice

Wine is so expensive in Paris, due to all the duties and taxes on it, that you would think the Parisians had decided to encourage people to follow the precepts of the divine Koran, which forbids drinking.

When I consider the dire effects of that liquor, I cannot help but regard it as the most fearsome gift that nature ever gave to men. If there is anything that has blackened the reputations of our monarchs, it is their intemperance; this is the source, the poisonous source, of their injustices and their cruelties.

I must say, to the shame of humankind, that the law forbids our princes to use wine, and yet they consume it to such an excess that they degrade themselves below the level of humanity. The use of it, however, is permitted to Christian princes, and it seems not to lead them to any wrongdoing. The human mind is a complete contradiction. In our licentiousness and debauchery we rebel against all precepts, and the law, created to render us more just, often serves only to make us more guilty.

But while I disapprove of the use of liquor that makes us lose our reason, I do not condemn those drinks that simply make us more cheerful. The wisdom of the East lies in searching out remedies for sorrow with as much vigor as for the most dangerous diseases. When some misfortune

24. The place referred to is the *Hospice des Quinze-Vingts*, a hospital for the blind, founded by King Louis IX in about 1260; it originally housed 300 ("quinze-vingts," or fifteen score) patients. It still exists today, but is now primarily an ophthalmological institute.

befalls a European, he has no other resource than reading a philosopher called Seneca;[25] but we Asiatics, wiser than them and better physicians as well, imbibe beverages that can cheer a man up and help him forget his sorrows.

There is nothing so depressing as the consolations we must draw from the necessity of evil, the futility of remedies, the inevitability of fate, the order of providence, and the general misfortune of the human condition. It is an absurdity, this attempt to reduce pain and evil by contemplating how we were all born into misery. It would be much wiser to try to lift the spirit up and out of such reflections, and consider man as a feeling creature instead of simply a reasoning one.

The soul, united with the body, is constantly being tyrannized by it. If the movement of the blood is too sluggish, if the humors are impure or insufficient in quantity, we fall into despondency and grief. But if we consume beverages that are capable of redressing the condition of the body, our soul again becomes capable of receiving the kind of external impressions that can cheer it, and the soul feels a secret pleasure in seeing its machine[26] regain its proper movement, so to speak, and its proper mode of life.

From Paris, the 25th of the moon of Zilcadé, 1713

Letter 34

Usbek to Ibben
At Smyrna

The women of Persia are more beautiful than those of France, but the French ones are nicer. It is difficult not to fall in love with the former, and just as difficult not to enjoy the latter. The former are more tender and more modest, while the latter are more gay and more playful.

Persian women's complexions are so superb because of the regulated lives they lead; they do not gamble, and they do not stay up late. They drink no wine whatsoever, and are almost never exposed to the air.

25. Seneca (c. 4 BC–65 AD) was a Roman stoic philosopher whose works were still widely read in Montesquieu's time.

26. Descartes had initiated the vogue of referring to the body as a "machine," to distinguish that part of the person from the soul or spirit.

Admittedly, the seraglio is better at ensuring good health than it is in providing pleasures; it is an even, smooth life, one without stimulation. Everything conduces to subordination and duty; the pleasures themselves are solemn, and the joys serious, and one's only taste of them comes by way of authority and dependence.

Even the men in Persia are less light-hearted than Frenchmen. One never sees that freedom of mind, that air of contentment that I find here in every social condition.

It is much worse in Turkey, where one can find whole families, moving down the generations from father to son, where no one has laughed since the foundation of the monarchy.

This Asiatic gravity comes partly from their habits of interacting with each other; people rarely see each other except in ceremonial situations. Friendship, that sweet engagement of the heart that makes life so much sweeter here, is practically unknown among them. They retreat to their houses, where there is always the same company waiting for them, and thus each family is, so to speak, isolated.

One day, when I was discussing this issue with a man from this country, he said to me: "What shocks me most about your way of life is that you are obliged to live among slaves, whose hearts and minds always reek of their base condition. These low-minded people weaken your own feelings of virtue, which come from nature, and since such people are around you from childhood on, they eventually destroy those sentiments altogether.

"After all, put aside your prejudices for a moment: what kind of education can one possibly receive from a miserable creature whose honor consists in guarding another man's women? From a creature who takes pride in this, the most vile employment a human can have? From one whose very fidelity makes him contemptible, for though it is his only virtue, it arises out of envy, jealousy, and despair? From one who, on fire with the desire to avenge himself on both sexes—of which he is the rejected dross—consents to being tyrannized by the stronger sex, provided that he can in turn make the weaker sex miserable? From one whose worth is in proportion to his imperfection, his ugliness, and his deformity, one who is esteemed precisely for his unworthiness? From a creature who is riveted for all his days to the harem doorway he is assigned to guard, riveted more strongly than the bolts and bars that secure it—and from one who boasts of living fifty years in this degraded position, where he is nothing more than the vile instrument of his master's jealousy?"

From Paris, the 14th of the moon of Zilhagé, 1713

Letter 35

Usbek to his cousin Gemchid,
Dervish at the glorious monastery of Tauris

What do you think of the Christians, sublime dervish? Do you think that, at the Day of Judgment, they will be trotted off to hell like the infidel Turks, who will serve as donkeys for the Jews? I know perfectly well that they will not go to dwell among the prophets, and that the great Ali did not come for their sakes. But since they had the bad luck to have no mosques in their countries, do you think that they will be condemned to eternal misery? And that God will punish them for having failed to practice a religion that He did not make known to them? I can tell you this: I have questioned many of these Christians, in order to see if they have any idea of the great Ali, the finest of all men, and I have found that they have never heard of him.

They are not at all like those infidels that our holy prophets put to the sword because they refused to believe in miracles from heaven. Rather, they are like those unhappy souls who lived in the darkness of idolatry in the days before the divine light came to shine upon the face of our great Prophet.

Moreover, when one examines their religion more closely, one can detect the seeds of our dogmas within it. I have often marveled at the secret ways of Providence, which seems to have wanted to prepare them in this way for the eventual general conversion. I have heard of a book one of their theologians wrote called *Polygamy Triumphant*, in which he proves that polygamy was commanded of Christians.[27] Their baptism is the image of the ablutions required by our sacred law, but the Christians' error is in assigning complete efficacy to this first ablution, thinking it suffices for all the others. Their priests and their monks pray, like us, seven times a day.[28] They hope to live forever in Paradise, where they will taste a thousand delights through the resurrection of the body. They have, like us, required fasts and mortifications through which they hope

27. The German pastor Johann Leyser published his *Polygamia Triumphatrix* in 1682 under the pseudonym of Theophilus Alatheus, and mocked and condemned as it was, it went through a number of reprintings. As the *Persian Letters* itself might suggest, European Christians were fascinated by the subject, and especially by the case of Muslim polygamy.

28. Montesquieu is in error here: the Muslim is called to prayer five times a day, not seven.

to influence divine mercy. They honor the good angels, and despise the evil ones. They have a holy belief in the miracles worked by God and His servants. They recognize, as we do, the insufficiency of their own merits, and their need for an intercessor between them and God. I see Mohammedanism everywhere here, though I do not see Mohammed. But the light of truth will come into the open and dissipate the shadows that surround it. A day will come when the Eternal will look down upon the earth and see only true believers. Time, which consumes everything, will also destroy all errors. All men will be surprised to see themselves standing together under a single standard. Everything, including the Law itself, will have been consummated, and the holy books will be raised up from the earth and carried away to the celestial archives.

From Paris, the 20th of the moon of Zilhagé, 1713

Letter 36

Usbek to Rhédi
At Venice

The use of coffee is widespread in Paris. There are a great many public houses that sell it. In some of these, one may learn the news, and in others, one can play chess. There is one where they prepare the coffee in such a manner that it turns everyone who drinks it into a wit—or at least, upon leaving the place, everyone is convinced that he is four times more clever than he was upon entering.

But what shocks me about these people is that they do not find a way to render their talents useful to their country, wasting them instead on childish trivia. For example, when I first came to Paris I found them all taking sides and heatedly arguing about the most meaningless topic imaginable, the reputation of an ancient Greek poet, whose place of birth and date of death have remained unknown for two thousand years.[29] Both sides agreed that he had been an excellent poet, so the only question

29. Montesquieu's satire here refers to the bitter, long drawn-out literary dispute known as the quarrel of the ancients and the moderns, which actually began a bit later than suggested here, with the publication of La Motte's translation of Homer's *Iliad* in 1714, and was indeed the topic of much coffeehouse discussion in the era.

was exactly how much excellence should be attributed to him. Everyone wanted to rate him, but among these distributors of reputation some carried more weight than others—and therein lay the quarrel. It was very animated, for they insulted each other so warmly, and came up with such bitter witticisms about each other that I had to marvel at the manner as well as the matter of the dispute. I said to myself that if someone were foolish enough to attack the reputation of some upstanding citizen in front of these people defending the ancient Greek's reputation, he would be rebuked immediately! And, I thought, such zeal in the cause of a long-dead man must be all the more fiery in defending a living one! But in any case, heaven forbid that I should anger the enemies of this poet, since two thousand years in the tomb has not been enough time for their implacable hatred to die down! They only beat the air now, but what would it be like if they were in the presence of a real enemy?

The ones I am talking about carry on their arguments in the vernacular, and thus they should be distinguished from another sort who make use of a barbaric tongue, which seems to add something to the fury and the obstinacy of the combatants. There are quarters in the city where one can see a kind of dense, dark mob of such people. They feed on subtle distinctions, obscure arguments, and false conclusions. One ought to die of starvation in such a trade, but it does in fact produce some return, for recently there was a whole nation of such people, chased out of their own land, who came across the seas to settle in France, bringing along with them nothing more to make their livelihood with than a striking talent for arguing.[30] Farewell.

From Paris, the last of the moon of Zilhagé, 1713

Letter 37

Usbek to Ibben
At Smyrna

The king of France is very old. Our histories show no comparable example of so long a reign by a monarch. They say he possesses, to a

30. Following England's Glorious Revolution of 1688, which was partly fueled by anti-Catholic sentiment, many Irish priests escaped to take refuge in France.

very great degree, the talent of making himself obeyed. He governs his family, court, and nation with the same finesse. People have often heard him say that of all the governments of the world, those of the Turks and of our own august Sultan give him the most pleasure—so highly does he rate oriental policies!

I have studied his character, and I have seen in it contradictions that I cannot resolve. For example, he has a minister who is only 18, and a mistress who is 80.[31] He loves his religion, but will not tolerate anyone telling him he should observe it with more rigor. Though he flees the noisy tumult of cities and says little himself, he spends every day, from morning to night, making people talk about him. He loves trophies and victories, but when he sees one of his good generals at the head of his troops, he is just as afraid as if the man were at the head of an enemy army. I believe he is the only man who ever lived who was both positively heaped with more wealth than any prince could ever hope for, and at the same time was overwhelmed by the most intolerable poverty.

He enjoys rewarding those who serve him, but he pays out just as generously for the assiduity, or more precisely the indolence of his courtiers as for the hard-fought campaigns waged by his captains. Sometimes he will prefer to favor the man who helps undress him or who passes a napkin to him when he is at the table rather than the man who has conquered cities or won battles for him. He does not believe that his royal grandeur should be limited by restricting the favors he gives, and without inquiring whether the man upon whom he is heaping honors has merited them, he simply assumes that his conferring them will make him deserving. Thus, he has been known to bestow a small pension on a man who ran two leagues to flee the enemy, and a fine governorship on another man who ran four.

He is a man of magnificence, especially in his building projects. There are more statues in his palace gardens than there are citizens in a large town. His palace guard is as strong as the one which guards the prince before whom all thrones totter. His armies are just as numerous, his resources just as great, and his finances just as inexhaustible.

From Paris, the 7th of the moon of Maharram, 1713

---

31. Louis XIV had appointed a number of very young ministers; the particular one in question here may be the Marquis de Cany. The mistress is Madame de Maintenon, who was born in 1635; Louis had in fact secretly married her sometime in 1685–1686.

Letter 38

Rica to Ibben
At Smyrna

It is a great debate among men as to whether it is better to withhold freedom from women or to grant it to them. It seems to me that there are good arguments on both sides. If the Europeans say that it is ungenerous to cause unhappiness to those we love, we Asiatics reply that there is something base about a man who gives up the authority that nature has given him over women. If they say that the sheer number of women we keep confined is troublesome, we reply that ten women who obey are less troublesome than one who disobeys. And if the Asiatics in turn assert that the Europeans cannot be truly happy with unfaithful women, they reply that the fidelity we enjoy does not prevent that sense of disgust that follows inevitably upon satisfied passion, and that our women are kept too close to us, that so tranquil a possession leaves us with nothing to desire, nothing to fear; and a little flirtation is like a pinch of salt, arousing the appetite and preventing spoilage. A wiser man than I am would be hard put to decide the question, for if we Asiatics do well by seeking out methods of reducing our anxieties, the Europeans do well by simply not feeling any.

After all, the Europeans say, when their marriages make them into unhappy husbands, they can simply turn and make themselves into happy lovers. For a man to complain reasonably about his wife's infidelity, only three people are required; but when there are four, the problem resolves itself.

A different question is whether women are subject to men under natural law. "No," a gentlemanly philosopher[32] told me the other day: "Nature never dictated such a law. Our domination of them is a veritable tyranny. They permit it only because they are gentler than we are and, as a result, more humane and more reasonable. These advantages would clearly give them superiority if we were reasonable, but they take it away because we are not.

"Now, while it is true that we exercise a tyrannical power over women, it is also true that they exercise a natural power over us: that of beauty, which nothing can resist. Our power is limited to our own country, but beauty's is universal. Why then do we men have such privilege? Is it

32. The gentlemanly (*galant*) philosopher is probably Bernard le Bovier de Fontenelle (1657–1757).

because we are the stronger? That is nothing but injustice. We employ every means we can to lessen their courage. Our powers would be equal, if our educations were. Let us test women in the areas that have not been enfeebled by their upbringing, and we would soon see just how much stronger we really are.

"It has to be admitted, even if it seems a shock to our customs, that among the most refined and cultured peoples, wives have always had authority over their husbands. This was established in law among the Egyptians, in honor of Isis, and among the Babylonians, in honor of Semiramis. It is said that the Romans ruled over all the nations of the world, but they were obedient to their wives. I will say nothing of the Sarmatians, who were essentially the servants of their wives; they were too barbaric for their example to be cited."[33]

So you see, my dear Ibben, that I have taken a liking to this country, where people love to maintain extraordinary opinions, and to reduce everything to paradox. The Prophet has settled this question, and has assigned the proper rights to each sex. Wives, he tells us, must honor their husbands, and their husbands must honor them, but the husbands have a degree of advantage over them.[34]

From Paris, the 26th of the moon of Gemmadi II, 1713

Letter 39

Hajji Ibbi[35] *to the Jew Ben Joshua, Muslim Proselyte*
At Smyrna

It seems to me, Ben Joshua, that there are always signs and wonders when extraordinary men are about to be born, as if Nature were suffering a kind of crisis, and the celestial power needed to put forth extra effort.

33. The Sarmatians were an Iron Age tribe in what is modern Iran. Herodotus (4. 110 ff.) narrates how they intermarried with the Amazons, and their women thus had unusual freedoms.

34. This last precept comes directly from the Koran, 2.228.

35. The epithet *hajji* is used for one who has completed the pilgrimage to Mecca.

There is nothing so wonderful as the birth of Mohammed. God, by the great decree of His providence, having resolved from the beginning to send this great Prophet to humankind so that he might enchain Satan, first created a light two thousand years before Adam passing down, from elect to elect, from ancestor to ancestor, until it finally reached Mohammed, as an authentic witness of his descent from the patriarchs.

It was also because of this same Prophet that God decreed that no child should be conceived unless the woman had become purified, and the man had undergone circumcision.

He came into this world circumcised, and joy shone on his face from the day of his birth. The earth trembled three times, as if it were giving birth itself; all the idols fell prostrate, and the thrones of kings were overturned. Lucifer was cast down into the depths of the sea, and it was only after swimming for forty days that he rose up out of the abyss and fled to Mount Cabes where, with his terrible voice, he called to the angels.

That night, God set up a barrier between man and woman that neither of them could pass. The arts of the magicians and necromancers became impotent. A voice could be heard coming from the heavens, saying, "I have sent my faithful friend unto the world."

According to the testimony of Ibn Abbas, the Arab historian, the generations of the birds, the clouds, the winds, and all the squadrons of angels came together in order to bring up this child, and they argued among themselves as to which should have the privilege. The birds said, in their twittering voices, that they were the best choice to raise him because they could most easily gather different fruits from different regions. The winds murmured, saying: "No, we are the ones best suited for the task because we can waft the finest scents to him from all parts of the earth." The clouds said, "No, no: he should be given into our care, because we can provide him with refreshing water at every moment." Up above, the indignant angels cried out, "But what would be left for us to do?" But then a voice from heaven was heard, putting an end to all the disputes: "He shall not be taken away from mortal hands, for blessed are the breasts that nourish him, and the hands that touch him, and the house that shelters him, and the bed that receives him at night."

After so much powerful testimony, my dear Joshua, a man would have to have a heart of iron not to believe in his holy law. What other signs could heaven give to authorize his divine mission, short of turning nature upside down and destroying the very men God wanted to persuade?

From Paris, the 20th of the moon of Rhegeb, 1713

Letter 40

Usbek to Ibben
At Smyrna

When a great man has died, people assemble in a mosque and listen to the funeral oration, which is a discourse in praise of the deceased, from which a listener would have real difficulty in trying to form a just estimate of the dead man's worth.

I would like to see funerals banned. We should weep for men at their birth, not at their death. What is the point of presenting those ceremonies, and all the dreary displays that go along with them, for a dying man in his final moments? The tears of his family and the sorrow on the faces of his friends only serve to worsen the fate he is about to suffer.

We are so blind that we do not know when we ought to grieve and when we ought to rejoice; almost all the sorrows we feel and all the joys too are false.

When I see the Mogul stupidly go every single year to have himself weighed like a cow, and when I see the people rejoice the fatter their prince has become—that is, the less capable of governing them—then I feel pity, Ibben, for human foolishness.

From Paris, the 20th of the moon of Rhegeb, 1713

Letter 41

The Chief Black Eunuch to Usbek

Ishmael, one of your black eunuchs, has just died, magnificent lord, and I see no alternative but to replace him. Considering that eunuchs are very hard to come by these days, I thought of making use of a black slave of yours who is here in the country, but I have so far been unable to persuade him to let himself be consecrated to this employment. Since I knew that this operation would be to his advantage in the long run, I wanted to exercise a little rigor with him. So in concert with your chief gardener, I gave orders that, even if it was against his will, he was to be put into the proper condition necessary to serve you in guarding what you love most, and to join me in those awe-inspiring places where otherwise he would dare not enter. But he began screaming as if we were about to burn him alive, and managed to slip out of our grip and avoid the fatal knife. I have just learned that he plans to write to you and plead for your mercy, saying that I only came up with this idea out of a spirit of vengeance for some jokes he had made about me. But I swear to you by the hundred thousand prophets that I have had no other aim than serving you as best as I could, which is the only thing dear to me, and the only thing I care about at all. I prostrate myself at your feet.

From the seraglio at Fatmé, the 7th of the moon of Maharram, 1713

Letter 42

Pharan to Usbek, his Sovereign Lord

If you were here, magnificent Lord, I would stand before you covered entirely with white paper, and even that would not be enough for me to write down all the insults that your chief black eunuch, the most wicked of men, has hurled at me since your departure.

On the pretext of some jokes that he claims I made about his miserable condition, he has attacked me with an inexhaustible vengeance. He has instigated the cruel superintendent of your gardens to give me impossible tasks ever since your departure, and even though a thousand times I thought I would die, I never once lost my fervor for serving you. How many times have I said to myself, "My master is the paragon of goodness, and I am the most miserable slave upon the face of the earth!"

I admit, magnificent lord, that I did not believe I was destined for even worse misery, but that traitor eunuch has decided to press his wickedness to even greater lengths. A few days ago, on his own authority, he told me I was to become one of the guardians of your sacred wives—that is to say, that I was to undergo an operation more cruel than death to me. Those who were given that operation at birth at the hands of cruel parents can console themselves, perhaps, at never having known what it is they have lost. But if I were made to descend below humanity, or were to be deprived of my humanity, I would die of grief, if I did not die from the barbarous act itself.

I kiss your feet, my sublime lord, in profound humility. Give commands such that I may feel the effects of your highly respected virtue, and do not let it be said that another man has been added to the ranks of the miserable on your orders.

From the gardens of Fatmé, the 7th of the moon of Maharram, 1713

Letter 43

Usbek to Pharan
At the gardens of Fatmé

Let your heart be joyful, and read these holy words; have the chief eunuch and the superintendent of the gardens kiss them. I forbid them to do anything to you: tell them to buy a eunuch to replace the one who died. Carry out your duties as if you had me always before your eyes; and know that though my bounty is great, great will be the punishment if you abuse my goodness.

From Paris, the 25th of the moon of Rhegeb, 1713

Letter 44

Usbek to Rhédi
At Venice

There are three classes or estates in France: the Church, the sword, and the robe. Each has a sovereign contempt for the others. Thus, for example, a man who ought to be scorned because he is a fool is scorned instead because he is a man of the robe.[36]

Everyone, right down to the meanest artisan, boasts of the excellence of the craft he has chosen; everyone sees himself as superior to anyone of a different profession, in direct proportion to the exalted idea he has formed of his own.

---

36. The term "men of the robe" or "nobles of the robe" (*noblesse du robe*) referred to the judicial elite, who held their ennobling offices as a kind of private property.

Men all resemble, more or less, that woman from the province of Erivan who, having received some favor from one of our monarchs, gave him a thousand thanks and, amid all the benedictions she showered upon him, expressed the hope that heaven might someday make him governor of Erivan.

I read in a travel account that a French vessel dropped anchor off the coast of Guinea, as some of the men on board wanted to go ashore and purchase some sheep. They were taken to the king, who dispensed justice to his subjects from under a tree. He sat on his throne—that is to say, on a wooden log—just as proudly as if he were seated on the throne of the great Mogul. He had three or four guards standing around him carrying wooden spears; an umbrella served as his canopy, shielding him from the heat of the sun. All the ornaments that he and the queen, his wife, wore consisted of their black skin and a few rings. This prince, whose vanity far outdid his poverty, asked the foreigners if he was much spoken of in France. He believed that his name must be known from pole to pole, and unlike that conqueror of whom it is said that he made the whole world be silent,[37] this one wanted to make the whole universe talk about him.

When the Khan of Tartary has finished dining, a herald proclaims that all the princes of the earth may now proceed to eat if they wish. And this barbarian—who eats nothing but milk, who has no house, who lives on banditry—this man regards all the kings of the earth as his slaves, and insults them regularly, twice a day.

From Paris, the 28th of the moon of Rhegeb, 1713

Letter 45

Rica to Usbek
At * * *

Yesterday morning while I was still in bed, I heard a rude knocking at my door, which was abruptly flung open by a man with whom I had only a casual social acquaintance, and who seemed to be beside himself.

---

37. The conqueror is Alexander the Great. According to the first book of Maccabees, "When the earth became quiet before him, he was exalted, and his heart was lifted up" (I Maccabees, 1:3).

The clothes he wore were worse than modest; his wig had not even been combed; he had not taken the time to have his waistcoat mended; and he had renounced, for that day, all the prudent precautions he normally took to disguise the battered state of his appearance.

"Get up," he said to me: "I need you for the whole day today, because I have a thousand purchases to make, and things will go much more smoothly if you are with me. First, we have to go to the Rue Saint Honoré to speak to a notary, who is going to sell me some land for five hundred thousand *livres*;[38] I want him to grant me the first refusal on the property. On my way here, I stopped for a moment in the Faubourg Saint Germain,[39] where I rented a house for two thousand *écus*, and I expect to finalize the contract today."

As soon as I was finished dressing, and just barely finished, my acquaintance hurried me out the door and down the stairs. "Let's get started," he said, "by buying a coach, and the horses to go with it." Soon we had purchased not only a coach but another hundred thousand francs' worth of merchandise, and all this in less than an hour. All this was done quickly, for my man did not bargain at all, did not keep track of his expenditures, and never paid in cash. I contemplated all this while puzzling over the man, finding in him a strange mixture of affluence and poverty, and I was not sure what to make of it. At last I could hold my peace no longer, and taking him off to one side I said to him, "Monsieur, who is going to pay for all this?" "I am," he said: "Come to my apartment, and I will show you immense treasures, and riches that are the envy of the grandest monarchs—but you will not envy them, for you will share them with me." I followed him. We climbed up five stories and then, using a ladder, we hoisted ourselves up to the sixth, which was a room open to the four winds, with nothing in it but two or three dozen earthenware pots filled with various liquids. "I got up early this morning," he said to me, "and the first thing I did was what I have been doing for twenty-five years now—that is, to inspect my work. I saw that the great day was here today, the day that would make me the richest man on earth. Do you see this ruby-colored liquid? It currently contains all the qualities that the philosophers have been seeking to perform the transmutation of metals. I extracted these grains from it, the ones you see here, which by their color are pure gold, though their weight is not quite perfect. This secret, which had been discovered by Nicolas Flamel,

38. The *livre* is an obsolete French currency, replaced by the franc in 1795.

39. The Faubourg Saint Germain was one of the most exclusive, and thus most expensive, areas of Paris.

but which Raymond Llull[40] and a million others have sought without success, has at last been revealed to me. I find myself today a most fortunate adept. May heaven help me to use the treasures it has given me, for its glory alone!"

I left in a state of rage, practically hurling myself down that stairway, leaving the rich man alone in his private poorhouse. Farewell, my dear Usbek. I will come to see you tomorrow, and if you wish, we can return together to Paris.

From Paris, the last of the moon of Rhegeb, 1713

Letter 46

Usbek to Rhédi
At Venice

I see people here disputing about religion endlessly, but it seems that at the same time they are competing to see who can practice it the least.

These people are no better Christians than others, and they are not better citizens either. And this is what bothers me, for, no matter what religion a man follows, its foremost duties are always observing the laws, loving others, and respecting one's parents.

In fact, the first objective of a religious man should be to please the God who established the religion he professes, should it not? And the surest way to succeed in that is undoubtedly to observe the rules of society and the duties of humanity. For, no matter what religion one professes, once we assume that such a religion is real, one must believe that God loves humankind, since He has established a religion to help make them happy; moreover, since He loves humankind, we will undoubtedly please Him if we do the same—that is, if we follow through on all the duties of charity and humanity, violating none of the laws under which we live.

---

40. Nicolas Flamel (1330–1418) was a French alchemist who had the posthumous reputation of having found the secret of turning metals into gold. Raymond Llull (c. 1232–1315) was an alchemist, astrologer, theologian, and polymath, originally from Majorca.

We are far surer of pleasing God in that way than in performing this or that ceremony, for ceremonies in themselves are of no value, except insofar as we suppose that God has commanded them. But even this is a matter upon which there is much disagreement, and since we must choose the ceremonies of one particular religion out of some two thousand, it is easy to be mistaken.

A man said this prayer to God every day: "Lord, I understand nothing of the endless disputes I hear regarding you. I want to serve you and do your will, but every man I consult wants me to serve you in his own way. I want to pray to you, but I do not know which language to use. I don't know what posture to adopt: some say I should pray standing up, others that I should sit, and yet others insist that I get down on my knees. And that is not all. Some say that I must wash myself every morning in cold water, while others maintain that you will look upon me with horror if I do not have a little piece of my flesh cut off. The other day, it so happened that I was eating a rabbit in a caravanserai. Three men seated around me soon made me tremble in fear, for all three insisted that I have grievously offended you: one[41] said it was because this animal was unclean; another,[42] because it had been strangled; and the third,[43] because it was not fish. A Brahmin was passing by, so I asked him to be the judge, and he said: 'They are all wrong; for evidently you did not kill this animal yourself.' 'Oh, but I did,' I said to him. 'Ah! In that case you have committed an abominable act, and God will never pardon you,' he said severely; 'for how do you know that the soul of your father had not passed into this animal?' All this, dear Lord, has left me unimaginably confused. I can scarcely move my head without the threat of offending you, but I want to please you, and devote this life you gave me to your service. I may be mistaken, but I think that perhaps the best method to achieve this is to live my life as a good citizen in the society into which you have had me born, and as a good father to the family you have given me."

From Paris, the 8th of the moon of Chahban, 1713

---

41. *A Jew* [Montesquieu's note].

42. *A Turk* [Montesquieu's note].

43. *An Armenian* [Montesquieu's note]. Montesquieu is evidently in error here, for Armenians do not forbid the eating of meat.

Letter 47

Zachi to Usbek
At Paris

I have great news to tell you: I have reconciled with Zéphis, and the seraglio, which had been divided by our quarrel, is now reunited. The only thing missing now from this place where peace reigns is you: come home, my dear Usbek, come home and make love reign triumphant.

I gave a great party for Zéphis, and I invited your mother, your wives, and your chief concubines; your aunts and many of your female cousins came too. They came on horseback, covered by the dark cloud of their veils and their clothing.

The next day, we all left for the countryside, where we hoped to feel freer. We mounted our camels, four of us to each box. Since we had made up the party on the spur of the moment, we did not have time to have the *courouc*[44] announced, but the chief eunuch, always ingenious, arranged for a different precaution: he had a thick curtain spread over the cloth that prevents us from being seen, ensuring that we could see no one at all.

When we arrived at the river we had to cross, each of us followed the custom of crossing inside a box, the box being carried over by boat—for we had heard that there would be many people near the river. One over-curious man approached too close to the area where we were confined, and he received a mortal blow, such that he will never again see the light of the sun. Another, who was found bathing naked in the water, met the same fate, and your faithful eunuchs sacrificed these two unfortunates to your honor and ours.

But listen to the rest of our adventure. When we were in the middle of the river such a strong wind came up, along with such dark clouds, that our sailors abandoned hope. Terrified by the situation, nearly all of us fainted. I remember hearing the voices of our eunuchs arguing, some saying that in order to evade the danger they needed to set us women free, but the chief eunuch said that he would die before his master would be dishonored, and that he would plunge his dagger into the breast of any man who would dare make such an outrageous suggestion. One of my slaves, completely beside herself, and only partly dressed, ran toward me to help me, but a black eunuch brutally grabbed hold of her

44. The word *courouc* was called out by the eunuchs and servants, warning others not to approach.

and forced her back to the place she had been. I fainted away, and only came to when the danger had passed.

How difficult these journeys are for us women! The men are only exposed to dangers that threaten their lives, while we must constantly fear for either our lives or our virtue. Farewell, my dear Usbek. I will adore you always.

From the seraglio at Fatmé, the 2nd of the moon of Rhamazan, 1713

Letter 48

Usbek to Rhédi
At Venice

Those who love to educate themselves are never idle. Though I have no pressing business to attend to, I am nonetheless continually occupied. I spend my whole life inquiring, and every evening I write down what has made an impression on me, what I have seen, and what I have heard in the course of the day. Everything interests me; everything surprises me. I am like a child, whose still-tender senses are vividly struck by the slightest of things they encounter.

You may not believe it, but we are received warmly in all sorts of social gatherings, and by all levels of society. I think this is largely due to the charm and natural gaiety of Rica, who seeks out all types of people, and is widely sought out in turn. Our foreignness no longer offends anyone, and we even enjoy the way some people are surprised to find us somewhat civilized—for the French cannot imagine that the climate in our part of the world could possibly produce real human beings. But still, I must admit that I find them worth the trouble it takes to disabuse them.

I spent several days in a country house outside Paris, the home of an important man who was delighted to entertain guests. His wife is a very pleasant woman who is both modest and witty, a combination not very likely to be found among our secluded Persian women.

Outsider that I was, I had nothing better to do than to study the endless crowd of people there, which never ceased to offer something new for me. I noticed a man whose simplicity of manner appealed to me; he took to me as well, and we spent a great deal of time together.

One day when we found ourselves together in the midst of a large gathering, we avoided the general conversation and began talking privately. I said to him, "You may find me more curious than polite, but I beg you to let me ask you some questions, because I am getting tired of understanding nothing and of being unable to figure out certain people. For two days now I have been trying to sort things out, and every single one of these people here has me so confused that it is like torture. I feel it would take me a thousand years to understand them; they are as closed off from me as the wives of our great monarch." He replied, "You need only ask, and I will explain everything. I am the more willing to do it because I can see you are a discreet man, who will not betray my trust."

"Who is that man," I asked, "who talks so much about all the great dinners he has given for important people, and who is on such familiar terms with your dukes, and who speaks so freely to those ministers of yours who are reputed to be so difficult to see? He is evidently a man of quality, but his looks are so vulgar that he does no honor to your people of quality; moreover, he appears quite uneducated to me. I am a foreigner, but it seems to me that there is, generally speaking, a politeness that is common to all nations; and I see no trace of it in him. Are your people of high rank less well-bred than others?" He laughed and replied, "That man is a tax farmer.[45] He is as much above all the others here in wealth as he is below them in birth. He would have the finest table in Paris, if he would only resolve never to eat at home. As you see, he is utterly impertinent, but he has an excellent cook, for whom he is grateful; you have heard him singing the man's praises all day."

I then asked him, "And that fat man dressed all in black, the one that lady just asked to have seated next to her? How can he wear such a gloomy outfit while his air is so light and witty, and his complexion so ruddy and vibrant? He smiles graciously when someone speaks to him, and his costume, though more modest than a woman's, is even more carefully arranged." He replied, "He is a preacher and, even worse, a spiritual director. And in that capacity, he knows more than the husbands do. He knows women's weaknesses; and they know that he has some himself."

"Really!" I exclaimed. "But he seems to be constantly talking about something called grace."

45. The collection of taxes had long been outsourced in France to private individuals who were allowed to keep any excess collected; by Montesquieu's time, the people who had the rights to collect taxes—*fermiers généraux*, or tax farmers—were extremely wealthy.

He replied, "No, not always. When he has the ear of a pretty woman, he would much rather speak about the fall from grace. He speaks like thunder from the pulpit, but when you find him alone, he is as gentle as a lamb." I said, "It would seem that he is highly respected, and that everyone holds him in great esteem."

"What? Respected? No, he is simply a necessary man. He can sweeten a retired, lonely life with his little nuggets of advice, his officious concern, his regular visits. He can cure you of a headache better than anyone living; an excellent man."

"Well, if I can continue to impose upon you, tell me who that is directly across from us, that ill-dressed man who makes such grimaces and seems to speak differently from the others. He shows no signs of witty speech; instead, he speaks in order to seem witty." He replied, "That is a poet, the most grotesque version of humanity that there is. Such people go about insisting that they were born the way they are, which is quite true, and always will be, for they are almost always the most ridiculous of men. And therefore, no one spares them: people heap contempt upon them from all sides. This one was drawn to the house by hunger, and the master and mistress of the place have treated him well, for they deny their goodness and decency to none. He wrote them an epithalamion for their wedding, which turned out to be the best thing he ever produced, for their marriage actually has been just as happy as his poem predicted.

"You may not believe it," he continued, "considering your Oriental prejudices, but we do have happy marriages here, and we do have women whose virtue is the most severe guardian. The couple of whom I just spoke enjoy an untroubled tranquility, loved and esteemed by all. There is only one thing: their natural goodness leads them to welcome every sort of person to their home, and some of these make for rather bad company. Not that I disapprove; after all, we must live with people the way they are, and sometimes the people who are considered the best company are in fact those with the most refined vices. Perhaps it is like poisons: the subtlest ones are also the most dangerous."

I lowered my voice and asked, "And who is that older man who seems so bad-tempered? I took him for a foreigner at first because, apart from his unusual dress, he criticizes everything in France, including your government." He replied, "That man is an old soldier, who makes his mark in society by his interminable war stories. He cannot endure the fact that France has won some battles where he was not present, or that people praise some siege where he was not in the trenches. He sees himself as so central to our history that he believes it ended where he did.

He thinks some wounds he incurred are as catastrophic as the dissolution of the monarchy. And, in contradiction to those philosophers who argue that we live in the present and that the past does not exist, he on the contrary lives only in the past, existing only in those campaigns in which he fought; he breathes the air of former days, like heroes living on after their great deeds."

I asked, "But then why did he leave the military?"

"Oh, he didn't quit the service," he replied; "the service quit him. They gave him some little post where he can narrate his adventures for the rest of his days. But he won't be advancing any farther: the path to honors is closed to him."

I asked, "Why is that?"

"We have a sort of ruling principle in France," he said, "that we should never promote officers who have patiently tolerated low-level assignments. We regard them as men whose minds have been narrowed by their focus on small things, and as a result have lost the capacity for great ones. We believe that a man who is not capable of becoming a general by the age of thirty will never be one—and that a man who cannot take in, at a single glance, all the complexities of a field of battle in all sorts of different situations, who cannot see at once all its advantages in victory and all its resources in defeat—such a man will never acquire that talent. And that is the reason why we reserve the outstanding posts for those great, sublime men to whom heaven has given both the heart and the genius of a hero; likewise, we reserve the subaltern employments for the men whose talents are best suited to them. These are the sort of men who have grown old fighting obscure wars, who at best will manage to keep doing what they have done their whole lives, and who should not be given new and difficult tasks when they are beginning to grow old."

A moment later curiosity pricked me again, and I said to him: "I will promise to stop asking you questions, if you will indulge me with just one more. Who is that tall young man with the extraordinary hairdo, little wit, and exceptional impertinence? Why does he speak so much more loudly than the others and seem to think he is so important?"

He replied, "He is a ladies' man." But at that point other people entered, some others got up and left, and someone began speaking with my friend, so I had to remain as uninstructed as I had been before I asked. But a little later by some strange coincidence the young man came and stood by me, and began to speak to me. "The weather is fine, monsieur; would you like to take a turn on the terrace?" I replied as civilly as I could, and we went outside together.

He said, "I've come out to the country as a favor to the lady of the house, with whom I'm on pretty intimate terms. Naturally, there is another lady who will not find this pleasant news, but what can you do? I see the prettiest women in Paris, but I never let myself become attached to any one of them, and I manage to keep them all fooled—because, just between you and me, I'm really not up to much, when it comes right down to it."

I said to him, "Apparently, monsieur, you have some assignment or some employment that keeps you from giving them more attention?"

"Not at all, monsieur. I have no other employment beyond enraging husbands and driving fathers to despair. And I enjoy frightening some woman who thinks she has caught me and keeping her at arms' length from me. There is a group of us who have divvied Paris up among us, and we like to get together and share all the details of our exploits."

I replied, "From what I can see, then, you make more noise than the bravest soldier, and command more esteem than a grave magistrate. But if you were in Persia, you would not enjoy these advantages; you would become someone more proper to guard women than to please them." My face had grown red with anger, and I believe that if I had gone on speaking to him, I would not have been able to keep from being uncivil.

What do you think of a country where such men are tolerated, and where they allow a man to follow a career like this? A place where infidelity, betrayal, abduction, and perfidy and injustice can actually make a man more esteemed? A place where they accord respect to a man for stealing a daughter from her father, or a wife from her husband, and breaking all the sweetest and holiest of bonds? Happy are the children of Ali, who defend their families from disgrace and seduction! The light of day is no more pure than the fire burning in the hearts of our wives, and our daughters can only tremble in fear when they think of the day that must deprive them of that virtue that makes them comparable to angels and incorporeal powers. Oh dear, native land, on whom the sun first sheds his rays, you have no part in the shame of those horrible crimes that makes that star begin to hide its face the closer it comes to the black West.

From Paris, the 5th of the moon of Rhamazan, 1713

Letter 49

Rica to Usbek
*At * * **

While I was in my room the other day, I saw a dervish come in, most bizarrely dressed. His beard hung down to the rope of his belt; his feet were bare; his habit was gray, coarse, and puckered into points here and there. The total effect was so freakish that my first thought was to send out to try to find a painter to let his imagination loose on it.

He began by making elaborate compliments to me, in the course of which I learned that he was a man of some merit and a Capuchin.[46] He went on, "I have been told, Monsieur, that you will be returning soon to the Persian court, where you hold a distinguished rank. I have come to ask your protection, and to beg you to obtain from the king a little dwelling near Casbin[47] for two or three religious."

"But Father," I asked him, "why do you want to go to Persia?"

He exclaimed, "Not me, monsieur! I would avoid such a thing altogether. I am the provincial here, and I would not trade my position for any other Capuchin office anywhere."

"Well, then, what the devil are you asking, exactly?"

He replied, "You see, if we had such a house, our priests in Italy could send out two or three of their religious."

I asked, "And evidently you know these men, these religious?"

"No, monsieur, I don't know them at all."

"Well then, what does it matter to you whether they go to Persia? This is a fine project, sending a couple of Capuchins to breathe the air around Casbin! How useful that would be for Europe and for Asia! And how necessary it is to get our monarchs involved! What a fine little colony this would be! Get out of here: you and your like were not made for transplanting, and you'd do best to keep on crawling around in the mud that engendered you."

From Paris, the 15th of the moon of Rhamazan, 1713

---

46. The Capuchin order of friars was founded in 1520, an offshoot of the Franciscans. They were a mendicant order: that is, they were to get their necessities by begging, and any ownership of goods was forbidden, as was even touching money. They became a powerful missionary force in the seventeenth century.

47. Casbin—or Qazvin—is an ancient Persian city, in what is today northwest Iran.

Letter 50

*Usbek to * * **[48]

I have observed some people among whom virtue was so natural that they were barely aware of it; they devoted themselves to their duty without having to force themselves, almost as if by instinct: far from discoursing at length about their rare qualities, they seemed not even to have noticed them. These are the kinds of people I love, not those people who are virtuous and seem stunned and delighted by the fact, and who think of good acts as miraculous events that make for a surprising narrative.

If modesty is a virtue necessary to those to whom heaven has given great talents, what should we think of those insects who dare to show the kind of pride that would dishonor truly great men?

I see people talking about themselves endlessly wherever I go; their conversation is like a mirror, always reflecting only one thing, their own impertinent selves. They will talk to you about the most trivial things that have happened to them, expecting that the interest they take in such things will make them seem fascinating to you. They have done everything, seen everything, said everything, thought everything: they are a universal model, a subject of inexhaustible analogies, a never-failing source of examples. Oh, how unsavory praise is, when it only reflects back upon the praiser!

A few days ago there was a man like that here who besieged us for two hours with talk of himself, his merits, and his talents; but since there is no such thing as truly perpetual motion, he eventually stopped talking. The conversation was open to us again, and we seized hold of it.

One of us, a man who seemed rather irritated, began by complaining about how boring some conversations can be. "Why must there always be some fool who describes nothing but himself, and who brings every comment others make back to himself?" At that, our speechifier abruptly broke back in: "You are so right. People should be more like me: I never praise myself. I am quite well off, of good birth, a generous man, and my friends all say that I have a fair amount of wit. But I never speak about any of that. If I do have some good qualities, the one that really stands out is my modesty."

I marveled at this fool, and while he continued speaking at full volume, I said quietly, "Happy is the man who is just vain enough to avoid

48. In editions before 1758, this letter is assigned to Rica.

speaking well of himself, who fears his listeners' reactions, and who keeps his own merits to himself, safe from the jealous pride of others!"

From Paris, the 20th of the moon of Rhamazan, 1713

Letter 51

Nargum, the Persian Envoy to Moscow, to Usbek
At Paris

A letter from Ispahan informs me that you have left Persia, and that you are currently in Paris. Why must I always learn your news from others?

I have been in this country for five years now, on the orders of the king of kings, and I have brought many important negotiations to fruition.

You know that the Russian Czar is the only one of the Christian princes to have interests in common with us: he is the enemy of the Turks, as are we.

His empire is vaster than ours, for it is a thousand leagues between Moscow and his furthest dominions on the border with China.

He is the absolute master of the lives and property of his subjects, all of whom are slaves, with the exception of four families. Even the lieutenant of the prophets, the king of kings, who uses the heavens for his footstool, has no more fearsome power than he does.

Considering the hideous climate here in Moscow, you would not think it much of a punishment to be banished, but whenever some prominent person falls into disgrace, he is sent to Siberia.

Just as the law of our Prophet forbids us to drink wine, that of the prince here forbids it to Muscovites.

They have a strange manner of greeting guests, one that is not at all Persian. Whenever a stranger enters one of their houses, the husband presents his wife, and the stranger kisses her—and this is considered a gesture of politeness toward the husband.

While the fathers usually have it written into the marriage contract of their daughters that the husband will not whip them, you would not believe how much Moscow women love to be beaten.[49] A Muscovite

49. *This custom has changed* [Montesquieu's note].

woman cannot quite believe that she truly possesses her husband's heart if he does not beat her regularly. Anything else on his part is seen as a sign of unpardonable indifference. Here is a letter that one of them recently sent to her mother:

> *Dear Mother,*
>
> *I am the unhappiest woman in the world. I have tried everything I could to make my husband love me, and nothing works. Yesterday, I had a thousand things that I needed to do around the house, so I left and stayed out all day long. I thought for sure that he would give me a royal beating when I returned, but he didn't say a thing. My sister gets very different treatment: her husband beats her every day; she cannot so much as look at a man without him smacking her for it. They are very much in love, and they understand each other perfectly.*
>
> *This is what makes her so haughty, but I am not going to let her look down on me much longer. I am determined to make my husband love me, no matter what the cost. I'm going to make him so furious that he will simply have to give me some sign of affection. No one will be able to say that I haven't been beaten, and that I live in a house where I don't matter. At the least little slap that he gives me, I will cry out at the top of my voice, so that people will think he's really going at it—and I think that if some neighbor came over to help me, I'd strangle him. I beg you, my dear mother, to make it clear to my husband that he is treating me very unworthily. My father, such a decent man, never behaved like this, and I can still recall thinking, when I was a little girl, that he loved you a bit too much. I embrace you, dear mother.*

Muscovites cannot leave the empire, even to travel. Kept separate thus from other nations by the laws of their country, they have preserved their ancient customs, and are so attached to them because they cannot believe there could be any others.

But the prince who reigns now[50] wants to change all that. He has had great disputes on the subject of his people's beards, and the clergy and monks have struggled mightily to retain their ignorance.

He wishes to make the arts flourish, and does everything he can to introduce Europe to the glories of his nation, largely ignored up to now and hardly known to anyone but itself.

Continually restless, he roams across his vast estates, everywhere leaving signs of his innate harshness.

---

50. Czar Peter the Great (1672–1725) strove to modernize Russia; his efforts ranged from the seemingly trivial—for example, he ordered that all courtiers should cut off their beards and look more like European gentlemen—to the more serious, such as reforming medieval tax and marriage laws. He visited Paris in 1717.

Then suddenly he quits them, as if they were too small to contain him, and goes off through Europe in search of other provinces and new kingdoms.

I embrace you, my dear Usbek. I beg you, send me news of yourself and your doings.

From Moscow, the 2nd of the moon of Chalval, 1713

Letter 52

Rica to Usbek
*At * * **

The other day I found myself among a group of people whom I greatly enjoyed. The group included women of all ages—one of eighty, one of sixty, and one of forty, who had a niece around twenty or twenty-two. Some instinct led me to approach the latter, and she whispered to me, "What do you think of my aunt? At her age, she still wants to find lovers, and she acts as if she is still pretty." I said, "Oh, she is wrong about that: a scheme like that is much more suitable for you."

A little later, I found myself next to the aunt, who said to me: "What do you think of that woman over there, the one who is at least sixty but still spent over an hour on her dress and hair today?" I replied, "She wasted her time; a woman would have to have charms like yours to justify such care."

I then went over to that poor sixty-year-old woman, feeling sorry for her in my heart, when she whispered to me: "Have you ever seen anything so ridiculous? Look at that eighty-year-old woman wearing those crimson-colored ribbons. She is trying to look young, and indeed she is succeeding, for she looks downright childish."

I said to myself, "Good Lord: do we only see the ridiculousness of others?" I thought, though, that perhaps we find a certain happiness in contemplating the weaknesses of others. But I was in the mood for entertaining myself, so I said to myself that, since we have climbed up so high, we might just as well descend, and we should start at the top of the chain, and approach the oldest of all the ladies present.

"Madame," I said to her, "you look so much like the woman I was just talking with that it would seem you must be sisters; you would seem to be about the same age." She replied, "Indeed, Monsieur, when the one of us dies, the other will be in great fear, for I believe there is no more than a couple of days between us."

Leaving this decrepit woman, I went back to the sixty-year-old. I said to her, "Madame, you must settle a bet that I have made: I have wagered that that woman"—and here I gestured toward the forty-year-old—"and you are the same age." She exclaimed, "Heavens, there are scarcely six months between us!"

Good, I thought; everything is working as I thought; let us continue. I stepped down another link in the chain to the forty-year-old woman. "Madame, do me the favor of telling me if you call that woman at the other table your niece just as a kind of joke? You are just as young as she is; in fact, there is something a little faded about her face, and not at all about yours. And then, there is that youthful color in your complexion . . ." She said, "I can explain. I am her aunt, but her mother was at least twenty-five years older than me; she and I had a different mother, and I heard my deceased sister say that her daughter and I were born in the same year."

"I thought it must be something like that, Madame," I said; "I was right to be puzzled."

My dear Usbek, women who feel that their time is coming to an end, that their charms are deserting them, want to recover their youth. Why wouldn't they make efforts to deceive others, considering that they expend so much effort on deceiving themselves, doing anything they can to avoid realizing this, the most appalling of realities?

From Paris, the 3rd of the moon of Chalval, 1713

Letter 53

Zélis to Usbek
At Paris

There has never been a stronger, more intense passion than that felt by Cosrou, the white eunuch, for my slave Zélide; he asks for her hand in marriage with such desperation that I cannot refuse him. And why should I refuse, when her mother does not object, and when Zélide herself appears to be satisfied with the idea of this false marriage to a mere shadow of a man?

What can she want with this miserable creature, who will have nothing in common with real husbands except for jealousy—who will emerge from his frigidity only to fall into a useless despair—who will always have her remember what he once was, only to remind her of what he is no longer—who, always ready to give himself but unable to do so, will endlessly deceive himself, and will endlessly deceive her, and in so doing will always remind her of the misery of her situation?

And then to have to live always with mere phantoms, with imagination—to find oneself always near pleasures, but never attaining them—to languish in the arms of a wretch, responding to his regrets rather than to his sighs!

What contempt a woman must feel for a man like that, one created only to be a guardian and never a possessor! I search for some sign of love, but I do not find it.

I speak freely to you, because I know you prefer my frankness and my free and open enjoyment of pleasure over the false modesty of my companions.

A thousand times I have heard you say that eunuchs enjoy a kind of sensuality unknown to us, and that nature compensates them for their loss, for nature has the resources to make up what is lacking in their condition; that while one can cease being a man, one cannot cease feeling, and that in this state one grows into a different kind of sense, so to speak, in order to experience a different kind of pleasure.

If all that is true, I suppose Zélide is less to be pitied. It is something, anyway, to live with someone who is not entirely wretched.

Send me your orders regarding this, and let me know if you wish the marriage to be performed in the seraglio. Farewell.

From the seraglio at Ispahan, the 5th of
the moon of Chalval, 1713

Letter 54

Rica to Usbek
*At * * **

This morning I was in my room, which, as you know, is only separated from the others by a very thin partition, and one moreover with many gaps in it, so that you can hear everything that is said in the neighboring rooms. A man was pacing back and forth and talking to another: "I don't know what's going on, but lately everything is against me. It's been three days since I came up with a witty retort, and I find myself confounded in every sort of conversation, so that nobody pays any attention to me or speaks to me at all, more than once or twice. I had prepared a few clever remarks to liven up my discourse, but no one gave me the chance to say them. I had a superb story all ready to tell, but whenever I was preparing to get started on it, the others slipped away—as if on purpose. I've had several witticisms in my head for four days now, with no chance to use them. If this keeps up, I'll end up being nothing but a fool; it seems like fate, and no one can help me avoid it. Yesterday, I had every expectation of being able to shine with three or four older ladies, who of course do not intimidate me at all, and I should have come out with the finest phrases in the world, but even though I spent over a quarter of an hour working at it, I was unable to steer the conversation: they continually changed the subject and, like the Fatal Sisters, cut off the thread of my discourse. If I do say so myself, it is hard work maintaining the reputation of a wit. I don't know how you have managed to succeed at it."

The other man replied, "An idea just occurred to me: let us work together on our wittiness; we can form a sort of partnership. Each day, we can decide what we're going to talk about, and we can help each other out so smoothly that, if someone else interrupts the flow of our ideas, we can work to get him to come around to what we were saying—and if he doesn't come around easily, we'll force him back to us. We'll determine in advance the spots where the hearers should express agreement, and spots where they should smile, and those where they should burst out in a hearty laugh. You'll see: we'll set the tone for every conversation, and everyone will admire our wit and the sharpness of our repartee. We can protect each other with little head signals. You'll shine today, and tomorrow it will be my turn. I'll accompany you to someone's home and as we climb the stairs, I'll exclaim: 'I have to tell you all about the brilliant thing monsieur here just said to a man in the street.' And with that I'll turn to you, and say 'that fellow didn't know what to say, he was so surprised.' Or, I'll recite a few of my verses, and you will say: 'I was there when he composed them; it was in the middle of a supper, and he didn't even need to pause and think.' And then sometimes you and I will have some fun at each other's expense, and people will say: 'just look at how they attack each other, and how each one defends himself. The gloves are off with those two! Let's just see how he'll respond to that one! Oh, marvelous: what presence of mind they have! This is a regular battle.'

But they won't know that we rehearsed the skirmish the day before. We must buy some of those books, those little anthologies of witty sayings, published for the benefit of those who have no wit and want to pretend that they do. Everything depends on having good models. I believe that, in less than six months, we'll be able to carry on a conversation of nothing but witticisms for an entire hour. But we need to pay attention to one item: that is, seeing that our wit gets reported by others. It's not enough to say a fine thing: it has to be picked up and repeated all over town; otherwise, it is lost, and there's nothing so depressing as observing some excellent phrase one has worked on deposited in the ear of a fool who lets it die there. True, there are some compensations for that situation: we might very well say some asinine things, and they might just as well remain incognito, but that is the only consolation. Well, there it is, my friend—this is the plan. Do as I say, and I promise you that you'll have a place in the Academy in six months; it will not take very long. And once you're there, you can lay aside your art, for then you'll be considered a man of wit, no matter what you say. People say that in France, as soon as a man joins an institution he has what they call *esprit de corps*:[51] you'll have it too, and the only thing I fear is that you will be embarrassed by all the applause."

From Paris, the 6th of the moon of Zilcadé, 1714

Letter 55

Rica to Ibben
At Smyrna

Among Europeans, the first quarter of an hour of a marriage smoothes out all the difficulties; the ultimate favors are always granted on the same date as the wedding ceremony. Women here are not like Persian women, who dispute every inch of the territory, sometimes for whole months. Here, nothing could be plainer: if they lose nothing, well, it is because they had nothing to lose. But—and this is a shameful thing—the very

51. Montesquieu puns on the word *esprit*, which in the rest of the letter means "wit." The phrase *esprit de corps* means a group's sense of cohesion or solidarity. The would-be clever man evidently fails to understand this.

moment of their defeat is always known, and without having to consult the stars, one can predict, almost to the hour, the birth of their infants.

French husbands almost never speak about their wives; this is because they are afraid that they might be speaking to men who know them better than they do.

Among them are some miserable ones who are inconsolable—the jealous husbands. And there are some who are hated by all—the jealous husbands. And there are some who are scorned by all—again, the jealous husbands.

And therefore, there is no country with a smaller number of jealous husbands than France. The serenity of the husbands is not based on their confidence in their wives; on the contrary, it is based on the bad opinion they have of them. All the wise precautions that the Asiatics take—the veils covering their faces, the prisons we keep them in, the vigilance of the eunuchs—all these seem to be methods more likely to stimulate the ingenuity of the sex rather than stunt it. Here, the husbands play their roles with a good grace, and look upon infidelity as something inevitable, destined by the stars. A man who wanted to be the sole possessor of his wife would be looked upon as a disturber of the public happiness, or like a madman who wanted to keep the sun from shining on any men other than himself.

Here, a husband who loves his wife is a man who hasn't enough merit to make himself beloved by some other woman; who abuses the law to make up for his own failure to attract a woman; who uses its advantages to the prejudice of society at large; who hoards what had been given to him only on a temporary basis; and who does his best to overturn the tacit social convention that provides for the happiness of both sexes. Being known as the husband of a pretty woman, a fact we strive to keep hidden in Asia, causes no anxiety here. A person feels free to find his entertainment wherever he likes. A prince will console himself for the loss of a castle by taking another: back in the time when the Turks took Baghdad, didn't we turn around and take the fortress of Kandahar from the Mogul?[52]

A man who tolerates his wife's infidelities is not at all disapproved of; on the contrary, people praise him for his prudence. Any dishonor lies solely in the details of a particular case.

This is not to say that there are no virtuous women, and they are considered distinguished; my guide always took pains to point them out to me. But every one of them is so ugly that one would have to be a saint not to end up hating virtue.

---

52. These events took place in, respectively, 1638 and 1649.

Considering everything I have said here, you will easily infer that the French do not pride themselves on their fidelity. They think that it is just as ridiculous for a man to swear to a woman that he will always love her, as it is to swear that he will always be healthy or happy. When they do promise a woman that they will love her always, they assume that for her part, she is also promising to keep herself always loveable, and if she breaks her promise, they are under no obligation to keep theirs.

From Paris, the 7th of the moon of Zilcadé, 1714

Letter 56

Usbek to Ibben
At Smyrna

Gambling is everywhere in Europe; one can be a professional gambler here, a title that substitutes for birth, wealth, and integrity. Any man sporting such a title is instantly granted entrée into the best levels of society, even though everyone involved knows that it is often a mistake to do so. But everyone seems to have agreed to remain incorrigible.

Women are especially addicted to it. In their youth, it is true, they rarely play, unless it is to advance pursuits dearer to their hearts; but the older they get, the more their passion for gaming seems to grow, and eventually that passion drives out all the others.

Ruining their husbands is their primary aim, and in order to succeed at it they have developed methods appropriate to every age, from the tenderest youth to the most decrepit old age: clothes and coaches get the process started, flirtation advances it, and gambling brings it to a happy conclusion.

I have often observed nine or ten women, or rather nine or ten centuries, all ranged around a gaming table. I have watched them, observing their hopes, their fears, their joys, and above all, their rages. You would think that nothing could ever calm them back down, and that their despair would only end with their lives; and you would have been uncertain whether they were paying off their creditors or their heirs.

It would seem that our holy Prophet had for his principal aim protecting us from all those things that can make us lose our reason: he forbade us to drink wine, which can drown our reason; and by an express command, he forbade us to play games of chance.[53] And when it was impossible for him to remove the causes of our irrational passions, he found ways to lessen them. Among us Persians, love carries with it no disturbances and no fury: it is rather a languid passion, leaving our souls in tranquility; having multiple wives reduces the dominion that one wife could hold over us, and it tempers the violence of our desires.

From Paris, the 10th of the moon of Zilhagé, 1714

Letter 57

Usbek to Rhédi
At Venice

The libertines here support an immense number of prostitutes, while the religiously devout support an immense number of dervishes. These dervishes take three vows: obedience, poverty, and chastity. People say that the first is the one most likely to be observed; as for the second, I can tell you it is entirely ignored; and as for the third, I leave it to you to judge.

But no matter how wealthy these dervishes are, they continue to insist on calling themselves poor—indeed, our glorious sultan would sooner renounce his sublime and magnificent titles. And they are right, for being *called* poor means they do not have to *be* poor.

The physicians, and some of these dervishes (the ones they call confessors), are always given either too much esteem or too much contempt. But those who expect to become heirs prefer physicians to confessors.[54]

The other day I visited a monastery for these dervishes. One of them, an old man whose white hair made him venerable, welcomed me very warmly. He showed me around the entire place. We went into the garden, where we began to converse. "Father," I said to him, "what is your own employment here in the community?" He replied, seeming very pleased with my question, "Monsieur, I am a casuist."

"A casuist?" I asked. "In my time so far in France, I have never heard of that title."

---

53. The prohibitions are in the Koran, 5:90–92.

54. The joke here is that the confessor would probably urge the dying to leave their goods to the church rather than to their heirs.

"What!" he exclaimed. "You don't know what a casuist is? Well, let me give you an idea of it; I'll explain it to your complete satisfaction. There are two kinds of sins: mortal sins, which exclude the sinner absolutely from paradise; and venial sins, which in fact do offend God, but do not irritate Him to the point of depriving the sinner of ultimate beatitude. Now, our whole art consists in distinguishing between these two kinds of sin, for, apart from a few libertines, every Christian wants to gain entry to paradise; but at the same time, everyone wants to get there as cheaply as possible. When one understands the mortal sins, one tries not to commit one of them, and that does the job nicely. But there are some men who do not aspire to perfection; they are not ambitious, and do not ask to have the first rank, so they are happy if they just barely manage to get into paradise. As long as they make it in, they are happy; their whole aim is no more than that. These are the people who take it by force,[55] rather than earn it, and who say to God: 'Lord, I have accomplished the letter of the law, and therefore you cannot renege on your promises. Since I have done nothing more than what you asked, I do not ask you to give me anything more than what you've promised.'

"Thus, we are necessary people, Monsieur. But this is not all: let me explain another very important point. The act itself is not the crime; the crime lies in the awareness of the person committing it. A person who does a wicked deed, as long as he does not know that it's wicked, has a perfectly clear conscience. And since there are an infinite number of equivocal actions, a casuist is able to confer upon them a degree of goodness beyond what they merit, simply by declaring them good. Provided the casuist can convince the person that his actions are not evil, he can remove all the taint of sinfulness.

"In telling you this, I am revealing to you the innermost secret of this career in which I have grown old. I want you to see the finer points: anything at all, even things that seem most unlikely, can be turned in such a way that they appear perfectly good."

I said, "My dear Father, all this is fine, but how do you reconcile yourself with heaven? If the Sophy[56] had a man at his court who did for him what you do against your God, someone who made fine distinctions between his commands, teaching his subjects which ones they have to obey and which ones they can violate, he would have such a man

---

55. See Matthew 11:12: "And from the days of John the Baptist to now, the kingdom of heaven suffereth violence, and the violent take it by force."

56. *Sophy* is one of the terms for the Persian monarch.

impaled on the spot." I bowed to the dervish, and walked away without waiting for his reply.

From Paris, the 23rd of the moon of Maharram, 1714

Letter 58

Rica to Rhédi
At Venice

There are many professions in Paris, my dear Rhédi. Here, a man will offer to help you out, for just a small sum, by showing you the secret of how to make gold.

Another promises you the ability to sleep with ethereal spirits, provided only that you abstain from women for thirty years first.

And you will encounter clairvoyants here of such power that they can tell you everything about yourself, so long as they first have just fifteen minutes alone with your domestics.

There are women here of such nimble skill that they can make the flower of their virginity perish and be reborn on a daily basis; and plucking it for the one-hundredth time gives them more pain than it did the first time.

There are others who, deploying their arts to heal all the damages wrought by time, know how to rescue a face whose beauty is tottering, and even how to bring a woman back from the very summit of old age, showing her how to descend smoothly to her sweetest youth.

All these people live—or strive somehow to live—in a city that is the veritable mother of invention.

The income of these citizens cannot be taxed, for it consists only of their wits and ingenuity; each has his own scheme, and each works it as best as he can.

Anyone who would try to number all the clerics here trying to get their hands on the revenues from a given mosque might as well try to number the grains of sand on the beach, or the slaves of our monarch.

An infinite number of self-styled Masters of languages, arts, and sciences offer to teach you what they do not know, and such a talent is quite a considerable thing, for it does not take much cleverness to teach what you know, but tremendous talent is necessary to teach what you do not.

The only way to die here is suddenly; death cannot exercise his empire here otherwise, for every corner of the city teems with people who have infallible remedies for every imaginable malady.

Every shop is hung with invisible nets for catching customers. One can, sometimes, end up with a bargain. A young shop girl will spend a whole hour coaxing a male customer, just to get him to purchase a box of toothpicks.

Everyone leaves this city a more cautious person than when he entered it: by dint of having to give up one's money to others, one learns eventually how to hang on to it—which is the only advantage this enchanting city offers to the foreign visitor.

From Paris, the 10th of the moon of Saphar, 1714

Letter 59

Rica to Usbek
At * * *

The other day I visited a home where a diverse group of people had gathered, and I found the conversation being dominated by two elderly women who had been laboring vainly all morning to find a way to look younger. "It cannot be denied," one of them said, "that men nowadays are very different from the men we used to see when we were young. Men then were polite, kind, easy to get along with; but these days, I find them intolerably coarse."

A man who suffered from gout picked up the theme. "Everything has changed, and times aren't what they used to be. Forty years ago, everyone was in good health, and we walked around cheerfully, asking only for a smile and a dance. But nowadays, everyone is intolerably low-spirited."

A moment passed, and the conversation turned to politics. An old gentleman said, "I swear, the State is no longer being governed. Just try to find a minister these days who is the equal of Colbert.[57] I knew him

57. Jean-Baptiste Colbert (1619–1683) was Minister of Finance under Louis XIV from 1665–1683; his far-reaching policies dramatically reformed the French economy.

well, that Colbert; he was a friend of mine; he saw to it that I received my pension before everyone else did—but now, just look at the state of our finances! Back then, everyone was comfortable, but today, I am ruined."

An ecclesiastic spoke up next. "Monsieur, you refer to the most miraculous days of our invincible monarch. Was there ever anything quite as grand as his efforts to exterminate heresy?"[58]

Another man, who had not yet spoken, said with an air of contentment, "And don't forget another triumph of those years, the abolition of dueling." Someone whispered to me, "a judicious remark, coming from a man who so fervently obeys the edict that allowed him to be beaten to within an inch of his life six months back, rather than break the law."[59]

Usbek, it seems to me that we always judge things by secretly relating them to our own concerns. I am not surprised that black men envision the devil as being a brilliant white color, and that they picture their gods as being black as coal—nor that certain peoples picture Venus as having breasts that hang down to her thighs—nor that all the idolaters have always pictured their gods in human form, ascribing to them all their own predilections. It has been well said that if triangles had a god, they would imagine him as having three sides.[60]

My dear Usbek, when I see human beings creeping about on this atom, this earth, which is after all only a tiny point in the universe, and proposing themselves as exact models for Providence, I am at a loss trying to reconcile such extravagant claims with such pettiness.

From Paris, the 14th of the moon of Saphar, 1714

58. The ecclesiastic is nostalgic for the era when Louis XIV revoked the Edict of Nantes, which had granted toleration to Protestants. The revocation, in 1685, resulted in a flood of emigration from France; in addition to being a moral disaster, the revocation also led to economic and social upheaval.

59. That is, the man was too cowardly to duel, and so instead he was beaten.

60. Vernière notes that the saying about the triangles and their god comes from Spinoza, but it may have been proverbial even earlier.

Letter 60

Usbek to Ibben
At Smyrna

You ask me whether there are Jews in France. As you know, wherever there is money, there will be Jews. You ask me what they do here. Exactly what they do in Persia: there is nothing that resembles an Asian Jew so closely as a European one.

Among the Christians here, they are just as they are among us, with that obstinate devotion to their religion that amounts almost to madness.

The Jewish religion is an old trunk from which two branches have sprouted that now cover the earth—that is, Islam and Christianity. Or rather, it is a mother who has given birth to two daughters who have paid her back with a thousand wounds; for when it comes to religion, those who are closest to each other are the worst enemies. But no matter how badly the daughters treat her, she goes on boasting of having brought them into the world; she makes use of the one or the other to reach out and embrace the whole world, just as her great age reaches back to embrace all time.

The Jews thus see themselves as the source of all holiness, the origin of all religion; and they look upon us as heretics who have dishonored the Law—or rather simply as rebel Jews.

If the change had been effected more gradually, they believe that they would have been seduced along with the others; but it came about so suddenly and in so violent a manner, such that one can point to the very hour and day of the one birth and of the other, that they find it scandalous in us that we have a specific age, and they continue to hold fast to a religion that is as old as the earth itself.

They have never enjoyed the kind of peace that they now experience in Europe. The Christians are beginning to abandon that old spirit of religious intolerance; it was a mistake to expel the Jews from Spain, just as it was to persecute the Christians in France whose beliefs differed only slightly from those of their king.[61] They have realized here that zeal for the advancement of one's religion is different from the attachment one ought to have for it, and that to love and observe one's faith, it is not necessary to hate and persecute those who do not observe it.

---

61. The Jews were expelled from Spain in 1492. The Christians persecuted in France were the Protestants, known as the Huguenots.

It would be a good thing if we Muslims thought about this issue the way the Christians do, and if once and for all there could be peace between Hali and Abu Bekr, and if we could leave it up to God to decide upon the merits of these holy prophets.[62] I would like to see them honored by acts of veneration and respect, and not by pointless preference; and I would like to see us merit their favor in whatever place God has put them, whether at His right hand or at the foot of his throne.

From Paris, the 18th of the moon of Saphar, 1714

Letter 61

Usbek to Rhédi
At Venice

I went into a famous church the other day, the one they call Notre-Dame. While I was admiring that splendid structure, I had occasion to fall into conversation with a priest, who like me had been drawn there out of curiosity. The talk turned to the tranquility associated with his profession. "Most people," he said to me, "envy the happiness of our condition, and they are right to do so. But there are irritations: we are not really so separated from the world, for we are called upon on a thousand occasions, and in that respect we have a difficult role to maintain.

"Worldly people are amazing: they cannot endure either our approval or our censure. If we try to correct them, they find us ridiculous; if we approve of them, they regard us as having debased ourselves. There is nothing more humiliating than the feeling that one has been a scandal even to an unbeliever. Therefore, we are obliged to conduct ourselves in an equivocal manner, and to deal with the freethinkers not in a firm, decided way, but by making them wonder what exactly we think of what they are saying. You have to be very clever to pull that off; that state of neutrality is difficult to maintain. The worldly man can say whatever he

62. Hali, Mohammed's son-in-law, and Abu Bekr, his father-in-law, here stand for Shia and Sunni Muslims. See also Note 8.

likes, and depending on the response to his little sallies, can either follow up or let it go, and in this way he has it much easier than we do.

"And that is not all. This happy, tranquil life of ours that everyone talks about evaporates the minute we go out into society. As soon as we appear there, we are forced into debate. For example, we are forced into trying to demonstrate the utility of prayer to a man who does not believe in God, the necessity of fasting to another who had denied the immortality of the soul his whole life. The enterprise is hard work, and the laughter is always at our expense. And moreover, we are endlessly tormented by a certain desire to attract others to share our views, a desire which is, so to speak, built into our profession. That too becomes ridiculous—as if one were to watch Europeans labor to enhance human nature by bleaching the skin of Africans. We are a trouble to the State, and a torment to ourselves, insofar as we try to make certain non-fundamental tenets of religion widely accepted. In that respect we resemble the Chinese conqueror who drove his subjects into general revolt by forcing them to cut their hair and fingernails.[63]

"Even our zeal for ensuring that those given into our charge perform the duties of our holy religion is a dangerous thing, and it cannot be carried out with too much prudence. There once was an emperor named Theodosius who put the entire population of a town to the sword, even the women and children. When he went on to enter the local church, a bishop by the name of Ambrose closed the doors upon him, calling him a sacrilegious murderer—which was indeed a heroic act.[64] This emperor, having gone on to do the penance called for by such a crime, and being admitted thenceforth into the church, went to sit among the priests. But the bishop made him leave—and that was the act of a fanatic. A person must temper his zeal. What did it matter to religion or to the State whether this prince sat with the priests or somewhere else?"

From Paris, the 1st of the moon of Rebiab I, 1714

---

63. This incident involved the Manchu emperor, Chun-Chi, in the mid-seventeenth century.

64. The Roman Emperor Theodosius the Great (347–395) had the citizens of Thessalonica massacred following an uprising in 390. The bishop of Milan, Ambrose, imposed extensive penance upon him before re-admitting him to the church.

Letter 62

Zélis to Usbek
At Paris

Your daughter having turned seven years old, I thought it was time to bring her into the inner rooms of the seraglio, rather than waiting until she was ten to entrust her to the black eunuchs. One can never begin too soon the process of depriving a child of her liberties and starting her holy education behind the sacred walls where modesty dwells.

For I cannot agree with those mothers who only confine their daughters when they are on the verge of marriage; who condemn their daughters to the seraglio, rather than consecrating them to it; and who thus force them violently to take on this way of life, rather than inspiring them to embrace it. Must everything in life be attained through reasoning, and nothing from the gentle paths of habituation?

It is futile to talk to us about the subordinate position in which nature has placed us, and it is not enough to make us feel it: we must be made to practice it, so that it can support us in that critical time when the passions begin to come to life within us and encourage us in the direction of independence.

If our only attachment to you were one of duty, we might sometimes forget that duty; if our only attachment were our feeling, a more powerful feeling might come along and weaken it. But when the laws give us to one man, they take all the others away from us, putting us so far away from all other men that they might as well be a hundred thousand leagues distant.

Nature, always industrious in finding ways to benefit men, did not stop in giving men desires; she wanted us to be desiring creatures as well, and wanted us to be the lively instruments of men's happiness. She set alight the passions within us, so that men might live in tranquility. If they should fall out of that state of peaceful indifference of theirs, nature has destined us as the ones to help them regain it—without ever being able to taste that blissful state into which we put them ourselves.

But for all that, Usbek, never imagine that your situation is a happier one than mine: I have enjoyed a thousand pleasures here that you have never known. My imagination has been working tirelessly to show me how great the value is of those pleasures: I have lived, while you have only languished.

Even within this prison where you have locked me, I am freer than you. If you were to double the guard you have placed on me, I would simply delight in your anxiety; and your suspicions, your jealousy, your worries are all just so many signs of your dependence.

So do continue, my dear Usbek: keep watch on me night and day, and do not limit yourself to ordinary precautions: increase my happiness by ensuring your own, and know that the only thing I fear is your indifference.

From the seraglio at Ispahan, the 2nd of the moon of Rebiab I, 1714

Letter 63

Rica to Usbek
At * * *

I am beginning to believe that you want to spend the rest of our life in the countryside. At first, I only lost you for three or four days, but it is now two weeks since I have seen you. True, you are staying in a charming house, among people you like, and can converse to your heart's content—and that is all it takes to make you forget everything else in the whole universe.

As for me, I continue to live the same life you saw me leading before. I go out into society, seeking to understand it. My thinking is gradually losing what remains of its Asiatic cast, and is adjusting easily now to European ways. I am no longer surprised to find five or six women in a house with five or six men; in fact, I am beginning to like it.

I have to admit it: I never knew women until I came here, and I have learned more about them here in a month than I would have in thirty years in the seraglio.

With us, people's characters are always alike, and that is because they are forced: you never see people as they really are, only as they are required to be. And with that kind of servitude of heart and mind, the only language you hear spoken is the language of fear, which is always the same—not the language of nature, which expresses itself with such variety, and which appears under so many different forms.

Dissimulation, that art so widely practiced and so very necessary among us, is unknown here: here, everything can be said, can be seen, can be heard. The heart reveals itself freely, just as the face does. In people's behavior—in their virtue as well as in their vice—there is always something artless.

In order to appeal to women here, one needs a certain talent quite different from the one they value even more—that is, a kind of witty banter that amuses them, for it seems to promise that they can have something at all times that in fact can only come along every once in a great while.

This banter, best suited to conversation around the dressing table, seems to have evolved to shape the general character of the nation: they banter in political councils, and at the head of an army, and in conversation with an ambassador. The most ridiculed professions are those that are presented as the most serious. Physicians would be much less ridiculed if they dressed less lugubriously, and if they killed off their patients while joking with them.

From Paris, the 10th of the moon of Rebiab I, 1714

Letter 64

The Chief Black Eunuch to Usbek
At Paris

I find myself in a difficult situation, my magnificent lord, and one that I scarcely know how to explain to you. The seraglio has fallen into frightful disorder and confusion. War has broken out among your wives; the eunuchs are divided; nothing is heard but complaints, murmurings, reproaches. My remonstrances are treated with contempt. Everything is permitted in this time of license, and my title is an empty one, carrying no authority within the seraglio.

Every single one of your women sees herself as better than all the others in terms of her birth, beauty, riches, wit, how much you love her; every one of them claims she deserves precedence on the basis of one or another of these. With every passing moment I lose more of that long-suffering patience of mine which, in fact, only served to make them all even more discontent. My prudence, even my forbearance—strange, rare virtues in a post such as mine—have been useless.

Shall I reveal to you, magnificent one, the cause of all these disorders? It lies entirely in your heart, in your tenderness toward your wives. If you would not restrain my hand—if, instead of merely remonstrating with them, I had your permission to punish them—if, instead of indulging them by listening to their weeping complaints, you sent them instead to come weep in front of me, one who is never moved by tears—then in short order, I would fit them with the yoke they ought to be wearing, and do away with their arrogant, independent tendencies.

Carried away at the age of fifteen from the depths of my native Africa, I was first sold to a master with more than twenty wives or concubines. Having observed my grave, taciturn air, he judged me fit for the seraglio, and gave orders that I should be readied for it; he forced me to undergo an operation that I at first found painful, but that I came to appreciate in time, for it gave me access to my masters' ear and to their trust. I entered into the seraglio, which was, for me, an entirely new world. The chief eunuch, the severest man I had ever known, ruled over it with absolute power. There was no idle chatter there, no divisions, no quarrels; a profound silence reigned in the place. Every woman went to bed at the same time every night of the year, and every one arose in the morning at the same hour. They went into the bath in good order, and came out at the slightest sign from us. The rest of the time, they were almost always confined to their individual rooms. He insisted on one rule, that they always maintain themselves in the strictest cleanliness, and he took the most indescribable precautions to ensure this; the slightest deviation from that rule was punished mercilessly. He would say, "I am a slave, but I am the slave of the man who is your master and mine, and I wield the power he has given me over you. It is he who chastises you, not me; I am merely the instrument he employs." Those women never entered into the master's room without having been summoned, and they received that favor with great joy, although they did not complain when deprived of it. And as for me, the least of the blacks in that tranquil seraglio—I was respected there a thousand times more than I am in yours, where I am in command of all.

When that great eunuch came to know me and my abilities, he took me under his wing, speaking of me to the master as of a man capable of good work, and capable of becoming his successor in the post. He was not concerned about my extreme youth, believing that my careful attentiveness would compensate for my lack of experience. What can I say? I made such rapid progress and came to be so trusted by him that he did not scruple to put into my hands the keys to that fearsome place that he had guarded so long. Under that great master, I learned the difficult art of command, forming myself to his rules of inflexible government. Under him, I studied the hearts of women. He taught me how to profit from their weaknesses, and never to be intimidated by their arrogant airs. He often took pleasure in watching me drive them into the farthest corners of obedience; then he would bring them back gently, ordering me to pretend to be, for a time, more pliant. But he was at his best in those moments when they were close to despair, wavering between entreaties and reproaches: he put up with their tears without being moved in the slightest, delighting in the knowledge of triumph. He would say, contentedly, "You see how one needs to govern women. I don't care how many there are; I could rule like this over as many women as the Grand Monarch has. How can a man hope to win their hearts, if his faithful eunuchs have not first broken their spirits?"

He was not just inflexible; he had a keen, penetrating mind. He could see through their schemes and their dissimulations; their studied gestures and affected expressions made no difference to him. He knew their most secret acts, their most secret words. He made use of certain ones in order to learn about other ones, and he liked to reward them for the slightest confidence. Since they only approached their husband when they were summoned, the chief eunuch called the ones he wanted to call, turning his master's gaze toward the one he had chosen, and this distinction was the reward for some secret she had told him. He had persuaded the master that it was best for discipline if he were allowed to do the choosing, so as to allow him the greatest authority possible. And that, magnificent one, is the way he governed what I believe was the best-run seraglio in all of Persia.

Untie my hands: permit me to force them to obey me, and in one week I will change all this confusion into order. Your own reputation demands it, and your security requires it.

From your seraglio at Ispahan, the 9th
of the moon of Rebiab I, 1714

Letter 65

Usbek to his wives
At the seraglio in Ispahan

I have been informed that the seraglio is in disorder, and that it is filled with quarrels and internal divisions. When I left, did I not exhort you all to live in peace with each other? You promised me this—were you trying to trick me?

Well, the trick would be upon you if I were to take the advice that the chief eunuch has given me, if I were to exercise my authority over you and force you to live in the way I exhorted you to.

But I do not wish to use violent methods—or at least not until I have exhausted all the alternatives. Therefore, behave the way you ought to, for your own good if not for my sake.

The chief eunuch has a very serious complaint: he tells me you have no respect for him. How can you reconcile your behavior with the modesty that your condition demands? In my absence, your virtue is entrusted to him: is that not true? That sacred treasure is deposited with him. But this contempt for him that you demonstrate seems to suggest that those who are entrusted with seeing that you live according to the laws of honor are simply an irritation to you.

Amend this behavior of yours, I urge you, and live in such a way that I may continue to reject the proposals that have been made to me regarding your freedom and your comfort.

I say this to you because I want to make you forget that I am your master, and remember only that I am your husband.

From Paris, the 5th of the moon of Chahban, 1714

Letter 66

Rica to * * *

Everyone talks about the sciences here, but I am not so sure that they are really all that well learned in them. A person who, when speaking as a philosopher, doubts everything dares not, when speaking as a theologian, deny anything;[65] and this walking contradiction is entirely pleased with himself, so long as everyone agrees with his subtle distinctions.

The mania afflicting most French people is the desire to be witty; and the mania afflicting those who want to be witty is the desire to write books.

However, this is a very bad idea: nature has so arranged things that the absurdities men say are passing things, but books give them

65. This could be a swipe at René Descartes, who as a philosopher famously began by putting everything in doubt, but who avoided doubt when it came to Christian dogma.

immortal life. A fool ought to be content to have annoyed those who live near him, but instead he wants the chance to torment future generations. He wants his absurdities to triumph over the complete oblivion that he really ought to have welcomed and enjoyed like a tomb. He wants posterity to be informed that he lived, and he wants it known for all time that he was a fool.

Of all these authors, the ones I despise the most are the compilers, the ones who rummage through the works of others and tear off strips to patch into their own books, like bits of turf in a lawn.[66] They are no better than the compositors who work for the printers, putting letters together so as to form a book; they have contributed nothing but the use of their hands. I think original books ought to be more respected, for I think it is a kind of profanation to take fragments out of their sanctuary and expose them to a contempt that they do not merit.

When a man has nothing new to say, why does he not simply keep quiet? Who needs all this repetition? "But I have a new order of things to contribute!" Well then, you seem a capable man! Come to my library, and I will give you employment: take the books from the top shelves and exchange them with the ones on the bottom: now there is a real masterpiece awaiting you!

I am writing to you about this, my dear * * *, because I am furious about a book I've just read, a book so fat that you would assume it must contain a universal science; but it has only wearied my brain, without putting one new thing into it. Farewell.

From Paris, the 8th of the moon of Chahban, 1714

Letter 67

Ibben to Usbek
At Paris

Three ships have come and gone without bringing me any news from you. Are you ill? Or do you enjoy making me worry?

66. There was a brisk trade in such compilations and anthologies in the eighteenth century, in both France and England.

If you do not care about me when you are in a country with no family and no ties, what will you be like when you return to your own people here in Persia? But perhaps I am mistaken. You are the likeable sort, the type who makes friends everywhere; the heart is a citizen of all nations, so how could a soul as fine as yours fail to make connections anywhere? I admit that I respect old, longstanding friendships, but I am not averse to forming new ones.

In whatever country I have visited, I have lived as if I were going to have to spend the rest of my life there: I have felt the same enthusiasm for virtuous men, and the same compassion, or rather tenderness, for the unfortunate, and the same esteem for those who have not been blinded by prosperity. This is my character, Usbek: wherever I encounter people, I form friendships.

There is a Guèbre[67] here who is, I believe, the dearest to me after you. He is the very soul of integrity. He was obliged to retire to this city for particular reasons, where he leads a peaceful life, supported by an honest trade, and married to a woman he loves. His whole life is marked by generous acts, and though he wishes to live a quiet life, there is more heroism in his heart than in those of the greatest monarchs.

I have spoken about you to him many times, and I show him all your letters; I observe that they give him pleasure, and I can see that you have made a friend out of a man you have never met.

What follows is a narrative of his most important adventures. He finds the idea of writing them down himself repugnant, but he was incapable of refusing me the pleasure of doing so, and now I confide the story to you.

The Story of Aphéridon and Astarte

I was born among the Guèbres, into a religion that may be the world's most ancient. I was unfortunate in that love awoke in me before reason did. I was only six years old, but I could not endure to be apart from my sister; my eyes were always fixed upon her, and whenever she had to leave me for a moment, she would return to find me in tears. Every day I grew a little older, and every day I loved her a little more. My father,

---

67. *Guèbre* (or Gabar) is another term for a Zoroastrian. Their sect, which had sprung up some two thousand years back, was now in the minority in Persia, and often persecuted by the Muslims. Montesquieu, following his sources, tends to depict them in positive terms, as did Voltaire, who wrote a tragedy about them, *Les Guèbres*, in 1769. For writers like Montesquieu and Voltaire, the Guèbres seem to stand for virtuous pagans.

surprised to see so strong a connection between us, would have liked to arrange a marriage between us, which would have been in accord with the ancient traditions of the Guèbres, as introduced by Cambyses.[68] But the fear of the Muslims, under whose yoke we live, prevented our people from even contemplating these holy alliances, which our religion not only permits but even enjoins upon us, alliances which are the innocent mirror of a union already formed by nature.

My father therefore, seeing how dangerous it would have been to follow my inclination and his own, resolved to extinguish a flame that he believed was just beginning but that in fact was already at its full height. He invented a trip that we had to take, and he brought me along with him, leaving my sister in the hands of a relative of his—for my mother had been dead for two years. I cannot express the despair this separation threw us into: I embraced my sister, her face bathed in tears, but not mine, for grief had rendered me insensible. We arrived at Tbilisi, and my father, after entrusting my education to a relative, left me and returned home.

Some time later I learned that he had made use of a friend's influence and put my sister into the king's harem, where she was in the service of a sultana. If I had learned of her death, I could not have been more overcome: not only must I lose all hope of seeing her again, but her entry into the harem would have required her turning Muslim—and, given the prejudices of that religion, she could now no longer contemplate me with anything but horror. Nonetheless, unable to continue to live in Tbilisi, tired of myself and of life, I returned to Ispahan. My first words there were bitter ones addressed to my father; I reproached him with having put his daughter in a place that required her to change her religion. I said to him, "You have brought down the wrath of God upon your family, and of the sun that shines upon you. You have done a worse thing than polluting the elements, for you have polluted the soul of your daughter, which had been just as pure. I will die of grief and love, and may my death be the only punishment God visits upon you!" With these words, I left, and for the next two years of my life I studied the outer walls of the harem, wondering in what part my sister might be; I exposed myself a thousand times to having my throat slit by one of the eunuchs who patrol outside that fearful place.

Eventually, my father died, and the sultana my sister served, observing her grow in beauty every day, and becoming jealous of her, had her

68. Cambyses was a sixth century BC king in Persia. Herodotus (Book III of the *History*) tells us that he married his sister, voiding the existing laws against incest.

married to a eunuch who desired her passionately. And thus it was that my sister came to leave the seraglio, moving into a house in Ispahan with her eunuch.

It took me three months to have the chance to speak with her, for the eunuch, the most jealous of men, kept putting me off with various pretexts. At last, I gained entrance into his harem, and he had me speak to her through a latticed screen. The eyes of a lynx would have been unable to make her out, so covered was she in garments and veils, and the only way I could recognize her was through her voice. Imagine my feelings, when I found myself so close to her, and yet so far away! But I kept it all inside, for I was being watched. I thought I saw her shed a few tears. Her husband tried to make some inept excuses for her, but I treated him like the meanest of slaves. He was confounded when he realized I was speaking to my sister in a language unknown to him—that is, ancient Persian, our holy language. I said to her, "Oh, my sister, is it true that you have turned your back on the religion of your forefathers? I know that in entering the harem, you had to profess the Muslim faith, but tell me the truth, did your heart consent to what your lips were forced to say, to leave behind a religion that permits me to love you? And for whom did you leave it, that religion so dear to us? For a wretch who still carries the marks of the chains he wore, a wretch who, if he were even a man, would be the lowest of all men."

She replied, "My brother, this man of whom you speak is my husband, and no matter how much contempt you have for him, I must honor him, and I would also be the lowest of all women if . . ." I interrupted her, exclaiming, "Oh, my sister! You are a Guèbre! He is not your spouse, nor could he be. If you have the faith of our fathers, you can only look upon him as a kind of monster."

"Alas," she said, "how distant that religion seems to me now! I had barely learned the precepts when I was forced to forget them. You can see that this language I speak to you is no longer familiar to me, and that I have a great deal of trouble in expressing myself through it. But you can rely on one thing: that the memory of our childhood together still fills me with happiness, and since that time, the only joys I have had have been false ones. Not a day has passed without thinking of you. You played a role, unknown to yourself, in my marriage, for I would not have entered into this except that it gave me hope to someday see you again. But oh, what this day has cost me, and will cost me yet more! For I can see you beside yourself with anger, and I can see my husband quivering with rage and jealousy. I will never see you again—I am probably speaking to you for the last time in my life right now—and if I am right about that, my dear brother, then that life of mine will not be a long one." At that, she was overcome with emotion, and finding herself unable to continue the conversation, she left me standing there, the most despairing of men.

Three or four days later, I again asked to see my sister. The barbarous eunuch would have liked to keep her from my sight, but apart from the fact that husbands of his sort do not enjoy the authority other husbands do, he was so madly in love with my sister that he could deny her nothing. I saw her in the same place, covered by the same veils, and accompanied by two slaves, which made me resort to our own language. I said to her, "My sister, why is it that I can only see you in this horrible situation? These walls closing you in, these bars and these locks, and these miserable guardians keeping watch over you—all of it puts me in a fury. How could you let yourself lose the sweet liberty your ancestors enjoyed? The only guarantee of virtue that your perfectly chaste mother gave to her husband was simply that very virtue: they lived happily together in mutual trust, and the simplicity of their life was for them a greater wealth than all the false tinsel that you seem to be enjoying so in this sumptuous house. In losing your religion, you have lost your liberty, your happiness, and that precious equality that is the honor of your sex. But what is even worse is that you have become, not a wife, for that is impossible, but a slave of a slave, the slave of one who has lost his very humanity."

She exclaimed, "Oh, my brother, have some respect for my husband and for the religion I have embraced. According to that religion, if I but listen to you or speak to you I am guilty of crime."

In a rage, I cried out, "What, my sister! So you actually believe in this religion?"

She said, "Oh, how good it would be for me if I did not believe in it! I am sacrificing too much not to believe in it, and if my doubts . . ." At that, she fell silent.

"Your doubts, my sister, are well founded, whatever they may be. What do you expect from a religion that makes you miserable in this world and gives you no hope for the next? Remember that our religion is the most ancient in the world, and that it has always flourished in Persia, having originated with the empire itself, so far back in time that no one can tell when it began, and that Mohammedanism only came to Persia by chance, and that the sect established itself not by persuasion but by conquest.[69] If our native princes had not been weak, you would see the cult of

69. The last pre-Islamic Persian empire, the Sassanid Empire, came to an end in the year 651 with the assassination of the Emperor Yazdegerd as he and his nobles were in flight from a Muslim army.

the ancient Magi still flourishing. Think back to those ancient centuries: everything from them speaks of Magism, and nothing of that Mohammedan sect, which was only in its infancy thousands of years later."

She replied, "But if my religion is newer than yours, it is also at least purer, for we worship only God, whereas you still worship the sun, the stars, fire, even the elements."

"I see, my sister, that living among the Muslims has taught you to slander our holy religion. We worship neither the stars nor the elements, and our forefathers did not worship them either; they never erected temples to them, nor offered them sacrifices. They only made of them a lesser religious cult, seeing them as among the works and manifestations of the divine. But my sister, in the name of the God who enlightens us, take this holy book I have brought, the book of Zoroaster, our lawgiver.[70] Read it without prejudice, and let its rays of enlightenment penetrate your heart. Think of your forefathers who honored the sun for so many years in the holy city of Balkh,[71] and, finally, think of me—for my only hopes for peace, for fortune, for life itself all rest upon your conversion." In a state of exalted emotion, I left her alone to decide upon the most important issue in my entire life.

I came back two days later. I maintained silence with her, and I simply waited for her to deliver the verdict—whether I would live or die. "You are loved, my brother," she said to me, "and loved by a Guèbre. I struggled for a long time, but, O gods, how love manages to overcome difficulties! Oh, how relieved I feel! I no longer have to fear loving you too much; I no longer have to impose bounds on my love, for the excess itself is legitimate. And oh, how perfectly this fits with the state of my heart! But now you, who have broken the chains that bound my spirit, when will you break the ones that tie my hands? I give myself to you, from this moment forward. Show me how dear this gift is to you by the speed with which you accept it. My brother, when I am finally able to embrace you, I think I might die in your arms."

I had never felt anything like the joy that her words aroused in me; in a second I had become, and felt myself to be, the happiest of men. I could see every desire I had had in my twenty-five years of life achieved, and I could see all the barriers against which I had labored so long vanish before my eyes. But once I grew a little accustomed to these fine new

---

70. The book is the *Avesta*, the collection of texts sacred to Zoroastrianism; some parts of it are said to date from before 500 BC. The dates of Zoroaster himself, who lived in eastern Persia, are disputed; he may have lived and taught as early as 1500 BC or as late as 500 BC.

71. Balkh is an ancient city in what is now northern Afghanistan.

feelings, I realized I was not nearly as close as I thought I was to obtaining my happiness, though indeed I had surmounted the greatest obstacle. I needed to out-maneuver the vigilance of her guards; I dared trust no one with the great secret of my life; I had only my sister, and she had only me. If I made any slips, I ran the risk of being impaled, but no torture was as painful as being without her. We agreed that she would send to me, asking for a clock that her father had left her, and that I would hide inside it both a file for her to saw through the bars on a window that faced onto the street, and a knotted rope for her to climb down with. And we agreed that I would not come visit her any more, but that every night I would keep watch by that window, waiting for her to execute her plan. For fifteen nights, I watched all night long without her being able to find the right moment, but on the sixteenth, I heard the sawing sound of the file; the work was interrupted several times, and each time the terror I felt was inexpressible. But after an hour, I saw her attaching the rope; she let herself down, and slipped into my waiting arms. I thought no more about danger: I stood still with her there for a long time. I took her to a place well outside of town where I had a horse ready; I put her up behind me, and off we went as swiftly as possible, racing away from that place that had been so painful to us both. Before daybreak, we arrived at the isolated home of a Guèbre who lived frugally, subsisting on what he grew himself. We did not think it wise to stay there long, and he advised us to take refuge in a dense forest nearby; we hid ourselves in the hollow trunk of an old oak, waiting for the talk about our escape to have died down. We lived for a time in that secluded spot, just the two of us, unwitnessed by any, repeating our vows of eternal love to each other over and over, waiting for the time when a Guèbre priest could perform the marriage ceremony prescribed by our holy books.

"Oh, my sister," I said to her, "how holy our union is! Nature has united us, and soon our holy law will unite us even more." Eventually a priest came to calm our amorous impatience. He performed all the wedding rites in the peasant's cottage: he gave us his blessing, and expressed a thousand wishes that we would be granted all the vigor of Gushtasp and all the holiness of Lohrasp.[72] Very soon afterward, we left Persia,

72. Both semi-legendary ancient Persian kings, Lohrasp was the father of Gushtasp. Gushtasp was the first to be converted, by Zoroaster himself, and he converted his father. Scholars have speculated that Gushtasp might have been the father of Darius the Great (550–486 BC). Montesquieu's text spells *Lohrasp* as *Hohoraspe*, which Vernière explains as a bizarre transcription error (146).

where we could not be really safe, and journeyed to Georgia. We lived there for a year, each day increasing our love for each other. But when my money ran out, I began to fear poverty, not for myself but for my sister, and I left her to go seek out help from our relatives. Never was there a more tender farewell. But my journey turned out to be not only futile but disastrous, for I learned that all our goods had been confiscated, and that my relatives had no wherewithal to help us; they could give me no more money than what was necessary for my journey back. And what despair awaited me then! I could not find my sister! A few days before my arrival, a troop of Tartars had made an incursion into the town where I had left her, and seeing her beauty, they took her with them, selling her to a group of Jews who were en route to Turkey, leaving behind only the little daughter who had been born to us a few months earlier. I set out after the Jews, and overtook them about three leagues distant, but my prayers and tears were in vain; they insisted on my paying them thirty tomans[73] for her, and would not reduce the price by even a single toman. After beseeching everyone I could for help, and begging for protection from priests both Turkish and Christian, I approached an Armenian merchant: I sold him my daughter and myself for thirty-five tomans. I returned to the Jews, giving them their thirty tomans, and giving the five remaining to my sister—though I had still not seen her at that point. "You are free, my sister," I told her; "I can embrace you now; here are five tomans for you. I only regret that I could not sell myself for more."

"What!" she exclaimed, "you have sold yourself?"

"Yes," I said.

"Oh, unlucky man, what have you done? Was I not unhappy enough, that you had to find a way to make me even more so? Your liberty was my only consolation, and now your bondage will lead me to my grave. Oh, my brother, how cruel your love is! And my daughter—I do not see her?"

"I have sold her as well," I said. We both broke down and burst into tears, unable to find the strength to say anything more. Eventually I

---

73. The toman was a gold coin in use in Persia; as a unit of currency, it was still in use in twentieth-century Iran; it has been replaced since the 1930s by the rial. The value of thirty tomans in Montesquieu's time would have been about 45 French livres or francs—not a queen's ransom, but far too high for the narrator to be able to meet. For comparison, Montesquieu's father paid 50 livres a year to cover the cost of wine for his two sons at their school in Juilly (Shackleton, p. 6).

went to find my master, and my sister arrived there at the same time; she threw herself at his feet.

She said, "I beg you, take me into servitude as well; I ask this of you the way others ask you for their liberty. Take me; you can sell me for more than you would be able to sell my husband." The struggle that followed between us brought tears to my master's eyes.

"Wretched man," she said, "did you think that I could accept my own liberty at the expense of yours? My lord, you see before you two unfortunate people who will die if you separate them. I give myself to you: pay me. Perhaps that money and my services will be able to obtain from you some day that for which I dare not ask you now. It is in your own interest not to separate us: for you see how his life depends upon mine." The Armenian, a sensitive man, was moved by our sufferings.

He said, "Serve me, the two of you, with fidelity and zeal for one year, and I promise you that I will grant you your freedom at that time. I can see that neither of you has deserved the sorrows that have befallen you. And if, when you have regained your liberty, you both become as happy as you deserve to be, if fortune smiles upon you, I am confident that you will make up the loss I suffer on your behalf." We both knelt and embraced his knees in gratitude, and we followed him on his journey. We consoled each other in the tasks that our servitude imposed upon us, and I was only too delighted when it happened that I could do my sister's work for her.

The appointed year came to an end; our master kept his word, and freed us both. We returned to Tbilisi. There I encountered an old friend of my father's, a man who successfully practiced medicine in that city. He lent me some money, which I used to finance some trading. Some business required my presence later in Smyrna, where I eventually established myself. I have lived there six years, and during that time I have come to enjoy the most amiable, sweetest social life possible: my family lives in peace and harmony, and I would not exchange my situation for that of all the kings in the world. And I have been fortunate enough to have met again with the Armenian merchant, whom I have been able to help out in significant ways.

From Smyrna, the 27th of the moon of
Gemmadi II, 1714

Letter 68

Rica to Usbek
*At * * **

The other day, I went to dine at the home of a judge, a man of law who had invited me over many times. After we had conversed on a wide variety of topics, I said to him, "Monsieur, it seems to me that your profession must be a very difficult one."

"Not as much as you'd think," he replied; "in fact, the way we manage it, it's really only a pastime."

"But how can that be? Isn't your mind always burdened with the affairs of other people? Are you not continually pestered by uninteresting things?"

"You are correct—those things are not at all interesting, for we take no interest in them whatsoever, and that alone proves that our profession is not as difficult as you think."

When I saw how offhand he was about it all, I continued, saying to him, "Monsieur, I have not seen your study."

"I can well believe that, because I don't have one. When I took on this position, I needed a lot of money to pay for it, so I sold my library. And the bookseller who bought it—quite a large number of volumes, by the way—left me nothing but this little account book. But then, I really don't regret losing them. We judges don't puff ourselves up with pointless learning. What need could I possibly have for a library full of law books? Practically every case is hypothetical and an exception to the general rule anyway."

"But, monsieur, isn't that because you are the ones who make everything an exception? After all, why do people all over the world have laws, if not to apply them? And how can anyone apply them if he doesn't know them?"

"Well, you wouldn't speak like this if you knew the courts. We have living law books there, known as lawyers; they work for us, and it is their job to instruct us."

I asked him, "But don't you suppose they often mislead you? So it would not be such a bad idea to arm yourselves against their assaults. They have weapons that they use to attack your justice, and you ought to have some with which you could defend yourself, so that you aren't walking into a battle with no armor on, against men armed and plated to the teeth."

From Paris, the 13th of the moon of Chahban, 1714

Letter 69

Usbek to Rhédi
At Venice

You would never have imagined that I could possibly become any more of a metaphysician than I already was, but it has happened, and you will agree with me, once you have come up for air from the deluge of philosophy I am about to unleash upon you.

The soberest philosophers who have reflected on the nature of God have concluded that He must be a supremely perfect being, but they have gone on to overdo the idea. They have enumerated all the perfections that a human being is capable of having and imagining, and have then applied them all to the divinity, without stopping to consider that some of these attributes contradict each other, and that they cannot all subsist within the same being without canceling each other out.

Western poets tell us of a painter who wanted to depict the goddess of beauty. He brought together all the most beautiful Greek women, and took the loveliest trait from each one of them, and from this he made a whole in order to give some idea of the most beautiful of all the goddesses.[74] Now, if a man therefore concluded that she was both blonde and brunette, that she had both black and blue eyes, that she was gentle and fiery, he would be naturally subject to ridicule.

God thus often lacks a perfection that would lead to a serious imperfection, but He is never limited except by Himself: He is His own necessity. Thus, for example, while God is all-powerful, He cannot break his promises, or deceive people. Often the impotence is not in Him, but in relative, contingent things, and this is the reason why He cannot change the essence of things.

Therefore it is no surprise that some of our sages have dared to deny the infinite foreknowledge of God, on this ground: that it is incompatible with His justice.

Daring as this idea of theirs is, it is well-adapted to metaphysical reasoning. Their principle states that God cannot possibly foresee things that depend upon the determination of free causes, for what has not yet happened does not exist, and therefore cannot be foreknown. For

74. Montesquieu alludes to a well-known story, originally in the *Natural History* (c. 78 AD) of Pliny the Elder, concerning the Greek painter Zeuxis, who used five different beautiful girls from the town of Croton to model for his portrait of Helen.

nothing, which has no properties whatsoever, cannot be perceived, and they think God cannot possibly read a will which does not exist, or see something in a person's mind[75] that does not exist there: before the mind has made a decision, the action which determines that decision is not there to be seen.

The mind is the agent of its own determination, but there are occasions when it is so undecided that it cannot tell what determination to make. Often it chooses an act solely in order to make use of its liberty, and God could not see this decision in advance, neither in the workings of the mind nor in the action that objects exert upon it.

How could God foresee things that depend upon free causes? He could only see them in one of two ways: first, by conjecture, which of course contradicts his infinite foreknowledge; and second, he could see them as necessary effects that infallibly follow upon the cause that produces them, but this is even more contradictory: for we hold it as a principle that the mind is free, but if this were the case, it would be no more free than a billiard ball that is struck by another is free to move or not to move.

But do not think that I want to set boundaries on God's knowledge. Just as He can make us act any way He wishes, so He knows all that He wishes to know. But while He is capable of seeing everything, He does not always avail Himself of that ability. In normal circumstances, He allows the creature the freedom to act or not to act, thereby allowing them to earn merit or blame, and for this reason He gives up His right to influence or determine the individual creature. But when He wants to know something, He knows it always. He needs only to will things to turn out the way He sees them, and to force creatures to conform to His will. And it is in this way that He plucks what will really happen from all the things that might happen, fixing by His decrees the future determinations of minds, and depriving them of the freedom to act or not to act that He had granted them.

If one could use an analogy to express something that is by nature inexpressible: a monarch does not know what his ambassador will do in an important affair. But if he wants to know, he has only to order the man to act in such and such a manner, and he can then rest assured that the thing will turn out exactly as he projects.

---

75. Montesquieu uses the word *âme*, which could equally well be translated as "soul" or "mind." Since the subject involves human psychology, I have used "mind," but the reader may wish to substitute "soul."

The Koran and the books of the Jews constantly deny the doctrine of absolute foreknowledge; in those books, God always seems not to know the future determinations that minds will make.[76] It seems this is the first truth that Moses taught humankind.

God placed Adam in the earthly paradise with the sole condition that he not eat a certain fruit—an absurd precept for a being who can foresee the future decisions that minds will make. Could such a being put conditions on his grace without turning it into a mockery? It is as if a man who hears that Baghdad has been captured were to say, "I will give you one hundred tomans if Baghdad is not captured." Would this not be a poor joke?

Well, my poor Rhédi, why so much philosophy? God is so high up that we cannot even see the clouds surrounding Him. We only know Him through the precepts He has given us. He is immense, spiritual, infinite. May His grandeur serve to reveal our smallness to us. To humble ourselves at all times is to worship Him.[77]

From Paris, the last day of the moon of Chahban, 1714

Letter 70

Zélis to Usbek
At Paris

Your good friend Soliman is in a state of desperation over an insult he has recently suffered. A foolish young man named Suphis had been seeking his daughter's hand in marriage for three months. He seemed to be content with what he knew of the daughter's appearance, having heard her described by women who had known her since infancy; a dowry was agreed upon, and everything was proceeding without incident. So yesterday, after the first ceremonies, the daughter left on

76. This generalization is incorrect, or at least overstated, with regard to both the Koran and the Old Testament ("the books of the Jews"). In the Koran, God's foreknowledge is asserted in sura 2:255, and in the Bible, it is asserted in a number of places, including the books of Deuteronomy (31:16) and Isaiah (49:18–25).

77. The final paragraph was added in the 1754 edition, perhaps in the feeling that some parts of the letter were coming too close to heresy or blasphemy.

horseback, accompanied by her eunuch, and fully veiled according to custom, from head to toe. But when she arrived at the home of her soon-to-be husband, he closed the door on her and swore that he would never admit her unless the dowry were increased. Relatives rushed back and forth, trying to reach some kind of settlement between the parties; and after a great deal of resistance, Soliman agreed to give a small gift to his new son-in-law. The marriage ceremonies went forward and were concluded, and the girl was brought to his bed, with a certain amount of violence. But an hour later, the young fool got up in a state of rage, slashing the girl's face in several places, claiming she had not been a virgin, and sending her back home to her father. There could be no greater affront than this. There are some people who insist that the girl is innocent. Fathers who experience insults like this must be the most unlucky people! If my daughter had been treated this way, I believe I would die of grief. Adieu.

From the seraglio at Fatmé, the 9th of
the moon of Gemmadi I, 1714

Letter 71

Usbek to Zélis

I grieve for Soliman, and all the more because the evil seems to be without remedy, for his son-in-law has only done what the law allows. This is a harsh law, in my view, for it exposes a family's honor to the whims of a fool. People say that there are certain ways of discovering the truth about such a matter, but this is an old error that has recently been revived among us, and our physicians provide compelling reasons for doubting the so-called certainty of those proofs. Even the Christians themselves find these proofs chimerical, and this despite the fact that their holy scriptures clearly insist upon them, their ancient lawgiver having asserted that the innocence or condemnation of every girl must depend upon them.[78]

---

78. The "lawgiver" is Moses, and the passage concerning the proofs of a bride's virginity is in Deuteronomy 22:13–22. Alluding to this brutal biblical passage hints—as Montesquieu does frequently in *Persian Letters*—that the western Christian is in no position to feel superior to the Persians.

I am pleased to hear of the care you are devoting to your own daughter's education. May God grant that her husband will find her as beautiful and as pure as Fatima[79]—that she have ten eunuchs to guard her—that she become the honor and the ornament of the seraglio to which she is destined—that above her head there be nothing but gilded ceilings, and beneath her feet nothing but superb carpets! And to crown all these wishes, may my own eyes see her in all her glory!

From Paris, the 5th of the moon of Chalval, 1714

Letter 72

Rica to Ibben
*At * * **

The other day, I found myself in a group that included a highly self-satisfied man. In the space of fifteen minutes he decided three questions of ethics, four historical problems, and five from physics. I have never met such a universal decisionist;[80] his mind was never troubled by the slightest doubt. We moved on from the sciences, and he proceeded to pronounce on current affairs. I wanted to catch him out, and I said to myself, "I'd better be careful and stick to the subject I know best, my own country." So I raised the topic of Persia, but before I had got scarcely four words out, he showed me that I was wrong twice, citing Tavernier and Chardin as authorities.[81] "Good God" I exclaimed to myself. "What kind of man is this? Soon he'll be showing that he knows the streets of Ispahan better than I do!" I learned what my role was: I kept my mouth shut, and let him continue to decide everything.

From Paris, the 8th of the moon of Zilcadé, 1715

---

79. Fatima was the daughter of Mohammed, and the wife of Ali.

80. Montesquieu's word is *décisionnaire*, a contemporary term for this particular kind of know-it-all.

81. Jean-Baptiste Tavernier (1605–1689) and Jean Chardin (1643–1713) were travelers whose books on Persia were Montesquieu's main sources. See the Introduction.

Letter 73

Rica to * * *

I had heard people speaking about a kind of tribunal called the French Academy. There can be no court in the world less respected than this one, for everyone says that as soon as it announces a decision, the people undo the verdict and instead impose new laws that the Academy must now follow.

Some time ago, to establish its authority, the Academy published a compilation of its decisions. This child of many fathers was already aged by the time it was born; and while it was legitimate, a bastard child that had already appeared almost smothered it in its cradle.[82]

The members who constitute this tribunal have but one charge, to chatter constantly. Eulogies sprout, as if out of nowhere, from their eternal babble; as soon as a person is initiated into the group's mysteries, he is seized by a rage for panegyric, a fury that never leaves him.

This beast has forty heads, each of them full of rhetoric, of metaphors and antitheses; with so many mouths, the beast can speak only in exclamations, and its ears are always attuned to cadences and harmonies. As for eyes, there really aren't any: the beast was evidently created to speak, not to see. It is not very steady on its feet, for time—which is its scourge—constantly throws it off balance, destroying everything it has created. It used to be said that it had rather greedy hands; I can say nothing about this, but leave it up to those who know more about the subject than I do.[83]

So there you have it, * * *, one of those oddities that we are spared in Persia. We have never gone in for concocting such bizarre institutions, looking instead to nature for our simple customs and manners.

From Paris, the 27th of the moon of Zilhagé, 1715

---

82. The reference is to the Academy's dictionary, a very slowly evolving project; it had been begun as early as the 1630s but was not published until 1694. In the meantime, one of the members, Antoine Furetière (1619–1688), announced that he was on the point of publishing his own dictionary; the other members were furious and expelled him in 1685. His dictionary was published in 1690, two years after his death and four years before the official one.

83. The allusion is too broad to pin down, but there were a number of stories circulating about the venality of Academy members.

Letter 74

Usbek to Rica
At * * *

A few days ago, a man I know said to me: "I promised to get you invited to some of the finer homes in Paris; today, I will take you to the home of a great lord, one of the men who best represents our nation."

"What does that mean, Monsieur? Is he more refined, more affable than the others?" "No," he replied. "Oh, I understand! He is one of those who must make his superiority known to everyone at all times; and if that's the case, then I really do not need to go there. I concede everything to him in advance, and I accept my condemnation."

But I had to go along anyway, and I saw there a terribly proud little man; he took a pinch of tobacco with such haughtiness, chewed it so pitilessly, spat with so much phlegm, and caressed his dogs in so offensive a manner that I could only ask myself: "Good God! If I acted like that at the court in Persia, I would have been acting the part of a great fool!" You and I, Rica, would have had to be very ill-natured indeed to heap hundreds of insults on every man who came to see us each day, trying to demonstrate their good will. They knew perfectly well that we were above them in status, and if they did not know it, the benefits they got from us would have demonstrated the fact. And since we therefore did not have to do anything to gain their respect, we did everything we could to make ourselves pleasant. We communicated with the least of them; surrounded on all sides by courtly magnificence, which tends to harden the heart, they found us men of feeling for others. They saw that it was only our hearts that were above them; in every way, we came down to their level and saw to their needs. But when the time arose to maintain the majesty of the prince in public ceremonies, when the time came to see to it that foreigners respected our nation, and when times of danger were upon us, in order to inspire the soldiers, then we ascended a hundred times higher than we had descended, bringing the fierce pride back into our faces. And by doing so, we represented the nation quite well.

From Paris, the 10th of the moon of Saphar, 1715

Letter 75

Usbek to Rhédi
At Venice

I have to admit it: I have not seen among the Christians that vigorous religious faith that is found among the Muslims. Among them there is a great gap between what they profess and what they believe, between belief and conviction, and between conviction and practice. Religion is less a subject of sanctification than a subject for debates, and everyone takes part. Courtiers, warriors, even women rise up against their ecclesiastics and ask them to provide proofs for things that they are determined not to believe. And this is not because they are all driven by reason, because they have taken the time and made the effort to examine the truth or falsehood of the religion they reject: no, it is because they are rebels who have felt the yoke approaching them and have shaken it off before they have even come to know it. Thus, they are no firmer in their unbelief than they are in their faith. They live in a state of constant flux and reflux, a tide that sweeps them ceaselessly from one side to the other. One of them said to me the other day, "I believe in the immortality of the soul only at certain times. My opinions depend entirely upon the state of my body—whether I feel a greater or lesser degree of vitality, whether my stomach is digesting well, whether the air I breathe is clean or unclean, whether my food is light or heavy—in any one circumstance, I might be a Spinozist, a Socinian, a Catholic, an unbeliever, or a votary. When the doctor is near my bedside, the confessor has the advantage. I know very well how to keep religion from getting in my way when I am feeling well, but I do allow it to console me when I am sick. Whenever I have no hope from any other source, religion presents itself, and its promises win me over; I would very much like to give myself up to it, and die in a state of hope."

Long ago the Christian princes freed all the slaves in their countries because, they said, Christianity makes all men equal. It is true, that religious act was very useful to them, for by it they weakened the power of the nobles, taking from them all the power they used to exert over the lower class of people. And later, they made conquests in countries where they saw that it would be to their advantage to keep slaves, and they permitted the buying and selling of them, forgetting all about that religious principle that had moved them so much in the past. How would I account for this—for something being true at one time, and an error at another? Why should we not do as the Christians did? We were foolish to give up on easy conquests in good climates simply because the water there was not pure enough for us, according to the principles of the holy Koran.[84]

I give thanks to almighty God, who has sent His great prophet Ali, that I profess a religion that is above all human concerns, being as pure as the heavens from which it descended.

From Paris, the 13th of the moon of Saphar, 1715

Letter 76

Usbek to his friend Ibben
At Smyrna

The laws in Europe are merciless toward those who kill themselves. They are made to die a second time, so to speak: they are dragged in disgrace through the streets and declared to be infamous, and all their goods are confiscated.

Ibben, these laws seem most unjust to me. When I am overcome with grief, with misery, with the scorn of others, why should I be prevented from putting an end to all these sorrows? Why should I be cruelly deprived of a remedy that lies in my hands?

Why do they make me labor for a society that I no longer wish to be a part of? Why should I be forced to adhere to a convention that I had no part in making? The basis of society is mutual advantage, but when I find it has become onerous to me, what is to prevent me from renouncing it? Life was given to me as a kind of favor; when it ceases to be that, I can put an end to it: when the cause ceases, the effect must too.

Would the prince want me to be his subject when I receive no advantages from that subjection? Can my fellow citizens demand such a wicked arrangement, comprised of my despair and their utility? Can God be unlike all other benefactors, and condemn me to accept the graces that cause me misery?

I am obliged to obey the laws when I am living under them—but when I no longer do so, can those laws continue to bind me?

---

84. *The Mohammedans do not bother to take Venice, because there is no water there for their purifications* [Montesquieu's note]. Rhédi had made this same point earlier, in Letter 31.

But some will object, you are meddling with the design of Providence. God has united your soul and body, and you wish to separate them: you are therefore opposing yourself to His designs, and fighting against Him.

But what does that really mean? Am I disturbing the providential order when I make some modifications to material objects, when, for example, I shape a round ball into a square—a ball that the basic laws of motion, those of creation and conservation, have made round? No, certainly not: I have only made use of the rights and powers that have been granted me. And in that sense I could make as many changes as I could imagine in the natural world, without anyone saying that I was opposing myself to Providence.

When my soul is at last separated from my body, will there be any less order, any less design in the universe? Can you believe that this new combination will be somehow less perfect, and less dependent upon general laws? Or that the world will have lost something? Or that the works of God are now less grand, or rather less immense?

Can you believe that my body, when it has become an ear of corn, or a worm, or a lawn, will be a work somehow less worthy of nature, or that my soul, disengaged now from everything earthly, will be less sublime?

All such ideas, my dear Ibben, have their source in human pride. We do not sense our own smallness, and despite what we really are, we want to think we count for something in the universe, that we matter to it, and that we are an object of importance within it. We imagine that the annihilation of a creature as perfect as ourselves would degrade the totality of nature. And we cannot conceive that one man the more or the less in the world—but what am I saying?—that all men together, one hundred million heads like ours, amount to a tiny, slender atom that God only perceives at all because of the immensity of his knowledge.

From Paris, the 15th of the moon of Saphar, 1715

Letter 77

Ibben to Usbek
At Paris

My dear Usbek, it seems to me that for a true Muslim, misfortunes are not so much punishments as warnings. The days that urge us to expiate our offenses are precious. The days of prosperity are the ones that ought to be cut short. Where does all this impatience come from, if not from wanting to see ourselves happy independently of Him who provides all happiness, He who is happiness itself?

If a being is composed of two beings, and if the necessity of conserving that union is a sign of needing to submit to the design of the Creator, one ought to make a religious law out of it. If that necessity of conserving that union is a better guarantee of men's behavior, then it ought to be made into a civil law.

From Smyrna, the last day of the moon of Saphar, 1715

Letter 78

Rica to Usbek
At * * *

I am sending you a copy of a letter written in Spain by a Frenchman. I think you will enjoy reading it.

> I have been traveling for six months in Spain and Portugal, living among peoples who despise all other peoples, except for the French—and they do the French the honor of hating them.
>
> Their gravity is the most notable characteristic of these two nations, and it manifests itself in two principal ways: either eyeglasses or moustaches.
>
> A man wearing glasses is self-evidently a man of consummate erudition, a man who has so buried himself in reading so many books that his eyesight has been weakened; and every nose so ornamented or so weighted can pass, indisputably, as the nose of a savant.
>
> As for the moustache, it is respectable in and of itself, regardless of the consequences, but sometimes it has been known to be the agent of great utility for the service of a prince and the honor of a nation, as was well demonstrated by a famous Portuguese general in the Indies.[85] Finding himself in need of money, he cut off one of his moustaches and sent it to

85. *Jean de Castro* [Montesquieu's note]. Juan de Castro (1500–1548) was governor of Portuguese India, of which Goa was the capital. The story about the moustache used as collateral is widely repeated, and is apparently true.

the inhabitants of Goa, asking a loan of twenty thousand pistoles[86] upon this collateral. The money was swiftly forthcoming, and the general later retrieved his moustache with honor.

One can readily imagine that people as grave and phlegmatic as these would also be proud, and they are. They typically base their pride on one of two very important things. Those who live in continental Spain and Portugal see themselves as lofty people if they are what is called "old Christians"—that is, if they are from Christian families that predate those whom the Inquisition in recent centuries persuaded to embrace the faith. Those who live in the Indies are no less self-delighted for having the sublime merit of being, as they call it, white-skinned. The proudest sultana in the seraglio of the Grand Sultan has never been as vain about her beauty as one of these old, foul, good-for-nothings, preening himself on the olive tint of his skin while he sprawls in the doorway, his arms crossed, in some little town in Mexico. A man of such consequence, a creature as perfect as this would not condescend to labor for all the treasure in the world, or dream of compromising the honor and dignity of his skin by some vile, mechanical exertion of effort.

For it is crucial to understand that, in Spain, when a man has achieved certain merits—when, for example, he can add to the qualities I have just mentioned, those of owning a long sword, or learning from his father the art of playing an out-of-tune guitar—with such accomplishments, he no longer works. His honor is expressed in the repose of his limbs. A man who sits in a chair for ten hours a day has exactly twice the consideration as one who sits only five, for it is through chairs that one acquires nobility.

But although these sworn enemies of work seem on the surface to exist in a tranquil, philosophic frame of mind, they are quite different within: they are always in love. They are the first men in the world to die a languid death beneath the window of a mistress, and any Spaniard who is not suffering from a head cold cannot be considered a gallant lover.

Their primary trait is religious devotion, and their secondary one is jealousy. They will go to great lengths to keep their wives away from a crippled soldier or a decrepit magistrate; but they willingly closet them privately with a fervent young novice who keeps his eyes lowered, or with a robust Franciscan who keeps his eyes raised.

They permit their wives to go out in public with their breasts exposed, but they do not want anyone to see their heels, or to be startled by the sight of their toes.

86. The *pistole* was a gold coin worth about ten *livres*.

People everywhere lament the cruelty of love, but even more so among Spanish men. Women heal them of their wounds, but only by giving them new ones, and they are often left with the long, painful memory of an extinguished passion.

They have their little politenesses which, in France, would seem out of place. For example, a captain never beats a soldier without first asking his permission, and the Inquisition never burns a Jew without apologizing to him.

Those Spaniards who are not burnt seem to be so attached to their Inquisition that it would be ill-mannered to take it away from them. I only wish that they would establish a different one: not for heretics, but one for the heresiarchs, who attribute the same spiritual efficacy to trivial monastic practices as they do to the seven sacraments, who worship everything they venerate, and who are so devout that they can scarcely be called Christians.

You can find intelligence and good sense among the Spanish, but do not bother trying to find it in their books. Look at their libraries: novels on one side, scholastic philosophers on the other, enough to make you think that the whole place was designed by some secret enemy of human reason.

The only good book they have produced is one that demonstrates how ridiculous all the others are.[87]

They have made huge discoveries in the new world, but they don't yet know their own continent. There are ports on their rivers that have not yet been discovered, and entirely unknown peoples living in their mountains.[88]

They say that the sun rises and sets within their lands, but one must also add that along the way, it passes over nothing but ruined, deserted countryside.

I would enjoy seeing, Usbek, a letter from Madrid written by a Spaniard who had traveled in France; I have a feeling it would avenge his country very well. What a wide field this would make for an objective, thoughtful writer! I imagine that he would begin his description of Paris like this:

---

87. The reference is to Cervantes' *Don Quixote.*

88. *The Batuecas* [Montesquieu's note]. He refers to a region outside Salamanca which, in his century, was still wild, isolated, and little known. The reference to unknown river ports is less clear. (In one edition, the word is *ponts*, bridges, but *ports* in the others. But "bridges" is no clearer.)

"There is a building here where they put the madmen. You would assume, therefore, that it must be the largest building in the city. But no, the remedy is too small for the sickness. No doubt the French, so vigorously condemned by their neighbors, lock up a few madmen in one building in order to convince the other countries that those outside the building are sane."

I will leave my imaginary Spaniard there. Farewell, my dear Usbek.

From Paris, the 17th of the moon of Saphar, 1715

Letter 79

The Chief Black Eunuch to Usbek
At Paris

Yesterday, some Armenians came to the seraglio bringing a young Circassian slave girl they wanted to sell.[89] I had her brought into the secret apartments, undressed her, and examined her with the practiced eye of a judge, and the more I examined her, the more charming I found her to be. A virginal modesty seemed to make her try to avoid my gaze, and I could see what it cost her to obey me. She blushed at being naked, even before me—me, exempt from the passions that might alarm modesty, and exempt from the empire women exert over men, ministering to modesty even in the freest moments, casting only a chaste gaze, capable of inspiring only innocence.

As soon as I judged her worthy of you, I lowered my eyes; I covered her in a scarlet mantle; I placed a golden ring on her finger; and I prostrated myself at her feet, worshipping her as the queen of your heart. I paid the Armenians, and hid her away from all eyes. Oh fortunate Usbek! You are the possessor of more beauties than all the palaces in the East. What a pleasure it will be for you, upon your return, to find the most ravishing creatures in all Persia! And to see within your seraglio the rebirth of the graces, even while time and continued ownership work to ruin them!

From the seraglio at Fatmé, the 1st of the moon of Rebiab I, 1715

---

89. Women from the Circassian region of the northern Caucasus became almost proverbial for their beauty, and were highly sought after for seraglios and for slaves; even as late as the nineteenth century, P.T. Barnum displayed "Circassian beauties" in his circus side shows.

Letter 80

Usbek to Rhédi
At Venice

Since I have been here in Europe, dear Rhédi, I have seen many kinds of governments. It is not like Asia, where the political rules are the same everywhere.

I have often asked myself what type of government conforms best to reason. It has seemed to me that the most perfect type is the one that reaches its objectives at the least cost, the one that leads men in the manner that best suits their inclinations.

If, under a mild government, the people are as submissive as they are under a harsh one, then the former is preferable, since it better conforms to reason, while harshness is foreign to reason.

Consider, my dear Rhédi, that in a state, the degree of cruelty employed in enforcing the laws does not make people obey them. In countries where punishments are moderate, people fear the laws as much as they do in places where they are tyrannical and hideous.

Whether a government is mild or cruel, punishment is always a matter of degrees: we inflict greater or lesser punishment based on the level of the crime. The imagination fits itself to the country in which one is living: a week in prison or a light fine will strike as much fear into the heart of a European raised in a country with a mild government, as does the loss of an arm to an Asiatic. People connect a certain degree of fear with a certain kind of punishment, and each of us feels differently: the terror of undergoing a disgrace will overwhelm a Frenchman, whereas it would not make a Turk lose a quarter of an hour's sleep.

In any case, I do not see that order, justice, and fairness are any better observed in Turkey, Persia, or the lands of the Mogul than they are in the republics of Holland, Venice, or even in England. I do not see that fewer crimes are committed, nor that men, intimidated by the magnitude of punishments, are any more submissive toward the laws.

On the contrary, I see a source of injustice and disturbance located in the heart of those very states.

I see the prince, who is himself the law, having less control than anywhere else.

I see that, in times of rigorous repression, there are always tumultuous upheavals, with no one in charge of them; and I see that once the state's violent authority has come to be despised, no one can possibly restore it.

I see that when there is no hope of amnesty, the disorder only deepens and grows.

I see that in states like these there is no such thing as a minor revolt, and that there is little or no interval between murmuring and outright sedition.

I see that great events need not have great causes. On the contrary, a minor incident can provoke a great revolution, often unforeseen both by the revolutionaries themselves and by those they overthrow.

When Osman, emperor of the Turks, was deposed, none of those who overthrew him intended to do so: they were only asking, as suppliants, for justice over some grievance. But then some unknown voice arose by chance out of the crowd: the name Mustapha was spoken, and suddenly Mustapha was emperor.[90]

From Paris, the 2nd of the moon of Rebiab I, 1715

Letter 81

Nargum, Persian Envoy to Moscow, to Usbek
At Paris

Out of all the nations in the world, my dear Usbek, none has ever surpassed the Tartars in glory or in the grandeur of their conquests. These people are the true dominators of the earth; all the others seem to have been created to serve them. They are both the founders and the destroyers of empires, and they have left the mark of their power upon the earth in every age. And in every age, they have been the scourge of nations.

The Tartars have twice conquered China, and they still hold sway over it.

They wield power over the vast tracts of land that compose the Mogul empire.

Masters of Persia, they have sat upon the throne of Cyrus and of Gushtasp.[91] They have conquered the Muscovite. Under the name of

90. The uprising leading to the execution of Sultan Osman II took place in 1622; he was succeeded by Mustapha I, who in turn was deposed a year later.

91. Cyrus the Great ruled Persia around 600 BC. On Gushtasp, see note 73 above.

Turks, they have made vast conquests in Europe, the near East, and Africa; and they still dominate these three parts of the world.

And, to speak of more distant times, from them sprang the peoples who overturned the Roman Empire.

What were the conquests of Alexander the Great, compared with those of Genghis Khan?

The only things they have lacked have been historians to celebrate the memory of all these marvels.

How many immortal acts have been buried in oblivion! How many empires were founded, whose origins we no longer know! That warlike nation, always completely preoccupied with its present glory, and always certain of becoming an immortal conqueror, never thought to preserve the memory of its conquests for the future.

From Moscow, the 4th of the moon of Rebiab I, 1715

Letter 82

Rica to Ibben
At Smyrna

While the French do a lot of talking, there is a species of taciturn dervishes among them known as Carthusians. I have heard it said that their tongues are cut out upon entering their monastery, and I think it would be a fine idea if the other dervishes would cut off whatever their profession makes useless to them.

But speaking of taciturn people, there are some even stranger types here, who have an extraordinary talent: that is, people who know how to talk without actually saying anything. They can maintain a two-hour conversation without your being able to decipher, repeat, or retain a single thing they've said.

Women love this sort of person, but not as much as they love another sort, those whom nature has gifted with the talent of smiling all the time, and who bestow a gracious approbation upon anything the lady says.

But they arrive at the very summit of their wit when they learn how to see subtleties everywhere, and detect a thousand little ingenuities in the most ordinary remarks.

I have known some others who are clever enough to bring inanimate objects into the conversation, to make their embroidered suit, their blonde wig, their snuff-box, their cane, and their gloves speak for them. It is always good to begin by arriving as noisily as possible with one's carriage out in the street, and then banging the doorknocker rudely; this preface gives a fine hint of the discourse that is to follow. After all, when the exordium is beautiful, it makes it easier to endure all the idiocies that have the good fortune to arrive a bit later.

I assure you that these little talents, for which we at home have no use, are mighty advantages for those who possess them here, and that a man of sense will never shine when in such company.

From Paris, the 6th of the moon of Rebiab II, 1715

Letter 83

Usbek to Rhédi
At Venice

If there is a God, my dear Rhédi, He necessarily must be just: if He were not, He would be the most wicked, the most imperfect of all beings.

Justice is the proper relationship that exists between two things. This relation is always the same, no matter what creature is viewing it, whether God, an angel, or a man.

It is true that men do not always perceive this relation, and in fact, even when they do see it, they often turn away from it; their self-interest is always uppermost in their minds. Justice raises its voice to speak, but finds it difficult to be heard above the roar of the passions.

Men are capable of injustice, because their self-interest leads them toward it, and because they prefer their own satisfaction to that of others. Everything always revolves around themselves. No evil is ever done gratuitously, for there is always a reason behind it, and that reason is always one of self-interest.

But it is impossible for God to do any injustice. Assuming that He sees justice, He must necessarily pursue it. Since He has no need of anything, and He is entirely sufficient unto Himself, if He were to do anything unjust, He would be the most evil of all creatures, being without the motive of self-interest.

Therefore, even if there were no God, we still ought to love justice—that is, we ought to do everything we can to resemble that Being of whom we have such a beautiful idea, that Being who, if He existed, would necessarily be just. Free ourselves as much as we like from the yoke of religion, we should never free ourselves from that of justice.

And this, Rhédi, is what makes me think that justice is eternal, entirely independent of human conventions. If it were dependent upon them, this would be a terrible truth, one that we would be bound to hide.

We are surrounded by men stronger than ourselves, men who could hurt us in a thousand different ways, and could do so most of the time with impunity. What a comfort it is to know that there is a principle residing in the hearts of all men that fights on our side, protecting us from their designs!

Without this principle, we would be in a state of constant fear, and we would walk past other men the way we walk past lions. We would not feel even for a moment that our goods, our honor, even our lives were safe.

This line of thinking ends by making me angry with those philosophers who represent God as a being who exercises a tyrannical power over us; they depict Him as acting in ways we would not, for fear of offending Him, and they ascribe to Him all the flaws that He punishes us for having. Their contradictory opinions have Him sometimes appear as an evil being, and sometimes as a being who hates evil and punishes it.

When a man examines his heart, what satisfaction it gives him to find himself just! This pleasure, austere though it be, ought to ravish him, for he sees himself as existing as far above those men who are not just as he is above tigers and bears. Yes, Rhédi: if I were to follow unswervingly that justice that I see before me, I would think myself the first of men.

From Paris, the 1st of the moon of Gemmadi I, 1715

Letter 84

*Rica to * * **

The other day, I went to the Invalides.[92] I would rather have been the one to erect this establishment, if I were the monarch, than to have won three battles. The hand of a great king is visible everywhere there. I think there is no place on earth more deserving of respect.

What a spectacle it is to see together in one place all those who sacrificed themselves for their country, who drew breath only to defend it, men who now feel the same spirit but not the same strength, and who desire only the chance to sacrifice themselves again!

What could be more admirable than the sight of these disabled warriors observing the same discipline in this sanctuary as they would in the face of the enemy, seeking out their final satisfaction in this imitation of war, and dividing their hearts and minds between the duties of religion and those of the military!

I would like to see the names of all those who have died for their country preserved in the temples, and inscribed in registers that would serve as the fountainhead of their grand, glorious reputations.

From Paris, the 15th of the moon of Gemmadi I, 1715

Letter 85

Usbek to Mirza
At Ispahan

You know, Mirza, how a group of ministers under Shah Suleiman came up with a plan either to expel all the Armenians from Persia or to force them to convert to Islam, on the assumption that our empire would remain polluted as long as it kept these infidels within its borders.[93]

92. The Hôtel des Invalides, built in the reign of Louis XIV, was originally a hospital for wounded soldiers, and this honor and care given to the soldier is the reason for the praise Rica gives it. The Invalides today is a large complex of buildings relating to France's military history.

93. Suleiman I reigned from 1666–1694. Montesquieu wants the reader to note the analogy between the treatment of Armenians in Persia and the

If this blindly pious idea had been carried out, it would have spelled the end of the greatness of Persia.

No one knows exactly how it failed. Neither those who came up with the proposal nor those who rejected it could see the consequences. Thus, chance came in and took over the role of reason and political wisdom, and saved the empire from a far greater jeopardy than it would have faced from the loss of any battle, or from the loss of any two cities.

Expelling the Armenians would have meant the immediate loss of all the businessmen and almost all the skilled workers in the kingdom. I am convinced that the great Shah Abbas[94] would rather have cut off his arms than sign such an order, and that sending away his most industrious subjects to the Mogul or other Indian kings would have been the equivalent of giving up half his holdings.

The persecution that our zealous Muslims carried out against the Guèbres forced them to leave en masse for India, depriving Persia of that hardworking people who were on the verge of conquering the sterility of our soil by dint of their own dedicated efforts.

But the zealots had yet another blow to strike: the ruination of our industry. Following this, the empire fell by itself, and with it that very religion that they had so wanted to have flourish.

If it is acceptable to speak freely, Mirza, I wonder if it isn't a good thing for a state to have many religions.

It has been observed that those inhabitants who follow a tolerated religion work harder and are more useful to the country than are those who follow the dominant one. The former are denied the honors that customarily come to the latter, and so they must distinguish themselves by affluence and by their possessions, which they can only acquire through hard work, and by taking on even the most difficult jobs.

Moreover, since all religions teach precepts that are useful to society, it is best if these precepts are observed zealously. Now, what is most likely to encourage such zeal, if not a multiplicity of religious faiths?

They are rivals, and utterly unforgiving of each other. Their jealousy extends to minute details: each man is constantly on his guard, fearful of doing something that will dishonor his side and expose it to the derision and unpardonable censures of the other side.

---

treatment of Protestants in France. Louis XIV revoked the Edict of Nantes in 1685, putting an end to the toleration of Protestants and commencing a wave of forced conversions and emigrations.

94. Abbas I, called The Great, reigned from 1587–1629.

And it has always been seen that introducing a new sect into a state is the surest way of correcting the abuses of the old.

It is pointless to argue that having many religions in a state is not in the prince's best interest. If all the religions in the world were brought together, it would do him no harm, for every single one of them preaches obedience and submission.

I admit that history is full of wars of religion. But one must be careful here: these wars were not caused by a multiplicity of religions, but rather by the spirit of intolerance shown by the dominant religion's believers.

This is the proselytizing spirit that the Jews caught from the Egyptians and which was passed on from them, like an epidemic illness, to the Muslims and Christians.

It is, then, a vertiginous insanity, the progress of which can only be regarded as a kind of total eclipse of human reason.

Finally, even if it were not inhumane to make such an assault on the consciences of others, with its thousands of self-replicating evil consequences, one would have to be mad to advise it. The man who wants me to change my religion does so only because he would never change his, no matter how much he was forced. And thus he thinks it strange that I will not do a thing he would not do for all the kingdoms of the world.

From Paris, the 26th of the moon of Gemmadi I, 1715

Letter 86

Rica to * * *

It appears that family members govern themselves here. The husband has only the shadow of authority over his wife, the father over his children, the master over his slaves. The law intervenes in every dispute between them, and you may be sure that the law never favors the jealous husband, the angry father, or the irritated master.

The other day, I went to the court of justice. On the way, you have to pass closely by an endless number of young female merchants who try to attract you with cajoling voices.[95] At first this spectacle is amusing,

95. To get to the law courts, one passed through the Galerie du Palais, which was filled with shops of various sorts.

but things soon turn dismal when you pass into the great halls, where men's suits are even more serious than the expressions on their faces. And finally one arrives at the sacred place where all the family's secrets are revealed, and where the most private acts are exposed to the light for all to see.

Here, a modest girl comes to narrate the torments she has suffered over her too-long-guarded virginity, the battles she has fought, and her mournful resistance; not only is she not proud of her victory, but she actually threatens an imminent defeat. And in order to make her father better acquainted with her needs, she exposes them now to everyone.

A shameless woman steps forth to make public the outrages she has visited upon her husband, as the rationale for why she should be granted a separation from him.

With a similar level of modesty, another woman comes to declare that she is tired of being considered a wife without the benefit of her marital rights. She reveals all the secrets of her married nights, and asks to be examined by a panel of experts in order to be given all the rights of a virgin again. There are even some who issue an open challenge to their husbands, demanding that they demonstrate their virility in public, a difficult thing in front of witnesses, and just as shameful for the wife who succeeds as for the husband who fails.[96]

An endless number of women, some ravished, some seduced, make men sound even worse than they are. The court echoes with tales involving love matters. The talk is always of angry fathers, misused daughters, unfaithful lovers, and outraged husbands.

As the law has it here, every child born during a marriage is assumed to be the husband's. Even if he has excellent reasons for not believing it, the law believes it for him, which relieves him of further inquiry and further suspicions.

The tribunal operates by majority vote, but people say that experience shows it would be much better to follow the minority, for there are precious few wise judges, and—as everyone knows—an infinite number of bad ones.

From Paris, the 1st of the moon of Gemmadi II, 1715

---

96. This is a reference to the ordeal known as the *preuve du congrès*, which had in fact been abolished in 1677, but there was a much-discussed case in 1714: the Marquise de Gesvre brought such a suit against her husband, asserting his impotence and seeking a divorce on those grounds.

Letter 87

*Rica to * * **

They say that the human is a social animal. If that is the case, then I would say that the Frenchman is the most human of all, the human *par excellence*, because he seems to have been designed purely for society.

Yet I have noticed some among them who are not just social, but seem to be entire societies unto themselves. They self-multiply and people all four corners of the town; a hundred men like this would make up a greater crowd than two thousand ordinary citizens. To the eyes of a foreigner, they could make up for the ravages of plague and famine. In schools they debate whether a body can be in more than one place at the same time, and men like this are the proof that the philosophers are seeking.

Such men are always in a hurry, because they have important business: asking everyone they meet where they are going and where they have come from.

No one can ever succeed in getting the idea out of their heads that politeness requires them to visit everyone they know every single day, and that having met someone that day in a public group somewhere does not count. For such encounters are too brief, and cannot satisfy the demands of proper ceremony.

They do more damage to people's front doors with their hammering than winds and tempests. If you were to examine the visiting ledgers of all the town's porters, you would find their names, mangled a thousand different ways in Swiss handwriting.[97] Their lives are one long line of post-funeral gatherings, where they express their condolences, or weddings, where they express congratulations. The king cannot grant some favor to one of his subjects without these people renting a carriage and hurrying over to express their joy. At day's end they return home to get some rest, in order to arise the next day and continue their weary duties.

One of them died of exhaustion the other day, and this epitaph was hung on his tomb:

> Here rests a man who never rested. He betook himself to five hundred and thirty funerals. He rejoiced at the births of two thousand, six hundred and eighty babies. He congratulated his friends on receiving pensions, which altogether totaled two million, six hundred thousand *livres*; and he never

97. Swiss immigrants were often employed as porters and doormen; their imperfect knowledge of Parisian pronunciation is the basis for the joke here.

repeated himself. He covered over four hundred leagues on city streets, and around five in the country. His talk was amusing: he had a repertoire of three hundred and sixty-five stories, and he also had ready one hundred and eighteen sayings drawn from the ancients, recollected from his youth, which he employed on especially important occasions. He died in his sixtieth year. I say no more, traveler; how could I ever finish telling you all that he did and all that he saw?

From Paris, the 3rd of the moon of Gemmadi II, 1715

Letter 88

Usbek to Rhédi
At Venice

In Paris, Liberty and Equality reign. Birth, virtue, even military glory, no matter how stunning—none of these can keep a man from being lost in the crowd. Jealousy based on rank is unknown here. They say that the greatest man in Paris is the one whose carriage has the best horses.

A great lord is a man who sees the king, speaks to the ministers, and has ancestry, debts, and a pension. If he can add to those the ability to hide his indolence behind a mask of busyness, or feign an addiction to pleasure, he believes himself the happiest of men.

In Persia, the only great men are those whom the monarch has invited to be part of the government. Here, there are some who are great due to their birth, but they have no influence. Kings are like skillful artisans who, in order to create their products, prefer to use the simplest tools.

The great goddess of the Frenchman is royal favor. The minister is the high priest, offering up many sacrificial victims to her. Those surrounding her, though, are not dressed in white robes: sometimes sacrificers and sometimes sacrificed, they all devote themselves to their idol, along with the entire population.

From Paris, the 9th of the moon of Gemmadi II, 1715

Letter 89

Usbek to Ibben
At Smyrna

The desire for glory is no different than the instinct all creatures have for their self-preservation. It seems as if we have extended our own being when we have managed to imprint it into the memory of others. We thereby acquire a new life, and this one becomes just as precious to us as the one heaven granted us.

But just as all men are not equally attached to life, so they are not all equally sensitive to glory. This noble passion is indeed always inscribed upon their hearts, but subsequent education and imagination can modify it in a thousand ways.

This difference between one man and another is even more pronounced between one people and another.

One might hold it as an axiom that, within a given state, the desire for glory grows in proportion to the liberty enjoyed by the subjects, and likewise diminishes along with it. Glory is never the companion of servitude.

A sensible man said this to me the other day: "In France, a person is in many respects freer than in Persia, and thus we love glory here that much more. This fortunate fantasy makes a Frenchman do things with pleasure and enthusiasm that your sultan could only get his subjects to do by dangling rewards and punishments constantly before their eyes.

"Moreover, among us, the prince is concerned for the glory of even the least of his subjects. We have a respected tribunal to maintain this honor,[98] the nation's sacred treasure, and the only one not under the sovereign's command. The sovereign would be acting contrary to his own interests if he did oversee this issue, for any subject whose honor was affronted by the monarch, for any reason whatsoever, would immediately quit the royal court and his employment, and return to his home.

"The difference between French soldiers and yours is that yours, who are all slaves and naturally cowardly, can only overcome the fear of death by the greater fear of punishment; this fear produces a new sort of terror in the man, rendering him stupefied. The French soldiers, on the other hand, rush forward to receive blows with joy, banishing their fear by a sense of satisfaction that is stronger than it.

98. The *tribunal des maréchaux de France* was established in the 1640s to pass judgment in matters of honor, and to eliminate the practice of the duel.

"But the very sanctuary of honor, reputation and virtue would seem to be found in republics, and in those countries where one can speak of real patriotism. In Rome, in Athens, in Sparta, honor was the sole recompense for the greatest services. An oak wreath, or a laurel, a statue, a eulogy: these were the immense reward for a victory in battle, or a conquered town.

"In such places, a man who had performed an act of greatness felt himself sufficiently recompensed by the act itself. Whenever he looked upon one of his compatriots, he could feel the pleasure of having been the man's benefactor; he reckoned the number of his services as being equal to the number of his fellow citizens. Every man is capable of doing good for another, but it is godlike to be able to contribute to the well-being of an entire society.

"Now, this noble emulation—is it not bound to be utterly extinct in the hearts of your Persians, for whom all employment and dignity must depend upon the whim of the sovereign? There, reputation and virtue are considered to be imaginary things if they are not accompanied by royal favors; in the presence or absence of such favors, reputation and virtue live or die. A man who enjoys public esteem today is never sure that he will not be in a state of dishonor tomorrow. Today, the general of an army—but tomorrow, perhaps the prince will take him for his cook, and then the only hope of praise left to the man will be for having made a good ragout."

From Paris, the 15th of the moon of Gemmadi II, 1715

Letter 90

Usbek to the same
At Smyrna

This general passion that the French nation has for glory has led to a certain something hard to define, which they call the point of honor. It is characteristic of every profession, but is especially marked among the military, where it is the point of honor *par excellence*. I find it very difficult to explain exactly what this is, because we have never had anything quite like it.

In earlier times, the French, and especially the nobles, obeyed virtually no laws except those of this point of honor, which regulated their entire lives, and they were so severe that a man could not omit even their most trivial details—to say nothing of actually transgressing against them—without incurring a consequence worse than death.

When it was a question of resolving some differences, the only method was the duel, which put an end to every difficulty. But the problem with this was that the duel often took place between people other than the ones directly involved.

No matter how little one man knew another, he was required to enter into the dispute and potentially to pay with his life, as if he were the outraged party. He always felt honored at having been chosen and at having been so flattered. And though he would not give four *pistoles* to a man to save him and his whole family from the gallows, nonetheless he would freely go and risk his life a thousand times over.

This method of coming to a decision was not very well conceived, for just because a man is more adroit or stronger than another does not mean he is more in the right.

Thus, the kings forbade dueling on pain of severe penalties, but in vain: honor always wants to be first, and it revolted, refusing to recognize any such laws.

The French thus live in quite a violent situation, for these same rules of honor oblige a man to avenge himself whenever he has been offended, but, at the same time, the laws will cruelly punish him when he does take revenge. If he obeys the laws of honor, he will die on the scaffold; if he obeys those of the justice system, he will be banished forever from the company of men. This is the only alternative he has: either to die or to be unworthy to live.

From Paris, the 18th of the moon of
Gemmadi II, 1715

Letter 91

Usbek to Rustan
At Ispahan

A man claiming to be a Persian ambassador has appeared here, and has insolently deceived two of the greatest monarchs on earth. He has given the French monarch the kind of gifts that ours would not dream of giving a king of Irimetta or of Georgia, and he has sullied the majesty of two empires by his petty-minded avarice.[99]

He has made himself ridiculous in front of a people who consider themselves the most polished in all Europe, and he has made it be said in the West that the King of Kings rules only over barbarians.

He has received honors which, by his actions and demeanor, he apparently did not want. The French court would appear to have more concern for the reputation of Persia than he himself, and has caused him to appear with some dignity before a people who have contempt for him.

Do not speak of this in Ispahan: spare this wretch's head. I do not want our ministers to punish him for what is clearly their own imprudence by making such a wretched choice for their ambassador.

From Paris, the last of the moon of Gemmadi II, 1715

Letter 92

Usbek to Rhédi
At Venice

The monarch who has reigned for so long is now no more.[100] He was constantly talked about during his life; everyone is silent now at his death. He was strong and brave right up to his last moment, and he apparently yielded only to fate. So died the great Shah Abbas, after having filled the whole earth with his name.

Do not imagine that a great event like this has only given rise to moral reflections. Everyone here thinks about his own affairs, and is maneuvering to gain some advantage from the change. The new king,

99. Mehemet Riza Beg, who visited Paris in 1715, was in fact an envoy of the Persian king, but his gifts were considered beneath the French king's dignity, and his embassy was conducted so awkwardly that he was the subject of gossip suggesting that he was an imposter. Louis XIV gave him a sumptuous reception, which is the subject of a painting in Versailles by Antoine Coypel.

100. *He died on September 1, 1715* [Montesquieu's note].

great-grandson of the deceased monarch, is only five years old, so a prince, his uncle, has been declared regent of the kingdom.[101]

The late king had made a will restricting the regent's powers, but this capable prince has gone to the Paris *parlement*, and pleading there all the rights due to him because of his birth, he has managed to overturn the will of the monarch who seemed to want to continue ruling even after his death.[102]

These *parlements* are comparable to those ruins that one walks through, kicking stones aside that once were part of a grand temple of some ancient national religion. Nowadays they only work with judicial matters, and their authority is always weak—until some unforeseen combination of events arises to return their power and vigor. Great bodies such as these follow the same destiny that all human things must: they give way before the depredations of time, which destroys everything, and to moral corruption, which weakens everything, and to supreme authority, which overthrows everything.

But the regent, who wants to be liked by the people, appears at the outset to have respected this lingering image of bygone public liberty, and, as if he were thinking of re-establishing the temple and the idol, he says he wants them to be seen as the essential support of the monarchy, and the foundation of all legitimate authority.[103]

From Paris, the 4th of the moon of Rhegeb, 1715

Letter 93

Usbek to his brother,
Santon at the Casbin monastery

I humble myself before you, holy santon,[104] and I prostrate myself; the sight of your footprints alone is the apple of my eye. Your holiness

101. Philippe, Duc d'Orléans, was regent until his death in 1723.

102. Louis XIV had stipulated that the regent would only be the chair of a council, but Orléans had this stipulation overturned. The powers of the various *parlements* had been much reduced under the reign of Louis, and now Orléans was able to ally himself with them, serving his self-interest as well as theirs.

103. Montesquieu was a member of the Bordeaux Parlement, serving as its *magistrat*, or head, from 1714–1726, so we can assume that Usbek speaks for him here.

104. A santon is a Muslim monk.

is so great that you appear to have the heart of our holy prophet; heaven is amazed at your austerities; the angels have looked down upon you from their heights and asked, "Why does he remain on the earth since his spirit is with us, flying high around the throne supported by clouds?"

And how could I fail to honor you, having learned from our wise men that dervishes, even those among the infidels, always have about them a holiness that makes them venerable to true believers? And since God has selected the purest souls from all the corners of the earth, and has separated them from the impious world, so that their mortifications and their fervent prayers will check his wrath before it falls upon the rebellious multitudes?

The Christians speak of the miracles worked by their first santons who took refuge by the thousands in the terrifying Theban desert, their leaders being Paul, Anthony, and Pacomius.[105] If what they say of them is true, their lives were as full of marvelous events as those of our most sacred imams. They went sometimes for as long as ten years without seeing another living man, but they lived day and night with demons. They were tormented endlessly by these evil spirits, finding them in their beds, at their tables; there was no escape from them. If all this is true, holy santon, we have to observe that no one has ever lived with worse company.

Sensible Christians look upon stories like these as quite natural allegories that can serve to call our attention to the miserable nature of the human condition. Even in the desert we would search in vain for a tranquil life, for temptations follow us at all times. Our passions, figured in these tales as demons, never leave us: these monsters of the heart, these illusions of the mind, these vain phantoms of error and untruth are always at work trying to seduce us, attacking us even in our fasting and our hair shirts—that is, in our very strength.

As for me, venerable santon, I know that God's messenger has put Satan in chains and hurled him into the abyss; he has purified the earth, which had been Satan's empire, and has made it a worthy place for angels and for prophets.

From Paris, the 9th of the moon of Chahban, 1715

---

105. Paul (called Paul the Hermit), Anthony, and Pacomius were early ascetics who lived in the Theban desert of Egypt. Paul was a semi-mythical figure whose dates are uncertain, but Anthony and Pacomius are much better documented: they lived in the fourth century, and they became models for later Christian monasticism.

Letter 94

Usbek to Rhédi
At Venice

I have never heard any discussion of international law that did not begin with a careful examination of the question of the origin of societies—which seems ridiculous to me. If people did not come together in groups, if they avoided and fled each other, we would need to ask why they separated themselves. But instead they are born tied to each other: a son is born to a father, and stays close to him: and that is society, and the cause of society.

International law is better known in Europe than in Asia, but one can add that its principles have been corrupted by the passions of princes, the forbearance of the people, and the flattery of writers.

This law, such as it is today, is a science that tells princes exactly how far they can go in violating justice without doing harm to their own interests. What a project this is, Rhédi, to come up with a system that hardens the conscience by making a system of iniquity, giving it rules and principles and computing its consequences!

The limitless power of our sublime sultans, which is a law unto itself, produces no more monsters than does this unworthy art that seeks to bend justice—which should be inflexible—into a desired shape.

One might say, Rhédi, that there are two totally different justices: the one operates at the level of the individual, and this is civil law; the other operates at the level of nations, tyrannizing over the affairs between peoples, and this is international law. As if international law were not itself a civil law—not one ruling over a particular country, but over all.

I will explain my thoughts on this in another letter.

From Paris, the 1st of the moon of Zilhagé, 1716

Letter 95

Usbek to the same

Judges are the ones who administer justice between citizen and citizen; but each nation should do the same between itself and another nation. And this second kind of justice must rest upon the same principles as the first.

Between nation and nation, a third party is rarely needed, because the subjects under dispute are almost always clear and easy to settle. The interests of two nations are normally so different that one only needs to be motivated by justice to discover the answer; one's personal interests are not normally affected, so that prejudice is easily avoidable.

It is very different when it comes to disputes between individuals. Since they live in society, their interests are so intermingled and confused, and there are so many different sorts of disputes, that it takes a third party to sort out and shine a light on what the individuals and their greed have obscured.

There are only two kinds of just wars: wars to repel an invading enemy, and wars to aid an ally who has been attacked.

There is nothing just about a war fought over a prince's personal quarrels, except where the case was so serious that it would warrant the death of the prince, or that of the nation that had committed the offence. Thus, a prince cannot go to war because someone has refused him an honor due to him, or because someone has been disrespectful toward his ambassadors, or for any similar reason—any more than an individual could justly kill someone who refuses him precedence. The reason is that a declaration of war is itself an act of justice, and justice always requires that the punishment suit the offence. Therefore, one must determine first whether he against whom one has declared war deserves to die: for to make war on someone is to will his capital punishment.

Within the realm of international law, war is the most severe act of justice, because it potentially has the effect of destroying a society.

Second in severity is the reprisal. Here too the one principle that must be observed is the suiting of the punishment to the crime.

A third act of justice is depriving a prince of the advantages he may expect from us, again proportioning the punishment to the offence.

A fourth act of justice—and the one that ought to be the most often used—is breaking off an alliance with the offending nation. This is the equivalent to banishment in civil law, a punishment the tribunals have used to remove guilty parties from society; thus the prince whose alliance we reject is like a banished person, no longer a member of our society.

There is no greater insult to a prince than breaking off an alliance with him, and there is no greater honor than contracting one with him. Among men, there is no greater glory, and indeed nothing more useful, than seeing others constantly attentive to our protection.

But any binding alliance we enter into must be a just one. Thus, an alliance between two nations for the purpose of oppressing a third is not legitimate, and it may be violated without crime.

An alliance with a tyrant does a prince no honor, and is unworthy of him. People tell of an Egyptian monarch who pointed out the king of Samos' tyranny and cruelty, exhorting him to mend his ways. When he did not, the Egyptian monarch sent word to him that he was renouncing his friendship and their alliance.[106]

Conquest in itself establishes no rights. If the people of the conquered nation survive, the conquest is a pledge of peace and the reparation of wrongs; if the people are destroyed or scattered, conquest is the monument of tyranny.

Peace treaties are so sacred among men that they almost seem to be the voice of nature itself reclaiming its rights. They are always legitimate, provided that the terms are such that both nations can preserve themselves. If this is not the case, the nation that finds it must perish, being deprived of its natural defenses by the peace treaty, can legitimately seek redress through war.

For nature has established differing degrees of strength and weakness among men, but she sometimes makes weakness equal to strength by adding despair to it.

And there you have it, dear Rhédi, what I call international law; this is the law of nations—or rather, the law of reason.

From Paris, the 4th of the moon of Zilhagé, 1716

Letter 96

The Chief Eunuch to Usbek
At Paris

A large number of yellow-skinned women have arrived here from the kingdom of Bijapur.[107] I have purchased one for your brother the governor of Mazanderan,[108] who sent me his sublime command last month, along with a hundred tomans.

106. In the mid-sixteenth century BC, King Ahmose of Egypt broke off his alliance with Polycrates of Samos; the story is told by the Greek historian Diodorus Siculus in Book I of his *Bibliotheca Historica* (c. 30 BC).

107. Bijapur was an independent kingdom—or rather sultanate—in India until 1686.

108. Mazanderan is a province bordering the Caspian Sea, in the north of what is now Iran.

I am an excellent judge of women, and they cannot deceive me, for my eyes are never clouded by impulses of my heart.

I have never seen such regular, perfect beauty. Her brilliant eyes light up her face, and enhance a complexion that would outdo all the charms of Circassia.[109]

The chief eunuch of an Ispahan merchant bid against me for her, but she turned her glance disdainfully away from him and seemed to seek me out, as if she wanted to say that a vile merchant was not worthy of her, and that she was destined for a more illustrious husband.

I must admit to you that I feel a secret joy when I think of this beautiful person's charms: I imagine her entering into your brother's seraglio, and I enjoy picturing to myself the astonishment on the faces of all the other wives—an imperious sorrow on some, a mute but even sadder affliction on some others, a malicious consolation on those who no longer have any hopes, and an angry ambition on those who still entertain hope.

I have set in motion, from one end of the kingdom to the other, a change in an entire seraglio. What passions I am about to excite! What fears and what misery I am stirring up!

But for all that inner turmoil, the surface will seem as tranquil as ever. Great revolutions such as this remain hidden deep within the heart. Sorrows are swallowed, and joys repressed. Obedience will be as exact as ever, and the rules as inflexible as ever. The sweet demeanor that is always expected will arise now out of the depths of despair.

We have observed that the greater the number of women we have to oversee, the fewer problems they give us. The greater necessity of pleasing, and the reduced opportunities for uniting together, the greater number of examples of submissive behavior—all these act as chains upon them. Each is always on the watch for failures among the others; it is as if they were working in concert with us to make and keep them more fully dependent. They do some of the work for us, and they point out things that we may have missed. But even more: they work to make their master turn against their rivals, never seeing how similar they are to those who are being punished.

But all this, magnificent lord, all this is nothing without the presence of the master. What can we do, wielding only this empty shadow of the authority that is never really ours? We cannot represent even half of yourself, and that only feebly; all we can employ is a hateful severity.

---

109. On Circassian beauty, see the note to Letter 79.

But you temper their fears with hopes, and you are a more absolute ruler when you caress than when you threaten.

Return then, magnificent lord, return and bring with you all the signs of your empire. Come back to soften and soothe desperate passions; come back to take away every excuse for weakness; come back to mollify discontented, murmuring love, and make duty itself an act of love; come back, finally, to lighten your faithful eunuchs' burden, which grows heavier every day.

From the seraglio at Ispahan, the 8th of the moon of Zilhagé, 1716

Letter 97

Usbek to Hassein,
Dervish of the Mountain of Jahrom[110]

O wise dervish, you whose inquisitive mind glitters with so much knowledge, hear what I have to say to you.

There are philosophers here who, to speak the truth, have not come close to attaining oriental wisdom: they have not been ravished up to the luminous throne, nor heard the ineffable words sung by the choirs of angels, nor tasted access to the divine ecstasy. Instead, left to themselves in the silence, deprived of knowledge of the sacred miracles, they simply follow the tracks of human reason.

And you would scarcely believe where this trail has led them. They have disentangled chaos, and have explained the divine architecture by simple mechanics. The Author of nature put matter into motion, and nothing else was required in order to produce the prodigious variety of objects we perceive in the universe.

Ordinary legislators propose laws for regulating human society, laws that are subject to change according to the ideas of the people who propose them and those who observe them. But these philosophers speak of general, immutable, eternal laws observed without exception and with an order, regularity, and infinite speed across the immensity of space.[111]

110. Jahrom is in what is today the province of Shiraz in southwestern Iran.

111. The laws of physics discussed in this letter derive from Descartes, especially his *Principes de la philosophie* (1644).

And what, o holy man, do you think these laws might be like? You might imagine that, in entering into the counsels of the eternal, you would be stunned by the sublimity of the mysteries; you might assume in advance that you could not possibly comprehend them, and that you will therefore simply admire them.

But you would soon change your mind. These laws do not dazzle with obfuscation and a false profundity. Indeed, their very simplicity has kept them misunderstood until now. But it is only after a great deal of reflection that people have come to see them in all their fecundity and in all their immense scope.

The first is that every body tends to follow a straight line, so long as it does not encounter another body that knocks it off course.[112] The second follows from the first: any body that circles around a center point tends to move away from it. This is because the further away it goes, the more its motion tends toward a straight line.

And there, sublime dervish, is the key to nature; these are the fertile principles from which seemingly endless consequences are derived.

The knowledge of five or six truths has produced a philosophy full of miracles, and has led them to the performance of almost as many marvels and prodigies as those our holy prophets tell of.

And I am convinced that among all our theologians, there is not one who would not be embarrassed if he were asked to compute the weight of the air surrounding the earth, or the total amount of rain that falls on its surface each year; not one who wouldn't have to ponder a long while before being able to say how far sound travels in an hour, or how long it takes a ray of sunlight to reach us, or how far it is from Earth to Saturn, or what the best sort of curve is in designing a ship for the best possible performance.

Perhaps if some holy writer had embellished the works of these philosophers with lofty, sublime rhetoric, mixing in powerful metaphors and mysterious allegories, he would have created a book scarcely inferior to our holy Koran.

But if I may tell you what I think, I really do not much like the ornate, figurative style. In our Koran, there are a great many trivial things, and no matter how much they are dressed up in forceful, vivid language, they will always seem petty to me. At first, it would seem that inspired texts are essentially divine ideas expressed in human language—but on the contrary, in our Koran we often find the language of God

112. Though we call this Newton's First Law, Newton borrowed it from his reading of Descartes.

and the ideas of men, as if God, by some amazing caprice, had dictated the words while man furnished the thoughts.

You will perhaps object that I am speaking too freely about our holiest possession, and you will ascribe it to the independence of mind found in this country. No: thanks be to heaven, my mind has not corrupted my heart, and as long as I live, Ali will be my prophet.

From Paris, the 10th of the moon of Chahban, 1716

Letter 98

Usbek to Ibben
At Smyrna

Fortune is more inconstant and unpredictable here than in any other country in the world. Every ten years, some revolution hurls the rich down into the ranks of the poor, and elevates the poor with rapid wings to the heights of riches. The one is stunned to see his poverty, the other his affluence. The newly rich praise the wisdom of Providence, while the newly poor lament the blindness of fate.

Those who are tax collectors find themselves swimming in a sea of treasure; there are few Tantalus types among them. They begin their profession in the utmost poverty, as despised as mud, but when they gain wealth, they also gain esteem; and therefore they do all they can to gain esteem.

They are currently in a terrible situation. A chamber of justice, or so it is called, was recently established, its goal being to strip them of all their wealth. They can neither hide nor avoid declaring all their effects, for they are obliged to declare everything, under pain of death, and they are thus forced to pass through a narrow strait, navigating between their lives and their money.[113] To make matters even worse, there is a minister who is known for his wit, and he honors them with his pleasantries, making jokes out of all the council's deliberations. You don't find every day a minister disposed to making the people laugh, and this one is to be congratulated on his efforts.[114]

---

113. On the institution of the "tax farmer," see the note to Letter 48. This chamber of justice was established by the Regent in 1716 in order to investigate abuses by the tax farmers, but it had little effect and was disbanded a year later.

114. The witty minister was Adrien Maurice, Duc de Noailles (1678–1766); he was president of the council of finance.

The class of lackeys is a more respectable one in France than elsewhere, for it is a breeding ground for great lords, and fills in the gaps left in the other classes. Those who make up this group take the places abandoned by the unfortunate nobility, ruined magistrates, and gentlemen killed in the course of wars. And when they cannot supply the loss themselves, they re-stock all the great families by means of their daughters, who act as a kind of manure, enriching the mountainous and arid lands.

I find, Ibben, that Providence is wonderful in the way it distributes riches. If it had given wealth only to good men, we would have come to associate wealth with virtue, and would not have seen how worthless it truly is. Instead, when we look at the sort of people who have the most wealth, we come to despise riches by first despising the rich.

From Paris, the 26th of the moon of Maharram, 1717

Letter 99

Rica to Rhédi
At Venice

I am amazed at how fashion constantly changes among the French. They have completely forgotten what they wore last summer, and they have no idea what they will be wearing this coming winter. But what is most amazing is what it costs a husband to keep his wife in the current fashion.

What good would it do for me to give you a detailed description of their clothes and accessories? A new fashion would come along and undo everything I said—as it undoes the work of all the tailors—and before you even received my letter, everything would have changed.

A woman who leaves Paris to spend six months in the country returns looking as antique as if she had been gone thirty years. A son cannot recognize the portrait of his mother, so bizarre does the outfit in which she was painted look to him; he thinks to himself that it must be some American woman depicted, or perhaps some fantasy on the painter's part.

Sometimes women's hairstyles get higher and higher, and then abruptly they descend again. There was a time when the coiffure was so tall that a woman's face appeared in about the middle of her person; at another time, her feet occupied that spot, balancing up in the air on the great pedestal of her heels. And you might not believe it, but architects have had to heighten, lower, or widen their doors to accommodate women's changing fashions; all the rules of their art must be attuned to fashion's caprices. One day you will see a quantity of beauty spots on a face, and the next day they will all have disappeared. In other times, women had waists and teeth, but today those are out of the question. In this changeable nation, whatever the wits may say about it, the daughters are made differently than their mothers.

And as it is with fashion, so it is with manners and modes of living: the French change their ways according to the age of their king. The monarch could even turn this into a serious nation, if he wanted to do so. He imprints his style on the court, the court on the city, the city on the provinces. The sovereign's soul is like a mold that gives its shape to all the others.

From Paris, the 8th of the moon of Saphar, 1717

Letter 100

Rica to the same

I was writing you the other day about the incredible changeability of the French and their fashion. You would not believe how obsessed they are with it: everything revolves around it, and it is the yardstick by which they measure other nations, and what is foreign always appears ridiculous to them. But I swear, the one thing I cannot reconcile is their fanatic devotion to their fashion and the inconstancy with which they change it on a daily basis.

When I tell you that they despise everything foreign, I hasten to add that this only applies to trivia; when it comes to serious matters, they distrust their own judgment so much that they practically abase themselves. They cheerfully admit that other nations are wiser, so long as you agree that they are the best dressed. They are willing to subject themselves to the laws of a rival nation, provided that French wig makers are allowed to set down the rules for foreign wigs. Nothing makes them prouder than to hear the taste of their chefs praised from north to south, and to see the rules of their hairdressers imported into every dressing room in Europe.

With such noble advantages, what should it matter to them that good sense comes from other countries, and that they have borrowed everything concerning government and politics from their neighbors?

What should we think of a kingdom, the oldest and most powerful in all Europe, that has been governed for more than a thousand years by laws not of its own making? If the French had been conquered, this would be explicable; but they were the conquerors.[115]

They have abandoned their ancient laws, which had been made by their first kings in national general assemblies; but what is most odd is that they have adopted, in their place, Roman laws, which had been created and codified by emperors who were those early kings' contemporaries.

And to make the acquisition complete, and to ensure that all good sense comes from other places, they have adopted all the Papal constitutions, integrating them into their law, thus creating for themselves a new form of servitude.[116]

True, they have recently drawn up a few statutes concerning towns and provinces, but these are almost all borrowed from Roman law.

The abundance of these adopted and, so to speak, naturalized laws is so great that it has overwhelmed the judges and justice itself. But those volumes of laws are nothing in comparison to the awe-inspiring army of annotators, commentators, and compilers, men as weak in their intellect as they are strong in numbers.

And this is not all. These foreign laws have introduced formalities in procedure that shame human reason. It would be difficult to decide whether such adherence to formalities is more pernicious in law or in medicine, if those wearing the lawyer's robes have done more harm than those wearing the physician's broad hat—if the one has ruined more people than the other has killed.

From Paris, the 17th of the moon of Saphar, 1717

---

115. French law had evolved in the course of the middle ages from a combination of Roman, Frankish, and Germanic sources. Montesquieu would have much more to say about the Roman and Germanic origins of French law in his later masterpiece, *The Spirit of the Laws* (*De l'esprit des lois*, 1748, especially Books 26–31).

116. See Letter 24 and the following, Letter 101, on the Papal constitution titled *Unigenitus*.

Letter 101

*Usbek to * * **

All the talk here is still about the *Constitution.*[117] The other day I visited a house where I encountered a fat, red-faced man[118] who said in a loud voice, "I have issued my teaching on the matter in a pastoral letter, so I am not going to respond to all of your points. But read it, that letter, and you will see that I have resolved all your doubts there. I really sweated over it," he went on, his hand wiping his forehead. "I needed all my doctrine for it, and I had to read through any number of Latin texts."

Another man replied, "I can well believe it, for it is a beautiful work, and I defy that Jesuit you see so often to do any better."

He replied, "Just read it, and you will be more fully instructed on all these matters in a quarter of an hour than if I had spoken to you all day long." This was the way he avoided entering into conversation and risking his self-importance. But under continued pressure, he was forced to come out of his hole, and he began uttering some of the greatest theological stupidities, one after another, all the while being supported in them by a dervish who treated him with the greatest respect. When a couple of men who were there contradicted one of his points, he said at once: "No, it is certain; we have made our judgment, and we are infallible judges."

I said to him at that point, "How are you infallible?" He said, "Why, can't you see, the Holy Spirit enlightens us."

"That's a good thing," I replied, "because considering the way you've spoken here today, you clearly need a great deal of enlightenment."

From Paris, the 18th of the moon of Rebiab I, 1717

---

117. On the Papal Constitution *Unigenitus*, see the note to Letter 24, and the fuller discussion in the Introduction.

118. Vernière suggests that the fat, red-faced man may be André-Hercule de Fleury, the bishop of Fréjus, who went on to become a cardinal and the chief minister of Louis XV. He was entirely in favor of *Unigenitus*.

Letter 102

Usbek to Ibben
At Smyrna

The most powerful states in Europe are those of the Emperor, and of the kings of France, Spain, and England. Italy and a great part of Germany are broken up into a number of smaller states whose princes are, properly speaking, martyrs to sovereignty. Our glorious sultans have more wives than some of these princes have subjects. Those in Italy, who are not at all united, have the greatest cause for lament: their states are as open as caravanserais, and they have to take in all comers. So they must attach themselves to the great princes, offering up their fear rather than their friendship.

Most governments in Europe are monarchies, or at least they are called that; I am not sure there has ever been a pure monarchy, and in any case pure monarchies are never able to stay that way for long. The pure monarchy is a turbulent state that always degenerates into either despotism or a republic. Power can never be equally shared between people and prince; the equilibrium is too delicate to maintain, and the power has to diminish on one side and grow on the other. But the advantage usually lies on the side of the prince, who commands the army.

The power, therefore, of the European kings is very great—indeed, nearly as great as they could possibly wish. But they do not exercise their power as extensively as our sultans do, in part because they do not wish to affront the mores and religion of their peoples, and in part because it is not in their interest to wield their power so widely.

With our princes, nothing brings them closer to the condition of the people than that immense power that they exercise over them; and nothing makes them more vulnerable to reversals and the caprices of fortune.

Their habit of putting to death all those who displease them, no matter how minor the offense, overthrows the proportion that there ought to be between crime and punishment, which is so to speak the soul of a state and the harmony of an empire. And that proportionality, so carefully observed by the Christian princes, gives them an infinite advantage over our sultans.

A Persian who, out of imprudence or sheer misfortune, incurs disgrace and the disfavor of his sultan, is certain to die; and the slightest misstep or the slightest whim can put him in that position. But if he attempts to assassinate the sovereign, or gives away secrets to the enemy, he will also surely die. Thus, he runs no greater risk in the latter case than in the former.

And therefore when he is in even the slightest disgrace, seeing certain death ahead of him, and seeing nothing worse, he naturally turns to subversion and to conspiring against the sovereign: it is the only chance he has.

It is very different with the nobility in Europe, for whom disgrace only means the loss of royal favor. They retire from the court and concentrate on leading a tranquil life, enjoying all the advantages of their birth. Since the only situations where they are executed are those of high treason, they greatly fear and avoid it, having considered how much they have to lose and how little to gain. Thus we see few revolutions here, and few princes die a violent death.

If our princes, with their unlimited authority, failed to take so many precautions to protect themselves, they would not survive a day; and if they did not have in their pay numberless troops to tyrannize over their subjects, their rule would not last a month.

It was only four or five centuries ago that a French king created a corps of guards, contrary to the custom of the times, to protect him from some assassins that a minor Asian prince had sent to kill him.[119] Until that time, kings lived calmly among their subjects, like fathers among their children.

The kings of France are so far from taking the lives of their subjects, as our sultans do, that on the contrary, wherever they go, they bring pardons for all criminals with them. It is sufficient for a man to look upon the august face of his prince to cease being unworthy of life. These monarchs are like the sun, bringing warmth and life everywhere.

From Paris, the 8th of the moon of Rebiab II, 1717

119. The French king was Philip Augustus (1165–1223). According to some chronicles, Richard the Lionheart of England hired the Persian group known as the Assassins to kill him. The "minor Asian prince" refers to the leader of the Assassins, Rashid El-Din, also known as The Old Man of the Mountains.

Letter 103

Usbek to the same

To follow up on my last letter, this is what an intelligent European was telling me the other day:

"The biggest mistake that the Asian kings make is to keep themselves hidden away the way they do. Their aim is to inspire more respect for them, but instead they only succeed in inspiring respect for royalty itself, and not the individual king; their subjects feel an attachment to the throne, but not to a particular person.

"That anonymous power that governs them always appears the same to the people. If ten kings in a row, who were known only by their names, had their throats cut one after the other, the people would sense no difference. It is as if they were governed by a succession of ghosts.

"If the detestable murderer of our great king Henri IV[120] had carried out the same act on a king in India, he would have gained control of the royal seal and an immense treasure that would have seemed to be amassed just for him; he would have taken up the reins of the empire, without a single one of the subjects even thinking to raise questions about the king, his family, or his children.

"It surprises us that there is rarely any change in the method of governing among Oriental princes. What can explain this, if not the fact that the method is tyrannical and hideous?

"Changes can only be made by the prince or by the people. But in the East, the princes take care to change nothing. After all, they have everything they could want, including such absolute power that any change they made could only be to their disadvantage.

"As for the subjects, if one of them should come up with some project or design, he could do nothing whatever against the State. He would have to be able to counterbalance, in one fell swoop, an enormous, unified power, and for this he lacks the time and the means. But all he would have to do is get to the source of that power—and then all he would need is a strong arm and an instant.

"The murderer ascends the throne while the monarch descends and falls from it, dead at his feet.

120. Henri IV was assassinated by François Ravaillac on May 14, 1610. Ravaillac was tortured at length, and eventually drawn and quartered in the Place de Grève in Paris.

"A malcontent in Europe fantasizes about acquiring some secret intelligence and giving it to the enemy, or of seizing some fort, or of fomenting some futile discontent among the people. But a malcontent in Asia goes straight to the prince, surprises him, strikes, and hurls him down, and in so doing effaces his entire previous life: in an instant, the slave has become the master, the usurper the legitimate ruler.

"Unfortunate is the king with only one head! It would seem that all the power is concentrated there, for the sole purpose of showing the first ambitious man who comes along where he can find it all in one place."[121]

From Paris, the 17th of the moon of Rebiab II, 1717

Letter 104

Usbek to the same

All the peoples of Europe are not equally submissive to their princes. For example, the impatient nature of the English people leaves their king very little time to establish his authority. Submission and obedience are the virtues they pride themselves upon the least. And on that topic, they say some extraordinary things. According to them, the only tie holding people together is gratitude: a husband and wife, a father and son are attached only by the love they bear one another, or by the benefits one brings the other, and these two grounds for gratitude lie at the origin of all kingdoms and all societies.

But if a prince, instead of wanting to ensure his subjects a happy life, seeks to overwhelm and destroy them, the foundation of obedience has ceased to exist. Nothing binds or attaches them to him, and they now return to their state of natural liberty. They maintain that limitless power can never be legitimate, because it has no legitimate origin. For, they say, we cannot grant another more power over us than we have over ourselves, and we do not have absolute power over ourselves. For example, we may not take our own lives; therefore, they conclude, there is no person on earth with such power.

---

121. There is an echo here of the sentiment attributed to the Roman emperor Caligula, who is said to have wished that the entire Roman populace had a single head, so that he could cut it off.

The crime of high treason, according to them, is nothing but the crime that the weakest commits against the strongest; it is simply an act of disobedience, whatever form the disobedience takes. And thus the people of England, finding themselves in a position of greater strength than their sovereign, declared him guilty of high treason for waging war against his subjects.[122] They are quite correct, therefore, in saying that it is easy to follow the precept of their Koran that tells them to be submissive to the powers that be,[123] because in fact it is impossible not to do this: for they are not asked to submit to the most virtuous, but only to the strongest.

The English say that one of their kings, having defeated and captured a prince who had fought him for the crown, began to reproach him for his disloyalty and treachery. But the other prince said, "It was only a moment ago that it was decided which of us was the traitor."[124]

A usurper declares all those who have not oppressed the country as he did to be rebels, and believing that there is no law where there are no judges, he orders the caprices of chance to be revered as if they were acts of Providence.

From Paris, the 20th of the moon of Rebiab II, 1717

Letter 105

Rhédi to Usbek
At Paris

In one of your letters, you spoke at length about the sciences and arts cultivated in the West. You may call me a barbarian, but I am not convinced that the good we get from them compensates for the misuses to which they are constantly being put.

I have heard people say that the invention of bombs alone has deprived all the European people of their liberty. Princes can no longer

122. Such arguments were made concerning the trial and execution of Charles I in 1649, and were more fully developed by later thinkers, notably John Locke in his *Treatise on Civil Government* (1690).

123. Romans 13.1: "Let everyone be subject to the governing authorities, for there is no authority except that which God has established. The authorities that exist have been established by God."

124. The defeated prince was Edward, son of Henry VI; he was captured by Edward IV after the battle of Tewkesbury in 1471.

trust the defense of towns to the citizens, who would surrender at the first bomb, so they have used this as a pretext for raising and maintaining large standing armies with which they have oppressed their subjects.

You know that since the invention of gunpowder, no place is impregnable—and that is to say, Usbek, that there is no place on earth where we are safe from injustice and violence.

I tremble at the thought that eventually someone will discover some new secret that will lead to an even more efficient way to kill even more people, perhaps to destroy entire populations and nations.

You have read the historians: pay heed to them. Almost every monarchy was established only because the sciences and arts were unknown, and every one was destroyed when they had become too widely cultivated. The ancient Persian empire furnishes us with our own example.

I have not been in Europe for very long, but I have heard sensible people talking about the harm done by chemistry.[125] It seems to be a fourth scourge upon mankind, but one that ruins us one by one and continually, while the other three—war, plague, and famine—destroy us in great numbers, but with intervals between bouts.

What good was the invention of the navigator's compass and the discovery of so many new peoples who give us their diseases rather than their wealth?[126] By general convention, gold and silver were established as the reference price for all merchandise and a way to gauge a product's value, and this was done because gold and silver were rare and otherwise useless. Why then do we seek to find more of them, and make them more common? Was it so we could indicate the value of something be two or three figures instead of one? That only makes it more inconvenient.

But from the other point of view, this invention was even more destructive to the newly discovered countries. Whole nations have been wiped out, and the ones who have escaped death have been reduced to so harsh a servitude that it makes a Muslim shudder.

Happy, then, are the ignorant children of Mohammed! Amiable simplicity, so dear to our holy prophet, you remind me always of the old days, and the tranquility that reigned in the hearts of our first fathers.

From Venice, the 5th of the moon of Rhamazan, 1717

---

125. Montesquieu is evidently thinking of newly invented medicines, some of which turned out to be lethal.

126. The diseases in question here probably include syphilis, widely understood to have been imported from America.

Letter 106

Usbek to Rhédi
At Venice

Either you do not say what you really think, or your actions are better than your words. You left your homeland to learn, and now you despise the instruction; you travel for self-enrichment to a country where the arts and sciences are cultivated, and you denounce them as pernicious. If I may say so, Rhédi, I am more in accord with you than you are with yourself.

Have you considered the barbarous and miserable state to which we would descend without the arts? You do not need to imagine it; you can actually see it. There are still countries on this earth where a passably trained ape could live with honor. He would soon find himself pretty much on a level with the other inhabitants, and they would see nothing eccentric, nothing bizarre about him. He would seem just like everybody else, and would even seem distinguished by his refinement.

You say that the arts were unknown to the founders of empires. I do not deny that barbarous people can spread themselves out, like a rushing torrent, across the earth, overwhelming with their ferocious armies the most civilized kingdoms. But do notice this: they go on either to learn the arts or to make their conquered people practice them, because otherwise they will not endure, and pass away as quickly as the sound of thunder and storm.

You say you fear the invention of some new, even crueler means of destruction than those we know already. No: if such a weapon were invented or discovered, it would be quickly prohibited by men's laws, and the unanimous consent of all the nations would bury that discovery again. There is no gain for princes in conquering by means of such destruction; they want subjects, not empty lands.

You lament the invention of gunpowder and bombs, and you find it strange that there is no place that is truly impregnable. Well, another way of saying this is that you find it strange that wars in our day are concluded more rapidly than they were in the past.

You must have observed in the histories you have read that since the invention of gunpowder, battles are much less bloody than they were, because there is less hand-to-hand combat.

And even when an art has proven harmful in some particular case, ought one to reject it altogether? Would you say, dear Rhédi, that the religion our holy prophet brought to us from heaven is pernicious, since it will eventually confound the unbelieving Christians?

You think that the arts make people soft, and thus cause the fall of empires. You refer to the ruin of the ancient Persians, which was the result of softness. But this does not prove anything, since the Greeks, who vanquished them many times, and subjugated them, cultivated the arts with infinitely more care than did the Persians.

When people claim that the arts make men effeminate, they cannot be referring to the people working in the arts, because those people are never lazy—and laziness is the vice that most saps courage.

So the question only involves the people who benefit from those arts. But in a civilized society, those who enjoy the fruits of one art have to work in another themselves, or otherwise be reduced to a shameful poverty. It follows, therefore, that laziness and softness are incompatible with the arts.

Paris is perhaps the most sensual city in the world, the place where pleasures are most refined—but it is also the place where life is perhaps the most difficult. For one man to live exquisitely, a hundred others must labor without letup. A woman takes it into her head that she wants to attend some assembly wearing a particular stylish outfit, and from that moment, fifty artisans sleep no more, having scarcely the leisure to eat and drink: she commands, and her command is obeyed more promptly than one of our own monarch's, for self-interest is the greatest monarch on earth.

This ardor for work, this passion for enriching oneself operates at all levels, from craftsmen up to the nobility. No one wants to be poorer than the one he sees immediately below him. In Paris, you can see men who have enough to live on until the Day of Judgment, and yet they go on working endlessly, even at the risk of shortening their lives, in order to make—as they will tell you—a living.

And that same spirit grips the whole nation; all you see around you are labor and industry. So where, exactly, are these effeminate people you speak about?

Let us imagine a country, Rhédi, where no arts are permitted except those absolutely necessary for agriculture, though that is already a huge number. And let us imagine that all those that support pleasures and fantasies are banned. I suggest to you that this would be one of the most miserable countries in the world.

Even if the inhabitants were courageous enough to renounce all those things that they need, the population would be in continual decline, and the State would become so weak that it would be very easy to conquer.

It would be easy to go into this in some detail, and to make you see that the income of individuals would quickly drop to nothing, and consequently so would that of the prince. There would be almost no more commercial relationships among the citizens, and there would be an end to the circulation of wealth and the rising incomes that arise from the arts' dependence upon each other. Each individual would live on his little patch of land, taking nothing more from it than what he absolutely needed to avoid dying of hunger. And since this often amounts to barely a twentieth of the State's revenues, it follows that the number of inhabitants would shrink until they were only a twentieth of their former numbers.

Look closely at the amount of income from industry. A man's capital produces for him, at most, a twentieth part of its value. But with one *pistole* worth of colored paints, a painter can create a picture worth fifty. The same is true of goldsmiths, wool and silk workers, and all sorts of craftsmen.

From all this one must conclude, Rhédi, that if a prince is going to be powerful, his people must live in luxury. He must labor to provide every kind of unnecessary luxury for them with just as much care as he does the necessities of life.

From Paris, the 14th of the moon of Chalval, 1717

Letter 107

Rica to Ibben
At Smyrna

I have seen the young king. His life is very precious to his subjects, and no less so to all of Europe, because of all the troubles that would break out if he were to die.[127] But kings are like gods; and while they live, one must think of them as immortal. The young king's looks are majestic but charming. A fine education seems to have been combined with a promising nature, foretelling a great prince to come.

---

127. In 1717, Louis XV was only seven years old and in uncertain health. If he were to die there was no obvious heir to the throne, and war would almost certainly have broken out.

They say that the character of a Western king can never be truly known until he has gone through two great tests: the choice of a mistress, and the choice of a confessor. Soon afterward begins their struggle for control of the king's mind, and the battles will be intense. For, with a young prince, these two powers are always rivals, but under an old one, they are reconciled and united. With a young prince, the dervish has a more difficult time: the king's very strength is his weakness, but the other one triumphs equally in his weakness and his strength.

When I first arrived in France, I found the old king utterly ruled by women; at his age, however, I think no monarch on earth had less use for them. One day, I heard a woman saying, "Something must be done for this young colonel; I can see his worth; I shall speak to the minister about him." Another said, "I am shocked that this young abbé has been neglected; he ought to be a bishop; he is a man of good birth, and I can testify as to his morals." Do not conclude, however, that the women saying these things were favorites of the king. Indeed, they probably had not spoken to him more than twice in their lives, even though it is easy enough in Europe to get an audience with a king. The point is that there is no one with any position at the court, or in Paris, or in the provinces who does not have a woman through whose hands pass all the favors, and sometimes all the injustices, that he dispenses. And these women all know each other, and together they form a kind of republic whose members are always actively helping and serving each other. It is like a new State within the State. And anyone at court, in Paris, or in the provinces who sees the workings of the ministers, magistrates, and prelates but does not know the women who govern them, is like a man who clearly sees a machine at work but does not know about the springs that make it work.

Do you imagine, Ibben, that a woman becomes the mistress of a minister just so she can sleep with him? What an idea! No, it is in order to present five or six requests to him every morning; and woman's natural goodness shows itself in her eagerness to do good to an infinite number of unlucky men, who in turn supply her with an income of some hundred thousand *livres* per year.

In Persia people complain that the kingdom is governed by two or three women, but it is much worse in France, where women in general govern, and not only usurp authority as a whole, but then go on to share it out among themselves.

From Paris, the last of the moon of Chalval, 1717

Letter 108

*Usbek to * * **

There is a kind of book here that we do not have in Persia, which seems to be very much in vogue right now: these books are called journals.[128] Reading them encourages one in idleness; one can run through some thirty volumes of them in half an hour, and find it a delightful pastime.

With the usual sort of book, the author has scarcely paid his opening compliments and dedications before the reader is overwhelmed and is forced to make his way, half dead with exhaustion, across an ocean of words. This author hopes to immortalize himself with a duodecimo, that one with a quarto; another with even higher hopes, sets his sights on a folio, and therefore he must expand his subject accordingly—which he does, pitilessly, with no concern for the poor reader who works himself almost to death trying to shorten what the author has been determined to lengthen.

I do not see, * * *, what merit there is in producing books like these. Certainly, I could make some myself, if I wanted to ruin my health—and the publisher.

The great mistake these journals make is in only treating of recent books, as if the truth were always something new. It seems to me that, until a man has read all of the ancients, he has no grounds for preferring the moderns.

But it is not enough that they impose upon themselves the law of only writing about books that are hot off the presses; no, they impose another law, which is to be tedious. They avoid any criticism of the books that they abstract, no matter how good the reasons for criticism might be. But after all, who would want to be bold enough to make ten or twelve new enemies every month?

Most authors are like poets: they are ready to tolerate a beating without complaint, but while they suffer blows to the body willingly, they are not willing to suffer the slightest criticism of their works. One must be very cautious then, and avoid hitting them in that especially touchy spot. Therefore the reviewers do just the opposite, and begin with great praise of the subject of the book, their first asinine move, and then

---

128. Literary journals in early eighteenth-century France printed mostly reviews and abstracts of new books, rather than original articles. Montesquieu subscribed to some half a dozen of them.

proceed to heap praise on the author, something they feel compelled to do. For they are dealing with living, breathing men who are ready and able to use their pens to annihilate the foolhardy journalist.

From Paris, the 5th of the moon of Zilcadé, 1718

Letter 109

Rica to * * *

The University of Paris is the eldest daughter of the kings of France, and eldest by far, being over nine hundred years old.[129] Thus, she slips into daydreams now and then.

People have told me that a while back she had a great controversy with some of the scholars regarding the letter Q,[130] which she wanted to have pronounced as a K.[131] The dispute got so heated that some of the scholars had their property confiscated, and ultimately the *parlement* had to step in and settle matters. It decreed, with all due solemnity, that all the subjects of the king of France could henceforth decide for themselves how they wanted to pronounce the letter. It was great sport to see two of the most respected bodies of Europe involved in a quarrel over a single letter of the alphabet!

It would seem, my dear * * *, that the intellects of sagacious men actually decrease when they are gathered together, so that the more wise men present, the less wisdom. These great institutions are always so absorbed in minutiae that the really essential things get left for last. I have heard that a king of Aragon[132] called together the assemblies of Catalonia and Aragon, and the first order of business was to decide in

129. Montesquieu follows the legendary origin of the University of Paris, dating it to the era of Charlemagne, but in fact it dates from the middle of the twelfth century.

130. *He refers to the Ramus controversy* [Montesquieu's note].

131. The issue involved the pronunciation of Latin, and the controversy was started by Peter Ramus (Pierre de la Ramée, 1515–1572), who argued that a "q" in Latin should be pronounced as if it had a "u" following it, as in the English word "require."

132. *This was in 1610* [Montesquieu's note]. In fact, the event took place in 1510, involving Frederick of Aragon.

which language the proceedings would take place. The dispute was so lively that the meeting came close to breaking up a thousand times, until finally an expedient was concocted: questions would be given in Catalan, and the answers would be in Aragonese.

From Paris, the 25th of the moon of Zilhagé, 1718

Letter 110

Rica to * * *

The role played by a pretty woman is more serious than is often acknowledged. Nothing can be more important than what happens each morning at her dressing table, among her maidservants. A general in the army does not employ any greater care when it comes to positioning the troops on the right flank, or ordering his reserve troops, than she does when positioning a beauty mark, which can always turn out to be a failure, but for which she has high hopes.

What a weight on one's mind, what concentration is required when it comes to sorting out the interests of two rival suitors, appearing unprejudiced to each while giving herself to both, and being the mediator of all their disputes—of which she is the cause!

What a burden to have to see that every party is a success, and to constantly be planning new ones, all the while trying to avoid all the dreadful accidents that could ruin them!

All that being the case, the hardest thing is not so much to be amused as to appear that way. You can bore women as much as you like and they will forgive you, so long as it looks as if they are having a fine time.

A few days ago, I was at a supper some ladies were giving in the country. On the way there, they kept saying, "at any rate, we must have a good time."

Our group turned out not to be a very good mix, and as a result everyone was quite serious. But one woman exclaimed, "Well, we certainly are amusing ourselves! In all of Paris, there simply can't be a party as merry as this one!" And just when my own boredom was beginning to overwhelm me, a woman shook my arm and said, "Isn't everyone in a fine mood tonight?" "Oh yes," I replied, yawning; "I'm ready to die from laughing so much." But my gloominess got the better of me, and I felt myself being led along, yawn by yawn, into a lethargic stupor, which put an end to all the party's pleasures for me.

From Paris, the 11th of the moon of Maharram, 1718

Letter 111[133]

Usbek to * * *

The deceased king's reign had gone on so long that its end made everyone forget how it began. Now it is the fashion to be fascinated with the events of his youthful years, and people only want to read memoirs from that era.[134]

Here is a speech given by one of the generals of the city of Paris[135] during a war council; but I confess that I do not understand much of it.

"Gentlemen, even though our troops have been repulsed with great losses, I believe it will be easy for us to recover. I have six couplets of a song ready for publication, and I am quite sure this will restore our equilibrium. I have chosen a number of superb, clear voices which, emanating from certain powerful chests, will move the people marvelously. I have set the words to a melody that has always had a very specific effect on people.

"If this is not sufficient, we can print up a poster showing Mazarin being hanged.[136]

"Fortunately for us, he speaks French badly, mutilating the language to the point where his fortunes are bound to deteriorate. We have

---

133. This letter did not appear in the first edition of 1721, but was added in the second. Its opening, however, was very different; the version given here is that of the final, 1754 edition.

134. This renewed interest in memoirs of the mid-seventeenth century was much stimulated by the publication of Cardinal de Retz' *Memoires* in 1717. De Retz was closely associated with the Fronde uprising and the period of civil war that followed (1648–1653).

135. The general is a member of the Fronde, the rebellious group that included disaffected aristocrats and many among the Paris bourgeoisie.

136. Cardinal Mazarin (1602–1661), an Italian, was the chief advisor to the young Louis XIV, and a vigorous supporter of royal absolutism; the members of the rebellious Fronde saw him, therefore, as their bitterest enemy.

not failed to notify the people of his ridiculous pronunciation.[137] We recently turned up a grammatical mistake of his so gross that people are laughing about it on every street corner.

"I am hopeful that within a week, the people will have turned the name Mazarin into a term for any beast that carries a load or pulls a cart.

"Since our defeat, our songs have caused him so much damage on the topic of original sin that in order to avoid losing half his followers, he has had to dismiss all his pages.[138]

"Therefore, be of good cheer; take heart; and be sure that our mockeries will soon force him to hightail it back across the mountains to Italy."

From Paris, the 4th of the moon of Chahban, 1718

Letter 112

Rhédi to Usbek
At Paris

During my stay in Europe, I have been reading the historians, both ancient and modern; I make comparisons between the various eras, and I take pleasure in seeing them in a kind of procession, so to speak, before my eyes. I especially concentrate on the great changes that make each era so different, and the earth so unlike what it was.

Perhaps you have not noticed one particular thing that continues to surprise me. How did the world come to be so sparsely populated compared to what it was in the past? How did nature come to reduce that

137. *The Cardinal, wishing to refer to an Arrêt d'Union* [decree of union], *speaking to the deputies at the Parlement, pronounced it as Arrêt d'Ognon* [decree of onion], *and the people made many a joke about this* [Montesquieu's note in the 1721 and 1722 editions].

138. The references of the joke here are in dispute. Mazarin's "original sin" may refer simply to his having been born in Italy, or it may refer to the rumors that he had been secretly married to the Regent, Anne of Austria, when Louis XIV was a boy. The reference to his pages may allude to the rumors that he was a pederast.

marvelous fertility of earlier eras? Can she already be in her old age, and is she falling into decline?[139]

I have spent over a year in Italy, seeing there the debris of ancient Italy, once so renowned. Although everyone lives in cities, they are actually quite deserted and depopulated; they seem to exist only to mark the places where those powerful cities we read about in history once stood.

Some people claim that the single city of Rome once contained as many people as a great kingdom in Europe contains today. Back then, there were Roman citizens who owned as many as ten or even twenty thousand slaves, not counting those who worked in his country homes. And since there were approximately four or five hundred thousand free citizens, the mind boggles at trying to compute the entire population.

There used to be powerful kingdoms in Sicily with large populations, which have entirely disappeared; the only significant things on the island now are its volcanoes.

Greece is so deserted that it contains today less than a hundredth part of its ancient population.

Spain, once so filled with people, now is filled with uninhabited countryside, and France is nothing compared to the ancient Gaul that Caesar described.

The northern countries are largely cleared out; and their people are no longer forced to separate, as in other times, and go off in swarms like bees to find new colonies and establish new nations and new homelands.

Poland and the Turkish holdings in Europe are almost empty of people.

In America, there is not the fiftieth part of the population that once made up their grand empires.

Asia is in no better condition.[140] Asia Minor once contained many powerful monarchies along with a number of enormous cities, but today there are only two or three. As for Asia proper, the part ruled by the Turks is depopulated. Those parts ruled by our kings, compared to what they were in the past, have only a small fraction of what they had in the days of Xerxes and Darius.

---

139. Montesquieu's belief in the dwindling population of the earth was widespread in his day. For a discussion of the idea and its origins, see David B. Young, "Libertarian Demography: Montesquieu's Essay on Depopulation in the *Lettres Persanes*," *Journal of the History of Ideas* 36.4 (Oct. 1975), 669–82.

140. By Asia, Montesquieu here means mainly what we call the Middle East and our northwest Asia and southeast Europe.

As for the smaller states around these great empires, they are truly deserted—for example, the kingdoms of Irimetta, Circassia, and Guriel.[141] Their princes today count barely fifty thousand subjects on their vast holdings.

Egypt has fared no better than the others.

In short, I look all around the globe and see nothing but ruin. It is as if the whole world were just beginning to recover from plague and famine.

Africa has always been so unknown that we cannot speak about it with as much precision as other parts of the world, but to focus simply on the Mediterranean countries, which have always been much better known, one can clearly see that they are greatly fallen from what they were in the days of Carthage and the Romans. The princes in that region today are so feeble that they are among the weakest in the world.

After making calculations that are as exact as possible with this sort of thing, I find that there are scarcely a tenth as many people on the earth today as there were in ancient times. What is even more shocking is that this depopulation is still ongoing. If it continues, in ten centuries the earth will be as uninhabited as a desert.

This, my dear Usbek, is the most terrible catastrophe ever visited upon the world. But we have hardly even perceived it, because it has happened so gradually, over the course of many centuries, which is the mark of some inner disease, a secret, hidden venom, a slow, wasting sickness afflicting human nature.

From Venice, the 10th of the moon of Rhegeb, 1718

Letter 113

Usbek to Rhédi
At Venice

The world, my dear Rhédi, is not incorruptible, and neither are the stars. The astronomers are the ocular witnesses of their changes, which are the natural effects of the universal motion of matter.

---

141. All three were small principalities in the Caucasus.

The earth, like the other planets, is subject to the laws of motion, undergoing a perpetual internal war among its basic elements. Sea and land appear to be locked in an eternal battle, and from this battle new combinations are produced continually.

Men, living in an environment so subject to change, are likewise in an uncertain state. They can be destroyed by a hundred thousand different causes, and these can work to raise or lower their numbers.

I am not speaking of those specific catastrophes that the historians describe, the ones that have destroyed whole towns and even whole kingdoms. There have been some of these that have brought the whole human race to the brink of total annihilation.

The histories are full of these universal plagues that have each, in their turn, wrought universal desolation. They speak of one in particular that was so violent that it scorched all the way down the roots of the plants, and was felt throughout the known world, as far off as China. One degree more, perhaps, and it would have wiped out all humankind.[142]

Not two centuries ago, the most shameful of all maladies made itself felt across Europe, Asia, and Africa, and it had astonishing effects in a short period of time; it would have meant the end of humankind if it had maintained that same furious pace.[143] Infected and overcome from infancy, unable to fulfill the duties society requires, the human race would have perished miserably.

What might have happened if the venom had been a bit more powerful? And it would have become so, no doubt, if a remedy just as powerful had not been discovered.[144] The disease attacked the reproductive organs, and might have gone on to attack reproduction itself.

But why talk about all the destruction that could have happened to humankind? Did it not in fact happen? Did the Flood not reduce our entire race to a single family?

Some philosophers distinguish between two creations: that of things, and that of humankind. They cannot comprehend that matter and created things are a mere six thousand years old,[145] or that God deferred

---

142. The reference is probably to the plague known as the Black Death in 1348.

143. The shameful malady is syphilis, believed to have been imported from the newly discovered Americas.

144. The remedy was the mercury cure.

145. This was the accepted age of the earth in Montesquieu's time, based on Biblical chronology, but it was beginning to be questioned. Spinoza,

the use of his power throughout eternity, making use of His creative power only yesterday. Was He unable to before then? Or perhaps He didn't want to? But if He could not have done it at one time, He could not have done it at another. Therefore, He must not have wanted to. But since there is no change in God, if we posit that He wanted to do something once, He must have wanted to do it at all times, since the very beginning.

However, all the historians speak of a first father; they all make us see the birth of human nature.[146] These philosophers think that Adam was preserved from some universal disaster, the way Noah was from the Flood, and that such great events on the earth have been frequent, from the creation till now?

But not all the destructions have been violent. We observe that certain places on earth no longer are inhabitable by humans. Perhaps the earth as a whole contains within it some general, slow-moving, imperceptible causes leading it to exhaustion.

I have preferred to send you these general ideas before responding in detail to your letter about depopulation over the last seventeen or eighteen centuries. I will show you in a future letter that there are moral causes, independent of physical ones, that have led to this effect.

From Paris, the 8th of the moon of Chahban, 1718

Letter 114

Usbek to the same

You seek the reason why the world is less populated now than it was in the past, but if you look into it carefully, you will see that the major cause is the change in the ways people live.

---

for example, posited that the world and God were coeternal. Montesquieu evidently had his doubts too, for the earlier editions began this sentence thus: "Those who understand nature and who have a rational idea of God cannot comprehend . . ."

146. In the earlier editions, before this sentence Montesquieu had added this: "We must not compute the years of the world. The number of grains of sand in the sea is no more than an instant in comparison."

Since the Roman world was divided up into Christian and Muslim, things have changed a great deal, because those two religions are far less favorable to the propagation of the species than was the religion of the Romans, those masters of the universe.

Polygamy was forbidden under the latter, and in that regard it had a very great advantage over the Mohammedan religion. And divorce was permitted, which gave it a different but equally important advantage over the Christian.

I find nothing so inconsistent as that plurality of wives that the holy Koran permits, and the requirement to satisfy them, which the same book teaches. "Look at your wives," says the Prophet; "you are as necessary to them as clothing, and they are as necessary to you as clothing."[147] Now here is a precept that is bound to render the Muslim man's life all too laborious. He who has the four wives established by the law, and only the same number of concubines or slaves—is he not in danger of being crushed to the ground by the weight of all that clothing?

"Your wives are your plowing fields," the Prophet says; "go therefore to your plowing fields, labor for the good of your soul, and you will find your reward."[148]

In my view, a good Muslim is like an athlete, destined to compete without respite; but he is an athlete who is soon weakened, enfeebled by his opening efforts, and who now languishes on the very field of victory, finding himself buried, so to speak, under his own triumphs.

Nature works slowly and, so to speak, frugally. Her operations are never violent, and she aims at temperance in all her works. She always proceeds regularly, measuredly, and when we try to hurry her, she soon turns languid, employing all her remaining strength just to survive, and losing altogether her productive virtues, her generative powers.

And this is the state of breakdown into which we are put by our great number of wives, more likely to exhaust than satisfy us. It is quite common among us to see a man with a big seraglio but with a very small number of children, and those children are often weak and unhealthy, having inherited their father's weariness.

That is not all: these wives, living in a state of enforced continence, have need of people to guard them, people who can only be eunuchs, for religion, jealousy, even reason itself would not permit anyone else to approach them. Now, these guardians have to be very numerous in order to maintain some tranquility in the midst of the incessant wars

147. Koran, sura 2, 187.

148. Koran, sura 2, 223.

that women wage against each other, as well as to keep outsiders away. Thus, a man with ten wives or concubines needs at least that many eunuchs to guard them. But what a loss to society, such a number of men who are dead from their birth! And what a drop in the population must be the inevitable result!

The slave girls who are in the seraglio to serve this great number of wives along with the eunuchs must necessarily grow old in a state of bitter virginity. They cannot marry as long as they stay there, and once their mistresses get used to them, they are almost never allowed to leave.

So this is how one individual man and his pleasures employ so many subjects of each sex, make them dead as far as the State is concerned, and render them useless for the propagation of the species.

Constantinople and Ispahan are the capitals of the two greatest empires in the world, and everything is drawn toward them, including so many people attired in so many different manners who come there from all parts of the earth. But the fact is that they are perishing, and would soon be destroyed if their sovereigns did not find ways to import almost entire nations of people, every century, to repopulate them. I will continue with this subject in another letter.

From Paris, the 13th of the moon of Chahban, 1718

Letter 115

Usbek to the same

The Romans did not have fewer slaves than we do; as a matter of fact, they had more, but they made better use of them.

Far from using forcible means to prevent their slaves from multiplying, they did everything in their power to encourage it. They brought them together in marriages as often as they could, and as a result their houses were filled with domestics of both sexes and all ages, and the State was filled with an innumerable population.

These children—who comprised part of their master's wealth—were born in large numbers in his house, and he had sole charge of feeding and educating them. The fathers, liberated from those concerns, could follow their natural bent and keep on propagating without fear of a too-large family.

As I said before, among us our slaves are entirely devoted to guarding our wives, and nothing else. From the point of view of the State, they exist in a condition of perpetual lethargy, and it is left up to the small number of free men, the heads of families, to cultivate all the arts and agriculture—tasks to which they devote as little time as possible.

It was not this way with the Romans. The republic made use of their slave population, to its great advantage. Each slave had his savings[149] which were subject to conditions set up by the master, but he could turn this money to whatever use his labor and resources suggested. Some opened banks, some went into shipping, some sold retail goods, and some applied themselves to the mechanical arts or to farming. But each of them tried with all his might to increase his capital, which procured him greater ease in his present servitude as well as hope for future freedom. And the end result was a hard-working people who stimulated the arts and industry.

These slaves, having become wealthy through their careful, hard work, were able to buy their freedom and become citizens. The republic thus continually renewed itself, receiving new families to replace the old ones that died off.

In my next letters, I will try to prove to you that the greater the population in a State, the healthier the commerce; and I will prove that the more commerce flourishes, the more the population grows: the two go hand in hand and inevitably reinforce each other.

If this is the case, how large would this prodigious number of slaves, always hardworking, grow to be? Industry and affluence gave birth to them and they, in turn, contributed to ever-greater industry and affluence.

From Paris, the 16th of the moon of Chahban, 1718

Letter 116

Usbek to the same

Until now, we have spoken only about Muslim countries, in seeking the reason why population has declined from what it was in the days of

149. This was the Roman *peculium*, an institution that allowed slaves to save money, which they put to various uses.

Roman domination. Let us turn now and examine the same phenomenon among the Christians.

The pagan religion permitted divorce, but it was forbidden by the Christian. This change, which at first seemed of so little consequence, slowly and imperceptibly had such terrible results that it is hard to believe.

This not only removed the sweetness of marriage, but did harm to its purpose: in trying to strengthen the bonds, it loosed them, and instead of uniting hearts, as it claimed to do, it ended up separating them forever.

The change took an act that was so free, an act that ought to have come from the heart, and made it into something governed by friction, necessity, and even the fatality of destiny. Distaste, personal feelings, the incompatibility of personalities—all these counted for nothing now. Now the heart—the most variable, inconstant thing in all nature—was to be fixed. Now two people, almost always very ill-matched people, were to be yoked together without the possibility of change, without hope, in the same way that cruel tyrants used to have living men fastened to dead bodies.

Nothing contributed more to mutual attachment than the ability to divorce. A husband and wife were able to endure domestic difficulties patiently, knowing that they had the power to put an end to them; and they often kept that power in hand for their entire lives without using it, simply because they knew that they were free to do so.

It is not this way with Christians, whose present woes make them despair of the future. The annoyances of marriage to them are lasting things, even, so to speak, eternal ones. And from that fact arises all the disgust, the discords, the mutual contempt, and the loss to posterity. Within the first three years of marriage the essential element becomes neglected, and the couple spends the next thirty years in frigidity, separated from each other privately—a separation perhaps more pernicious than a public one would be. They live on, each alone, and all this to the disadvantage of future generations. Soon enough a man, tired of the eternal wife, will avail himself of prostitutes, a shameful kind of commerce, and one pernicious to society; it does not fulfill the main aim of marriage, but merely simulates its pleasures.

If one of the two people bound together like this cannot or does not want to have children, whether because of age or temperament, that one buries the two of them together, making the spouse equally infertile.

It is therefore not surprising to see that among the Christians, so many marriages produce very few children. Divorce is abolished;

ill-matched couples have no remedy; and wives no longer pass, as they did among the Romans, through the hands of successive husbands who made the best possible use of them.

I would dare to predict that in a republic such as ancient Sparta, where the citizens were subject to many subtle and unusual laws, and in which the only family was that of the republic itself, if a law had declared that men would change their wives every year, the population would have soon grown beyond counting.

It is difficult to say what it was that brought the Christians to the point of abolishing divorce. Marriage, in every country around the world, is a contract governed by many different conventions, and the only conventions that ought to be banned are the ones that undermine its main purpose. But the Christians do not see it this way, and so they have trouble saying exactly what marriage is. They do not see it as consisting in sensual pleasure; instead, as I have said, they seem to have wanted to ban that aspect as fully as they could. Instead, marriage for them is an image, a symbol, something mysterious—something I do not understand.

From Paris, the 19th of the moon of Chahban, 1718

Letter 117

Usbek to the same

The prohibition of divorce is not the only reason for the depopulation of Christian countries; just as important is the enormous number of eunuchs they have living among them.

I am referring to the priests and dervishes, of both sexes, who take vows of lifelong celibacy. Among Christians, this is the virtue *par excellence*, which I cannot fathom, since it is a virtue that leads to nothing.

If you ask me, their theologians and scholars contradict themselves when they say that marriage is a holy state, but that celibacy, which is the exact opposite, is even holier. And when it comes to precepts and fundamental dogma, what is good is always the best.

The number of these people professing celibacy is very great.[150] In earlier times, fathers condemned their children to it from the cradle;

150. Vernière notes that in 1667 there were 270,000 religious in France, a number that had shrunk to 200,000 by 1776 (p. 246).

now, they commit themselves at the age of fourteen, which is almost the same thing.

This profession of celibacy has wiped out more men than all the plagues and all the bloodiest wars ever did. In every religious house there is an eternal family, one in which no one is ever born, and which depends on all the others for its upkeep. These houses are always open, like so many abysses into which future generations are flung.

This is very different from the Roman approach, which erected penal laws against those who refused the marriage laws, and those who wanted to enjoy a personal liberty so contrary to the public good.[151]

I speak only of Catholic countries. In the Protestant religion, everyone is free to have children; they tolerate neither priest nor dervish. And when Protestantism was being established, and people were going back to the ways of the early Church, if the founders had not been afraid of being accused of incontinence, they would no doubt have rendered the practice of marriage universal and softened the yoke by removing the one barrier that separates the Nazarene from Mohammed on this point.

But in any case, it is clear that their religion gives Protestants an infinite advantage over the Catholics.

I predict that, given the present state of Europe, it is impossible that Catholicism can survive another five hundred years.

Before the decline of Spain's power, the Catholics were much stronger than the Protestants. But the latter have gradually arrived at a level of equality. The Protestants will continue to become richer and stronger, and the Catholics weaker.

The Protestant countries are bound to be, and actually are, more populous than the Catholic ones. And from this it follows, first, that the taxes collected are much greater, since the number of people paying taxes is greater; second, that the lands are better cultivated; and finally, that commerce is more flourishing, because there are more people with fortunes to make, and since they have more needs, more resources for meeting those needs have sprung up. When there are only enough people sufficient for agriculture, commerce dies off, just as when there are only enough for commerce, agriculture suffers; in other words, both must fall at the same time, since a person cannot devote himself to one without neglecting the other.

In the Catholic countries, not only has the cultivation of the earth been forsaken, but people's industriousness itself has become pernicious,

151. The emperor Augustus decreed two laws, *Julia* and *Papia Poppaea*, rewarding fruitful marriages and penalizing unmarried people.

for it consists only in learning five or six words in a dead language. Once a man has managed that feat, he no longer has to worry about earning his fortune; he finds a comfortable life in the cloister, a life that would have cost him much sweat and difficulty outside it.

And that is not all. The dervishes control nearly all the wealth in the State; it is a society of misers who always take and never give. They accumulate their revenues continually to build up their stock of capital. So much wealth falls therefore, so to speak, into a state of paralysis—no more circulation, no more commerce, no more arts, no more manufacturing.

There is not a single Protestant prince who does not impose far greater taxes on his subjects than the Pope does on his. The latter, however, are poor, while the others live in opulence. Commerce brings everything to life with the ones, while monasticism brings death to everything with the others.

From Paris, the 26th of the moon of Chahban, 1718

Letter 118

Usbek to the same

We have nothing more to say about Asia and Europe; let us turn to Africa. But we can really only speak of its coastal areas, for we know so little of the interior.

The countries of the Barbary Coast, where Islam is established, are less populous than they were in the time of the Romans, for the reasons I have already given. As for the Guinea coast, their population must be violently declining, for the petty rulers and village chiefs there are selling their subjects to the European princes for the purpose of sending them to their colonies in America.

What is striking is that this America, which is absorbing so many new inhabitants, is practically unpopulated itself, and profits not at all from the continual losses in Africa. These slaves, transported to a new climate, perish by the thousands. And the work in the mines (which employ both native and imported workers), the poisonous vapors exhaled there, and the need to use mercury all the time combine to destroy them utterly.[152]

152. Montesquieu is referring to the mines in Peru, but he is inaccurate in assuming that African slave labor was used there.

Nothing seems quite as outrageous as killing off an endless number of men in order to dig silver and gold out of the ground: these metals are completely useless, and they are only valuable because we have chosen to use them as symbols of wealth.

From Paris, the last of the moon of Chahban, 1718

Letter 119

Usbek to the same

The fertility of a nation can sometimes depend on the smallest change in circumstances, so that all that may be necessary is a new turn in the people's imagination in order to make the population dramatically increase.

The Jews, constantly exterminated and constantly rising again, have overcome their losses and their continual destruction by the single hope that exists in every one of their families—that from them might be born the powerful king who will rule over all the earth.

The ancient kings of Persia had so many thousands of subjects only because of that precept taught by the religion of the magi, that the acts that most please God are creating a child, cultivating a field, and planting a tree.

If China contains so many people today, it is the result of a certain way of thinking: children consider their fathers as gods, and respect them as such in this life, honoring them after their deaths with sacrifices, through which they believe that their souls, annihilated in the Tian,[153] will take on a new life; as a result, each is moved to want to augment his family, so submissive in this life and so necessary in the next.

On the other hand, the Muslim countries are becoming progressively less populous because of an idea that, holy as it might be, does not fail to have pernicious effects when it becomes rooted so deeply in our minds. We view ourselves as travelers who are always thinking of another country, and therefore it seems outlandish to us to create useful, lasting things, to be concerned for the future well-being of our children, or to

153. *Tian* is an ancient Chinese word for the cosmos, often identified with a condition or region like the Western idea of Heaven.

work at any project intended to last beyond this short, fleeting earthly life. Because our minds are untroubled about the present and unworried about the future, we don't take the trouble to repair public buildings, to clear uncultivated lands or to improve those that could benefit from our attention. We live in a state of general insensibility, leaving everything up to Providence.

In Europe, it was the spirit of vanity that led to the unjust law of primogeniture, so unfavorable to procreation because it focuses a father's entire attention on just one of his children, encouraging him to turn his back on the others; it obliges him to solidify the fortune to the one, and oppose helping the others; and finally, it eliminates the equality of citizens, which is the source of all prosperity.

From Paris, the 4th of the moon of Rhamazan, 1718

Letter 120

Usbek to the same

The countries inhabited by savages are usually very thinly populated, due to their aversion to work and agriculture. This unhappy aversion is so strong that, when they want to put a curse on one of their enemies, they can wish him nothing worse than to be reduced to working a field; they believe the only pursuits noble enough to be worthy of them are hunting and fishing.

But since there are often years when hunting and fishing are less productive, they are ravaged by frequent famines. Moreover, there are no countries so abundant in game and fish that they can provide sustenance for an entire population, because animals flee heavily populated areas.

The villages of savages, each with some two or three hundred inhabitants, are detached from each other, having as few interests in common as two great empires, and cannot be self-sustaining. For they lack the resources of large States, in which all the different parties are interdependent and offer mutual assistance.

And there is another custom among the savages, even more pernicious: this is the cruel habit of the women aborting their pregnancies because they do not want their bodies to be unattractive to their husbands.

Here, they have terrible laws against this kind of moral disorder, bordering on the fanatical. Every girl who fails to report her pregnancy to the magistrate is punished with death if her fetus dies. Modesty, shame, even an accident—none of these will excuse her.[154]

From Paris, the 9th of the moon of Rhamazan, 1718

Letter 121

Usbek to the same

The usual effect of colonies is to weaken the country that sets them up, without increasing the population of the colony.

People should stay where they are. When people exchange a good climate for a bad one, diseases creep in, and other diseases arise simply from making the change.

The air is like plants: it is charged with particles of the soil of each region. It works on us so as to fix our temperament. When we are transported to another country, we become sick. Our bodily fluids are accustomed to a certain consistency, and our solids to a certain disposition, and both to a certain degree of movement, and they are unable to tolerate new ones, resisting every change.[155]

When a country is unpopulated, we may assume that there is some unwholesomeness in the nature of the terrain or in the climate, and therefore, when men are uprooted from a happy environment and sent to such a place, the consequence will be just the opposite of what was planned.

The Romans knew this from experience: they sent all their criminals to Sardinia, and Jews as well. They needed to find consolation for losing such people, and it was easily found in the contempt they had for the wretches.

The great Shah Abbas, desiring to deprive the Turks of the resources for keeping large armies on the borders, transported nearly all of the Armenians from their country, sending some twenty thousand families

154. A French law stating that every pregnancy had to be reported was decreed in 1556, and it had been reiterated as recently as 1708.

155. This paragraph was added in 1754.

to the province of Gilan,[156] where they all perished in a short period of time.

All the attempts to import people to repopulate Constantinople have been failures.

The huge numbers of blacks, as we have noted, did nothing at all to increase the population of America.

Since the destruction of the Jews under Hadrian, Palestine is uninhabited.[157]

We must conclude that the large-scale destructions of populations are irreparable, because once a people are brought to such a low point, they stay there; if they are to recover, it will take centuries.

But if at such a low point even the slightest of the circumstances I have described were to come into play, not only would there be no recovery, but the low point would actually worsen to the point of annihilation.

The results of the expulsion of the Moors from Spain are just as evident today as they were at the beginning; far from filling in the void they left, that void only grows larger every day.[158]

Since the devastation of America, the Spanish, who have taken the place of the previous inhabitants, have not been able to repopulate the country. On the contrary, by some strange fate that I think would be better called divine justice, the destroyers are destroying themselves, and are being wiped out further every day.

Princes should not, therefore, dream any longer of populating great countries by means of colonies. I know that they have occasionally succeeded, for there are some climates so beneficial that the species always multiplies there—witness those islands[159] that were settled by sick people abandoned there by ships, where the abandoned ones soon regained their health.

But when such colonies flourish, far from increasing the prince's power, they only divide it, unless they are very small, such as those where some troops are sent to occupy a place for reasons of commerce.

The Carthaginians had discovered America, like the Spaniards, or at least some of the larger islands, with which they did a great deal of

---

156. Gilan is today a province of Iran, on the coast of the Caspian Sea.

157. The Roman emperor Hadrian put down a Jewish revolt in the year 135, and forced all Jews out of Jerusalem.

158. King Philip III of Spain expelled the Moors in 1610.

159. *The author is perhaps referring to the Isle of Bourbon* [Montesquieu's note]. We know the island today as Réunion; Montesquieu had read a story to this effect in Étienne de Flacourt's 1658 history of Madagascar.

commerce; but when they saw the number of their inhabitants diminishing, the wise republic forbade its citizens to trade or even sail there.

I would go so far as to say that, instead of sending Spaniards to the Indies, they really ought to be gathering up Indians and half-breeds and sending them back to Spain; the monarchy ought to bring all its dispersed people together, and if Spain were to keep only half of its great colonies, it would become the most formidable power in Europe.

An empire can be compared to a tree. When the branches grow too long, they take all the sap out of the trunk, and the tree is good only for shade.

There is no better cure for a prince's mania for conquering distant lands than the examples of the Portuguese and the Spanish.

These two nations, having made incredibly rapid conquests of immense kingdoms, and as a result more surprised at their victories than the vanquished were at their defeat, looked for methods to maintain their gains. Each chose a different path.

The Spanish, despairing of the conquered nations' remaining loyal, decided to exterminate them and repopulate the kingdoms with loyal Spaniards; and never has a more horrible plan been more efficiently carried out. A nation, whose people were as numerous as the entire population of Europe, have disappeared from the face of the earth upon the arrival of these barbarians who seemed, in discovering the Indies, to want nothing more than to reveal to all humankind the heights of cruelty.

Through this barbarism, they retained their domination over the country. You may judge from this how deadly conquest is, given the deadliness of its effects. For after all, this solution was the only one available to them. How could they have hoped to maintain the obedience of millions of people? How could they have sustained a civil war so far away? What would have happened if they had allowed enough time for this people to overcome their amazement at these newly arrived gods, and their fear at their gunpowder?

As for the Portuguese, they took the opposite approach, and employed no cruelty. As a result, they were chased out of every land they discovered. The Dutch fomented rebellion among the natives, and they profited from it.

What prince would envy the results of these conquests? Who would want conquests under these conditions? The ones were soon chased away, and the others laid the new lands waste, turning their own country into a desert as well.

It is the fate of heroes to ruin themselves in conquering countries that they soon go on to lose, or in subjugating nations that they are then obliged to destroy—like that madman who was obsessed with buying statues that he then hurled into the sea, and mirrors that he soon broke.[160]

From Paris, the 18th of the moon of Rhamazan, 1718

Letter 122

Usbek to the same

A mild government contributes marvelously to the propagation of the species. Republics demonstrate the truth of this every day, and Switzerland and Holland more than most, though they are the two worst countries in Europe if you judge them by their terrain—and yet they are the two most populous.

Nothing attracts foreigners more than liberty, and the affluence that always follows it. The former is something people seek out for its own sake, and our needs draw us to those countries where we may find the latter.

The species multiplies under conditions where there is an abundance that provides for children without diminishing the livelihood of the parents.

The very equality among citizens, which usually produces an equality in their fortunes, carries with it abundance and life, nourishing all parts of the body politic and spreading throughout.

It is not the same in those countries living under an arbitrary power. There, the prince, the courtesans, and a few individuals own all the wealth, while everyone else is left to groan under extreme poverty.

If a man is ill at ease, and believes that his children will be even poorer than he is, he will not marry; or, if he does marry, he will fear having too many children, which could end up ruining him financially, and seeing them go on to live at a level even worse than their father's.

True, the rustic or peasant once married reproduces indifferently, whether he is rich or poor; these considerations do not touch him. He always has his heritage to hand down to his children—his tools for working the land—and so nothing prevents him from following the blind instincts of nature.

---

160. Scholars have been unable to trace this story about the madman.

But in a State, what good is a large number of children languishing in poverty? They never prosper, and die off in nearly the same numbers as they are born; weak and debilitated, they perish individually in a thousand different ways, or else they are dispatched in great numbers by the frequent epidemics that misery and poor diet are constantly producing. The ones who escape reach adulthood weak, and they remain unhealthy the rest of their lives.

Men are like plants, never growing and flourishing unless they are well cultivated. Among the poor, the species suffers and perhaps in some cases degenerates.

France furnishes a powerful example of all this. In the recent wars, all the young men of families feared being made to enlist in the militia, and this caused them to marry,[161] which they did, at too tender an age and without sufficient income. From such marriages issued many children that are nowhere to be seen today, for poverty, hunger, and disease have carried them off.

If such things can be said of so healthy a climate, and of a country as civilized as France, what could be said of other states?

From Paris, the 23rd of the moon of Rhamazan, 1718

Letter 123

Usbek to the mullah, Mehemet Ali,
Guardian of the three tombs at Qum

What good are the fasts of the imams and the hair shirts worn by the mullahs? The hand of God has smitten the children of the Law twice; the sun has darkened, and seems to light up only their defeats. Their armies assemble, but they are dispersed like so much dust.

The Ottoman Empire is staggered by the two greatest blows it has received.[162] A Christian mufti supports it only with difficulty. The Grand Vizier of Germany is the scourge of God, sent to chastise the

161. An ordinance forbade the militias from enrolling married men.

162. These two blows are the military defeats that led to the losses of the cities of Timisoara in 1716 and Belgrade in 1717, both in modern Romania.

sectaries of Omar.[163] He carries the wrath of heaven with him everywhere, as punishment for their rebellion and their perfidy.

Sacred spirit of the imams, you weep night and day over the children of the Prophet led astray by the detestable Omar; you are moved with sorrow at the sight of their misery; you yearn for their conversion, not their damnation; you want to see them all united under the banner of Ali through the tears of saints, not scattered in the mountains and the deserts, fleeing the infidels in terror.

From Paris, the 1st of the moon of Chalval, 1718

Letter 124

Usbek to Rhédi
At Venice

What can be the motive behind these immense gifts that princes shower upon their courtiers?[164] Are they trying to strengthen their attachment? But these men are already bought and paid for. And while they may attract a few by buying them, they lose countless others by impoverishing them.

When I consider the situation princes are in, always surrounded by greedy, insatiable men, I can only feel sorry for them, and all the more when I see that they do not have the strength to resist the requests—which always end up being onerous to those others who request nothing.

I can never hear of these generosities, these gifts and pensions that they hand out, without having a thousand reflections come up and crowd themselves into my mind. I feel as if I am hearing the following ordinance being proclaimed:

163. The "Christian mufti" is Cardinal Alberoni of Spain, who encouraged the Turks in their struggles with the Empire, including the armies of Eugene, Duke of Savoy (the "Grand Vizier"). Omar and Abu Bekr are the founders of the Sunni form of Islam; Usbek, a follower of Shia, pointedly uses the word "sectaries" to refer to the Sunnis.

164. This letter was added to the second edition of 1721, where it was numbered 60, and dated 1715. It would be natural to assume, given that date, that the letter was a criticism of the (almost legendary) munificence of Louis XIV. Placing it here makes its satire more general, relating to monarchs as a class.

"The indefatigable courage of some of our subjects in petitioning us for pensions having unceasingly exercised our royal munificence, we have finally ceded to the multitude of requests which they have presented to us, and which have always been the principal concern of the crown. They have pointed out that they have never once failed to attend our *levée* since our accession to the throne; that we have always found them standing in our hallways as immovable as posts; and that by dint of climbing up on the highest shoulders available, they have achieved the sight of our Royal Serenity. We have even received a number of requests from members of the fair sex, begging us to remember that they are notoriously difficult to maintain; some of the superannuated ones have begged us, their heads shaking with age, to note that they were the very ornaments of the court of our predecessors; and finally, if the military generals have rendered the State fearsome by means of their great warlike feats, these women have rendered the court no less celebrated by means of their intrigues. Therefore, desiring to treat the supplicants with generosity and to answer all their prayers, we proclaim the following decree:

"That every working man who has five children withhold every day one fifth of their bread. We command the heads of households to make the reduction of each child's portion as precisely as possible.

"We expressly forbid all those who are engaged in trying to improve the estates they have inherited, or who are renting their lands out for farming, to do any repairs of any kind whatsoever.

"We decree that all people who work in the low and mechanical trades and who have never attended a *levée* of our majesty shall buy clothing for themselves, their wives, and their children not more than once every four years; moreover, we most strictly forbid them from having those little celebrations that they are used to having in their homes on the major holidays.

"And since we are informed that the good citizens of our towns are entirely occupied with providing for the establishment of their daughters, who have distinguished themselves in the eyes of the State only by their pathetic, irritating modesty, we hereby command that they wait to marry them off until, having reached the maximum age for marriage established by law, they come to them to demand it. We forbid our magistrates to provide for the education of their children."

From Paris, the 1st of the moon of Chalval, 1718

Letter 125

Rica to * * *

With all religions, it is a touchy matter to specify what sorts of pleasures in the afterlife await those who have lived a good life on earth. Of course, it is easy enough to detail at great length the horrors that await the sinners, but for virtuous people it is not so clear what one ought to promise. It seems to be in the very nature of pleasures that they be of short duration, and the mind has great difficulty in imagining any other sort.

I have seen descriptions of paradise that would make any man of sense avoid going there. Some say the happy spirits in the afterlife engage in an endless bout of flute playing; others that it is an interminable walking about. Others depict them as endlessly dreaming about their mistresses down here, apparently thinking that a hundred million years is too short a time for us to lose our taste for these amorous adventures.

In this regard, I am reminded of a story I heard from a man who had spent time in the land of the Mogul. It goes to show that Indian priests are no less sterile than the others when it comes to the ideas they have of paradise.

A woman who had recently lost her husband paid a ceremonial visit to the governor of her town, asking permission to burn herself. But because this cruel custom had been abolished as fully as possible in lands ruled by Mohammedans, he refused her request absolutely.

When she saw that her entreaties were useless, she flew into a terrible rage. "Look," she exclaimed, "and see how frustrated we are! It isn't permitted for a poor wife to burn herself when she feels like doing so! Have you ever seen anything like it? My mother, my aunt, my sisters have all burned themselves perfectly well. But when I come to ask permission of this miserable governor, he says no and starts yelling at me like a madman!"

By chance, a young bonze was standing nearby.[165] The governor asked him, "You, infidel! Are you the one who has put this idea in this woman's head?" "No," he replied; "I have never spoken to her. But if she were to ask me, I would tell her to make the sacrifice. She would be performing an action agreeable to the god Brahma, and she would be well compensated for it: in the next life, she would find her husband waiting,

165. A *bonze* is a Buddhist priest. Montesquieu evidently confuses the term with Brahmin, a Hindu priest.

and the two of them would begin a second life together." The woman, surprised at this, spoke up: "What are you saying? I will find my husband again? Oh, in that case, I won't burn myself. He was jealous, bad-tempered, and so old that, unless the god Brahma were to perform some kind of miracle on him, he surely would have no use for me. Me burn myself for him! I wouldn't burn the tip of my finger, even if it would bring him back from the pit of Hell. Two old bonzes talked me into this, and knowing perfectly well what our life together had been like, they carefully omitted telling me all this. And if the god Brahma doesn't have anything better than this to offer me, I am happy to renounce that particular bliss. Honored sir, I will convert to Islam. And as for you," she said, turning to the bonze, "you can go, if you like, and tell my husband that I am doing just fine without him."

From Paris, the 2nd of the moon of Chalval, 1718

Letter 126

Rica to Usbek
At * * *

I await your arrival here tomorrow, but I am nonetheless sending you now these letters of yours from Ispahan. My own letters tell me that the ambassador of the Great Mogul has been ordered into exile. They add that the prince, the king's uncle who was in charge of his education, has been arrested, and that they have imprisoned him in a castle under heavy guard and stripped him of all his honors.[166] I am moved by the afflictions of this prince, and I feel sorry for him.

166. This is a lightly disguised reference to a major event in France in 1718, known as the Cellamare conspiracy. It involved the Prince of Cellamare, Antonio del Giudice, who was the Spanish ambassador to France, and a number of others who conspired to unseat Philippe, Duc d'Orléans, as Regent. The Duc de Maine, uncle and tutor to the young Louis XV, was involved, captured, and imprisoned, along with a number of others. The affair contributed to increasing tensions between France and Spain, and France declared war in 1719. All were given a general pardon, however, in 1720.

I admit, Usbek, that I have never been able to see another person weep without being moved myself. My own humanity is touched by these unfortunates—and indeed, it is as if their very misfortune is what makes them human. Even the great and powerful ones, whom I detest when they are at their heights: I feel compassion for them as soon as they are fallen.

But then, what good would such affection do them when they are in their prosperity? It would feel too much as if we were on an equal footing. They would much rather have our respect, which does not have to be repaid. But once they are stripped of their grandeur, they have only our tears to remind them of their lost happiness.

I find something naïve and also something grand in the words of a prince who, having fallen into the hands of his enemies and seeing his courtiers weeping for him, said to them: "I can tell by your tears that I am still your king."[167]

From Paris, the 3rd of the moon of Chalval, 1718

Letter 127

Rica to Ibben
At Smyrna

You have heard a great deal about the famous king of Sweden. He was laying siege to a town in a kingdom they call Norway. When he visited the trenches, alone with an engineer, he was shot in the head and killed. His Prime Minister was immediately arrested, the councils met, and he was condemned to death.[168]

He was accused of a grievous crime: slandering the nation and making the people lose confidence in their king. In my view, a crime like this deserves a thousand deaths.

For, after all, if it is a wicked thing to blacken the character of the least of his subjects in the mind of the prince, how much worse it is to

167. The words are attributed to the ancient Persian monarch Darius III, when he had been defeated by Alexander the Great in 330 BC.

168. Charles XII of Sweden was killed during the siege of Frederikshald in 1718, and his Prime Minister, Baron von Görtz, was executed the following year.

blacken the character of the entire nation, so that it loses the good will of the man whom Providence has chosen to rule over it!

I would like it if men were to speak to kings the way the angels do to our holy Prophet.

You know how, at those sacred banquets where the King of Kings descends from his most sublime throne in order to speak with us, his slaves, I make it a strict rule for myself to keep my restless tongue under control. No one has ever heard me utter so much as a single word that could be at all hurtful to the least of his subjects. And while I have sometimes had to abandon discretion, I never ceased to be a decent and upstanding man; in that trial of one's faithfulness, I may have risked my life, but never my virtue.

I do not know why it is, but there has never been a prince so evil that his chief minister was not even worse; whatever wicked action he performs, it has almost always been suggested to him: and so it is that a prince's ambition is always less dangerous than the base souls of his counselors. But how can it be that a man who was only yesterday placed in a ministry, and who may be turned out of it tomorrow, manage to turn so quickly into the enemy not only of himself but of his family, his country, and the people—and even of those yet unborn, the descendants of those he is intent upon oppressing?

A prince has his passions, and the minister stirs them up; this is how he conducts his ministry. He has no other goal, nor even any interest in any other one. The courtiers seduce the prince by means of flattery, but the minister's flattery is his counsel, the schemes he inspires, and by the principles he teaches—a far more dangerous seduction.

From Paris, the 25th of the moon of Saphar, 1719

Letter 128

Rica to Usbek
*At * * **

The other day, I was crossing the Pont Neuf with one of my friends, when he encountered an acquaintance of his. He told me the man was a geometrician, and he certainly looked the part, for he was deeply lost in thought, so much so that my friend had to grab hold of his sleeve and shake his arm in order to get him to notice us.[169] He had been utterly preoccupied with determining the properties of a curve that had been frustrating him for a week now. They exchanged a great many pleasantries, as well as some literary news. Their conversation continued until they reached the door of a café, which I entered with them.

I noticed that our geometrician was warmly greeted by everyone, and that the waiters paid much more attention to him than to the two musketeers seated in a corner. And as for him, he clearly found the place to his liking, for his face lit up and he even smiled, as if there was nothing of the geometrician about him.

Nonetheless, his highly precise mind was continually weighing and evaluating everything that was said in the conversation. He was like someone who walks through a garden, wielding his sword so as to cut off the head of every flower that rose up above the others. A martyr to his own precision, anything odd or irregular bothered him, the way someone with delicate eyesight is pained by too much light. Nothing was indifferent to him, provided that it was true. And thus his conversation was quite peculiar. That day, he had come back to town from the country with a man who had been to see a superb chateau with magnificent gardens, but he himself had seen only a building that was sixty feet long and thirty-five wide, and a ten-acre grove of trees in the shape of an irregular rectangle. He would have preferred to find the rules of perspective more carefully observed, so that the walkways in the grove would appear to be all the same width, and he could have provided an infallible method for achieving this. He was quite pleased with a sundial of unusual construction he had seen there, but he got very annoyed with a gentleman sitting next to me, who asked if the sundial used the Babylonian system of hours.[170] Another person, one of those obsessed with the news of the day, brought up the bombardment of Fontarabia,[171] and he instantly provided us with a description of the arcs that the bombs followed in the air; delighted with that knowledge alone, he had no interest

169. The geometrician here prefigures the mathematicians of Laputa in Swift's *Gulliver's Travels* (1726), who are so absorbed in mathematical reverie that their servants must slap them with a bladder to get them to notice someone trying to speak to them.

170. The "Babylonian system" refers to a sundial that measured the hours by available daylight; since this is variable and less precise, the very idea irritates the geometrician.

171. Fontarabia in Spain (today, Hondarribia or Fuenterrabia) was besieged and taken for France by the Duke of Berwick in 1719.

in knowing what the outcome of the bombardment was. Another man was lamenting that he had been ruined by a flood the previous winter, to which the geometrician replied, "I am very pleased to hear it, for it means that my calculations were correct, and that last year saw at least two more inches of rain than normal."

A moment later he left, and we followed. Since he walked very rapidly and failed to look where he was going, he ran directly into another man; they collided roughly, and each one recoiled in direct proportion to his velocity and mass. When they had both recovered somewhat from the shock, the other man, holding his forehead, said to the geometrician, "I am happy that you have run into me like this, because I have good news to tell you: I have just published my Horace." "What!" said the geometrician. "He has been available for two thousand years already." The other said, "No, you misunderstand me. What I have just published is a translation of that ancient author. I have been working on translations now for twenty years."

The geometrician exclaimed, "But sir, are you telling me that for twenty years now you have not thought for yourself? You speak for others, and they think for you?" The learned man replied, "Monsieur, you must see that I have done a great public service in making the works of great authors available for readers!" He said, "That is not exactly what I mean. I cherish, as much as the next man, those geniuses whose work you misrepresent. But you do not resemble them in the slightest, for no matter how long or how much you translate, no one will ever translate you!

"Translations are like copper coins that are technically worth the same as gold ones, and may be even more widely used than the gold; but they are always inferior, and never have the same weight.

"You say that you want to give a new birth to the illustrious dead, and I admit that you do give them a sort of body; but you do not give them real life; the soul that would animate them is always lacking.

"Wouldn't it be better if you devoted yourself to seeking out some of those splendid truths that mathematics is constantly revealing to us?"

After this little piece of counsel, the two men parted, and not, I suspect, on the best of terms with each other.

From Paris, the last of the moon of Rebiab II, 1719

Letter 129

Usbek to Rhédi
At Venice

Most lawmakers have been men of limited abilities, thrust into positions of leadership by mere chance, who have rarely consulted anything other than their own prejudices and whims.

They seem to have failed to see the grandeur and dignity of their work. They have amused themselves in creating foolish regulations, the kind of thing that satisfies petty minds but only brings them into disrepute among men of sense.

They throw themselves into pointless details, particular cases—the hallmark of a narrow mind, which only sees things in their parts and cannot take a more general view.

Sometimes they have affected a language of their own, an absurdity for a lawmaker: how can people observe the law if they cannot understand it?

Often, they have abolished existing laws when it was not necessary to do so—which is to say, they have thrown their nations into the confusion that always accompanies such changes.

It is true that, through some quirk of human nature and not through the workings of the human mind, it is sometimes necessary to change certain laws. But this is rare, and when the need does arise, the hand that makes the change should tremble: there should be an air of solemnity and a host of precautions, so that the people naturally conclude that there is a certain sanctity to the laws, since abrogating them requires so many formalities.

Often the lawmakers have written overly subtle laws, basing them on logic rather than on natural equity. The end result is that such laws are considered overly harsh, and people have wanted to have them set aside for the sake of fairness; but this remedy introduces a new problem. Whatever the laws are, they must always be followed as if they were a kind of public conscience to which individuals always ought to conform.

But one must admit that certain laws show a great deal of wisdom, such as those that grant fathers great authority over their children. Nothing is better at relieving the magistrates and courts, and nothing contributes more to the tranquility of a state, for customs are always more effective than laws in producing good citizens.

Of all the types of power, this is the one that is the least abused; it is the most sacred of magistracies; it is the only one that is born out of no conventions, but rather precedes all of them.

It has been observed that in lands where a greater degree of reward and punishment is given to fathers, families are better regulated. Fathers are the image of the Creator of the universe who, while he is capable of leading men solely by his love, does not hesitate to make use of both hope and fear.

I cannot conclude this letter without noting a bizarre aspect of French thinking. It is said that they have retained an infinite number of Roman laws that are useless or worse, but they have failed to institute paternal power, which the Romans considered the first legitimate authority.

From Paris, the 4th of the moon of Gemmadi II, 1719

Letter 130

Rica to * * *

In this letter, I shall introduce you to a certain species here that they call the *nouvellistes,* who gather in a magnificent garden where they combine their indolence with busyness.[172] They are quite useless to the state, and all their talk of the last fifty years now has had exactly the same effect as fifty years of silence would have had. But they see themselves as terribly important, always talking about great projects and major issues of policy.

The basis of all their conversations is a frivolous, foolish curiosity; there is no ministerial cabinet so secret that they do not believe they have managed to penetrate it. They cannot believe that there is anything they do not know: they know how many wives our august sultan has, how many children he sires each year, and, though they have no espionage

172. There is no good English equivalent for the word *nouvelliste*; some translations have used the word "newsmonger," but as this letter makes clear, that term is not adequate for these people who, in an era of increasingly rapid communication, had become obsessed with the latest news. These *nouvellistes,* though satirized here, did in fact play a significant role in the informal communication network of eighteenth-century France, and in the development of public opinion. They gathered in, among other places, the large public gardens outside the Luxembourg and Tuileries palaces. The *nouvellistes* are discussed in some detail in Robert Darnton's *The Devil in the Holy Water* (Philadelphia: U of Pennsylvania Press, 2010).

resources, they are fully informed as to all the methods he uses to humble the Turkish and Mogul emperors.

As soon as they have exhausted the present, they turn their attention to the future and rush ahead of Providence, returning to inform it of all men's doings. They take up a particular general and after having praised him for a thousand absurd things that he never did, they prepare a thousand others for him—which he will not do either.

They make armies fly through the air like cranes, and city walls fall like cards. They have bridges crossing every river, secret routes through every mountain range, and vast arsenals hidden in burning deserts. All they lack is good sense.

A man who lodges with me received this letter from a *nouvelliste*; it seemed quite an unusual thing, so I kept it. Here is what it said:

Monsieur,

I rarely make mistakes when it comes to current affairs. On the first of January, 1711, I predicted that the Emperor Joseph would die in the course of that year. Now, since he was in excellent health, I thought people would laugh at me if I made my prediction too obvious, and so I used rather enigmatic terms—but people in the know could tell what I meant. On the 17th day of April of that year, he died of smallpox.

When war was declared between the emperor and the Turks,[173] I sought out our people in the various nooks and crannies of the Tuileries; I assembled them next to the fountain, and I predicted the siege of Belgrade to them, as well as its fall. I was fortunate in having my prediction come about. True, around the middle of the siege I bet one hundred *pistoles* that the city would fall on the 18th of August,[174] and in fact it held out until the following day; but could any losing bet be closer to winning?

When I heard that the Spanish fleet was sailing for Sardinia, I knew that they would be victorious: I said so at the time, and I was proven right. Puffed up with my success, I added that this victorious fleet would embark for Finale, in order to conquer the Milanese. When my prediction met with some scoffing, I determined to do something splendid to support it: I bet fifty *pistoles* on it, and I lost again, because that devil Alberoni,[175] ignoring the treaty, sent his fleet to Sicily and at once fooled two great statesmen, the Duke of Savoy and myself.

---

173. This is the war of 1716–1718, discussed in Letter 123, which ended in disaster for the Turks.

174. *1717* [Montesquieu's note].

175. For Alberoni, see the notes to Letter 123.

All this, monsieur, has nonplussed me so that I have sworn to carry on predicting, but never again to wager. In earlier days, we gentlemen of the Tuileries were innocent of wagering, and indeed the late Count L***[176] would not have allowed it. But now, ever since a set of young upstarts has taken to joining us, we hardly know where we are anymore. The minute one of us opens his mouth to pass on a bit of news, one of these young men leaps up to offer a wager against it.

The other day, as I was unfolding my sheet of notes and adjusting my spectacles, one of these young loudmouths waited for my first pause for breath, and exclaimed, "I'll bet a hundred *pistoles* against it!" I pretended not to hear this outrage, and I went on, in a louder voice, saying "The *maréchal* of ***, having learned . . ." "It's false," he interrupted; "you always hand out the most absurd bits of news; there's no sense at all in it." Well, I beg you, monsieur, to do me the honor of lending me thirty *pistoles*, for, I must admit, all this betting has me in a bit of trouble. I enclose copies of two letters I wrote to the minister. I remain yours, etc.

Letters from a *nouvelliste* to a minister

My Lord,

I am the most zealous subject the king has ever had. I am the one responsible for having one of my friends carry out a plan I came up with, for writing a book that proves that Louis the Great is the greatest of all monarchs who have been called great. I have been working for some time now on another project, one which will do even more honor to our nation, if your Excellency would grant me the privilege.[177] My plan is to prove that, since the beginnings of the monarchy, the French have never been defeated, and anything that historians have said to the contrary is nothing but falsehood. I am quite often obliged to correct the historians, and I must flatter myself a bit in saying that I am a superb critic. I remain yours, etc.

My Lord,

Due to our sad loss of the Count L***, we entreat you now to have the goodness to allow us to elect a new president. Our assemblies are increasingly marked by disorder, and affairs of state are not receiving the same serious attention that they used to. The young men among us are quite without discipline and have no respect for their elders; it is a veritable council of

176. The comte Joachim de Lionne, who died in 1716, was a habitué of the Tuileries garden and something of a patron to the *nouvellistes*; he had a considerable network of his own for gathering news.

177. A *privilege* in this context means the permission to print a book.

Rehoboam, with youth dominating over age.[178] It does us no good to remind them that we were frequenting the Tuileries for twenty years before they were born; I fear that they will drive us all out in the end. And if we are obliged to depart this place, where we have so many times done honor to the spirits of the great French heroes of the past, we will be forced to take our assembly to the King's Garden[179] or some even more remote place. I am, yours, etc.

From Paris, the 7th of the moon of Gemmadi II, 1719

Letter 131

Rhédi to Rica
At Paris

One of the subjects that has intrigued me most since coming to Europe is the history and origin of republics. As you know, most Asians have no idea that this kind of government exists; indeed, their imaginations have not been strong enough for them to have thought that there could be any kind of government besides despotism.[180]

The earliest governments we know of were monarchies; it was only by chance, and through the long succession of centuries, that republics came to be formed.

After Greece had been devastated by floods, new inhabitants came to re-people the land. Most came from Egypt and from the neighboring Asian countries, and since those places were ruled by kings, the new arrivals used the same government. But the tyranny of kings grew too heavy, and the yoke was thrown off, so that out of the debris of all those kingdoms arose the republics which were to flourish in Greece, the sole civilized land in the midst of barbarians.

The love of liberty and the hatred of kings kept Greece independent for a long time, spreading republican government far and wide. The

---

178. In I Kings 12:8, Solomon's son and heir, Rehoboam, forsakes the advice of the elders in favor of the young.

179. Today, the King's Garden is the botanical garden on the Left Bank, known as the *Jardin des plantes*.

180. It was common to associate Eastern and Middle-Eastern governments with despotism. See the Introduction for further discussion of the idea, one central to much political thought in the European eighteenth century.

Greek cities found allies in Asia Minor, and set up colonies there as free as themselves, using them as ramparts against the schemes of the Persian kings. And that is not all: the Greeks populated Italy, Spain, and perhaps even Gaul. We know that the great Hesperia, so famous among the ancients and regarded as the land of happiness, was Greece at first.[181] The Greeks sought this blessed land, and failing to find it at home, they went to look in Italy; those in Italy later went to Spain, and those in Spain to Bétique[182] or Portugal, and thus all these different regions took on the name of Hesperia among the ancients. These Greek colonies retained the spirit of liberty from their beautiful country of origin, and thus there was rarely a monarchy to be seen in Italy, Spain, or Gaul in those distant days. As you will see in a moment, the people of the north and of Germany were no less free, and if we do find traces of royalty in their early histories, it is because the chiefs of armies or republics were later mistaken for kings.

All this was the case in Europe, but Asia and Africa were always overrun by despotism, except in those few cities we mentioned in Asia Minor, and the republic of Carthage in Africa.

The world was divided between two powerful republics, Rome and Carthage; nothing is better known than the story of the beginnings of the Roman republic, and nothing is less known than the origin of Carthage. We know nothing of the succession of Carthaginian princes after Dido, or how they came to lose their power. The tremendous growth of the Roman Empire would have been a great gift to the world if it had not been for the injustice of their drawing so sharp a distinction between the Roman citizen and the vanquished peoples, and if they had given their provincial governors less sweeping powers, and if those sacred laws that were erected to fend off tyranny had been observed, and finally, if the government had not stifled those laws by using the very treasure they had amassed by their injustice.

Caesar suppressed the Roman republic, forcing it to submit to arbitrary power.

Europe long groaned under violent, military governments, and Roman mildness was changed into cruel oppression.

---

181. In ancient mythology, the Hesperides (daughters of Hesperus, the evening star) were nymphs who lived in a blessed garden far to the west; later, the term was applied to the garden as well.

182. Bétique, or Betica, was a region in south central Spain. Montesquieu uses the location again in Letter 142.

But then numberless unknown tribes poured out of the north like a torrent flooding into Roman provinces; and finding that it was just as easy to make actual conquests as it was to carry out raids, they dismembered the empire, founding their own kingdoms. These were free peoples, and so they limited their kings' authority, so that their kings were, properly speaking, closer to what we would call chiefs or generals. Thus these kingdoms, though established by force, did not feel the weight of a conqueror's yoke. When the peoples of Asia, such as the Turks and the Tartars, made conquests, since they were controlled by a single sovereign, they thought only of adding to his subjects and establishing his authority by violence. But the people of the north, having been free in their own countries, restricted their chiefs' authority when they spread into the Roman provinces. Some of these peoples, such as the Vandals in Africa and the Goths in Spain, deposed their kings when they were not satisfied with them, and among others, the prince's authority was limited in a thousand different ways. A great number of nobles shared in the authority, and wars could not be declared without their consent; spoils were divided between the chief and his soldiers, with no additional tax for the prince; and laws were made by a national assembly. These were the fundamental principles of all those states that were formed out of the debris of the Roman Empire.

From Venice, the 20th of the moon of Rhegeb, 1719

Letter 132

Rica to * * *

Some five or six months ago, I went into a coffee house and noticed that everyone was listening to a well-dressed man speaking. He was saying how enjoyable life in Paris was, and he deplored his own situation, which required him to live in the provinces. He said, "My lands are worth fifteen thousand *livres* in rents, and I would rather have only a quarter of that, if I could get it in cash and transferable letters of credit. It's no good putting more pressure on my farmers, because that would only load them with the added expense of lawsuits; and doing that only makes them less able to pay me. I have never been able to put my hands on a hundred *pistoles* at a time. If I owed someone ten thousand francs, my lands would be confiscated and I would be thrown into the poorhouse."

I left without having paid much attention to all this, but yesterday, finding myself in the same neighborhood, I went into the same place, and this time I saw a very serious looking man with a pale, long face; he seemed sad and thoughtful as he sat there among some five or six chattering men, and abruptly he interrupted them in a loud voice: "Yes, gentlemen, I am ruined. I no longer have enough to live on. For at the moment I have two hundred thousand *livres* in bank notes, and a hundred thousand in silver *écus*: I am in terrible straits. I thought I was wealthy, and here I am, ready for the poorhouse. If I at least owned some small piece of land that I could retire to, I would be sure of being able to make a living—but the land I own would fit in this hat."[183]

I happened to turn my gaze in another direction and saw a man grimacing like someone possessed. "After something like this, who will I ever be able to trust?" he cried. "A no-good traitor I thought was my friend—I lent the man some money, and he paid it back! What a vicious betrayal! From now on, I don't care what he does: he'll never have my respect again."[184]

And close by him was a poorly dressed man who raised his eyes to the heavens and said, "May God bless the projects of our ministers! May we see the shares rise up to two thousand, and all the lackeys in Paris richer than their masters!"[185] I was curious enough to ask who the man was. They told me, "He is a very impoverished man, with a similarly impoverished kind of career: he is a genealogist, and he believes that if things keep going the way they are, his trade will make him rich, for all the newly wealthy people will have need of him in order to polish up their ancestry and create coats of arms for their coaches. He believes that he will be creating an endless supply of new nobility, and he is positively

---

183. The two speakers reflect different aspects of the economic chaos that the policies of John Law helped create. The first speaker refers to the dramatic fall in land values, and the second laments the drop in currency value. Montesquieu's letter is dated 1719, but the currency problems did not begin to develop until 1720. See the Introduction for more background on Law and his financial system.

184. The point here is that the new banknotes Law introduced are actually worth less than the ones the speaker originally lent.

185. The reference is to shares in Law's Mississippi stock venture, which, for a time, did seem to produce huge returns, making ordinary small investors dream of sudden wealth—until the bubble burst in 1720.

shaking with joy as he imagines the clients who will be lining up to see him."

Finally I saw an old, pale, dried-up sort of man come in; I recognized him as one of the *nouvellistes* even before he sat down. He was not one of those who are always convinced that things will turn out well, who are always predicting victories and trophies. No, this was the opposite type, one of the tremblers who never have anything but bad news to relate. He said, "Things are going badly with regard to the war in Spain; we have no cavalry on the frontier, and it looks as if Prince Pio—who has a very large cavalry—will force all of Languedoc to pay tribute."[186] Sitting across from me was a poorly dressed thinker who looked at the *nouvelliste* with an expression of pity, and the louder the one held forth, the more the other shook his head. I went over to him, and he whispered to me: "Look at that fool, haranguing us for an hour now with his fears for Languedoc, whereas I just yesterday discovered a sunspot that, if it continues to grow, will bring an end to all life on earth—and you don't hear me saying a thing."

From Paris, the 17th of the moon of Rhamazan, 1719

Letter 133

*Rica to * * **

The other day, I visited a large library in a convent of dervishes, who are officially in charge of it but who are required to open it to the public at certain hours.[187]

Upon entering, I encountered a solemn-looking man walking among the innumerable books. I went up to him and begged him to tell me what was in some of these books, particularly the ones that seemed to be the most treasured. He said, "Monsieur, I am like a stranger in a

---

186. Prince Pio di Savoia-y-Corte Real was the leader of the Spanish forces, and did indeed threaten Languedoc in 1719, though this came to naught when the war was negotiated to a close in 1720.

187. This sequence of five letters satirizing modern learning takes place in what scholars believe to be the library of the Abbey of St. Victor in Paris, which had been opened to the public in 1707. The Abbey dated back to the early twelfth century, but was destroyed during the Revolution.

foreign country here; I do not know anyone. Many people come up to me and ask questions similar to yours, but as you must understand, I am not about to read all these books just to be able to answer them. My librarian can tell you what you want to know, for he busies himself day and night deciphering what you see all around us. The man is good for nothing as well as being a real burden on us, because he does not work for the abbey. But wait—I hear the bell sounding for mealtime. Those who, like myself, are the heads of religious communities ought always to be the first at all our daily events." And with that, the monk pushed me out the door and closed it; he disappeared so quickly that I wondered if he had wings.

From Paris, the 21st of the moon of Rhamazan, 1719

Letter 134

Rica to the same

The next day I came back to that same library, and this time I encountered a very different sort of man. His air was unpretentious, his appearance intelligent, and his manner quite friendly. As soon as I expressed my curiosity, he set himself not only to satisfying it but, even more, seeing that I was a foreigner, he wished to instruct me.

"Father," I said to him, "what are these large volumes occupying this entire wall of the library?" He replied, "These are all interpretations of Holy Scripture." "What a great number of them!" I exclaimed. "Scripture must have been very obscure before, and it must be very clear by now. Are there any doubtful points remaining? Could any point possibly still be contested?"

"Oh," he replied, "only too many of them, only too many, good Lord! There are as many such points as there are lines."

"Really?" I asked. "But then what were all these authors doing?"

"These authors," he replied, "were all searching through Scripture not for what we should believe, but for what they already believed themselves. They never regarded it as a book containing dogmas that they should accept, but only as a work that could lend some authority to their own ideas. And in the furtherance of that end, they corrupted every meaning and tortured every passage. It is like a country upon which every sect descends for pillage; it is a battlefield upon which enemy nations meet for combat, attacking and skirmishing in every possible way.

"Now, nearby you will find ascetic, devotional books; then, books on morality, a great deal more useful; then theology, doubly unintelligible due to the material discussed and the manner of the discussion; then, the works of the mystics, that is, the devout with some passion in their hearts."

I interrupted: "Oh, wait, Father, don't go so fast. Tell me a little more about these mystics."

He replied, "Monsieur, devotion warms a heart that is disposed to passion, sending vapors up to the brain and heating it, and thence these ecstasies, these ravishments. This state is the delirium of devotion; often it becomes perfected, or rather corrupted, into quietism.[188] You understand that a quietist is simply a man who combines madness, devotion, and libertinism.

"Here are the casuists, who open the secrets of the night up to the light of day.[189] Their imagination gives shape to all the monsters that the demon of love can produce, and putting them together and comparing them in all different ways, they make such monsters the object of all their thoughts. They are fortunate if their hearts do not become complicit in such matters, and if they do not themselves slip into becoming accomplices to all the improper things they describe so nakedly and naively.

"You see, Monsieur, that I think for myself, and I say what I think. I am by nature naïve and unguarded, and even more so with you as a foreigner who wants to learn the truth about things. If I wanted to, I

188. Quietism was the term given to a highly controversial form of mystical devotion, holding that perfection could be achieved by completely abandoning the will and surrendering to the divine presence. Its most famous exponents were Madame Guyon (1648–1717) and her distinguished disciple, François Fénelon (1651–1715). The movement was condemned as heretical, and Montesquieu clearly mocks it here. The satirical point is that Quietism, with its emotionalism, leads to loose morality, though that was not at all true of Madame Guyon or Fénelon.

189. For an earlier attack on casuists, see Letter 57. Antoine Adam suggests that Montesquieu here refers to a book on matrimony from 1637 by a Spanish Jesuit named Sanchez, which, some said, improperly brought things that should remain private into the light. The complete, three-volume work was in fact first printed in 1605, and its subject matter made it somewhat scandalous.

could be speaking to you in awestruck language, saying nothing but things like, 'This is divine, that is respectable, this is marvelous.' And as a result one of two things would happen: either you would believe me, or I would become degraded in your eyes."

We stopped there, for some business came up that required the dervish, and we broke off our conversation in order to pick it up the following day.

From Paris, the 23rd of the moon of Rhamazan, 1719

Letter 135

Rica to the same

I returned at the designated time, and my man picked things up at exactly the point where we had left off. "Here," he said, "are the grammarians, the annotators, and the commentators." I said, "Father, surely all these men have not been able to dispense with good sense altogether?"

"Oh yes they have; there is not a hint of it anywhere, and their works are none the worse for the lack, which is very lucky for them."

I said, "True enough, and I know of quite a few philosophers who ought to have taken up this kind of writing."

"Here are the orators," he continued, "who have the power to persuade without reasons; and the geometers, who force a man to be persuaded against his will, convincing him through a kind of tyranny.

"Here are the metaphysical books, treating of grand subjects; the infinite comes up constantly. And here are the books of physics, which find nothing more worthy of marveling at in the vast economy of the universe than the workings of a simple machine made by an artisan.

"Here, books of medicine, monuments to the fragility of nature and the power of art. They make you tremble even when they treat of the slightest malady, so good are they at evoking the impending presence of death. But then they also make us feel perfectly secure when they discuss the powers of the various remedies, giving us the sense that we are practically immortal.

"Right next to them are the anatomy books, which contain not so much description of the parts of the human body as the barbarous names that have been given to them, and as a result the patient is not cured of his disease, nor the doctor of his ignorance.

"Here we have the alchemists, who inhabit sometimes the poorhouse and sometimes the madhouse, both of which suit them perfectly.[190]

"Here are books on the science of—or rather, on our ignorance about—the occult, such as those that contain material on black magic: detestable in most people's view, and pitiable in my own. The same applies to the books on judicial astrology."[191]

I interrupted with some heat: "What are you saying, Father? Books on judicial astrology? We use this very widely in Persia. It rules all the acts of our lives, and determines all our endeavors; astrologers act as our directors, and in fact they even influence matters of state."

"Well, if that is the case, you live under a yoke far heavier than that of reason. Yours is the strangest of all dominions. I feel sorry for a family, let alone a nation, that allows itself to be dominated by the planets."

I replied, "We use astrology the way you use algebra. Each nation has its own science that helps it shape its politics. All the astrologists put together have never made as big a mess in Persia as one of your algebra experts has made here.[192] And do you really believe that the fortuitous confluence of the stars is a less certain rule to live by than the fine ideas of your famous systematizer? If a vote were to be taken both in France and in Persia, astrology would come out with a decisive victory, and your economic calculators would be thoroughly humiliated; indeed, what bad decision could not be laid at their doors?"

Our conversation was interrupted, and we had to part.

From Paris, the 26th of the moon of Rhamazan, 1719

Letter 136

Rica to the same

In our next conversation, my scholarly acquaintance led me into a private room. "Here are the books on modern history," he said. "To begin with, see here the historians of the Church and the popes—books I read in order to edify myself, but which end up having the opposite effect.

190. Alchemists were satirized in Letter 45.

191. Judicial astrology involves making predictions based on the stars.

192. The reference is to John Law and his economic system.

"Over here are the ones written on the decadence of the powerful Roman Empire, which had been formed out of the debris of many monarchies, and whose fall gave rise to just as many new ones. An endless number of barbaric nations, as unknown as the lands they inhabited, all suddenly appeared and overwhelmed the Empire, ravaging it and cutting it up into pieces, founding from it all the kingdoms you see presently in Europe. Strictly speaking, these peoples were not actually barbarians because they were free, but they became so, submitting themselves to absolute power and thus abandoning that sweet liberty that accords so well with reason, humanity, and nature.

"Here are the histories of Germany, which is only a shadow of its former empire.[193] It is, I believe, the only power on earth that has not been weakened by internal divisions, the only one that grows stronger in proportion to its losses, and the only one whose victories have given it little profit but whose defeats have made it unconquerable.

"Here we have the histories of France, in which we read how the power of the kings grew, died out twice, was reborn twice, then languished for several centuries, and then quietly gathered its strength from various quarters and rose up into its peak period—just like those rivers that peter out here and there along their courses, or sometimes dip down underground for a space, but then reappear, enlarged now by other rivers flowing into them, sweeping away everything that stands in their way.

"Over here, you can see the Spanish nation springing out from the mountains, its Muslim princes slowly becoming subjugated, just the opposite of the rapidity with which they had made their conquests. A single monarchy emerged out of the union of many smaller kingdoms, but eventually its own grandeur and empty opulence overwhelmed it, and it lost both power and reputation, retaining nothing but its pride, based on its earlier strength.

"And here are the histories of England, where we see liberty constantly emerging even from the flames of discord and sedition, the prince always tottering on his unshakeable throne. Theirs is an impatient nation, but wise in their very fury, master of the seas today—a thing once unheard of—and now melding commerce together with empire.

"Close by, you will find the histories of that other queen of the ocean, the republic of Holland, so respected in Europe and so powerful in Asia, where even its merchants find kings prostrating themselves before them.

193. The "former empire" is the Holy Roman Empire.

"The histories of Italy show us a nation that was once master of the world, and is today the slave of every other nation; its princes are weak and divided, the only remnant of sovereignty remaining to them being a tradition of empty statecraft.

"Here, see the histories of the republics—of Switzerland, the very image of liberty; of Venice, resourceless apart from its economy; and of Genoa, whose greatness lies only in its buildings.

"Here are the histories of the north, Poland among them, which has so badly misused its liberty and its ability to elect its kings that it seems to be trying to console its neighboring nations, which have lost both the one and the other."

At this point, we separated, agreeing to meet again the next day.

From Paris, the 2nd of the moon of Chalval, 1719

Letter 137

Rica to the same

The next day, he led me into another room. "Here," he said, "are the poets; which is to say, the authors who make a career out of putting shackles on common sense and crushing reason beneath the weight of ornament—the way women used to be buried beneath their finery and jewels. You know about poetry: it is not at all rare in the east, where the sun seems to overheat the imagination.

"And here are the epic poems."

"Wait—just what is an epic poem?"

"To tell you the truth, I really don't know. The connoisseurs say that only two have ever been written, and that all the others that call themselves by the name do not deserve it; but about this too I know nothing. They say, moreover, that it is impossible to write a new epic, which is certainly surprising.[194]

"Here we have the dramatic poets who, in my opinion, are the very best kind, and masters of the human passions. There are two kinds: the

194. The two epics are Homer's *Iliad* and *Odyssey*. Whether epic was still possible in the modern world was a frequently debated point among literary theorists. For another depiction of how the ancient Greeks were venerated in the era, see Letter 36.

comic, who move us gently, and the tragic, who disturb us with their violent intensity.

"Here are the lyric poets, the ones I detest just as much as I admire the others, for they devote all their art to creating mere harmonious extravagances.

"Next, we find the authors of idylls and eclogues, who are admired even among the members of the royal court, giving them the illusion of a tranquility they themselves do not possess, and all of it dressed up in shepherds' clothing.[195]

"Of all the authors we have seen, here are the most dangerous: the writers who hone their epigrams, like slender little arrows that make a deep, incurable wound.

"Here you see the romances, whose authors are a species of poet, for they wreak havoc on both the language of reason and that of the heart. They spend their time seeking out nature, but miss it every time; their heroes are as likely to be found in the natural world as winged dragons or hippogriffs."[196]

I said to him, "I have seen some of your romances, and if you were to see some of ours, you would be even more astonished. They are just as unnatural, but our customs make them even more tedious: a lover has to go through ten years of passion before he can even see the face of his mistress. But the authors are compelled to make their readers go through these boring preliminaries. Now, it is impossible to diversify the plot's events, so the author has recourse to an even worse artifice than the problem it is supposed to fix—that is, miracles. I am quite sure that you would never praise some magician making an army spring forth from underground, or some hero who singlehandedly slaughters an army of a hundred thousand men. But this describes our romances: these lifeless, constantly repeated adventures bore us to tears, and their absurd miracles are offensive to our reason."[197]

From Paris, the 6th of the moon of Chalval, 1719

---

195. The taste for pastoral poetry among the elite in France continued throughout the century, finding its ultimate expression in Marie Antoinette's having a pastoral landscape created at Versailles where she and her guests could play at being shepherds.

196. The word translated here as "romances" is *romans*, a word which today means novels, but the context makes it clear that Montesquieu means the old style romances, which were still in vogue at the time, and which were not bound by the constraints of realism.

197. Rica's reference might be to Antoine Galland's recent translation of the *Arabian Nights* (1704–1717), but as so often, the criticism might equally be directed back against the French, hinting at the use of the fantastic and miraculous in recent French romances.

Letter 138

Rica to Ibben
At Smyrna

The ministers here follow each other, destroying their predecessors, as regularly as the seasons: over the last three years, I have seen the finance system change four times. In Turkey and Persia, taxes are levied and raised in the same way as they were back when the empires were founded, but that is not at all the case here. True, we do not put quite so much thought into it as the westerners do. We think that the only difference between administering the revenues of a prince and those of some individual is simply the difference between counting a hundred thousand tomans and a hundred, but here they approach the issue with a great deal more technical expertise and mystery. All the great geniuses need to work at the issue night and day, and they must be constantly giving birth—with all the pains of giving birth—to new financial projects. They then go seek the counsel of countless other men, who do the work for them without even being asked. The geniuses must retire and live in the depths of offices impenetrable to the upper classes and held sacred by the lower; their heads must always be kept stuffed full of important secrets, miraculous schemes, new systems; and, being entirely absorbed in their own meditations, they must give up the use of speech, and often of politeness as well.

The moment the late king closed his eyes in death, people were busy establishing a new administration. Everyone felt that things were going badly, but no one knew what to do to improve them. The unlimited authority of the previous ministers had not had good results, so they decided the power should be divided. Toward this end, they set up six or seven councils, which resulted in perhaps the best, most sensible government France had seen. It did not last long—just like the benefits it created.[198]

Upon the death of the king, France was like a body overwhelmed with a thousand diseases. Then N*** took scalpel in hand, cut off the useless growths, and applied a number of topical remedies. But there remained an inner illness, resisting the cure. A foreigner came along

198. Louis XIV had died on the first of September, 1715. Philip, Duc d'Orléans, the Regent, at first reluctant to rule as a king, established the seven councils (a system called the *polysynode*) in October of that same year, and then abolished them in 1718.

then, attempting the cure; after all too many violent remedies, he believed he had gotten the patient back to health—but all he had managed was to make the body swell up.[199]

All those who were wealthy six months ago are now in poverty, and those who could not afford bread are now gorging themselves on riches. Never have the two extremes come so close together. The foreigner has flipped the state inside out the way a tailor does a coat: what used to be hidden inside is now on the outside, and what used to be outside is now inside. What unhoped-for fortunes, unbelievable even to those who have made them! God has never before brought people up so high from nothingness. How many valets today are being served by their erstwhile comrades—and perhaps tomorrow by the men who used to be their masters!

All this produces many bizarre things. Lackeys who made their fortune under the preceding reign now brag about their birth. They look down with contempt upon those who remove their livery in a certain street, sneering at the very people they had been themselves six months before.[200] They cry out at the top of their lungs, "The nobility is being ruined! What disorder in the state! What confusion in the ranks of society! Every day we see some nobody making a fortune!" And I can promise you that these latter will have their revenge upon the ones who succeed them, and that in thirty years' time we will hear plenty from those new aristocrats too.

From Paris, the 1st of the moon of Zilcadé, 1720

Letter 139

Rica to the same

Now here is a fine example of marital tenderness, not just in a woman but in a queen. The Queen of Sweden, desiring at all costs that her

199. N* * * is the Maréchal de Noailles, (the "witty minister" of Letter 98), who presided over the council of finance until 1718. The foreigner is the Scotsman, John Law (see Letter 132).

200. The "certain street" is the Rue Quincampoix, where Law's offices were. To "remove one's livery" is to give up a life of service, to become independent. Contemporary engravings suggest that crowds were constantly milling about on the Rue Quincampoix, seeking the latest economic news for any possible advantage.

husband should share the crown, has tried to remove any difficulties by issuing an edict to all the states promising to renounce her own rule if he is elected.[201]

It is now sixty-some years since another queen, this one named Christina, abdicated the throne in order to devote herself to philosophy.[202] I do not know which case excites more wonder.

While I believe, in general, that each person should remain in the place to which nature assigned him, and while I cannot approve of that weakness in some people who believe they are above their station and seek to leave it behind them, like deserting one's post—still, I am struck by the greatness of soul we observe in these two princesses, and to see the mind of the one and the heart of the other superior to their destiny. Christina dreamed of *knowing*, in an era when so many others only thought of enjoying; and the other could only enjoy by entrusting the entirety of her happiness to the hands of her august spouse.

From Paris, the 27th of the moon of Maharram, 1720

Letter 140

Rica to Usbek
*At * * **

The *parlement* of Paris has just been exiled to a little town called Pontoise. The Council had sent it a declaration to register, one which would have brought dishonor upon the body, and it therefore registered it in a manner that dishonored the Council.[203]

---

201. When King Charles XII of Sweden died, his sister, Ulrika Eleonora, was elected to the throne in 1719, and renounced her claim in favor of her husband, Frederick of Hesse-Castel on March 20, 1720. If we take the date of this letter literally—March 27, 1720—then Rica could only have learned about it via the *nouvellistes* or one of their news sheets.

202. Queen Christina of Sweden had abdicated, for this very reason, in 1654.

203. On the *parlements*, see Letter 92 and notes, as well as the Introduction. In this case, the Finance Council had submitted a declaration removing a great deal of paper money from circulation. The exile to Pontoise lasted from July 20 (the day before the date on this letter) to early December of 1720.

Some of the kingdom's other *parlements* are being threatened with similar treatment.

Institutions like these are always unpopular; they never approach their king except to tell him unhappy truths, and while whole crowds of courtiers are there to tell him endlessly how happy his people are under his rule, groups like this give the lie to such flattery, instead carrying to the throne all the groans and tears that they have had to listen to.

The truth is a heavy burden, my dear Usbek, when one has to carry it to princes! They need to remember that the ones carrying such a burden are forced to do so, and that they would never resolve to take on so sad and painful a task if they were not compelled to do so by their duty, their respect, and even their love.

From Paris, the 21st of the moon of Gemmadi I, 1720

Letter 141

Rica to the same

I plan to come and see you toward the end of the week. How good it will be to spend some days with you!

A few days ago, I was introduced to a woman of the court who had taken a fancy to have a look at my foreign appearance. I found her quite beautiful, worthy of our own monarch, and deserving of a noble place in the sacred regions of his heart.

She asked me a thousand questions about the customs and the way of life of the Persians. It seemed to me as if the life of the seraglio was not to her taste, and that she even found the idea of a man being shared among ten or twelve women repugnant. She would be unable to see the happiness of the one without envy, and the condition of the others without pity. She loves reading, especially poetry and fiction, and asked me to tell her about ours. What I said only whetted her curiosity, and she begged me to make a translation of some part of one of the books I had brought with me. I did so, and I sent her, a few days later, a Persian tale. Perhaps it will amuse you to see it dressed in a foreign language.

In the days of Sheik Ali Khan[204] in Persia, there lived a woman named Zuléma. She knew the entirety of the holy Koran by heart; there was no dervish with any better understanding than hers of the traditions of the holy prophets; the Arab scholars could say nothing so mysterious that she would not comprehend its entire meaning at once. And to all that knowledge she joined so cheerful a manner that when she spoke, it was uncertain whether she meant to instruct or entertain.

One day, she was with her companions in one of the rooms of the seraglio, and one of the other women asked what she thought about the other life, and whether she agreed with that longstanding tradition among our scholars that paradise is only for men.[205]

"This is the common belief," she told them. "Nothing has been left undone in the effort to degrade our sex. There is even a nation that is spread throughout Persia, called the Jewish nation, which insists, on the authority of its holy books, that we have no soul.

"These hurtful opinions have no other source than the pride of men, who want to carry their superiority with them all the way to the afterlife, never thinking that on the great Day of Judgment, all creatures will appear before God as nothing, with no special distinctions among them, except for whatever qualities virtue has created within them.

"God will suffer no limits to his rewards, and just as men who have lived well and made good use of their dominion over us here below will find themselves in a paradise full of beauties so celestial, so ravishing, that if a mortal were to see them, he would kill himself at once in order to enjoy them—just so, those virtuous women will be in a place filled with delights, where they will be intoxicated with a torrent of pleasures, including divine men who will submit themselves to them. Each of them will have her own seraglio, in which her men will be enclosed, and eunuchs even more faithful than ours will be there to guard them.

"I have read," she added, "in an Arab book about a man named Ibrahim who was insufferably jealous. He had twelve extremely beautiful wives, and treated them very harshly. He put no trust in his eunuchs nor in the walls of the seraglio, keeping them instead almost always under lock and key, enclosed within their separate rooms without being able to see or speak with each other, for he was jealous even of an innocent friendship. Everything he did bespoke this natural brutality of his. A

---

204. This is apparently the Ali Khan who served as Grand Vizier under Suleiman III (1666–1694); he is mentioned in the book by Chardin that Montesquieu so frequently uses.

205. In Letter 24, Rica subscribes to this belief.

gentle word never passed his lips, and he never made the slightest sign, unless it were to add some new rigor to their condition of slavery.

"One day when they were all assembled within a single room in the seraglio, one of them—braver than the rest—reproached him for his bad nature. She said, 'When one so insistently seeks out methods to make oneself feared, he will always end up with some that end up making him hated. We are all so miserable that we cannot help wishing for some change. Others in my situation would wish for your death, but I desire only my own and, having no other hope of being separated from you, it seems to me that my death would be sweet.' Such talk, which ought to have moved him, instead threw him into a furious rage: he drew his dagger and plunged it directly into her breast. With her dying voice, she said, 'My dear companions, if heaven has pity on my virtue, you will be avenged.' And at that she departed this unhappy life and went to the place of delights, where women who have spent their lives well enjoy an endless bliss.

"The first thing she saw was a sunny meadow, its green enlivened by the richest colors of flowers. A stream, its waters clearer than crystal, wandered through the meadow, making a thousand twists and turns. Then she went into a set of charming groves, whose silence was disturbed only by the sweet singing of birds. She then saw splendid gardens, which nature had ornamented with all her simplicity and all her magnificence. And finally she came to a superb palace that had been prepared for her, stocked with celestial men to give her pleasure.

"Two of them stepped forward to undress her, while others helped her into a bath and perfumed her with the most delicious essences. Later they gave her clothes infinitely richer than her own, and then led her into a great room where she found a fire burning with aromatic wood, and a table covered with the most exquisite foods. Everything seemed to be working in concert to ravish her senses: to one side of her, she heard music as divine as it was tender, and on the other, all she could see were the dances of her divine men, whose only wish was to please her. All such pleasures, however, only served to draw her insensibly toward even greater pleasures. They brought her into her bedroom and, after having undressed her again, they carried her to a superb bed where two of the most beautiful men received her into their arms. She was intoxicated with it all, and her ecstasies surpassed even her desires. 'I am beside myself,' she said to them. 'I would believe I were dying, if I were not sure of my immortality. It is too much now—leave me. I am overcome with the violence of these pleasures. Yes, now you are calming my senses a little; I can breathe again, and I feel myself again. Who has taken away the torches? May I not gaze on your divine beauty? May I not see . . . But why see? You are taking me back to my first raptures. O gods! How wonderful these shadows are! What—I will be immortal, and immortal with you? I will be . . . No, please give me some rest, for I can see perfectly well that you are the kind of men who will never ask for rest for yourselves.'

"After several repeated commands, she was obeyed—but only when she seriously wanted to be. She lay back languidly, falling asleep in their arms. Two minutes of sleep put an end to her fatigue; she felt two kisses, which immediately inflamed her and made her open her eyes. She said, 'I am uneasy; I am afraid you no longer love me.' But this was a fear she did not want to feel for long, so they soon gave her all the assurances she could possibly desire. 'I understand now,' she cried. 'Forgive me; I am sure of you now. You speak nothing, but you prove your love better than anything you could possibly say. Oh yes, I confess it: no one has ever loved so much. And now, look: you are arguing about which of you will have the honor of persuading me! Oh, if you compete with each other—if you combine that ambition with the pleasure of overcoming me, I am lost: you will both be the victors, and I will be the only one vanquished. But I will sell that victory dearly!'

"All this was only interrupted by the coming of the dawn. Her faithful, amiable domestics came into the bedroom and got the two young men out of bed; they were led away by two old men to a place where they would be guarded for her pleasure. Then she got up, and appeared to her adoring court in a charming, simple *déshabillé*, and soon after was covered in the most sumptuous of ornaments. The night had made her more beautiful, making her coloring more lively and her expression more graceful. The day passed with nothing but dances, concerts, feasts, games, and promenades, and people noticed that Anaïs stole away from time to time and flew to her two young heroes; after a time alone with them, she would return to the group she had left, and every time her expression would be more serene. Finally, when night came, they lost her altogether; she went to close herself up in the seraglio where, she said, she wanted to become better acquainted with the immortal captives who were going to be living with her for eternity. She visited the secluded, charming apartments, where she counted fifty miraculously beautiful slaves. All night long she wandered from chamber to chamber, everywhere receiving homage that was always different yet always the same.

"And this is how the immortal Anaïs passed her life, sometimes in glittering pleasures, sometimes in solitary ones, admired by a brilliant group or by a hopelessly smitten lover. Sometimes she would leave her enchanted palace to visit a woodland grotto; flowers seemed to spring up beneath her feet, and amusements crowded around her.

"She had lived in this happy state for more than a week and, being so consistently beside herself with pleasure, she had not entertained a single thought: she had taken joy in her happiness without really knowing it, and without having had a single one of those tranquil moments where the soul takes stock of itself, so to speak, and listens to itself when the passions have gone silent.

"The fortunate ones have such sharp pleasures that they rarely enjoy that freedom of mind, and this is why, being attached so intensely to the things of the present, they lose entirely the memory of things past, and no longer even think about having known or loved anything in another life.

"But Anaïs had the true mind of a philosopher, and had passed much of her life in meditation, her thoughts extending far beyond what would have been expected of a woman left to herself. The austere life that her husband had forced her to lead had had this one advantage.

"It had been this strength of mind that had led her to despise that fear that dominated all her companions, and even death itself, which had only been the end of her pains and the beginning of her happiness.

"Thus she slowly emerged from the intoxication of pleasure, and spent time alone in one of her palace apartments, allowing herself time to reflect delightfully on her past condition and on her present blessedness. She could not help feeling sorry for the misery of her companions: we continue to feel the sufferings that we have shared with others. Anaïs had no boundaries when it came to her compassion: feeling ever more tenderly toward those unhappy women, she felt inspired to try to help them.

"She turned to one of the young men who was near her and commanded him to take on the appearance of her husband, to go to the seraglio and make himself master there, and to chase the real husband out of the place. And she told him to stay there until she recalled him.

"He obeyed immediately. He flew down through the air and arrived at the seraglio of Ibrahim, who was not there at the time. He knocked, and every door was opened to him; the eunuchs prostrated themselves at his feet. He hurried to the apartments where the wives of Ibrahim were imprisoned; on his way, he had stolen all the keys from the pockets of that jealous man, to whom he was invisible. He entered, and surprised them all immediately by his gentle, friendly demeanor; and soon after that, he surprised them even more by his eagerness and by the rapidity of his endeavors. Everyone was astonished, and they would have taken it all to be a dream if it had not been so very real.

"While these novel scenes were being played out in the seraglio, Ibrahim was storming at the locked door, howling out his name and shouting. After a great deal of difficulty, he finally entered, throwing the eunuchs into extreme confusion. He strode along rapidly, but he jumped back dumbstruck when he saw the false Ibrahim, his exact double, taking all the liberties that the master of the place would take. He cried out for help, wanting the eunuchs to help him kill this imposter, but they did not obey him. He had only one feeble resource left to him—to rely upon the judgment of his wives. Within an hour, the false Ibrahim had seduced every one of the judges. The other one was chased away, and dragged unceremoniously out of the seraglio; he would have been killed a thousand times over if his rival had not ordered that his life be spared. Finally, the new Ibrahim, master of the field of battle, showed himself more and more worthy of the choice they had made, distinguishing himself by unheard-of miracles.

"The wives exclaimed, 'You are not like Ibrahim!' And the triumphant Ibrahim replied, 'No, say instead that that imposter is not like me. What would a man have to do to be your husband, if what I do is insufficient?'

"'Oh, we have no reason to doubt,' said the wives. 'If you are not Ibrahim, it is enough for us that you have earned the right to be him: you have been more Ibrahim in one day than he has been over these last ten years.'

"He replied, 'Promise me then that you will declare in my favor against that imposter.'

"They all said with one voice, 'never fear: we swear eternal fidelity to you. We have had nothing but abuse for such a long time. That traitor never believed in our virtue; the only thing he believed in was his own weakness. Now we see that all men are not made like him; instead, they are much more like you. If you only knew how much you make us hate him!'

"The false Ibrahim replied, 'Ah, I will give you new objects for your hatred; you still do not fully realize all the wrong he has done to you.'

"They replied, 'We can judge his injustice by the scale of your vengeance.' 'Yes, you are right,' said the divine man; 'I have fit the punishment to the crime, and I am very glad that you are pleased with my method of punishment.'

"The wives said, 'But what will we do if that imposter comes back?'

"He answered, 'It would be very difficult for him to fool you, I believe. Given how close I am to you, no kind of trickery would work, but in any case I will send him so far away that you will never again hear of him. From now on, I will take it upon myself to assure your happiness. I will never be jealous; I know I can trust you without giving you any troubles. I have a high enough opinion of my own merits to believe that you will remain faithful to me—and if you will not be virtuous for me, for whom could you be?'

"This conversation between him and the women went on for a long time; they were more struck by the difference between the two Ibrahims than by their similarity, but they never dreamed of seeking any explanation for these marvels. At length, the desperate husband returned to trouble them. He found his entire household in a state of joyfulness, and his wives were more skeptical of him than ever. Such a place was no home for a jealous man, and he left in a fury. The next instant, the false Ibrahim swept him up and carried him through the air, depositing him two thousand leagues away.

"O gods! What desolation these wives fell into whenever their dear Ibrahim was absent! The eunuchs quickly recovered their natural severity, and the whole household was in tears; they would imagine at times that everything that had happened was only a dream. They would sit looking at each other and retell even the tiniest details of these strange events. And then at last, the heavenly Ibrahim returned, more loveable than ever, and then it seemed that his journey had not been so difficult to bear. The new master conducted himself in a manner so opposite from the old one that it surprised all the neighbors. He dismissed all the eunuchs, opening his house up to everyone; he would not even have his wives veil themselves. It was a remarkable thing to see them at the feasts among the men, just as free as they were. Ibrahim thought—quite correctly—that the customs of the country did not apply to citizens like himself. But he spared no expense, and with his great profusion he dissipated the entire fortune of the jealous man who, returning three years later from the distant lands to which he had been transported, found nothing there but the wives—and thirty-six infants."

From Paris, the 26th of the moon of Gemmadi I, 1720

Letter 142

Rica to Usbek
*At * * **

Here is a letter I received yesterday from a scholar; I think you will find it remarkable.

Monsieur,

Six months ago, a very rich uncle of mine left me five or six thousand *livres*, along with a superbly furnished house. It is a pleasant thing to have some wealth, as long as one knows how to make the best use of it. I am not an ambitious man, nor do I have much taste for pleasures; I am almost always shut up in my study, where I live the life of a scholar. This is the kind of place where a true aficionado of antiquity will be found.

When my uncle had closed his eyes for the last time, I very much wanted to have him buried according to the rituals followed by the ancient Greeks and Romans. But I had no access to lachrymatories,[206] urns, or ancient lamps.

But since then, I have managed to acquire these precious rarities. A few days ago, I sold my silver tableware to buy an earthen lamp that had belonged to a stoic philosopher. I gave up all the mirrors with which my uncle had covered almost every wall in all the rooms, just in order to get a small, slightly cracked mirror once used by Virgil, and I was delighted to see my own face reflected in it, instead of that of the swan of Mantua. That is not all: I spent one hundred *louis d'or*[207] for five or six pieces of a two-thousand-year-old currency. I believe there is not a single piece of furniture anywhere in my house that is later than the period of the decline of the Empire. I have a small room filled with very precious, very expensive manuscripts, and though it is destroying my eyesight to read them, I would much rather make use of them than of printed versions, which are less correct and which anybody can read. Though I almost never go out, I still have an extreme desire to know all the ancient roadways that the Romans built. There is one fairly close to me, built by a proconsul of the Gauls some twelve hundred years ago; whenever

206. The lachrymatory was a small vase, supposed to hold the tears of the mourners, buried along with the deceased in Roman tombs.

207. While the franc and the *livre* were silver, the gold coin known as the *louis d'or* was so named for having the face of the king stamped on one side. Its value fluctuated, but was usually set at 20 francs.

I leave to visit my country house, I always take that road, though it is in terrible shape and takes me over a league out of my way. It enrages me to see that they have erected wooden poles along the route to show how far it is to the neighboring towns. It is so depressing to see these miserable markers instead of the ancient columns that were there in the past. I plan to have them re-erected by my heirs; I will write it into my will, and that will force them to do it. Monsieur, if you have any Persian manuscripts, it would give me great pleasure if you would allow me to buy them; I will pay you whatever price you like, and I will sweeten the bargain by including some of my own works, from which you will see that I am by no means a useless member of the republic of letters. You will find it of interest to read in an essay of mine that the wreaths that were used in the olden days for triumphal processions were oak and not laurel; you will find it wonderful, as well, to read my proof, using the most scholarly speculation drawn from the gravest of the Greek authors, that Cambyses was wounded in his left leg and not his right. Elsewhere, I demonstrate that a short forehead was considered especially beautiful among the Romans. And I will send you a quarto volume that explicates one particular verse in the sixth book of Virgil's *Aeneid.* You will not receive all this for a few days yet, but for now I will content myself by sharing with you a fragment from an ancient Greek mythologist, which has never been published, and which I discovered in a dusty library. I must break off now in order to attend to a very important task I have at hand: it involves restoring a fine passage in Pliny the naturalist, which the copyists of the fifth century have strangely garbled. I am, etc.

Fragment from an Ancient Mythologist

On an island near the Orcades was born an infant whose father was Aeolus, god of the winds, and whose mother was a Caledonian nymph.[208] It is said of him that he learned all by himself how to count on his fingers, and that by the time he was four, he could distinguish so perfectly among different metals that when his mother tried to give him a brass ring instead of a gold one, he threw it on the ground.

When he had grown up, his father taught him the secret of confining the wind inside goatskin bags, which he then sold to travelers. But since his merchandise was not very highly prized in his homeland, he left and began to travel the world, accompanied by the blind god of chance.

---

208. The passage is a satire on John Law and his financial system. Law was a Scot; Orcades is the Latin form of Orkney, the group of islands off the north of Scotland, and Caledonia is an ancient name for Scotland.

In his voyages, he learned that in Bétique,[209] gold is found everywhere, and he quickly turned his steps in that direction. But Saturn, who had reigned there for a great while, did not receive him well.[210] But when that god had quitted the earth, he went forth into all the crossroads and proclaimed in a loud, hoarse voice: "People of Bétique, you think you are rich because you own gold and silver. I pity you for your error. Believe me, and leave the country of vile metals, and come instead into the empire of the imagination, where I will promise you such riches that will astonish you." And with that he opened up a great many of the goatskins he had brought with him, distributing his merchandise to anyone who desired it.

The next day, he returned to those same crossroads, crying out: "People of Bétique, do you want to be rich? Imagine that I am very rich, and that you are too. Every morning, make yourself imagine that your fortune has doubled overnight; then get up and, if you have creditors, go and pay them with the money that you have imagined, and tell them to do some imagining themselves."

A few days later, he came back again, speaking in this way: "People of Bétique, I see that your imagination is not as strong as it was at first. Let yourselves be guided by mine. I will place a great banner before your eyes every morning, and it shall be for you a source of riches. You will find only four words written on it, but they will be filled with meaning, for they will regulate the dowries of your wives, the inheritances of your children, and the number of your servants.[211] And as for you," he said, turning to those nearest to him, "as for you, my dear children (and I may call you that, since you have received from me a second birth), my banner will determine the size of your carriages, the sumptuousness of your feasts, and the number and pensions of your mistresses."

A few days after this, he came to the crossroads out of breath and beside himself with rage, and he cried out: "People of Bétique, I have

---

209. Bétique, mentioned also in Letter 131, is an ancient Roman province of Spain, roughly the same as Andalusia today. In this case, though, Bétique actually means France. The term had been used in the same way by Fénelon in his allegorical romance, *Télémaque* (1699).

210. Saturn is Louis XIV. Law had visited Paris in 1699–1700, 1706, and again in 1714, just before the death of Louis. It was only with the coming of the Regency that Law found favor and, in 1716, set up his Banque Générale in the Rue Quincampoix.

211. The four words are "*Le cours des actions*": the price of shares, presumably in the venture known as the Compagnie des Indes. The current price would be posted daily at Law's offices in the Rue Quincampoix.

counseled you to imagine, and you have not done it. Very well: now I order you to." With that, he abruptly left, but he had second thoughts, and he came back. "I believe that some of you have been contemptible enough to have held onto your gold and silver. Never mind the silver, but as for the gold . . . as for the gold . . . Oh, this makes me so indignant . . . I swear to you on my sacred goatskins that if those individuals fail to bring their gold to me, I will punish them severely." Then he added, in his most persuasive tones: "Do you believe that I actually want to keep those miserable metals of yours? It was a sign of my honesty when, a few days ago, you brought them all to me and I immediately gave you half back."[212]

The next day, he was seen coming from a distance, and people heard him speak in his sweetest, most insinuating voice: "People of Bétique, I understand that you have stored part of your treasure in foreign countries. I beg you, do have it all sent to me; it will give me pleasure, and I will be forever grateful."

The son of Aeolus thus spoke to people who had no inclination to laugh, but they could not help it as they listened to him, which left him much confused. But, plucking up his courage, he hazarded one more try. "I know that you have some precious stones; in the name of Jupiter, get rid of them; nothing will impoverish you like those sorts of things—so get rid of them, I say unto you. And if you cannot do it yourselves, I can give you the names of some excellent businessmen who will handle it for you. What riches will be showered down upon you if you only do what I advise! Yes, I will promise to give you every bit of the purest contents of my goatskins."

Finally, he got up on a platform and, in his most assured voice, said to them: "People of Bétique, I have compared the happy state in which you all are now with the one you were in when I first came here, and I find you the richest people on the face of the earth. But in order to make your fortune complete, allow me first to take half of everything you own." With these words, the son of Aeolus vanished as if on wings, leaving his listeners in indescribable dismay, which made him return the next day, speaking to them thus: "I see that my discourse yesterday

212. In March of 1720, a government edict declared that gold and silver coins would no longer be honored as of May 1 for gold, and August 1 for silver; everyone was to convert to paper money. As this passage suggests, those who had holdings in gold found their net worth declining precipitously. A series of edicts followed over the summer, keeping the country's financial system in constant upheaval.

displeased you in the extreme. Well then, imagine that I never said anything. True, half is too much. All we need to do is deploy some other expedients to get to the goal I had in mind. Let us all put all our wealth together in one place; this should be easy enough, since there isn't much of it left." And at that, three-fourths of the wealth disappeared.

From Paris, the 9th of the moon of Chahban, 1720

Letter 143

Rica to Nathanaël Levi, Jewish Physician
At Leghorn

You ask what I think of the healing powers of amulets and talismans. But why do you ask me? You are a Jew, and I am a Mohammedan—which is to say, we are both very credulous people.

I always carry with me over two thousand passages from the holy Koran; I keep a small packet tied to my arm, containing the names of more than two hundred dervishes; and the names of Ali, Fatmé, and all the pure ones are tucked away in more than twenty places in my clothing.

However, I by no means disapprove of those who reject the powers we attribute to certain words. We find it harder to respond to their arguments than they do to our experiences.

Out of long habit, I wear all the holy strips of cloth in order to conform to the universal practice; it seems to me that, if they do not have any more power than the rings and other ornaments people wear, they cannot have any less. But you, you place complete confidence in certain mysterious letters, and without that safeguard, you would be in a perpetual state of fear.[213]

How miserable human beings are! They flutter back and forth between false hopes and ridiculous fears, and instead of relying on their reason, they create monsters that frighten them, or phantoms that seduce them.

What effect do you think the arrangement of certain letters can have? And what negative effect can come of arranging them differently? What

213. The reference is to the symbolism given to Hebrew letters in the Kabbalah.

is their relation to the winds, that they can soften the tempests—to artillery's gunpowder, that they can undo its powers—to what physicians call the peccant humour and the morbific cause of illnesses, that they can bring about cures?

What is strange is how those who exhaust their reason by finding some connection between events and occult causes work just as hard preventing themselves from seeing the true cause.

You will tell me that certain charms have won battles—and in turn, I will tell you that you are blind if you do not see in the terrain itself, in the numbers or in the bravery of the soldiers, or in the experience of the captains, sufficient causes to create the effect whose cause you are determined to ignore.

I will grant, for the moment, that marvelous things may happen, but grant me, in my turn, the possibility that no such things happen—for this too is possible. What you grant me does not prevent the two armies from fighting, so would you argue then that if they do, neither side can be victorious?

Do you believe that the outcome remains uncertain until some invisible power comes along to determine it? That all the blows struck in the battle were futile, all the prudence vain, all the courage useless?

And as for those sudden attacks of panic you find so hard to explain: do you not think that they might be produced by the sight of death, taking on a thousand forms all over the field? Do you think that in an army of a hundred thousand, there might not be a single fearful man? And do you think that his losing heart cannot cause others to do so? And that the second man, in deserting a third, does not influence the latter to desert a fourth? It does not require any more than this for despair to seize an entire army, and even to seize it more easily, the larger it is.

Everyone knows this, and everyone knows that men, like all creatures concerned with self-preservation, love life passionately. We know this as a general truth—and yet we ask ourselves what could be the reason why, in certain cases, they fear losing their lives?

The sacred books of all nations are full of accounts of these supernatural panics and terrors, but I cannot imagine anything more pointless: in order to determine whether there was a supernatural cause for something which could have had any of a hundred thousand natural causes, one must first have found some way to rule out all of those, and this is impossible.

I say no more about it, Nathanaël; in my view, it does not merit serious discussion.

From Paris, the 20th of the moon of Chahban, 1720

P.S. As I was finishing this letter, I heard someone in the street shouting that he was selling a letter from a provincial doctor to a Parisian one (for here, all such trivia gets printed, and people buy it). I thought it would be a good idea to send it to you, for it touches upon our subject.[214]

Letter from a Physician in the Provinces to a Physician in Paris

There was a patient in our town who had not slept for thirty-five days. His doctor prescribed opium, but he could not persuade himself to take it. When he had the cup in his hand, he was more uncertain than ever. Finally, he said to his doctor, "Monsieur, please have mercy on me, just until tomorrow: I know a man who is not a medical practitioner but who has an innumerable supply of remedies for insomnia at his home. Please allow me to send and inquire of him, and if I do not get some sleep tonight, I promise that I will return to you." Having dismissed the doctor, the patient had his curtains closed and said to a servant boy, "Here, go find Monsieur Anis[215] and tell him to come see me."

Monsieur Anis arrives. "My dear Anis, I am dying; I am unable to sleep. Don't you have something in your shop like *The C. of G.*, or some pious work written by someone like R. P. J. that you have been unable to sell?[216] For it is often true that the ones hardest to sell are the best remedies."

The bookseller replied, "Monsieur, I have in my shop and at your service *The Holy Court* by Father Caussin in six volumes.[217] I can have it sent to you, and I hope that you will find it efficacious. If you would

214. The editions before 1758 add this sentence to the end of the paragraph: "There are many things in it that I do not understand, but you, being a doctor, will surely understand the language of your colleagues."

215. Monsieur Anis is an only slightly disguised version of the printer and bookseller Jean Anisson (1640–1721), who had been director of the Imprimerie Royale, the first major national printing office in Europe. By the date of this letter, 1720, he operated a shop specializing in religious books.

216. *The C. of G.* is probably a geographical book titled *La Connaissance du Globe* by Pierre du Val (1677), though scholars are unsure of this. R. P. J. stands for *Révérend Père Jesuit*—and thus by implication, any book written by a Jesuit will cure insomnia.

217. Père Nicolas Caussin wrote, among many other learned works, the *Cour Sainte, ou Institution chrétienne des grands* (1625).

like the works of the Reverend Father Rodriguès, a Spanish Jesuit,[218] I will certainly send them. But trust me, stick with Father Caussin: one of Caussin's sentences will do you as much good as a whole page of *The C. of G.*"

With that, Monsieur Anis rushed off to seek the remedy in his bookshop. *The Holy Court* arrives: the dust is shaken off it, and the patient's son, a young schoolboy, begins to read from it, and the effect is almost immediate. By the second page, his pronunciation begins to slur, and soon everyone in the room begins to grow sleepy; and one minute later, they are all snoring except the patient, but he too succumbs after a lengthy trial.

The next day, the doctor arrives. "Well!" he says. "Did you take my opium?" No one says anything in reply, but the wife, the daughter, and the little boy all have joyous expressions on their faces as they point to Father Caussin. The doctor asks what this is, and they say, "Hurray for Father Caussin! We must send off to have him bound.[219] Who would have thought? Who would have believed it? It's a miracle. Here, Doctor, have a look at Father Caussin: this is the volume that put our father to sleep." And they explained the whole thing to him.[220]

The doctor was a subtle man, versed in the mysteries of the Kabbalah and the occult powers of words and spirits, and all this made quite an impression on him. After some reflection, he resolved to completely change his practice. He said to himself, "Now here is an extraordinary fact. I must try to take the experiment a bit further. Why shouldn't it be possible for one mind to transmit its own qualities to the things it works upon? Indeed, do we not see it around us every day? It is at least worth the attempt. I am sick to death of apothecaries: their syrups, their potions and all their Galenic drugs only ruin the health of patients. Let us, therefore, change our method: let us give the powers of the mind a try." And employing this idea, he opened a new pharmacy, as you will

218. Père Alonso Rodriguès (1526–1616) was a teacher and spiritual advisor. His best known work on ascetic devotion was translated into French and into English, with the English title of *The Practice of Christian and Religious Perfection* (1609; trans. 1612).

219. Books were typically sold in loose sheets, and the customer would have them bound if he so wished.

220. The remainder of this letter is broadly comic, containing material that Montesquieu evidently came to feel embarrassed about. He omitted it altogether in the 1754 edition; the editors of the 1758 edition reinserted it, but put it in a footnote.

see from the following, which are descriptions of the principal remedies he devised:

Laxative Tisane

Take three pages of the Logic of Aristotle in Greek, two pages of the most demanding treatise on scholastic theology (such as those by the subtle Scotus), four of Paracelsus, one of Avicenna, six of Averroes, three of Porphyry, and the same number from Plotinus and from Iambilichus. Infuse all of them for twenty-four hours, and take four times a day.

A Stronger Laxative

Take ten A*** of C*** concerning the B*** of C*** of the I***.[221] Distill them in a hot water bath; place one drop of the harsh, bitter liquid that results in a glass of water; drink the entire glass with confidence.

Emetic

Take six speeches, any dozen funeral orations (any will serve, except for those of Monsieur de N***[222]), a collection of current operas, fifty romances, and thirty contemporary memoirs; blend them all in a flask. Let them simmer for two days, and then distill the mixture over a gentle fire.

And, if this is not enough:

A Stronger One

Take one sheet of the marbled paper that was used as a cover for a collection of poems from the J*** F***.[223] Infuse it for a period of three minutes; heat a spoonful of it, and swallow.

---

221. The abbreviations can be interpreted various ways, but they probably stand for Acts (in the sense of decrees or communiqués) of the Council of the Bank and Company of the Indies. This would be another dig at the financial schemes and policies of John Law, including the communications of his joint stock company.

222. The bishop of Nîmes, Esprit Fléchier (1632–1710), a highly regarded preacher, a respected historian, and a member of the Académie Française.

223. The Jeux Floraux ("floral games") is a poetry society founded in 1323 and still operating today, holding an annual competition; it is based in Toulouse.

A Very Simple Remedy for Asthma

Read all the works of the reverend Father Maimbourg,[224] an ex-Jesuit, stopping to breathe only at the end of each sentence, and you will slowly come to feel your breathing ability much improved, with no need to repeat the treatment.

For Prevention of Mange, Scabies, Ringworm, and Horse Farcy[225]

Take three of Aristotle's categories, two degrees of metaphysics, one philosophical distinction, six verses of Chapelain, one sentence drawn from the letters of Monsieur l'Abbé de Saint-Cyran[226]; write them all down on a slip of paper, fold it up, attach it to a ribbon, and wear it around your neck.

A Miraculous Drug of Violent Fermentation, with Smoke, Heat, and Flame[227]

Blend an infusion of Quesnel with one of Lallemant[228]; allow the fermentation to take place, which will involve a great deal of violence, impetus, and noise while the acids battle against and penetrate within the alkaline salts; fiery vapors will evaporate. Pour the fermented liquor into an alembic: nothing will come out of it, and nothing will remain in it—only a death's head.

---

224. Louis Maimbourg (1610–1686) was a Jesuit historian and controversialist; Pope Innocent XI expelled him from the Jesuit order for having defended the Gallican liberties (that is, the independence of the French Catholic church)—an act for which Louis XIV rewarded him.

225. Farcy is a contagious horse disease which can be communicated to humans.

226. Jean Chapelain (1595–1674) was a poet, scholar, critic, and one of the chief theoreticians of literary Neoclassicism. Jean du Vergier de Hauranne, Abbé of Saint-Cyran (1581–1643), was a monk who had been friends with Cornelius Jansen, and was responsible for introducing Jansenism into France.

227. This and the remaining prescriptions are in Latin in the original.

228. Pasquier Quesnel (1634–1719) was a major Jansenist theologian; when the Papal Constitution *Unigenitus* was issued, the heresies it condemned came from Quesnel's writings, though many of his theses could be found in the works of Jansen as well. The Jesuit Jacques-Philippe Lallemant (1660–1748) attacked Quesnel and defended *Unigenitus* in a number of books.

A Laxative

Take two pages from the soothing Molina, six from the laxative Escobar, and one from Vasquez as a softener; soak in four pints of common water. When half evaporated, strain and express, and into the result dissolve three pages from Bauny as a corrosive and one from Tamburini as a cleanser.[229]

Use as an enema.

For Chlorosis, which the Vulgar Call Green-Sickness or Love-Sickness

Take four illustrations from Aretino and two pages from the book on marriage by the Reverend Thomas Sanchez.[230] Soak in five pints of common water.

Use as a laxative.

These are the drugs that our physician put into use, with the kind of success one can imagine. He did not want (he said) to ruin his patients financially by using rare and largely unobtainable remedies—such as, for example, a dedicatory epistle that makes no one yawn, or a too-short preface, or a pastoral letter that the bishop himself actually wrote, or a book by a Jansenist who was either scorned by another Jansenist or admired by a Jesuit. He maintained that remedies such as those were nothing but quackery, for which he felt an insurmountable antipathy.

Letter 144

Rica to Usbek[231]

A few days ago, I was a guest in a country house where I met two scholars who are widely celebrated here. They were marvels to me. The

229. Molina, Escobar, Bauny, and Tamburini were all theologians whose works are casuistic—and therefore Jesuit.

230. Pietro Aretino (1492–1556) wrote, among other things, a great deal of highly sexual comic poetry; illustrated versions would by definition be more or less pornographic. For the Spanish Jesuit Sanchez, see note to Letter 134.

231. This letter first appeared in the 1754 edition as one of the supplementary letters, but was then and thereafter often misprinted as "Usbek to Rica." The opening of the third paragraph shows that the letter is addressed to Usbek.

conversation of the first one always reduced itself to this: "What I have said is true because I said it." The conversation of the second took a different turn: "What I have not said is not true, because I have not said it."

I liked the first one well enough, for a man's being opinionated does not bother me at all—but an impertinent man bothers me a great deal. The first one defended his opinions, which is his business; the second one attacked the opinions of others, which is other people's business.

Oh, my dear Usbek! How ill-suited vanity is to those who have been endowed with a greater dose of it than is necessary for self-preservation! People like this want so badly to be liked that they make themselves dislikeable. They seek out ways to seem superior, but they do not even rise to the level of the ordinary.

Modest men, let me embrace you. You make life pleasant and charming. You believe that you have nothing, but in my eyes you have everything. You believe that you humble no one, but in fact you humble everyone. And when I compare you in my mind with these conceited men I see all around me, I pull them down from their lofty thrones and prostrate them at your feet.

From Paris, the 22nd of the moon of Chahban, 1720

Letter 145

Usbek to * * *

A man of intelligence is usually rather difficult in society. He likes very few people, and he is bored with the great number of people he refers to as "bad company." His contempt is eventually impossible to disguise, and then they all turn into his enemies.

Confident of charming people whenever he likes, he too often neglects doing so.

He tends to criticize, because he notices more than other people do, and he feels more deeply as well.

He always runs through all his fortune, because he can so readily think of ways to make it all back.

He fails in all his enterprises, because he takes so many risks. He is farsighted, but this means the things he sees are too distant. Moreover, at the beginning of an enterprise, he is less struck by the difficulties of the task than by the many ways he can imagine of overcoming them by using only his own resources.

He ignores the little details, which are often the determinants of success or failure in all great affairs.

The ordinary man, in contrast, tries to pay attention to everything: he knows perfectly well that he dare not overlook anything.

Universal approval usually goes to the ordinary man. It is a pleasure to applaud him, and a delight to withhold applause from the other man. The man of intellect is envied, which means that people will pardon nothing in him. People will grant every excuse to the ordinary man; vanity is on his side.

But if the intelligent man has so many disadvantages, what shall we say about the harsh conditions of the true scholars?

I never think about all this without recalling a letter from one of them to a friend. Here it is:

> Monsieur,
>
> I am a man who spends every night gazing through a thirty-foot telescope at the great orbs rolling through the sky, and when I want to relax, I take out my microscope and study a mite or a moth.
>
> I am not at all wealthy; I have only a single room, and I dare not light a fire there because I have my thermometer there, and the heat would raise its reading. Last winter, I thought I would die of cold; even though my thermometer reading, which was very low, suggested that my hands were going to freeze, I was not deterred. And I have the consolation of knowing the precise temperatures for every day in the last year.
>
> I do not communicate with others much, and indeed I know no one out of all the people I observe around me. But there is one man at Stockholm, another at Leipzig, and another at London, men I have never seen and no doubt never will see, with whom I carry on so thorough a correspondence that I cannot let a single post go by without writing them.
>
> But even though I know no one in my neighborhood, I have such a bad reputation here that I will soon be obliged to move. Some five years ago, I was rudely insulted by one of the neighbor women who claimed it was her dog that I dissected. A butcher's wife, who happened to be there at the time, joined in. And while the latter heaped insults upon me, the former picked up stones and began hurling them at me and at Doctor ***, who was with me, and who suffered a terrible blow upon the frontal occipital bone, as a result of which the seat of reason within him was severely shaken.

Ever since then, whenever some dog goes missing in the street, everyone assumes I have had something to do with it. One good bourgeois woman, having lost her little dog which, she said, she loved more than she loved her own children, came into my room the other day and fainted away; not finding her dog there, she reported me to the magistrate. I believe I shall never be delivered from the annoying malice of these women who, with their yapping voices, are constantly deafening me with funeral orations for every automaton that has died over the last ten years.[232]

I remain, etc.

In earlier days, all scholars were accused of magic. I am not surprised: everyone says to himself, "I have taken natural talents as far as they can be taken, but there is another scholar in advance of me: there must be witchcraft in it."

Today such accusations are discredited, so the accusers have taken a different tack: a scholar today can scarcely avoid being called either irreligious or heretical. And even if he is absolved of it by the people, it doesn't matter: the wound has been inflicted, and it will never entirely heal. It will always remain a sore spot with him. And thirty years later an adversary will come up to him and say with some modesty, "God forbid that I would imply that what they said of you is true; but you were obliged to defend yourself . . ." And at that point, even his justification is turned against him.

If he writes some historical study, even if he has a noble spirit and a pure heart, he will undergo a thousand persecutions. They will haul him before the magistrate over some incident that happened a thousand years ago. And they will want to prove that his pen is captive, if it is not for sale outright.

However, he is better off than those cowardly men who sell out their faith for a miserable government pension—who, once all their impostures are totaled up, profit less than an obol from them—who overturn the Empire's constitution, taking power away from one group and giving it to another, by taking from the people and giving to the princes—who bring long-dead rights back to life, by flattering the passions that are current and the vices that are on the throne—imposing all the more

232. Calling dogs automatons derives from Cartesian philosophy, which held that animals are basically machine-like and have no consciousness and no souls. For an overview of the idea, see Peter Harrison, "Descartes on Animals," *The Philosophical Quarterly* 42 (1992), 219–27.

unworthily on posterity, which has no means of negating their false statements.[233]

But it is not enough for an author to have fought off all these insults, nor that he has to live in constant anxiety about the success of his works. The book that has cost him so much finally appears, and it is immediately the object of criticism from all directions. How can he avoid it? He has had a thought, and he has supported it in writing: how could he know that some man two hundred leagues away has published exactly the opposite thought? But thus begins a war.

Still, if only he could hope to gain some respect! But no. At best, he is esteemed by those who work in the same field as he. A philosopher looks with sovereign contempt on someone whose mind is stocked with facts; and in turn, he is regarded as a visionary by the man with a strong memory.

As for those who proudly proclaim their own ignorance, they would like to see the entire human race buried as deeply in oblivion as they will be themselves.

When a man lacks a certain talent, he consoles himself by developing a contempt for it. He wishes to remove the obstacle standing between himself and merit, and in doing so, he finds himself on the same level with those whose work he had found so formidable.

And finally, in order to achieve even the most doubtful reputation, he must sacrifice all pleasures and give up his health as well.

From Paris, the 26th of the moon of Chahban, 1720

Letter 146

Usbek to Rhédi
At Venice

For a long time, people have said that honesty is of the essence in a good minister.

---

233. The following passage was added to the second edition of 1721, and then removed in the 1754 edition: "But what shall I say about this century, in which I see a scholar serving at the discretion of a bookseller? In which I see a man who deserves to have statues erected to him forced to labor night and day to make the fortune of a miserable businessman? His works could have been of use to posterity, but instead they must be hurried due to avarice, the end entirely subordinated to the means."

A private person can enjoy the obscurity of his position; he only discredits himself in the eyes of a few people, and remains hidden from all others. But a minister who lacks probity has as many witnesses and as many judges as the people he governs.

Do I dare say it? The greatest evil that a dishonest minister does is not in harming his prince, or in ruining his people. There is another, in my view a thousand times worse, and that is the bad example that he sets.

You know that I traveled in India for a long time.[234] I saw there a naturally generous nation become perverted—all the way up from the lowest of subjects to the very greatest—by the wicked example of a minister. I saw a people there for whom generosity, probity, candor, and good faith were natural, and I saw them abruptly change to become the very worst of people. The evil was contagious, sparing not even the healthiest members of the body politic. I saw the most virtuous men turn around and perform unworthy acts, violating the principles of justice on the empty pretext that the same violation had been done to them.

They invoked vile laws to justify the foulest acts, and they labeled injustice and perfidy as "necessity."

I have seen faith in contracts annulled, the most sacred conventions wiped away, all the laws of the family turned upside down. I have seen greedy debtors, proud and insolent in their poverty, the disgraceful instruments of the fury of the laws and the harshness of the times, pretending to make a payment instead of actually making one and thrusting the knife into the flesh of their benefactors.

And I have seen others, even more shamefully, buying for practically nothing or, rather, picking up oak leaves from the ground and using them to impoverish widows and orphans.[235]

I have seen an insatiable lust for wealth born suddenly in every heart. I have seen the sudden emergence of a detestable conspiracy to get rich, not through honest work and decent industry, but through the ruination of the prince, the State, and the citizens.

I have seen a respectable citizen of these miserable times who could only go to sleep every night if he were able to declare, "Today, I ruined a family; tomorrow, I will ruin another."

---

234. "India" here clearly stands for France, and the wicked minister in question is John Law, whose financial system led to the abuses the letter goes on to enumerate.

235. The oak leaves could be shares of stock in Law's company, or the paper money that he had had issued. The implication is that something inherently worthless has been allowed to usurp the place of real money.

Another said, "I am going off with a man dressed in black, carrying a writing tablet in his hand and a piece of sharpened steel on his ear, to assassinate all those to whom I owe debts."[236]

Another said, "I see that my business affairs are going quite well. It is true that when I went to make a payment three days ago, I left an entire family in tears, I eliminated the dowries of two decent girls, and deprived a little boy of his education. The father will die of grief, and the mother of sorrow: but I have done nothing more than what the law permits."

What greater crime can there be than this of a minister who corrupts the morals of an entire nation, degrades the most generous spirits, tarnishes the glow of high office, and darkens virtue herself, dragging down even the highest of nobles into the general state of contempt?

What will posterity say, when they must blush for the shame of their forefathers? What will the next generation say when they compare the iron of their ancestors with the gold of those who gave them birth? I am certain that the nobles of the future will wipe from their family trees the dishonor of those who disgrace them, and leave this present generation in the hideous nothingness it has made of itself.[237]

From Paris, the 11th of the moon of Rhamazan, 1720

Letter 147

The Chief Eunuch to Usbek
At Paris

Things have degenerated to an intolerable state: your wives have come to imagine that your absence gives them complete impunity. Terrible things have happened. I tremble at the thought of the story I must tell you.

---

236. The man in black is an official of the law; his weapon is his pen, tucked behind his ear.

237. With this, the terrible aftermath of John Law's financial reign, we come to the end of the events in the West. The remaining letters are out of order—the first is three years previous—but they form a distinct plot sequence, showing the worsening effects of Usbek's absence. As the dates suggest, part of the problem is the great delay in letters passing from Paris to Ispahan and back.

A few days ago, Zélis was going to the mosque when she let her veil fall, allowing her face to be seen by everyone.

I found Zachi in bed with one of her slaves, something utterly forbidden by the laws of the seraglio.

By the sheerest chance, I came across a letter, which I am sending to you; I have been unable to discover to whom it was addressed.

Yesterday evening, a young man was discovered in the seraglio garden; he escaped by climbing over the wall.

Add to all this whatever has not come to my knowledge, and you will see that you have surely been betrayed. I await your orders, and until the happy moment when I receive them, I remain in a dangerous situation. But if you fail to put all your wives under my complete command, I will not answer for any of them, and every day I will have more unhappy news to send you.

From the seraglio at Ispahan, the 1st of the moon of Rhegeb, 1717

Letter 148

Usbek to the Chief Eunuch
At the seraglio in Ispahan

With this letter I give you complete, unlimited power over the entire seraglio. Your command is identical with my own. Let fear and terror accompany you. Hasten from apartment to apartment, carrying punishment and chastisement with you. Let all live under constant fear, and let all fall weeping at the sight of you. Interrogate every member of the seraglio, beginning with the slaves. Do not spare the women I love; every one of them must submit to your terrible tribunal. Bring the most hidden of secrets forth into the light of day, purify that polluted place, and bring back the virtue that has been banished. From this moment on, even the slightest faults will be on your head. I suspect Zélis is the one who wrote the letter you found: investigate all this with the eyes of a lynx.

*From * * *, the 11th of the moon of Zilhagé, 1718*

Letter 149

Narsit to Usbek
At Paris

O great lord, the chief eunuch has just died. Because I am the oldest of your slaves, I have taken his place until you make it known upon whom you wish to cast your eyes.

Two days after his death, I was given one of the letters you had addressed to him. I have been very careful not to open it; I have put it away with respect, still sealed, until you make known to me what your sacred will shall be.

Yesterday, a slave came in the middle of the night to tell me that he had discovered a young man in the seraglio. I arose and investigated, and found that it was only a dream.

I kiss your feet, O sublime lord, and I beg you to count upon my zeal, my experience, and my years.

From the seraglio at Ispahan, the 5th of the moon of Gemmadi I, 1718

Letter 150

Usbek to Narsit
At the seraglio in Ispahan

Miserable creature that you are! You have in your hands letters that contain orders that are to be carried out promptly and violently: the least delay puts me into despair, and there you sit calmly, under an absurd pretext!

Horrible things have happened; it may be that half of my slaves deserve to die. I am sending you the letter that the chief eunuch sent me before his death. If you had opened the packet addressed to him, you would have found bloody commands within. Read them, those commands, and if you do not carry them out, you will die.

*From * * *, the 25th of the moon of Chalval, 1718*

Letter 151

Solim to Usbek
At Paris

If I remained silent any longer, I would be as guilty as those criminals you have within your seraglio.

I was the confidant of the chief eunuch, the most faithful of your slaves. When he saw that he was approaching his end, he called me and said these words to me: "I am dying, and the only sorrow I feel as I quit this life is that I have lived to see the wives of my master become criminals. May heaven protect him from the evils that I see coming! And after my death, may my menacing ghost appear to remind these wicked ones of their duty, and to intimidate them further! Here are the keys to this dreadful place; take them to the oldest of the blacks. But if he fails to be vigilant enough after my death, consider how to inform the master." And with these words, he expired in my arms.

I know what he wrote you, some time before his death, about the conduct of your wives. There is a letter here in the seraglio that would have brought terror with it if only it had been opened. What you have written since was intercepted three leagues away from here. I do not know why, but everything is turning out unluckily.

But your wives no longer behave with any restraint at all. Since the death of the chief eunuch, it is as if everything were permitted. Only Roxane has remained dutiful and has retained her modesty. Morals grow more corrupted every day. The faces of your wives no longer reveal that masculine, austere virtue that they used to. Instead there is some new joyousness prevailing here lately, which I believe to be an infallible sign of some new indulgence. In the littlest things I can see new, heretofore unheard-of liberties being taken. Even among your slaves there is a certain laziness with regard to their duties and the rules, which surprises me: they no longer show that zest for serving you that used to animate the entire seraglio.

Your wives have been in the country for a week, at one of your most isolated houses. I hear that the slave in charge has been corrupted, and that the day before they arrived, he had two men hidden for them in an alcove in the stone wall in the main chamber, from which they come out at night, when the rest of us are in bed. The old eunuch who is currently our leader is an imbecile, who will believe anything they tell him.

I feel a rage within me to avenge all these betrayals. And if heaven permits, for the good of your service, that you should find me capable of taking over, I can promise you that if your wives will not be virtuous, they will at least be faithful.

From the seraglio at Ispahan, the 6th of the moon of Rebiab I, 1719

Letter 152

Narsit to Usbek
At Paris

Roxane and Zélis wanted to go to the country, and I thought I should not refuse them. Fortunate Usbek! You have faithful wives, and vigilant slaves. I am in command here, a place that virtue itself seems to have chosen as her haven. Rest assured that nothing will happen here that would be an offense to your eyes.

One bad thing did happen, and it has been truly annoying to me. Some Armenian merchants recently arrived in Ispahan, having carried with them one of your letters to me. I sent a slave to pick it up, but he was robbed on his way back, and the letter has been lost. Write me again promptly, for I imagine that, in this time of change, you must have important things to tell me.

From the seraglio at Fatmé, the 6th of the moon of Rebiab I, 1719

Letter 153

Usbek to Solim
At the seraglio in Ispahan

I place a sword in your hand. I entrust to you that which is now the dearest thing in the world to me—my vengeance. Enter into this new employment, but leave your heart and your pity behind. I will write to my wives to give you their blind obedience. In the chaos of all these crimes, they will fall prostrate before your gaze. I must place in you all my hope of happiness and repose. Give me back the seraglio that I left. But begin with expiation: exterminate the guilty, and make those who are tempted to be guilty tremble in fear. For such critical service, what rewards might you not expect from your master? It only depends upon you now to see yourself raised up higher than ever, and with all the recompense you could ever have desired.

From Paris, the 4th of the moon of Chahban, 1719

Letter 154

Usbek to his wives
At the seraglio in Ispahan

May this letter be like the thunder that bursts forth in the midst of lightning and tempest! Solim is your chief eunuch, not for guarding you, but for punishing you. Let all the seraglio abase itself before him. He must judge your past actions, and for the future, he will make you live under a yoke so heavy that you will pine for your lost liberty, even if you do not regret your lost virtue.

From Paris, the 4th of the moon of Chahban, 1719

Letter 155

Usbek to Nessir
At Ispahan

Happy is he who, fully knowing the price of a good and tranquil life, can let his heart rest in the bosom of his family, and never know any other land than the one in which he was born!

I am living in a barbarous place, where everything that oppresses me is constantly present, and everything that interests me is absent. I am consumed with a grim sadness, and feel myself falling into a frightful despondency. I feel as if I were being annihilated, and I only find myself again whenever a dark feeling of jealousy comes over me, a feeling that gives birth to fears and suspicions, to hatred and regret.

You know me, Nessir; you have always seen into my heart as into your own. I would pity you, if I thought you knew how deplorable my state is. I must sometimes wait six months for news of my seraglio, and I count every passing second, my impatience making them stretch out longer and longer. And when at last what I have waited for arrives, my heart pounds within me, and my hand trembles at opening the fatal letter. This very anxiety, though it renders me so desperate, is nonetheless the happiest state available to me, and I fear falling from it by a blow that will be crueler to me than a thousand deaths.

Whatever reasons I had for leaving my native country, and though I owe my life to my flight, I can no longer go on with this horrible exile. Will I not die all the same, the victim of all my sorrows? I have urged Rica a thousand times to leave this foreign land, but he opposes all my suggestions. He keeps me here under a thousand different pretexts. It is as if he has forgotten his homeland, or rather, as if he has forgotten me, so insensitive is he to my unhappiness.

Oh, how miserable I am! I want to return to my country, but perhaps only to become even more miserable there! And what will I do there? I will be delivering my head to my enemies. And that is not all: I will enter into my seraglio, and I will have to ask for news of what dire things have happened there in my absence—and if I discover the guilty ones, what will become of me? And since the very idea of it so overwhelms me here, so far away, what will it be like when I am there? What will happen if I am forced to see, if I am forced to hear, what I cannot even imagine without shuddering? And finally, what if I have to mete out punishments that will only serve as permanent signs of my own confusion and despair?

I will be locking myself up behind walls more terrible for me than for the women who are kept there, for I will be bringing all my suspicions along with me, and all their acts of attentiveness will not remove a single one of them. In my bed, in their arms, I will feel only my anxieties; at a time when fretting is inappropriate, my jealousy will allow me no escape. Shameful dregs of the human race, vile slaves whose hearts have been forever closed to the tender feelings of love—you would not howl so over your situation if you knew the misery of mine.

From Paris, the 4th of the moon of Chahban, 1719

Letter 156

Roxane to Usbek
At Paris

Horror, darkness, and dread reign here in the seraglio, and a frightful mourning is everywhere: a tiger is furiously raging at us here at every moment. He has put two white eunuchs to death, even though they proclaimed their innocence to the end. He has sold off a great number of our slaves, and forced us to exchange the remaining ones among ourselves. Zachi and Zélis have each been shamefully treated alone in their rooms in the darkness of night; this unclean one has not hesitated to lay his vile hands upon them. He keeps us all locked up in our apartments, and even though we are alone here, he forces us to wear the veil at all times. We are not allowed to speak to each other, and it would be a crime for us to write; the only freedom left to us is that of weeping.

A whole troop of new eunuchs has come into the seraglio, and they plague us night and day. Our sleep is constantly being interrupted by their suspicions, whether real or feigned. The only thing that consoles me is that this will not last long, and that all these miseries will end with my life, which will not be long, cruel Usbek: I will not even allow you the time to make these outrages stop.

From the seraglio at Ispahan, the 2nd of
the moon of Maharram, 1720

Letter 157

Zachi to Usbek
At Paris

Oh God! A barbarian has outraged me even in the way he punished me! He has inflicted a punishment that begins by putting my chastity into question—that leads into the most extreme humiliation—that drags us down, so to speak, to the level of infancy.

My soul, at first almost annihilated with shame, recovered itself and began to feel indignation, while my cries echoed from the vaulted ceilings of my apartment. They could all hear me pleading for mercy from the vilest of human beings, trying to make him feel pity, but he only became even more inexorable.

Since that time, his insolent and servile soul has elevated itself over mine. His presence, his gaze, his words, all these evils overwhelm me. When I am alone, I at least have the consolation of weeping, but when he comes into my sight, I am seized with an impotent fury, and I fall into despair.

This tiger dares to say that you are the author of his barbarities. He wants to make me cease loving you, and he pollutes even my deepest feelings. When he pronounces the name of the one I love, I can no longer complain; all I can do is die.

I have endured your absence, and I have maintained my love, due to the strength of that love. My nights, my days, my moments—everything has been for you. I was proud of that love, and your love for me made me respected here. But now . . . No, I can no longer endure the humiliation into which I have descended. If I am innocent, return and love me, and if I am guilty, then return, so that I may die at your feet.

From the seraglio at Ispahan, the 2nd of the moon of Maharram, 1720

Letter 158

Zélis to Usbek
At Paris

A thousand leagues from me, you judge me guilty; a thousand leagues from me, you punish me.

If a barbaric eunuch lays his vile hands on me, it is at your command. It is the tyrant who performs the outrage, not the one who obeys his orders and carries out the tyranny.

You may, in your imagination, redouble your mistreatment of me. My heart is tranquil, since it is no longer in love with you. Your soul degrades itself, and you have become cruel. Rest assured that you will never be happy. Farewell.

From the seraglio at Ispahan, the 2nd of the moon of Maharram, 1720

Letter 159

Solim to Usbek
At Paris

I grieve for myself, o magnificent lord, and I grieve for you: never has a faithful servant descended into the horrible despair that I have. I can only tremble as I write them, but here are your miseries, as well as mine.

I swear by all the prophets in heaven that since you entrusted your wives to me, I have watched over them night and day, and that I never relaxed my anxieties, not even for a moment. I began my ministry with punishments, and although I later suspended them, I never compromised my natural severity.

But what am I saying? Why am I boasting to you about this faithfulness of mine, which has turned out to be futile? Forget all of my past service; look upon me as a traitor, and punish me for all the crimes that I have been unable to prevent.

Roxane, the proud Roxane—oh, God!—who can be trusted now? You suspected Zélis, and you felt entirely secure concerning Roxane: as it turns out, that fierce virtue of hers was only a cruel deception, a veil over her treachery. I surprised her in the arms of a young man who, upon being discovered, rushed upon me; he stabbed me twice with a dagger, and the eunuchs, hearing the commotion, ran in and surrounded him. He defended himself a long time, wounding many of them, and he even tried to get back into the bedroom in order, as he said, to die in the sight of Roxane. But finally our numbers were too much for him, and he fell dead at our feet.

I do not know, o sublime lord, whether I should wait to hear your severe commands. You have put vengeance into my hands, and I must not let it languish there.

From the seraglio at Ispahan, the 8th of the moon of Rebiab I, 1720

Letter 160

Solim to Usbek
At Paris

I have made my decision: your miseries will be wiped away. I will begin the punishment.

And I feel already a secret, inner joy: my soul and yours are going to find peace. We are going to exterminate this crime, in such a way that even innocence itself will turn pale.

O you women, who seem to have been created only in order to despise your senses, and feel indignant about your own desires—you eternal victims of shame and modesty—if only I could bring you in your thousands into this unhappy seraglio, so that you could see with astonished eyes all the blood I am about to spill!

From the seraglio at Ispahan, the 8th of the moon of Rebiab I, 1720

Letter 161

Roxane to Usbek
At Paris

Yes, I have betrayed you. I have corrupted your eunuchs; I have amused myself with your jealousy, and I found a way to make a place of delight and pleasure out of this hideous seraglio of yours.

I am going to die. The poison will circulate through my veins—for, what would I do in this life, when the only man who could make me want to live is no more? I die, but my shade's flight upward will be well accompanied: I have just dispatched all those unholy guardians, the ones who spilled the noblest blood in the world.

How could you ever have thought that I was credulous enough to believe I was put in this world to adore you and your whims? That while you permitted everything for yourself, you had the right to thwart all my desires? No: I was able to live in that servitude, but I was always free. I altered your rules so that they fit the laws of nature, and my mind has always maintained its independence.

You ought to thank me for the sacrifice I made for you, for having abased myself so low as to make you think I was faithful to you; for keeping hidden within my heart what I ought to have proclaimed to the whole world; and finally, for having profaned the name of virtue by letting it be applied to the way I tolerated your whims.

You were surprised not to find all the transports of love in me? If you had really known me, you would have seen nothing in me but rage and hatred.

But you have long enjoyed the advantage of believing that a heart such as mine would submit itself to you. We were both happy: you thought me duped, and I was duping you.

This kind of talk will no doubt seem new to you. Can it be that after overwhelming you with sorrows, I will manage to make you admire my courage? But it is done now; the poison is working within me, and I am losing my strength—the pen drops from my hand—I feel even my hatred weakening—and I am dying.

From the seraglio at Ispahan, the 8th of the moon of Rebiab I, 1720

BIBLIOGRAPHY

Works in English

Articles

Altman, Janet Gurkin. "Strategic Timing: Women's Questions, Domestic Servitude, and the Dating Game in Montesquieu." *Eighteenth-Century Fiction* 13.2–3 (2001): 325–48. MLA International Bibliography. Web. 19 July 2013.

Aravamudan, Srinivas. "Response: Exoticism beyond Cosmopolitanism?" *Eighteenth-Century Fiction* 25.1 (2012): 227–42. Project MUSE. Web. 20 June 2013.

Baird, Robert J. "Late Secularism." *Social Text* 18.3 (2000): 123–36. Project MUSE. Web. 20 June 2013.

Baktır, Hasan. "A Dialogic Enlightenment Perspective; Approach to the Ottoman and European Relations in Pseudo-Oriental Letters." *Turkish Studies* 3.4 (2008): 193–211. MLA International Bibliography. Web. 19 July 2013.

Beecher, Jonathan. "Variations on a Dystopian Theme: Melville's 'Encantadas.'" *Utopian Studies* 11, no. 2 (2000): 88–95. JSTOR. Web. 22 June 2013.

Behdad, Ali. "The Eroticized Orient: Images of the Harem in Montesquieu and His Precursors." *Stanford French Review* 13.2–3 (1989): 109–26. MLA International Bibliography. Web. 19 July 2013.

Bell, Dorian. "Balzac's Algeria: Realism and the Colonial." *Nineteenth-Century French Studies* 40.1 (2011): 35–56. Project MUSE. Web. 20 June 2013.

Bellhouse, Mary L. "Femininity and Commerce in the Eighteenth Century: Rousseau's Criticism of a Literary Ruse by Montesquieu." *Polity* 13, no. 2 (Winter 1980): 285–99. JSTOR. Web. 20 June 2013.

Bensmaia, Reda. "The Phantom Mediators: Reflections on the Nature of the Violence in Algeria." *Diacritics* 27.2 (1997): 85–97. Project MUSE. Web. 20 June 2013.

Betts, C. J. "Constructing Utilitarianism: Montesquieu on Suttee in the *Lettres Persanes*." *French Studies* 51.1 (1997): 19–29. MLA International Bibliography. Web. 19 July 2013.

———. "Lettres Persanes, Lettres Anglaises: Some Reflections." *Studies on Voltaire and the Eighteenth Century* 304 (1992): 874–75. MLA International Bibliography. Web. 19 July 2013.

———. "Some Doubtful Passages in the Text of Montesquieu's *Lettres Persanes*." *Studies on Voltaire and the Eighteenth Century* 230 (1985): 181–88. MLA International Bibliography. Web. 19 July 2013.

Biti, Vladimir. "The Divided Legacy of the Republic of Letters: Emancipation and Trauma." *Journal of Literature and Trauma Studies* 1.2 (2012): 1–30. Project MUSE. Web. 20 June 2013.

Boer, Inge E. "Despotism from under the Veil: Masculine and Feminine Readings of the Despot and the Harem." *Cultural Critique* 32 (Winter 1995–1996): 43–73. JSTOR. Web. 22 June 2013.

Bradford, Clare. "Representing Islam: Female Subjects in Suzanne Fisher Staples's Novels." *Children's Literature Association Quarterly* 32.1 (2007): 47–62. Project MUSE. Web. 20 June 2013.

Brady, Patrick. "The *Lettres Persanes*: Rococo or Neo-Classical?" *Studies on Voltaire and the Eighteenth Century* 53 (1967): 47–77. MLA International Bibliography. Web. 19 July 2013.

Braun, Theodore. "'La Chaine Secrète': A Decade of Interpretations." *French Studies* 42.3 (1988): 278–91. MLA International Bibliography. Web. 19 July 2013.

Carr, J. L. "The Secret Chain of the *Lettres persanes*." *Studies on Voltaire and the Eighteenth Century, Volume LVII: Transactions of the Second International Congress on the Enlightenment.* Ed. Theodore Besterman. Geneva: Droz, 1967. 333–44. Print.

Chew, Samuel C. "An English Precursor of Rousseau." *Modern Language Notes* 32.6 (1917): 321–37. MLA International Bibliography. Web. 19 July 2013.

Choudhury, Mita. "Despotic Habits: The Critique of Power and Its Abuses in an Eighteenth-Century Convent." *French Historical Studies* 23.1 (2000): 33–65. Project MUSE. Web. 20 June 2013.

Cocks, Edmond. "The Servitude Theory of Population." *The American Scholar* 43, no. 3 (Summer 1974): 472–80. JSTOR. Web. 22 June 2013.

Coleman, Patrick. "Œuvres Complètes de Montesquieu, *Lettres Persanes*." *French Studies* 60.1 (2006): 111–12. Print.

Coller, Ian. "East of Enlightenment: Regulating Cosmopolitanism between Istanbul and Paris in the Eighteenth Century." *Journal of World History* 21.3 (2010): 447–70. Project MUSE. Web. 19 June 2013.

Crisafulli, Alessandro S. "Montesquieu's Story of the Troglodytes: Its Background, Meaning, and Significance." *PMLA: Publications of the Modern*

Language Association of America 58.2 (1943): 372–92. MLA International Bibliography. Web. 19 July 2013.

———. "A Neglected English Imitation of Montesquieu's *Lettres Persanes.*" *Modern Language Quarterly* 14 (1953): 209–16. MLA International Bibliography. Web. 19 July 2013.

———. "Parallels to Ideas in the *Lettres Persanes.*" *PMLA: Publications of the Modern Language Association of America* 52.3 (1937): 773–77. MLA International Bibliography. Web. 19 July 2013.

Crumpacker, Mary M. "The Secret Chain of the *Lettres Persanes*, and the Mystery of the B Edition." *Studies on Voltaire and the Eighteenth Century* 102 (1973): 121–41. MLA International Bibliography. Web. 19 July 2013.

Curley, Edwin. "From Locke's Letter to Montesquieu's *Lettres.*" *Midwest Studies in Philosophy* 26.1 (2002): 280–306. Academic Search Premier. Web. 20 June 2013.

Curthoys, Ned. "A Diasporic Reading of *Nathan the Wise.*" *Comparative Literature Studies* 47.1 (2010): 70–95. Project MUSE. Web. 20 June 2013.

Darby, Robert. "Captivity and Captivation: Gullivers in Brobdingnag." *Eighteenth-Century Life* 27.3 (2003): 124–39. Project MUSE. Web. 20 June 2013.

Davidson, Levette Jay. "Forerunners of Goldsmith's *The Citizen of the World.*" *Modern Language Notes* 36, no. 4 (April 1921): 215–20. JSTOR. Web. 22 June 2013.

De Bruyn, Frans. "Anti-Semitism, Millenarianism, and Radical Dissent in Edmund Burke's *Reflections on the Revolution in France.*" *Eighteenth-Century Studies* 34.4 (2001): 577–600. Project MUSE. Web. 20 June 2013.

Diken, Bülent, and Carsten Bagge Laustsen. "Postal Economies of the Orient." *Millennium* 30.3 (2001): 761–84. Academic Search Premier. Web. 20 June 2013.

Dobie, Madeleine. "Embodying Oriental Women: Representation and Voyeurism in Montesquieu, Montagu and Ingres." *Cincinnati Romance Review* 13 (1994): 51–60. MLA International Bibliography. Web. 19 July 2013.

———. "'Langage Inconnu': Montesquieu, Graffigny and the Writing of Exile." *Romanic Review* 87.2 (1996): 209–24. MLA International Bibliography. Web. 19 July 2013.

Docker, John. "The Enlightenment and Genocide." *Journal of Narrative Theory* 33, no. 3 (Fall 2003): 292–314. JSTOR. Web. 22 June 2013.

Douthwaite, Julia. "Female Voices and Critical Strategies: Montesquieu, Mme de Graffigny, and Mme de Charrière." *French Literature Series* 16 (1989): 64–77. MLA International Bibliography. Web. 19 July 2013.

Drennon, Herbert. "The *Persian Letters:* A Glance at Montesquieu and His Politics." *Mississippi Quarterly: The Journal of Southern Culture* 11 (1958): 83–94. ProQuest. Web. 20 June 2013.

Falvey, John. "Aspects of Fictional Creation in the *Lettres Persanes*, and of the Aesthetic of the Rationalist Novel." *Romanic Review* 56 (1965): 248–61. MLA International Bibliography. Web. 19 July 2013.

Finnane, Antonia. "Yangzhou's 'Mondernity': Fashion and Consumption in the Early-Nineteenth-Century World." *Positions: East Asia Cultures Critique* 11.2 (2003): 395–425. Project MUSE. Web. 20 June 2013.

Frautschi, R. L. "The Would-Be Invisible Chain in *Lettres persanes*." *The French Review* 40, no. 5 (April 1967): 604–12. JSTOR. Web. 22 June 2013.

Gearhart, Suzanne. "The Place and Sense of the 'Outsider': Structuralism and the *Lettres Persanes*." *MLN* 92, no. 4, French Issue (May 1977): 724–48. JSTOR. Web. 19 June 2013.

Germann, Jennifer Grant. "Fecund Fathers and Missing Mothers: Louis XV, Marie Leszczinska, and the Politics of Royal Parentage in the 1720s." *Studies in Eighteenth-Century Culture* 1.1 (2007): 105–26. Project MUSE. Web. 20 June 2013.

Ghachem, Malick W. "Montesquieu in the Caribbean: The Colonial Enlightenment between 'Code Noir' and 'Code Civil.'" *Historical Reflections / Réflexions Historiques* 25, no. 2, Postmodernism and the French Enlightenment (Summer 1999): 183–210. JSTOR. Web. 22 June 2013.

Gilbert, Alan. "'Internal Restlessness': Individuality and Community in Montesquieu." *Political Theory* 22, no. 1 (February 1994): 45–70. JSTOR. Web. 22 June 2013.

Gonthier, Ursula Haskins. "Persians, Politics and Politeness: Montesquieu Reads Shaftesbury." *Nottingham French* Studies 48.3 (2009): 8–19. MLA International Bibliography. Web. 19 July 2013.

Goodman, Dena. "The Martin Guerre Story: A Non-Persian Source for Persian Letter CXLI." *Journal of the History of Ideas* 51, no. 2 (April–June 1990): 311–16. JSTOR. Web. 19 June 2013.

———. "Towards a Critical Vocabulary for Interpretive Fictions of the Eighteenth Century." *Romance Quarterly* 31.3 (1984): 259–68. MLA International Bibliography. Web. 19 July 2013.

Green, F. C. "Montesquieu the Novelist and Some Imitations of the *Lettres Persanes*." *The Modern Language Review* 20, no. 1 (January 1925): 32–42. JSTOR. Web. 22 June 2013.

Gunny, Ahmad. "Montesquieu's View of Islam in the *Lettres Persanes*." *Studies on Voltaire and the Eighteenth Century* 174 (1978): 151–66. MLA International Bibliography. Web. 19 July 2013.

Hakim, Zeina. "Whose Story?: The Game of Fiction in Early Eighteenth-Century French Literature." *Studies in Eighteenth-Century Culture* 41.1 (2012): 195–209. Project MUSE. Web. 20 June 2013.

Hart, Francis R. "Johnson as Philosophic Traveler: The Perfecting of an Idea." *ELH* 36, no. 4 (December 1969): 679–95. JSTOR. Web. 22 June 2013.

Hatzenberger, Antoine. "Kazanistan: John Rawls's Oriental Utopia." *Utopian Studies* 24.1 (2013): 105–18. Project MUSE. Web. 20 June 2013.

Higonnet, Margaret. "Frames of Female Suicide." *Studies in the Novel* 32.2 (2000): 229–42. MLA International Bibliography. Web. 19 July 2013.

Hilger, Stephanie M. "Comment peut-on être Péruvienne?: Françoise de Graffigny, a Strategic *Femme de Lettres*." *College Literature* 32.2 (2005): 62–82. Project MUSE. Web. 19 June 2013.

Hodson, Christopher. "'A Bondage So Harsh': Acadian Labor in the French Caribbean, 1763–1766." *Early American Studies* 5.1 (2007): 95–131. Project MUSE. Web. 20 June 2013.

Hou, Hongxun. "Montesquieu and China." *Contemporary Chinese Thought* 22.1 (1990): 11–31. Print.

Hulliung, Mark. "Patriarchalism and Its Early Enemies." *Political Theory* 2, no. 4 (November 1974): 410–19. JSTOR. Web. 22 June 2013.

Hundert, E. J. "Sexual Politics and the Allegory of Identity in Montesquieu's 'Persian Letters.'" *The Eighteenth Century* 31, no. 2 (Summer 1990): 101–15. JSTOR. Web. 19 June 2013.

Hundert, E. J., and Paul Nelles. "Liberty and Theatrical Space in Montesquieu's Political Theory: The Poetics of Public Life in the *Persian Letters*." *Political Theory* 17, no. 2 (May 1989): 223–46. JSTOR. Web. 19 June 2013.

Jennings, Jeremy. "The Debate about Luxury in Eighteenth- and Nineteenth-Century French Political Thought." *Journal of the History of Ideas* 68.1 (2007): 79–105. Project MUSE. Web. 19 June 2013.

Joncus, Berta. "'Ich bin eine Englanderin, zur Freyheit geboren': Blonde and the Enlightened Female in Mozart's *Die Entfahrung aus dem Serail*." *The Opera Quarterly* 26.4 (2010): 552–87. Project MUSE. Web. 20 June 2013.

Kelly, George Armstrong. "Conceptual Sources of the Terror." *Eighteenth-Century Studies* 14, no. 1 (Autumn 1980): 18–36. JSTOR. Web. 22 June 2013.

Kenshur, Oscar. "Virtue and Defilement: Moral Rationalism and Sexual Prohibitions in the 'Lettres Persanes.'" *Studies on Voltaire and the Eighteenth Century* (2001): 69–111. Print.

Kessler, Sanford. "Religion and Liberalism in Montesquieu's *Persian Letters*." *Polity* 15, no. 3 (Spring 1983): 380–96. JSTOR. Web. 19 June 2013.

Kettler, David. "Montesquieu on Love: Notes on the *Persian Letters*." *The American Political Science Review* 58, no. 3 (September 1964): 658–61. JSTOR. Web. 19 June 2013.

Knight, Charles A. "The Images of Nations in Eighteenth-Century Satire." *Eighteenth-Century Studies* 22, no. 4 (Summer 1989): 489–511. JSTOR. Web. 22 June 2013.

Kra, Pauline. "Montesquieu's *Lettres persanes* and George Lyttelton's *Letters from a Persian in England*." *Studies on Voltaire and the Eighteenth Century* 304 (1992): 871–74. ProQuest. Web. 20 June 2013.

———. "Multiplicity of Voices in the *Lettres persanes*." *Revue belge de philologie et d'histoire* 70, no. 3 (1992): 694–705. Persée. Web. 22 June 2013.

———. "The Name Rica and the Veil in Montesquieu's *Lettres persanes*." *Studi Francesi* 42.1 [124] (1998): 78–79. MLA International Bibliography. Web. 19 July 2013.

———. "The Role of the Harem in Imitations of Montesquieu's *Lettres persanes*." *Studies on Voltaire and the Eighteenth Century* 182 (1979): 273–83. MLA International Bibliography. Web. 19 July 2013.

Kwass, Michael. "Consumption and the World of Ideas: Consumer Revolution and the Moral Economy of the Marquis de Mirabeau." *Eighteenth-Century Studies* 37.2 (2004): 187–213. Project MUSE. Web. 19 June 2013.

Lavaque-Manty, Mika. "Liberal Feminism, Gender and Montesquieu." *Conference Papers—Midwestern Political Science Association* (2004): 1–28. Academic Search Premier. Web. 20 June 2013.

Lowe, Lisa. "Rereadings in Orientalism: Oriental Inventions and Inventions of the Orient in Montesquieu's *Lettres persanes*." *Cultural Critique* 15 (Spring 1990): 115–43. JSTOR. Web. 22 June 2013.

Mallinson, G. J. "Usbek, Language and Power: Images of Authority in Montesquieu's *Lettres persanes*." *French Forum* 18, no. 1 (January 1993): 23–36. JSTOR. Web. 22 June 2013.

Malueg, Sara Ellen Procius. "Commentary on Papers by Shelby O. Spruell and Ann M. Moore." *Proceedings of the Annual Meeting of the Western Society for French History* 8 (1981): 159–64. MLA International Bibliography. Web. 19 July 2013.

Mander, Jenny. "Nothing to Write Home About?: The Linguistic Limits of the Enlightenment's Global Journey." *Invitation au Voyage: Studies in Honour of Peter France*. (2000). Print.

Marso, Lori J. "The Stories of Citizens: Rousseau, Montesquieu, and de Staël Challenge Enlightenment Reason." *Polity* 30, no. 3 (Spring 1998): 435–63. JSTOR. Web. 20 June 2013.

Maslan, Susan. "The Dream of the Feeling Citizen: Law and Emotion in Corneille and Montesquieu." *Substance* 35.1 (2006): 69–84. Project MUSE. Web. 19 June 2013.

McAlpin, Mary. "Between Men for All Eternity: Feminocentrism in Montesquieu's *Lettres persanes*." *Eighteenth-Century Life* 24.1 (2000): 45–61. Project MUSE. Web. 19 June 2013.

McWilliams, Susan Jane. "Montesquieu's *Persian Letters*: Travel, Translation, and the Problems of Political Theory." *Conference Papers—American Political Science Association* (2003): 1–28. Academic Search Premier. Web. 20 June 2013.

Mirsepassi, Ali. "New Geographies of Modernity." *Comparative Studies of South Asia, Africa and the Middle East* 26.1 (2006): 1–15. Project MUSE. Web. 20 June 2013.

Moraru, Christian. "Reading, Writing, Being: Persians, Parisians, and the Scandal of Identity." *Symploke* 17.1 (2009): 247–53. Project MUSE. Web. 19 June 2013.

Mosher, Michael. "Double Exposures: The Philosophical Intentions of Montesquieu's *Persian Letters.*" *Conference Papers—Midwestern Political Science Association* (2004): 1–23. Academic Search Premier. Web. 20 June 2013.

———. "The Judgmental Gaze of European Women: Gender, Sexuality, and the Critique of Republican Rule." *Political Theory* 22, no. 1 (February 1994): 25–44. JSTOR. Web. 22 June 2013.

———. "Montesquieu's *Persian Letters* and the Cavellian Skeptic: Insight and Blindness in the Enlightenment." *Conference Papers—American Political Science Association* (2007): 1–30. Academic Search Premier. Web. 20 June 2013.

Nanquette, Laetitia. "French New Orientalist Narratives from the 'Natives': Reading More Than Chahdortt Djavann in Paris." *Comparative Studies of South Asia, Africa and the Middle East* 29.2 (2009): 269–80. Project MUSE. Web. 19 June 2013.

Neiman, Morris. "A Hebrew Imitation of Montesquieu's *Lettres persanes.*" *Jewish Social Studies* 37, no. 2 (Spring 1975): 163–69. JSTOR. Web. 20 June 2013.

Newmark, Kevin. "Leaving Home without It." *Stanford French Review* 11.1 (1987): 17–32. MLA International Bibliography. Web. 19 July 2013.

Oake, Roger B. "Polygamy in the *Lettres persanes.*" *Romanic Review* 32 (1941): 56–62. MLA International Bibliography. Web. 19 July 2013.

Pachter, Henry M. "A Philosophy for the New Left." *Salmagundi* 17 (Fall 1971): 114–24. JSTOR. Web. 22 June 2013.

Pacini, Giulia. "Righteous Letters: Vindications of Two Refugees in *Lettres d'une Péruvienne* and Its Unauthorized Sequel, *Lettres taïtiennes.*" *Eighteenth-Century Fiction* 188.2 (2005): 169–85. Project MUSE. Web. 20 June 2013.

Palmeri, Frank. "Conjectural History and Satire: Narrative as Historical Argument from Mandeville to Malthus (and Foucault)." *Narrative* 14.1 (2006): 64–84. Project MUSE. Web. 20 June 2013.

Pangborn, Matthew. "Royall Tyler's *The Algerine Captive*, America, and the Blind Man of Philosophy." *Arizona Quarterly* 67.3 (2011): 1–27. Project MUSE. Web. 20 June 2013.

Pelli, Moshe. "The Epistolary Story in Haskalah Literature: Isaac Euchel's 'Igrot Meshulam.'" *Jewish Quarterly Review* 93.3 (2003): 431–69. Project MUSE. Web. 10 Aug. 2013.

Pucci, Suzanne L. "Orientalism and Representations of Exteriority in Montesquieu's *Lettres persanes.*" *The Eighteenth Century* 26, no. 3 (Fall 1985): 263–79. JSTOR. Web. 22 June 2013.

Radasanu, Andrea. "Montesquieu's Enlightenment Critique of Divine Love." *Conference Papers—American Political Science Association* (2007): 1–16. Academic Search Premier. Web. 20 June 2013.

Rahihieh, Nasrin. "'How to Be Persian Abroad?': An Old Question in the Postmodern Age." *Iranian Studies* 26, no. 1/2 (Winter–Spring 1993): 165–68. JSTOR. Web. 22 June 2013.

Ram, Harsha. "Russia and the Oriental Despot." *India International Centre Quarterly* 21, no. 2/3, The Russian Enigma (Summer/Monsoon 1994): 31–46. JSTOR. Web. 22 June 2013.

Ranum, Orest. "Personality and Politics in the Persian Letters." *Political Science Quarterly* 84, no. 4 (December 1969): 606–27. JSTOR. Web. 19 June 2013.

Richardson, Alan. "Astarté: Byron's *Manfred* and Montesquieu's *Lettres Persanes.*" *Keats-Shelley Journal* 40 (1991): 19–22. JSTOR. Web. 22 June 2013.

Roddick, Nick. "The Structure of the *Lettres Persanes.*" *French Studies* 28 (1974): 396–407. MLA International Bibliography. Web. 19 July 2013.

Rogers, Katharine M. "Subversion of Patriarchy in *Les Lettres persanes.*" *Philological Quarterly* 65.1 (1986): 61–78. MLA International Bibliography. Web. 19 July 2013.

Roosbroeck, G. L. van. "Additional Persian Letters before Montesquieu." *Romanic Review* 23 (1932): 243–48. MLA International Bibliography. Web. 19 July 2013.

Ruddy, F. S. "International Law and The Enlightenment: Vattel and the 18th Century." *The International Lawyer* 3, no. 4 (July 1969): 839–58. JSTOR. Web. 22 June 2013.

Russo, Elena. "Monstrous Virtue: Montesquieu's Considérations sur les Romains." *Romanic Review* 90.3 (1999): 333–52. MLA International Bibliography. Web. 19 July 2013.

Saint-Amand, Pierre. "Original Vengeance: Politics, Anthropology, and the French Enlightenment." *Eighteenth-Century Studies* 26, no. 3 (Spring 1993): 399–417. JSTOR. Web. 22 June 2013.

Schaub, Diana J. "Montesquieu on Slavery." *Perspectives on Political Science* 34.2 (Spring 2005): 70. Expanded Academic ASAP Infotrac. Web. 19 June 2013.

Shackleton, Robert. "The Moslem Chronology of the *Lettres persanes.*" *French Studies* 8 (January 1954): 17–27.

Shklar, Judith N. "Putting Cruelty First." *Daedalus* 111, no. 3, Representations and Realities (Summer 1982): 17–27. JSTOR. Web. 22 June 2013.

Spruell, Shelby O. "The Metaphorical Use of Sexual Repression to Represent Political Oppression in Montesquieu's *Persian Letters.*" *Proceedings of the Annual Meeting of the Western Society for French History* 8 (1981): 147–58. ProQuest. Web. 20 June 2013.

Stilwell, Jama. "A New View of the Eighteenth-Century 'Abduction' Opera: Edification and Escape at the Parisian Théâtres de la Foire." *Music and Letters* 91.1 (2010): 51–82. Project MUSE. Web. 20 June 2013.

Strong, Susan C. "Why a Secret Chain? Oriental Topoi and the Essential Mystery of the *Lettres persanes*." *Studies on Voltaire and the Eighteenth Century* 230 (1985): 167–79. MLA International Bibliography. Web. 19 July 2013.

Strong, Tracy B. "Nietzsche and the Political: Tyranny, Tragedy, Cultural Revolution, and Democracy." *The Journal of Nietzsche Studies* 35.1 (2008): 48–66. Project MUSE. Web. 20 June 2013.

Sznaider, Natan. "Rewriting the *Persian Letters*." *British Journal of Sociology* 61.3 (2010): 627–33. SocINDEX with Full Text. Web. 19 June 2013.

Tenenbaum, Susan. "Montesquieu and Mme. de Stael: The Woman as a Factor in Political Analysis." *Political Theory* 1, no. 1 (February 1973): 92–103. JSTOR. Web. 22 June 2013.

Thomas, Downing A. "Economy and Identity in Graffigny's *Lettres d'une Péruvienne*." *South Central Review* 10, no. 4 (Winter 1993): 55–72. JSTOR. Web. 22 June 2013.

———. "Negotiating Taste in Montesquieu." *Eighteenth-Century Studies* 39.1 (2005): 71–90. Project MUSE. Web. 19 June 2013.

Thomas, Ruth P. "Montesquieu's Harem and Diderot's Convent: The Woman as Prisoner." *The French Review* 52, no. 1 (October 1978): 36–45. JSTOR. Web. 19 June 2013.

Tomaselli, Sylvana. "Moral Philosophy and Population Questions in Eighteenth-Century Europe." *Population and Development Review* 14, Supplement: Population and Resources in Western Intellectual Traditions (1988): 7–29. JSTOR. Web. 22 June 2013.

Trumpener, Katie. "Rewriting Roxane: Orientalism and Intertextuality in Montesquieu's *Lettres persanes* and Defoe's *The Fortunate Mistress*." *Stanford French Review* 11.2 (1987): 177–91. MLA International Bibliography. Web. 19 July 2013.

Vambery, Arminius and David Mandler. "Arminius Vambery: How I Decided to Travel to Europe, and Why I Wrote My Memoirs." *Shofar* 25.3 (2007): 16–22. Project MUSE. Web. 20 June 2013.

Vartanian, Aram. "Eroticism and Politics in the *Lettres persanes*." *Romanic Review* 60 (1969): 23–33. MLA International Bibliography. Web. 19 July 2013.

Vazsonyi, Nicholas. "Montesquieu, Friedrich Carl von Moser, and the 'National Spirit Debate' in Germany, 1765–1767." *German Studies Review* 22, no. 2 (May 1999): 225–46. JSTOR. Web. 22 June 2013.

Walsh, Jonathan. "A Cultural Numismatics: The 'Chain' of Economics in Montesquieu's *Lettres persanes*." *Australian Journal of French Studies* 46.1–2 (2009): 139–54. MLA International Bibliography. Web. 19 July 2013.

Wellington, Marie. "Montesquieu's Troglodytes and Voltaire's Quakers: A Case of Ideological Kinship." *Dalhousie French Studies* 28 (Fall 1994): 29–41. JSTOR. Web. 22 June 2013.

Winston, Michael. "Medicine, Marriage, and Human Degeneration in the French Enlightenment." *Eighteenth-Century Studies* 38.2 (2005): 263–81. Project MUSE. Web. 19 June 2013.

Wolloch, Nathaniel. "'Facts, or Conjectures': Antoine-Yves Goguet's Historiography." *Journal of the History of Ideas* 68.3 (2007): 429–49. Project MUSE. Web. 20 June 2013.

Yeazell, Ruth Bernard. "Harems for Mozart and Rossini." *Raritan* 16.4 (1997): 86–105. MLA International Bibliography. Web. 19 July 2013.

Young, David B. "Libertarian Demography: Montesquieu's Essay on Depopulation in the *Lettres persanes*." *Journal of the History of Ideas* 36, no. 4 (October–December 1975): 669–82. JSTOR. Web. 22 June 2013.

———. "Montesquieu and Watteau as Regency Social Critics." *Liberal & Fine Arts Review* 5.2 (1985): 3–19. MLA International Bibliography. Web. 19 July 2013.

Zarifopol-Johnston, Ilinca. "Found in Translation: The Two Lives of E. M. Cioran; or How Can One Be a Comparatist?" *Comparative Literature Studies* 44.1 (2007): 20–37. Project MUSE. Web. 20 June 2013.

Zonana, Joyce. "The Sultan and the Slave: Feminist Orientalism and the Structure of *Jane Eyre*." *Signs* 18, no. 3 (Spring 1993): 592–617. JSTOR. Web. 22 June 2013.

Books

Aravamudan, Srinivas. *Enlightenment Orientalism: Resisting the Rise of the Novel.* Chicago: University of Chicago Press, 2012. Print.

Atkinson, Geoffroy. *The Sentimental Revolution: French Writers of 1690–1740.* Ed. Abraham C. Keller. Seattle: University of Washington Press, 1965. Print.

Berman, Marshall. *The Politics of Authenticity: Radical Individualism and the Emergence of Modern Society*. New York: Atheneum, 1970. Print.

Besterman, Theodore. *The Invisible Chain of the* Lettres persanes. Geneva: Institut et Musée Voltaire, 1963. Print.

Blum, Carol. *Strength in Numbers: Population, Reproduction, and Power in Eighteenth-Century France*. Baltimore: Johns Hopkins University Press, 2002. Print.

Boer, Inge E., and Mieke Bal. *Disorienting Vision: Rereading Stereotypes in French Orientalist Texts and Images*. Amsterdam: Rodopi, 2004. Print.

Bomer, John M. *The Presence of Montaigne in the* Lettres persanes. Birmingham, AL: Summa Publications, 1988. Print.

Conroy, Peter V. *Montesquieu Revisited.* New York: Twayne Publishers, 1992. Print.

Cook, Elizabeth Heckendorn. *Epistolary Bodies: Gender and Genre in the Eighteenth-Century Republic of Letters.* Stanford, CA: Stanford University Press, 1996. Print.

Dainotto, Roberto M. *Europe (in Theory).* Durham, NC: Duke University Press, 2007. Print.

Dobie, Madeleine. *Foreign Bodies: Gender, Language, and Culture in French Orientalism.* Stanford, CA: Stanford University Press, 2001. Print.

Euben, Roxanne L. *Journeys to the Other Shore: Muslim and Western Travelers in Search of Knowledge.* Princeton, NJ: Princeton University Press, 2006. Print.

Frail, Robert J. *A Singular Duality: Literary Relations between France and England in the Eighteenth Century.* New York: AMS, 2007. Print.

France, Peter. *Politeness and Its Discontents: Problems in French Classical Culture.* Cambridge: Cambridge University Press, 1992. Print.

Freeman, Kathryn S. *British Women Writers and the Asiatic Society of Bengal.* Abingdon: Ashgate, 2014.

Fritz, Paul, and Richard E. Morton. *Woman in the 18th Century, and Other Essays.* Toronto: S. Stevens, 1976. Print.

Goldsmith, Elizabeth C. *Writing the Female Voice: Essays on Epistolary Literature.* Boston: Northeastern University Press, 1989. Print.

Gonthier, Ursula H. *Montesquieu and England: Enlightened Exchanges, 1689–1755.* London: Pickering & Chatto, 2010. Print.

Goodman, Dena. *Criticism in Action: Enlightenment Experiments in Political Writing.* Ithaca, NY: Cornell University Press, 1989. Print.

Grimsley, Ronald. *The Idea of Nature in the* Lettres persanes. London: French Studies, 1951. Print.

Grosrichard, Alain. *The Sultan's Court: European Fantasies of the East.* Trans. Liz Heron. London: Verso, 1998. Print.

Harari, Josuè V. *Scenarios of the Imaginary: Theorizing the French Enlightenment.* Ithaca, NY: Cornell University Press, 1987. Print.

Keener, Frederick M. *The Chain of Becoming: The Philosophical Tale, the Novel, and a Neglected Realism of the Enlightenment: Swift, Montesquieu, Voltaire, Johnson, and Austen.* New York: Columbia University Press, 1983. Print.

Kingston, Rebecca. *Montesquieu and His Legacy.* Albany, NY: SUNY Press, 2009. Print.

Knight, Charles A. *The Literature of Satire.* Cambridge: Cambridge University Press, 2004. Print.

Kra, Pauline. *The Invisible Chain of the* Lettres persanes. (Volume 23 of Studies on Voltaire and the Eighteenth Century.) Geneva: Institut et Musée Voltaire, 1963. Print.

———. *Religion in Montesquieu's* Lettres persanes. Geneva: Institut et Musée Voltaire, 1970. Print.

Loy, J. Robert. *The Persian Letters*. New York: Meridian, 1961. Print.

Mirsepassi, Ali. *Intellectual Discourse and the Politics of Modernization: Negotiating Modernity in Iran*. Cambridge: Cambridge University Press, 2000. Print.

Mornet, Daniel. *French Thought in the Eighteenth Century*. Hamden, CT: Archon Books, 1969. Print.

Pohl, Nicole, and Brenda Tooley. *Gender and Utopia in the Eighteenth Century: Essays in English and French Utopian Writing*. Aldershot, England: Ashgate, 2007. Web.

Pucci, Suzanne R. *Sites of the Spectator: Emerging Literary and Cultural Practice in Eighteenth-Century France*. Oxford, England: Voltaire Foundation, 2001. Print.

Richter, Melvin. *The Political Theory of Montesquieu*. Cambridge: Cambridge University Press, 1977. Print.

Romanowski, Sylvie. *Through Strangers' Eyes: Fictional Foreigners in Old Regime France*. West Lafayette, IN: Purdue University Press, 2005. Print.

Runyon, Randolph Paul. *The Art of the* Persian Letters*: Unlocking Montesquieu's "Secret Chain."* Newark, DE: University of Delaware Press, 2005. Print.

Russo, Elena. *Styles of Enlightenment: Taste, Politics, and Authorship in Eighteenth-Century France*. Baltimore: Johns Hopkins University Press, 2007. Print.

Schaub, Diana J. *Erotic Liberalism: Women and Revolution in Montesquieu's* Persian Letters. Lanham, MD: Rowman & Littlefield, 1995. Print.

Shackleton, Robert. *Essays on Montesquieu and on the Enlightenment*. Oxford, England: Voltaire Foundation at the Taylor Institution, 1988. Print.

Sonenscher, Michael. *Before the Deluge: Public Debt, Inequality, and the Intellectual Origins of the French Revolution*. Princeton: Princeton University Press, 2007. Print.

Tarek El-Ariss. *Trials of Arab Modernity: Literary Affects and the New Political*. New York: Fordham University Press, 2013. Print.

Thibaudet, Albert. *French Literature from 1795 to Our Era*. Trans. by Charles Lam Markmann. New York: Funk and Wagnalls, 1938. Print.

Todorov, Tzvetan. *On Human Diversity: Nationalism, Racism, and Exoticism in French Thought*. Cambridge, MA: Harvard University Press, 1993. Print.

Van Roosbroeck, Gustave Leopold. *Persian Letters before Montesquieu*. New York: Institute of French Studies, 1932. Print.

Whittuck, Charles A. *The "Good Man" of the XVIIIth Century: A Monograph on XVIIIth Century Didactic Literature*. London: G. Allen, 1901. Print.

Young, David B. *Montesquieu's Standard and His Relativism in the* Lettres persanes*: Their Origins, Significance, and Development*. Dissertation. New York: Columbia University, 1971. Print.

Chapters in Books

Anderson, Perry. "Persian Letters (Montesquieu, 1721)." *The Novel: Volume 2: Forms and Themes*. Ed. Franco Moretti. Princeton, NJ: Princeton University Press, 2006. 161–72. Print.

Betts, C. J. "Montesquieu: *Lettres persanes.*" *Early Deism in France: From the so-called 'déistes' of Lyon (1564) to Voltaire's* Lettres philosophiques *(1734)*. International Archives of the History of Ideas, vol. 4. The Hague: Martinus Nijhoff Publishers, 1984. Print.

Boase, Alan M. "The Interpretation of *Lettres persanes.*" *The French Mind.* Ed. Will G. Moore. Oxford, England: Oxford University Press, 1952. 162–69. Print.

Braun, Theodore E. D. "Montesquieu, *Lettres persanes*, and Chaos." *Disrupted Patterns: On Chaos and Disorder in the Enlightenment.* Eds. Theodore E. D. Braun, John A. McCarthy, and N. Katherine Hayles. Amsterdam: Rodopi, 2000. 79–90. Print.

Cook, Elizabeth Heckendorn. "The Limping Woman and the Public Sphere." *Body and Text in the Eighteenth Century*. Eds. Veronica Kelly and Dorothea von Mücke. Stanford, CA: Stanford University Press, 1994. 23–44. Print.

Crisafulli, Alessandro S. "The Journal des Sçavans and the *Lettres persanes.*" *Literature and History in the Age of Ideas: Essays on the French Enlightenment Presented to George R. Havens.* Ed. Charles G. S. Williams. Columbus, OH: Ohio University Press, 1975. 59–66. Print.

De Carolis, Chetro. "'Une Chaîne Secrète et en Quelque Façon Inconnue': The Delegation of Power and Word in the *Lettres persanes.*" *French Orientalism: Culture, Politics, and the Imagined Other*. Eds. Desmond Hosford and Chong J. Wojtkowski. Newcastle upon Tyne, England: Cambridge Scholars, 2010. 183–200. Print.

DiPiero, Thomas. "The Spirit of Laws (of Desire)." *Illicit Sex: Identity Politics in Early Modern Culture*. Eds. Thomas DiPiero and Pat Gill. Athens, GA: University of Georgia Press, 1997. 25–44. Print.

Douthwaite, Julia. "The Exotic Other Becomes Cultural Critic: Montesquieu's *Lettres persanes* and Mme de Graffigny's *Lettres d'une Pèruvienne.*" *Exotic Women: Literary Heroines and Cultural Strategies in Ancien Règime France.* Philadelphia: University of Pennsylvania Press, 1992. 74–139. Print.

Elmarsafy, Ziad. "Conclusion: Towards Democracy." *Freedom, Slavery, and Absolutism: Corneille, Pascal, Racine*. Lewisburg, PA: Bucknell University Press, 2003. Print.

Fairbairn, A. W. "False Attributions of the *Lettres persanes.*" *Studies in the French Eighteenth Century: Presented to John Lough by Colleagues, Pupils and Friends.* Eds. D. J. Mossop, G. E. Rodmell, and D. B. Wilson. Durham, NC: University of Durham, 1978. 52–65. Print.

Kenshur, Oscar. "Virtue and Defilement: Moral Rationalism and Sexual Prohibitions in the *Lettres persanes.*" *Voltaire; Religion and Ideology; Women's Studies; History of the Book; Passion in the Eighteenth Century.* Ed. Anthony Strugnell. Oxford, England: Voltaire Foundation, 2001. 69–111. Print.

Kra, Pauline. "Montesquieu and Women." *French Women and the Age of Enlightenment.* Eds. Samia I. Spencer, Germaine Brée, and Elizabeth Fox-Genovese. Bloomington, IN: Indiana University Press, 1984. 272–84. Print.

Mason, Sheila. "New Perspectives on the *Lettres persanes*: Montesquieu and Lady Mary Wortley Montagu." *Eastern Voyages, Western Visions: French Writing and Painting of the Orient.* Ed. Margaret Topping. Oxford, England: Peter Lang, 2004. 113–33. Print.

———. "The Riddle of Roxane." *Woman and Society in Eighteenth-Century France: Essays in Honour of John Stephenson Spink.* Eds. Eva Jacobs, W. H. Barber, Jean H. Bloch, F. W. Leakey, and Eileen LeBreton. London: Athlone Press, 1979. 28–41. Print.

McAlpin, Mary. "Utopia in the Seraglio: Feminist Hermeneutics and Montesquieu's *Lettres persanes.*" *Gender and Utopia in the Eighteenth Century: Essays in English and French Utopian Writing.* Eds. Nicole Pohl and Brenda Tooley. Aldershot, England: Ashgate, 2007. 87–106. Print.

O'Reilly, Robert F. "The Structure and Meaning of the *Lettres persanes.*" *Studies on Voltaire and the Eighteenth Century.* Ed. Theodore Besterman. Geneva: Institut et Musée Voltaire, 1969. 91–131. Print.

Proulx, Patrice J. "Literary Border Crossing: Reconceptualizing Montesquieu's *Lettres persanes* in Lise Gauvin's *Lettres d'une autre* and Chahdortt Djavann's *Comment peut-on être français?*" *Transatlantic Passages: Literary and Cultural Relations between Quebec and Francophone Europe.* Eds. Paula Ruth Gilbert and Miléna Santoro. Montreal, QC: McGill-Queen's University Press, 2010. 122–35. Print.

Pucci, Suzanne Rodin. "The Discrete Charms of the Exotic: Fictions of the Harem in Eighteenth-Century France." *Exoticism in the Enlightenment.* Eds. G. S. Rousseau and Roy Porter. Manchester, England: Manchester University Press, 1990. 145–74. Print.

———. "Letters from the Harem: Veiled Figures of Writing in Montesquieu's *Lettres persanes.*" *Writing the Female Voice: Essays on Epistolary Literature.* Ed. Elizabeth Goldsmith. Boston: Northeastern University Press, 1989. 114–34. Print.

Richards, Earl Jeffrey. "The Referential Quality of National Images in Literary Texts: The Case of Montesquieu's *Lettres persanes.*" *Europa Provincia Mundi.* Eds. Joep Leerssen and Karl Ulrich Syndram. Amsterdam: Rodopi, 1992. 309–19. Print.

Romanowski, Sylvie. "Montesquieu's *Lettres persanes* and the Libertine Traditions." *Libertinage and the Art of Writing II*. Ed. David Rubin. New York: AMS, 1992. 59–68. Print.

Shackleton, Robert. "A Supposed Letter of Montesquieu in 1795." *Studies in Eighteenth-Century French Literature*. Eds. J. H. Fox, M. H. Waddicor, and D. A. Watts. Exeter, England: University of Exeter, 1975. 225–310. Print.

Shanley, Mary, and Peter Stillman. "Political and Marital Despotism: Montesquieu's *Persian Letters*." *The Family in Political Thought*. Ed. Jean Bethke Elshtain. Amherst: University of Massachusetts Press, 1982. 67–79. Print.

Van Kley, Dale K. "The Century of *Unigenitus*." *The Religious Origins of the French Revolution: From Calvin to the Civil Constitution, 1560–1791*. New Haven, CT: Yale University Press, 1996. Print.

Werner, Stephen. "Comedy and Modernity: The *Lettres persanes*." *Montesquieu and the Spirit of Modernity*. Eds. David W. Carrithers and Patrick Coleman. Oxford, England: Voltaire Foundation, 2002. 37–46. Print.

Works in French

Articles

Barrière, P. "Les éléments personnels et les éléments bordelais dans les 'Lettres persanes'." *Revue d'Histoire littéraire de la France* 51, no. 1 (1951): 17–36. JSTOR. Web. 22 June 2013.

Benet, Robert. "Du regard de l'Autre dans les *Lettres persanes*: Investigation, voilement, dévoilement." *L'Information littéraire* 44.3 (1992): 6–13. MLA International Bibliography. Web. 19 July 2013.

Benrekassa, Georges. "Le parcours ideologique des *Lettres persanes*: figures de la socialité et discours politique." *Europe* 574 (1977): 60–79. MLA International Bibliography. Web. 19 July 2013.

Bercovici, Daniel. "La vertu dans les *Lettres persanes*: significations du mot." *Language Quarterly* 16.1–2 (1977): 53–54. MLA International Bibliography. Web. 19 July 2013.

Bissière, Michèle. "Graffigny, Riccoboni, et la tradition des *Lettres persanes*." *Postscript: Publication of the Philological Association of the Carolinas* 12 (1995): 9–21. MLA International Bibliography. Web. 19 July 2013.

Bleton, Paul. "Ce qu'espionner veut dire." *Belphégor: Littérature Populaire et Culture Médiatique* 10.1 (2011): [no pagination]. MLA International Bibliography. Web. 19 July 2013.

Blum, Carol. "Une controverse nataliste en France au XVIIIe siècle: La polygamie." *Population (French Edition)* 53, no. 1/2, Population et histoire (January–April 1998): 93–112. JSTOR. Web. 22 June 2013.

Bolzinger, André. "Folies cosmopolites." *L'Évolution Psychiatrique* 68, no. 3 (July 2003): 447–55. SciVerse. Web. 22 June 2013.

Bonnel, Roland G. "Le despotisme dans les *Lettres persanes*." *Studies on Voltaire and the Eighteenth Century* 278 (1990): 79–103. MLA International Bibliography. Web. 19 July 2013.

Cambou, Pierre. "L'esprit et la loi dans les *Lettres persanes*: une pratique ironique des lumières." *Littératures* 42 (2000): 37–51. MLA International Bibliography. Web. 19 July 2013.

Carayol, Elisabeth. "Des Lettres persanes oubliées." *Revue d'Histoire littéraire de la France* 65, no. 1 (January–March 1965): 15–26. JSTOR. Web. 22 June 2013.

Chamayou, Anne. "Les *Lettres persanes* ou l'esprit des livres." *L'Esprit Créateur* 40.4 (2000): 13–24. Project MUSE. Web. 22 June 2013.

Coulet, Henri. "Le style imitatif dans le roman épistolaire français des siècles classiques." *Revue d'Histoire littéraire de la France* 85, no. 1 (January–February 1985): 3–17. JSTOR. Web. 22 June 2013.

Courtois, Jean-Patrice. "Comment Roxane devient philosophe: romanesque de l'illisible et sexuation des concepts dans les Lettres persanes." *La Lecture Littéraire* 3 (1999): 27–47. MLA International Bibliography. Web. 19 July 2013.

Crisafulli, Alessandro S. "L'observateur oriental avant les *Lettres persanes*." *Lettres Romanes* 8 (1954): 91–113. MLA International Bibliography. Web. 19 July 2013.

Dagen, Jean. "La chaîne de raisons dans les *Lettres persanes*." *Littératures* 17 (1987): 71–83. MLA International Bibliography. Web. 19 July 2013.

Dimoff, Paul. "La place dans l'œuvre de Montesquieu de 'l'Essai touchant les lois naturelles'." *Revue d'Histoire littéraire de la France* 57, no. 4 (October–December 1957): 481–93. JSTOR. Web. 22 June 2013.

Drévillon, Hervé. "L'âme est à Dieu et l'honneur à nous. Honneur et distinction de soi dans la société d'Ancien Régime." *Revue Historique* 654 (April 2010): 361–95. JSTOR. Web. 22 June 2013.

Durand-Sendrail, Béatrice. "Mirage des lumières: politique du regard dans les *Lettres persanes*." *L'Esprit Créateur* 28.4 (1988): 69–81. MLA International Bibliography. Web. 19 July 2013.

Edmunds, Bruce. "Absence et présence dans les *Lettres persanes*." *Constructions* (1988): 75–88. MLA International Bibliography. Web. 19 July 2013.

Estève, Laurent. "L'ironie du droit naturel: pour une nouvelle lecture du livre XV, 5." *Kairos* 14 (1999): 91–112. MLA International Bibliography. Web. 19 July 2013.

Eubanks, Peter. "Montesquieu et l'intériorisation de la religion." *Romance Notes* 51.2 (2011): 191–98. Project MUSE. Web. 22 June 2013.

Faguet, E., and Simone Goyard-Fabre. "De la philosophie de Montesquieu et de son actualité." *Revue de Métaphysique et de Morale* 76, no. 3 (July–September 1971): 292–322. JSTOR. Web. 22 June 2013.

Fricker, Yves. "Les 'Lettres persanes' et les origines de la pensée sociologique." *Revue européenne des sciences sociales* 41, no. 126, Sociologie et relativisme: Hommage à Jacques Coenen-Huther (2003): 53–60. JSTOR. Web. 22 June 2013.

Gaillard, Aurélia. "Montesquieu et le conte oriental: L'expérimentation du renversement." *Féeries: Études sur le conte merveilleux, XVIIe–XIXe siècle* 2 (2004): 109–24. MLA International Bibliography. Web. 19 July 2013.

Garagnon, Jean. "Montaigne et Montesquieu: une source pour la lettre persane XLIV?" *French Studies Bulletin* 97 (2005): 17–19. MLA International Bibliography. Web. 19 July 2013.

Gaulin, Michel. "Montesquieu et l'attribution de la lettre XXXIV des *Lettres persanes*." *Studies on Voltaire and the Eighteenth Century* 79 (1971): 73–78. MLA International Bibliography. Web. 19 July 2013.

Goulemot, Jean Marie. "Vision du devenir historique et formes de la révolution dans les *Lettres persanes*." *Dix-Huitième Siècle* 21 (1989): 13–22. MLA International Bibliography. Web. 19 July 2013.

Hawkins, R. L. "Une vingtaine de lettres inédites." *Revue d'Histoire littéraire de la France* 43 (1936): 113–23. MLA International Bibliography. Web. 19 July 2013.

Hoffman, Paul. "Usbek Métaphysicien. Recherches sur les significations de la 69e 'Lettre persane'." *Revue d'Histoire littéraire de la France* 92, no. 5 (September–October 1992): 779–800. JSTOR. Web. 22 June 2013.

Hopp, Lajos. "*Lettres persanes* et *Lettres de Turquie*." *French Studies* 21 (1967): 220–28. MLA International Bibliography. Web. 19 July 2013.

Hubert, René. "La notion du devenir historique dans la philosophie de Montesquieu." *Revue de Métaphysique et de Morale* 46, no. 4 (October 1939): 587–610. JSTOR. Web. 22 June 2013.

Kehrès, Jean-Marc. "Travestissement discursif et discours utopique: Marivaux et les digressions de Marianne." *French Forum* 33.3 (2008): 17–34. Project MUSE. Web. 10 August 2013.

Kempf, Roger. "Les *Lettres persanes* ou le corps absent." *Tel Quel* 22 (1965): 81–86. MLA International Bibliography. Web. 19 July 2013.

Labbens, Jean. "La Religion dans la modernité selon Montesquieu." *Archives de sciences sociales des religions* 40, no. 89 (January–March 1995): 9–25. JSTOR. Web. 22 June 2013.

Laufer, Roger. "La réussite romanesque et la signification des 'Lettres persanes' de Montesquieu." *Revue d'Histoire littéraire de la France* 61, no. 2 (April–June 1961): 188–203. JSTOR. Web. 22 June 2013.

Leigh, R. A. "Le thème de la justice dans les *Lettres persanes*." *Cahiers de l'Association Internationale des Études Françaises* 35 (1983): 201–19. MLA International Bibliography. Web. 19 July 2013.

Magné, Bernard. "Une source de la Lettre persane XXXVIII? 'L'égalité des deux sexes' de Poullain de la Barre." *Revue d'Histoire littéraire de la France* 68, no. 3/4, Dix-Huitième Siècle (May–August 1968): 407–14. JSTOR. Web. 22 June 2013.

Mahmoud, Parvine. "Les Persans de Montesquieu." *The French Review* 34, no. 1 (October 1960): 44–50. JSTOR. Web. 22 June 2013.

Mass, Edgar. "Le développement textuel et les lectures contemporaines des *Lettres persanes*." *Cahiers de l'Association Internationale des Études Françaises* 35 (1983): 185–200. MLA International Bibliography. Web. 19 July 2013.

Melani, Nivea. "La structure des *Lettres persanes*." *Annali Istituto Universitario Orientale, Napoli, Sezione Romanza* 10 (1968): 39–94. MLA International Bibliography. Web. 19 July 2013.

Mercier, Roger. "Le roman dans les *Lettres persanes*: structure et signification." *Revue des Sciences Humaines* 107 (1962): 345–56. MLA International Bibliography. Web. 19 July 2013.

Moschetto, Bruno-François. "La ville des lumières comme source de la réflexion politique dans les *Lettres persanes*." *AUMLA: Journal of the Australasian Universities Language and Literature Association* 109 (2008): 121–32. MLA International Bibliography. Web. 19 July 2013.

Pascal, Jean-Noël. "Montesquieu romancier après les *Lettres persanes*: note sur Arsace et Isménie, histoire orientale." *Littératures* 17 (1987): 85–91. MLA International Bibliography. Web. 19 July 2013.

Pedersen, John. "La liberté dans les 'Lettres persanes'." *Revue Romane* 25.2 (1990): 404–13. MLA International Bibliography. Web. 19 July 2013.

Perrin-Naffakh, Anne-Marie. "Persifler l'extravagance: procédés d'ironie dans une lettre persane." *L'Information Grammaticale* 36 (1988): 30–33. MLA International Bibliography. Web. 19 July 2013.

Picard, Bernard. "La Pensée et l'action dans les *Lettres persanes*." *The French Review* 42, no. 6 (May 1969): 857–64. JSTOR. Web. 22 June 2013.

Pomeau, René. "Une correspondance inédite de Montesquieu." *Revue d'Histoire littéraire de la France* 82, no. 2 (1982): 186–262. MLA International Bibliography. Web. 19 July 2013.

———. "Montesquieu et ses correspondants." *Revue d'Histoire littéraire de la France* 82, no. 2 (1982): 179–85. MLA International Bibliography. Web. 19 July 2013.

Raymond, Agnes G. "Encore quelques réflexions sur la 'chaine secrète' des *Lettres persanes.*" *Studies on Voltaire and the Eighteenth Century* 89 (1972): 1337–47. MLA International Bibliography. Web. 19 July 2013.

Romanowski, Sylvie. "La quête du savoir dans les *Lettres persanes.*" *Eighteenth-Century Fiction* 3, no. 2 (January 1991): 93–111. Project MUSE. Web. 22 June 2013.

Rosset, François. "Les nœuds du langage dans les *Lettres d'une Péruvienne.*" *Revue d'Histoire littéraire de la France* 96, no. 6 (November–December 1996): 1106–27. JSTOR. Web. 22 June 2013.

Saint-Amand, Pierre. "Le Voyage du Philosophe."*Modern Language Studies* 21, no. 1 (Winter 1991): 66–73. JSTOR. Web. 22 June 2013.

Sanfey, Darach. "L'attribution de la lettre CXLIV des *Lettres persanes.*" *Travaux de Littérature* 6 (1993): 173–92. MLA International Bibliography. Web. 19 July 2013.

Schwarzbach, Bertram Eugene. "*A quo?*: Datation de l'*Opinion des anciens sur les juifs*; *Ad quem?*: Une source des *Lettres persanes.*" *Lettre Clandestine* 5 (1996): 33–41. MLA International Bibliography. Web. 19 July 2013.

Singerman, Alan J. "Réflexions sur une métaphore: le sérail dans les *Lettres persanes.*" *Studies on Voltaire and the Eighteenth Century* 185 (1980): 181–98. MLA International Bibliography. Web. 19 July 2013.

Stewart, Philip. "Toujours Usbek." *Eighteenth-Century Fiction* 11.2 (1999): 141–50. Project MUSE. Web. 22 June 2013.

Testud, Pierre. "Les 'Lettres persanes,' roman épistolaire." *Revue d'Histoire littéraire de la France* 66, no. 4 (October–December 1966): 642–56. JSTOR. Web. 22 June 2013.

Vallois, Marie-Claire. "'Rêverie orientale' et géopolitique du corps féminin chez Montesquieu." *Romance Quarterly* 38, no. 3 (August 1991): 363–72. EBSCO MegaFILE. Web. 22 June 2013.

Viselli, Sante A. "Le Troglodyte image fictive du Sauvage canadien." *L'Homme et la nature/Man and Nature* 5 (1986): 191–200. Print.

Waterson, Karolyn. "La Bruyère's Travel Literature: An Old World Sinfonietta." *Dalhousie French Studies* 27, Réflexions sur le genre moraliste au dix-septième siècle (Summer 1994): 123–41. JSTOR. Web. 22 June 2013.

Books

Dédéyan, Charles. *Montesquieu, ou, L'alibi persan.* Paris: Sedes, 1988. Print.

Grimal, P. *Lettres persanes.* Paris: Colin, 1961. Print.

Grosrichard, Alain. *Structure du serail: La fiction du despotisme asiatique dans l'Occident classique.* Paris: Seuil, 1979. Print.

Vernière, Paul. *Lettres persanes*. Paris: Garnier, 1961. Print.

Waddicor, Mark Hurlstone. *Montesquieu, Lettres persanes*. London: Arnold, 1977. Print.

Book Chapters

Berthiaume, Pierre. "Les *Lettres persanes* ou l'exotisme sans l'exotisme." *Indigenes and Exoticism/Indigènes et exotisme*. Eds. Alex J. Dick, Jo-Ann McEachern, and Nicholas Hudson. Kelowna, BC: Academic, for Canadian Society for Eighteenth-Century Studies, 2005. 1–18. Print.

Chabut, Marie-Hélène. "Livre, lecture et dé-lire dans les *Lettres persanes*." *L'epreuve du lecteur: Livres et lectures dans le roman d'Ancien Régime*. Eds. Jan Herman, Paul Pelckmans, and Nicole Boursier. Louvain, Belgium: Peeters, 1995. 200–207. Print.

Charara, Youmna. "La Formation d'une série romanesque au XVIIIe siècle: Les réécritures des 'Lettres persanes'." *Poétique de la pensée: Études sur l'âge classique et le siècle philosophique: En hommage à Jean Dagen*. Eds. Béatrice Guion, et al. Paris: Champion, 2006. 201–18. Print.

Falzoni, Franca Marcato. "D'une littérature à l'autre: *Lettres d'une autre* de Lise Gauvin." *La deriva delle francofonie: L'altérité dans la littérature québécoise*. Ed. Carla Fratta. Bologna, Italy: Cooperativa Libraria Universitaria Editrice Bologna, 1987. 211–24. Print.

Gallouët, Catherine. "Le corps noir dans la fiction narrative du XVIIIe siècle: Voltaire, Montesquieu, Behn, de la Place, Castilhon, de Duras." *Le corps romanesque: images et usages topiques sous l'Ancien Régime*. Eds. Monique Moser-Verrey, Lucie Desjardins, and Chantal Turbide. Quebec, QC: PU Laval, 2009. 103–18. Print.

Goulemot, Jean. "Bonheur et désenchantement dans les *Lettres persanes*." *La Quête du bonheur et l'expression de la douleur dans la littérature et la pensée françaises*. Eds. Carminella Biondi, et al. Geneva: Droz, 1995. 107–12. Print.

Jaugin, E. "Morales et incertitudes romanesques dans les *Lettres persanes*." *Autour du roman: Études présentées à Nicole Cazauran*. Paris: Presse de l'École normale supérieure, 1990. 169–85. Print.

Lemaire, Jacques. "L'Apparicion Maistre Jean De Meun d'Honoré Bouvet et les *Lettres persanes* de Montesquieu: Points de convergence." *Études sur le XVIIIe siècle*. Eds. Roland Mortier and Herve Hasquin. Brussels: Les éditions de l'Université de Bruxelles, 1978. 59–71. Print.

Macé, Laurence. "Les *Lettres persanes* devant l'Index: une censure 'posthume'." *Montesquieu en 2005*. Ed. Catherine Volpilhac-Auger. Oxford, England: Voltaire Foundation, 2005. 48–59. Print.

Mercier-Faivre, Anne-Marie. "Une lecture fantasmatique de la *Gazette d'Amsterdam* au temps des *Lettres persanes* (1720–1721): le cas du despo-

APPENDIX: THE LEGACY OF MONTESQUIEU'S *PERSIAN LETTERS*

When Montesquieu published his *Persian Letters* in 1721, the book very quickly became a huge success, spawning a host of imitators hoping to capitalize on its popularity, though few could match Montesquieu's artistry and intelligence. But many of these imitations remain of interest today, in part because what Montesquieu started had enormous potential for later writers who wanted to look at European realities through an "oriental" prism in order to achieve a fresh perspective. A sampling from four of those later works is provided here.

1) George Lyttelton, *Letters from a Persian in England to His Friend at Ispahan* (1735)

Montesquieu's *Persian Letters* was translated into English in 1722, the year following its original publication, by John Ozell, a prolific translator. The book slowly became popular in England as well, being reprinted in 1730, and at that point one of its most attentive readers was George Lyttelton (1709–1773). Lyttelton, born into a family with political and aristocratic connections, became involved with politics while still young, and in his twenties he crafted his book as a direct and open imitation of Montesquieu, setting his Persian traveler in England. Lyttelton's book refers directly to Montesquieu, and at moments attempts to be a continuation of it; for example, a sequence of eleven letters continues Usbek's story about the Troglodytes. Lyttelton's *Letters from a Persian in England* found a wide public and was reprinted many times throughout the eighteenth century. The selections below illustrate both the form and manner of Lyttelton's imitation and the differences between him and Montesquieu: Lyttelton's satire is gentler by far than Montesquieu's, shading off at times almost into a panegyric on England's constitution and mores (such as Letter 78 below).

These selections are from the 1793 edition; the book continued selling well after Lyttelton's death. The text and punctuation below are slightly modernized, but some of the eighteenth-century spelling and its use of italics have been retained to give the reader some flavor of the original.

Letter 22

Selim to Mirza at Ispahan
From London

There is a very pretty, fair-complexioned girl, who lodges in a house over against me. She was always staring at me from her window, and seemed to solicit my regards by a thousand little airs that I cannot describe, but which touched me still more than all her beauty: at last I became so enamored of her that I resolved to demand her in marriage. Accordingly, I went to visit her in form, and was received by her mother, a widow gentlewoman, who desired very civilly to know my business.

'Madam,' said I, 'I have a garden at Ispahan adorned with the finest flowers in the east; I have the Persian jasmine, the Indian rose, the violet of Media, and the tulip of Candahar: but I have lately beheld an English lily more fair than all these, and far more sweet, which I desire to transplant into my garden. This lily, Madam, is now in your possession; and I come a suppliant to you, that I may obtain it.'

The old lady, not conceiving what I meant, began to assure me very faithfully that I was mistaken, for she had neither lily nor rose belonging to her.

'The lily,' returned I, 'is your lovely daughter, whom I come to ask of you for my wife.'

'What do you propose to settle on her?' replied she. 'That is the first point to be considered.'

'I will do by her very handsomely,' answered I; 'I will settle upon her—*two black eunuchs*, an expert old midwife, and six or seven very adroit female slaves.'

'Two *blacks*,' answered she, 'are well enough; but I should think *two French footmen* would be *genteeler*.

'However, Sir, we will not quarrel about her *equipage*. The question is, what *provision* you think of making.'

'Do not trouble yourself about that,' returned I; 'she shall have *meat* enough, I warrant you; plenty of *rice*, and the best *sherbet*[1] in all Persia.'

1. Sherbet was a drink made of fruit juices and water.

'Do not tell me of *rice* and *sherbet*,' said the old woman; 'I ask what *jointure* you will give her?'

This word stopped me short, for I did not know what a *jointure* signified. At last she explained herself by demanding of me how her daughter was to live if I should die.

'I have an Indian wife,' answered I, 'that intends to burn herself as soon as I expire; but I would not recommend that method to your daughter.'

'How!' said she; 'you are married then already!'—'Yes,' said I; 'in Persia we are allowed to *take* as many women as we can *keep*: and some, I am sure, of the most fashionable men in England, do the same only leaving out the *ceremony*.'

'It is a very wicked practice,' answered she; 'but since it is your religion so to do, and that my daughter's *fortune* is too small to get a husband among Christians, I am not much averse to give her to you upon reasonable terms, because I am told you are very *rich*.'

She had scarce spoke these words, when my little mistress, who had been listening to our discourse behind the screen, came out from her concealment, and told her mother that if so many women were to live together, she was sure there would be no peace in the family, and therefore she desired her to insist on a good *pin-money* (that is to say, as the term was explained to me, a great *independent allowance*) in case her husband and she should *disagree*.

'What,' said I, 'young lady, do you think already of *separating your* interests from *mine*? And must I be obliged to pay my wife *for living ill with me*, as much as I should *for living well*?

'No, by Hali! I will never wed a woman who is so determined to *rebel* against her husband, that she *articles* for it in the very contract of her marriage!'

Letter 48

Selim to Mirza at Ispahan
From London

I was this morning with some gentlemen of my acquaintance, who were talking of the attempt that had been made not long ago of setting up a press at Constantinople, and the opposition it had met with from the *Mufti*. They applied to me to know what I thought of it, and whether in Persia also it was our religion that deprived us of so useful an art.

I told them, that policy had more part than religion in that affair; that the press was a very dangerous engine, and the abuses of it made us justly apprehend ill consequences from it.

'You are in the right,' said one of the company; 'for this single reason, *because your government is a despotick one*. But in a free country the press may be very useful, as long as it is under no partial restraint: for it is of great consequence that the people should be informed of every thing that concerns them; and, without printing, such knowledge could not circulate either so easily or so fast. And to argue against any branch of liberty from the ill use that may be made of it, is to argue against liberty itself, since all is capable of being abused. Nor can any part of freedom be more important, or better worth contending for, than that by which the spirit of it is *preserved, supported*, and *diffused*. By this appeal to the judgment of the people, we lay some restraint upon those ministers who may have found means to secure themselves from any other *less incorruptible tribunal*; and sure they have no reason to complain if the *publick* exercises a right which cannot be denied without avowing that their conduct will not bear enquiry. For though the best administration may be attacked by calumny, I can hardly believe it would be hurt by it, because I have known a great deal of it employed to very little purpose against gentlemen in opposition to ministers who had nothing to defend them but the force of truth. I do not mean by this to justify any scurrilities upon the *personal characters* either of magistrates or private men, or any *libel properly so called*. Against such abuses of the press the laws have provided a remedy; and let the laws take their course; it is for the interest of liberty they should do so, as well as for the security and honor of government: but let them not be strained into oppression by *forced constructions*, or *extraordinary acts of power*, alike repugnant to natural justice, and to the spirit of a free state. Such arbitrary practices no provocation can justify, no precedents warrant, no danger excuse.'

The gentleman who spoke thus was contradicted by another of the company; who, with great warmth, and many arguments, maintained that the licentiousness of the press was grown of late to such a dangerous height as to require *extraordinary remedies*; and that, if it were put under the inspection of some discreet and judicious person, it would be far more beneficial to the *publick*.

'I agree to it,' answered he, 'upon one condition, viz. That there may be likewise *an inspector for* THE PEOPLE, as well as one for the *court*; but if *nothing* is to be licensed on one side, and *every thing* on the other, it would be vastly better for us to adopt the eastern policy, and allow *no printing here at all*, than to leave it under such *a partial direction*.'

Letter 49

Selim to Mirza at Ispahan
From London

The same gentleman, who, as I told thee in my last, argued so strongly for the liberty of the press, went on with his discourse in the following manner.

'If we have so much reason to be unwilling, that what we *print* should be under the *inspection* of the court, how much more may we complain of a new power assumed within these last fifty years by all the courts in Europe, of *inspecting private letters*, and invading the *liberty of the post*? The secrecy and safety of correspondence is a point of such consequence to mankind, that the least interruption of it would be criminal, without an evident *necessity*; but that of course, from one year to another, there should be a constant breach of it *publickly* avowed, is such a violation of the rights of society, as one cannot but wonder at *even in this age.*'

'You may well wonder,' said I to him, 'when I myself am quite amazed to hear of such a thing; the like of which was never practiced among *us*, whom you English reproach with being *slaves*. But I beg you to inform me what it was that could induce a free people to give up all the secrets of their business, and private thoughts, to the curiosity and discretion of a minister, or his inferior tools in office?'

'They never gave them up,' answered he; 'but those gentlemen have exercised this power by their own authority, under the pretense of discovering plots against the state.'—'No doubt,' said one of the company, 'it is a great advantage and ease to the government, to be acquainted at all times with the sentiments of considerable persons, because it is possible they may have some ill intent.'—'It is very true,' replied the other; 'and it might be still a *greater* ease and advantage to the government to have a *licensed spy* in every house, who should report the most private conversations, and let the minister thoroughly into the secrets of every family in the kingdom. This would effectually detect and prevent conspiracies: but would any body come into it on that account?

'Is it not making a bad compliment to a government, to suppose that it could not be secured without such measures as are inconsistent with the end for which it is designed?

'But such in general is the wretched turn of modern policy; the most sacred ties of society are often infringed to promote some present interest, without considering how fatal it may prove in its remoter consequences, and how greatly we may want those useful barriers we have so lightly broken down.'

Letter 77

Selim to Mirza at Ispahan
From London

I am going, in the confidence of friendship, to give thee a proof of the weakness of human nature, and the unaccountable capriciousness of our passions. Since I delivered up Zélis to her husband, I have not enjoyed a moment's peace. Her beauty, which I saw without emotion while she continued *in my power*, now she is *out of it*, has fired me to that degree that I have almost lost my reason. I cannot bear to see her in the possession of the man to whom I gave her: if shame, if despair, did not hinder it, I should ask him for her again. In this uneasiness and disorder of my mind, there remains but one part for me to take: I must fly from her charms and my own weakness; I must retire into Persia, and endeavor, by absence and different objects, to efface the impressions she has made. Alas! What shall I find there? A seraglio composed of beautiful *slaves*; the *mercenary prostitutes*, or *reluctant victims*, to gross and tyrannical lust! What *rational commerce* can I hope for with *these*, what *true affection*, what *solid peace*, what *heart-felt delight*? But, were Zélis my wife, *in such a wife* I should find the most *endeared*, most *pleasing*, most *faithful friend*. All the precautions of eastern jealousy would then be unnecessary; those wretched precautions, which, while they bar the door against dishonor, shut out esteem, the life of friendship; and confidence, the soul of love.

Thou wilt be surprised at my talking thus: but what I feel for Zélis, and what I have seen in England, has overcome my native prejudices: I have seen here wives, over whose conduct, though perfectly free, *religion*, *honor*, and *love*, are stricter guards than legions of eunuchs, or walls of brass: I have seen, by consequence, *much happier husbands* than any Persian can possibly be. We will discourse on this subject more fully when I am with thee: and it will be my greatest pleasure, to try to remove out of thy mind all those prepossessions of which my own has been cured by my abode in this country. If I bring thee home *truth*, I am sure thou wilt think that I have traveled to better purpose, than if I came back fraught with the gold of Peru, or the diamonds of Golconda.

I have more than completed the four years stay I proposed making in England; and am now determined to pass through France as far as Marseilles, and embark from thence for the Levant, as soon as the business with which I am charged on the part of some of my friends, with the Turkey merchants there, will permit. It is my fixed resolution to go away without giving Zélis the least intimation of the cause of my departure: Abdallah shall never know that I am his *rival*; it would take too much from the character of a *friend.* Thou art the only one to whom I dare confide my folly; and since it has hurt nobody but myself, I hope thou wilt rather pity than blame me for it.

Letter 78

Selim to Mirza at Ispahan
From London

I am just on the point of leaving England: Abdallah and Zélis have received my adieus. The combat is past; my resolutions strengthen, and thou mayest expect ere long to see thy friend, with a *mind* a good deal altered by his travels; but a *heart,* which to *thee,* to his *country,* and to his *duty,* is still *the same.*

It would be unjust and ungrateful in me to quit *this island,* without expressing a very high esteem of the *good sense, sincerity,* and *good-nature,* I have found among *the English*: to these qualities I might also add *politeness,* which certainly they have as good a title to as *any of their neighbors*; but I am afraid that this accomplishment has been acquired too much at the expense of other virtues more solid and essential. Of their *industry,* their commerce is a proof; and for their *valor,* let their *enemies* declare it. Of their *faults* I will at present say no more, but that many of them are *newly introduced,* and so contrary to the genius of the people, that one would hope they might be easily rooted out. They are undoubtedly, all circumstances considered, a very *great,* a very *powerful* and *happy* nation; but how long they shall *continue so,* depends entirely on the *preservation of their liberty.* To the *constitution* of their government alone are attached all these blessings and advantages: should *that* ever be *depraved* or *corrupted,* they must expect to become the most *contemptible* and most *unhappy* of mankind. For what can so much aggravate the wretchedness of an oppressed and ruined people, as the remembrance of former freedom and prosperity? All the images and traces of their liberty, which it is probable no change will quite destroy, must be a perpetual reproach and torment to them, for having so degenerately parted with *their birthright.* And, if slavery is to be endured, where is the man that would not rather chuse it under the warm sun of Agra or Ispahan, than in the northern climate of England?

I have therefore taken my leave of my friends here, with this affectionate, well-meant advice, That they should vigilantly *watch over their constitution*, and guard it by those strong bulwarks which alone are able to secure it, *a firm union of all honest men, justice upon publick offenders, national and private frugality.*

2) Voltaire, *Zadig, or Destiny: An Oriental Tale* (1747)[2]

Voltaire (1694–1778) was one of the most important thinkers and writers of the century, and certainly one of its most original minds, but he too got caught up in the vogue for "oriental" tales, and *Zadig* is one of his best efforts in the genre.

The selections below illustrate the particular brand of satire that Voltaire deployed. Like Montesquieu, he sets his story in an exotic Persian locale in order to make points about contemporary France. Voltaire insists upon the connection with France even more than Montesquieu did, as we see below in the characters of Arnou and Yebor. Instead of an epistolary form, though, he opts for a straightforward narrative, using a seemingly objective third-person point of view. *Zadig* is in many respects a playful tale with a cheerful cynicism, but it also has many serious points to make about human relationships, religion, and free will. Women come in for harsh satire, and religion, whenever it falls into the hands of clerics, turns out to be at best absurd and at worst barbaric.

Setting his tale in this long ago, faraway time and place allows Voltaire to be more outspoken about sensitive topics than he could be otherwise. But the setting has other benefits too, allowing the author to write something more in the vein of a fable or parable than a realistic narrative. And that fable quality, in turn, allows Voltaire to present what he sees as some universal truths about human nature.

Chapter 1: The One-Eyed Man

In the days of King Moabdar, there was a young man in Babylon named Zadig; he had been gifted with a good nature at birth, and this had only been strengthened by education. Though young and rich, he knew how to keep his passions under control; he had no affectations; he had no interest in always being right, and he knew the respect that was due to human weaknesses. It was surprising to see that with all his intelligence, he never hurled insults or railed at all those vague, disconnected, noisy assertions, those rash slanders and ignorant decisions, those gross jokes

2. Translated by Raymond N. MacKenzie.

and that pointless clamor of words that comprised what was called "conversation" in Babylon. He had learned in the first book of Zoroaster that love of self is like a balloon swollen up with wind, and that pricking it results in tempests bursting forth from it. Above all, Zadig never prided himself on treating women with contempt and subjugating them. He was generous; he had no fear of being kind to ingrates, in this regard following the maxim of Zoroaster: "When you eat, give some to the dogs, even if they bite you in return." He was as wise as a person can be, for he desired to live among the wise. Instructed in the sciences of the ancient Chaldeans, he was not uninformed about the physical principles of nature, such as they were understood in those days, and he had as much metaphysical knowledge as people have had throughout all the ages—which is to say, hardly any. He firmly believed that a year consisted of three hundred and sixty-five and a quarter days, despite the new philosophy of his time, and that the sun was at the center of the world; and when the chief magi told him, in insultingly haughty tones, that his beliefs were all wrong, and when they added that to believe that the sun revolved under its own power and that a year had twelve months was to be an enemy of the state, he kept quiet, without anger and without contempt.

Zadig, possessed of great riches and, as a result, many friends, being in good health, handsome, with an open and moderate mind and a sincere, noble heart, believed that he could be happy. He was going to marry Sémire, whose beauty, birth, and fortune made her the premier mate in all Babylon. He had a solid, virtuous attachment to her, and Sémire loved him passionately. The happy day that was to unite them was near when, walking together near one of the gates of the city, beneath the palm trees that adorn the Euphrates river, they saw a group of men with sabers and arrows approaching them. These were dependents of young Orcan, the nephew of a minister, who his uncle's courtiers had led to believe that he could do whatever he liked. He had none of the graces nor the virtues of Zadig, but believing himself to be the worthier one, he was furious at not being more favored at court. This jealousy, born out of nothing more than his own vanity, led him to believe that he was madly in love with Sémire. He wanted to carry her off. The abductors seized her, and in the violence of their struggle, they wounded her, making the blood flow from a person whose very sight would have softened the tigers on Mount Imaüs. She pierced the heavens with her cries.

She called out, "My dear husband! They are tearing me away from the one I adore!" She had no concern for her own danger; her only thoughts were for her poor Zadig. The latter meanwhile defended her with all the force that valor and love can provide. Aided only by two slaves, he put the ravishers to flight and brought Sémire back to her home, bleeding and in a faint; when she opened her eyes, she saw her liberator.

She said to him, "Oh, Zadig, I loved you as my husband, but now I love you as the man to whom I owe my honor and my life." Never had there been a heart as moved as that of Sémire. Never had a more beautiful mouth spoken sentiments more touching than those burning words, which are inspired by the sense of the greatest of favors and by the tenderest transports of the worthiest of loves. Her wound was slight; she was soon healed. Zadig was wounded more seriously; an arrow striking close to his eye had left a deep gash. Sémire asked nothing of the gods except the curing of her beloved. Night and day, her eyes were bathed in tears: she awaited the moment when Zadig would be able to take joy in the sight of her. But an abscess, taking root in the wounded eye, made everyone fear. They sent to Memphis for the great physician Hermès, who came with a large retinue. He visited the sick man and declared that he would lose the eye, and he predicted the very day and hour when this doleful incident would take place.

"If it had been the right eye," he said, "I would have cured it, but wounds to the left eye are incurable." All Babylon, while lamenting the fate of Zadig, admired the profundity of Hermès' science. Two days later, the abscess broke on its own. Zadig was perfectly healed. Hermès wrote a book in which he proved that it should not have healed. Zadig did not read a word of it; but as soon as he was well enough to go out, he prepared himself to visit the woman who was all his hope for happiness in life, and for whom alone he desired to have the sight of his eyes. Sémire had been in the country for three days. On the road, he learned that the beautiful lady, having declared vigorously that she had an insurmountable aversion to one-eyed men, was going to marry Orcan that very night. Hearing this, he fell to the ground in a faint; his grief brought him close to the grave; he remained ill a long time; but at last, reason brought him out of his affliction, and the sheer atrocity of what he had undergone somehow consoled him.

"Since I have undergone such cruelty at the whim of a woman of the court," he said to himself, "I must instead marry someone from the citizenry." He chose Azora, the city's wisest and best-born girl; he married her, and lived for a month with her in the sweetest and tenderest union possible. But he noticed a certain frivolity in her, and a decided tendency to believe that the best-looking men were always the most virtuous and the wisest.

Chapter 2: The Nose

One day, Azora returned home from a walk in a rage, muttering angry exclamations. "What is the matter, my dear wife?" Zadig asked her. "What can have put you in such a state?"

"Alas!" she said. "You would be in the same state as I am if you had seen the spectacle I just witnessed. I went to give some consolation to the young widow, Cosrou, who had just finished erecting a funeral monument for her young husband beside the river that borders the meadow. In her grief, she made a vow to the gods to remain at the tomb as long as the water of the stream continued to flow past it."

"Well," said Zadig, "this sounds like a fine, respectable wife, and one who truly loved her husband!"

"Ah," she replied, "if only you knew what she was doing when I came to visit her!"

"What was it, my beautiful Azora?"

"She was having the stream's course redirected." With that, she broke out in a torrent of invective against the young widow so long, and a flood of reproaches so violent, that this great show of her own virtue began to displease Zadig.

He had a friend, named Cador, who was one of those young men his wife saw as having more integrity and merit than others. Zadig took him into his confidence and assured himself, as far as he could, of his fidelity by means of a generous gift. Azora, having spent two days in the country with one of her friends, came back to the house on the third day. The servants, all in tears, announced that her husband had died unexpectedly the night before, and that they had not dared to bring this awful news to her, and that they had just buried Zadig in the tomb of his fathers, toward the back of the garden. She wept, tore her hair, and swore that she would die. That evening, Cador asked permission to speak with her, and they wept together. The next day, they wept less and dined together. Cador confided to her that his friend had left him the greater part of his fortune, and gave her to understand that he would make himself perfectly happy if he shared it with her. The lady wept, became angry, then grew milder; their supper was longer than their dinner; they confided in each other more and more; Azora sang the praises of the deceased; but she did admit that he had certain faults from which Cador was quite free.

During the supper, Cador suddenly complained of a violent pain in his spleen; the lady, anxious and assiduous, had the servants bring in all the essences with which she perfumed herself, in the hope that one of them might be good for pain in the spleen; she lamented bitterly that the great Hermès was no longer in Babylon; and she even deigned to touch the spot that was causing Cador such intense pain.

"Have you always been subject to this cruel malady?" she asked him with the greatest compassion.

Cador replied, "It has almost taken me to the grave sometimes, and there is only one remedy for it: that is to apply the nose of a man who died the day before directly to the painful spot."

"That is certainly a strange remedy," said Azora.

"Not any stranger," he said, "than the sachets that Arnou[3] uses against apoplexy." This reasoning, together with the extreme merits of the young man, decided the lady at last.

"After all," she said, "when my husband passes from the world of yesterday to the world of tomorrow on the bridge of Chinivar, will the angel Asraël be any less inclined to carry him, simply because his nose is going to be a little shorter in the second life than it was in the first?"

With that, she took a razor; she proceeded to the tomb of her husband, watering it with her tears, and finding Zadig stretched out there, she approached to cut off his nose. Zadig sat up, protecting his nose with one hand and snatching away the razor with the other.

"Madame," he said to her, "curse no more about the young widow Cosrou; your plan to cut off my nose is quite a bit worse than hers of changing the course of a stream."

From Chapter 4: The Envious Man

Zadig hoped to let philosophy and friendship console him for the evils that fortune had inflicted upon him. In a suburb of Babylon, there was a tastefully decorated house in which all the arts and pleasures that an upstanding person could desire were gathered together. In the morning, its library was open to all scholars, and in the evening, its dinner table was open to a worthy company. But he soon learned how dangerous scholars can be. A great dispute arose concerning a Zoroastrian law forbidding the eating of griffin.

Some asked, "How can eating griffin be forbidden, when griffins do not exist?"

Others replied, "They must exist, since Zoroaster does not want us to eat them."

3. *"In those days, there was a man in Babylon named Arnou, who cured and even prevented apoplexies, in the newspapers, by means of a sachet hung from the neck."* [Voltaire's note. The reference is to a contemporary French physician named Arnoult.]

Zadig wanted to bring both groups into concord, so he said to them: "If there are griffins, let us by all means avoid eating them. If there are none, we should avoid eating them all the more, and thus we will all be obedient to Zoroaster."

One scholar, who had written a thirteen-volume work on the properties of griffins, and who was one of the greatest theurgists, hurried off to denounce Zadig to an arch-magus named Yebor,[4] the stupidest of the Chaldeans and therefore the most fanatical. This man would have had Zadig impaled for the greater glory of the sun, after which he would have recited his Zoroastrian breviary in the most satisfied of tones. But Zadig's friend Cador (and one friend is worth more than a hundred priests) went to see Yebor, and said to him:

"Long live the sun and the griffins! But avoid punishing Zadig: he is a saint, with griffins in his barnyard—and he never eats them. But his accuser is a heretic who dares to maintain that rabbits have cloven feet, and that they are not unclean."[5]

"Well then!" exclaimed Yebor, shaking his bald head, "we shall have to impale Zadig for having thought bad thoughts about griffins, and the other for having spoken bad things about rabbits."

Cador smoothed everything over by means of a maid of honor who had borne him a child, and who had powerful influence with the college of mages. Nobody ended up being impaled, an outcome which caused some muttering among many of the learned men, who felt this was a bad omen presaging the decadence of Babylon.

Zadig exclaimed, "Where is happiness to be found? Everything conspires to persecute me in this world, even creatures that do not exist." And he cursed scholars, resolving henceforth to live only with good people.

Chapter 11: The Pyre

Sétoc was delighted, and made his slave into his intimate friend.[6] He could no more get along without him than the Babylonian king before,

4. Yebor is an anagram of Boyer. Jean-François Boyer (1675–1755) was the bishop of Mirepoix and a member of the Académie Française; he worked to keep Voltaire out of the Académie on the grounds of his irreverence toward religion, and as a result Voltaire always saw him as a personal enemy.

5. The satire here implicitly touches on the Bible: a complicated set of rules involving whether animals with cloven feet can be eaten is given in Deuteronomy 14: 6–8.

6. After a series of misadventures involving a disastrous love affair with the Babylonian king's wife, Zadig is captured and sold into slavery. He is purchased by an Arab merchant, Sétoc, who he soon impresses with his intelligence.

and Zadig was happy to find that Sétoc had no wife. He saw that his master possessed a natural bent toward goodness, a considerable rectitude, and good sense as well. He was irritated to see that he worshipped the celestial army, that is, the sun, moon, and stars, as was the ancient custom in Arabia. He broached the subject discreetly a few times. At last he said that they were only bodies like any others, and merited not more worship than did a tree or a rock.

"But," said Sétoc, "these are eternal beings, from whom we have derived all our advantages; they are the life force of nature; they regulate the seasons; and moreover, they reside so far away from us that one cannot help but revere them."

Zadig replied, "You get more benefits from the waters of the Red Sea, which bring you merchandise from India. Why is that sea not just as ancient as the stars? And if you adore that which is far distant from you, you ought to adore the land of the Ganges, which is at the far corners of the world."

"No," said Sétoc; "the stars are so brilliant that I cannot help but adore them."

When night came, Zadig lit a great number of candles in the tent where he was going to dine with Sétoc; and when his master appeared, he threw himself down on his knees before the lighted tapers, addressing them thus: "Eternal and brilliant lights, be propitious to me always." Having said these words, he sat down at the table without looking at Sétoc.

Sétoc, surprised by all this, asked, "What are you doing?"

"I am doing just as you did," Zadig replied. "I am adoring these candles, and neglecting both their master and my own."

Sétoc understood the profound point of the parable. He let the wisdom of his slave penetrate his soul; he no longer wasted incense on created things, but preserved it for his adoration of the eternal Being who had created them.

There was in those days an atrocious custom in Arabia, which had come originally from Scythia, became established in India through the influence of the Brahmans, and now threatened to spread throughout the entire Orient. When a married man died, and his beloved wife wanted to be holy, she burned herself alive in public on the corpse of her husband. This was a solemn rite called the Widow's Pyre. The tribe that had the most burned wives was the most prestigious.

An Arab belonging to Sétoc's tribe having died, his widow, named Almona, who was deeply devout, announced the day and the hour when she would throw herself into the flames to the sound of drums and trumpets. Zadig remonstrated with Sétoc, telling him how contrary it was to the good of humankind, and how they were burning every day young widows who could instead be contributing children to the State, or at least bringing up the children they already had, and he made him see how so barbaric a custom should be abolished, if it were possible to do so.

Sétoc replied, "Women have had the right to burn themselves for more than a thousand years. Who among us would dare to change a law that time has consecrated thus? Is there anything more respectable than a well-established abuse?"

"Reason is even older," said Zadig. "Go speak to the chiefs of the tribes, and I will seek out the young widow."

He had himself introduced to her; and after he had gained her good opinion of him by praising her beauty, and after telling her what a pity it was to throw such charms into the flames, he went on to praise her resolution and her courage.

He asked her, "So then, you must love your deceased husband prodigiously?"

"Me? Not at all," replied the Arab lady. "He was brutal, jealous, a man impossible to tolerate. But I am firmly resolved to throw myself onto the flaming pyre."

"I suppose, then," said Zadig, "that there must be some truly delicious pleasure in being burned alive."

"Ah!" she exclaimed, "the thought of it makes nature shudder, but one has to do it nonetheless. I am a devout woman; my reputation would be ruined, and I would be a laughingstock if I failed to burn myself."

Zadig, having brought her to acknowledge that she was going to burn herself for others, and out of vanity, spoke with her for a long while in a manner calculated to make her love life a little bit, and he managed also to inspire a certain warmth in her toward the man talking to her.

"What would you do," he asked her, "if you could rid yourself of the vanity of burning yourself?"

"Alas," the lady said, "I believe I would beg you to marry me."

Zadig still had a vivid enough memory of Queen Astarté to be able to elude that declaration; he set off at once to the chiefs of the tribes, telling them what had happened, and advising them to enact a law forbidding a young widow to burn herself until she had had one full hour in privacy with a young man. And since then, not one woman burned herself in Arabia. Thanks were owed to Zadig for having destroyed in a single day so cruel a custom, and one that had endured for centuries. And so it was that he became the benefactor of Arabia.

3) Oliver Goldsmith, *The Citizen of the World* (1762)

One of the many French imitators of Montesquieu was Jean-Baptiste de Boyer, Marquis d'Argens (1704–1771), who produced volumes titled *Lettres Juives* (Jewish Letters, 1738) and *Lettres Chinoises* (Chinese Letters, 1741). The *Lettres Chinoises* was translated into English in 1755, and that translation inspired a struggling young Irish writer, Oliver Goldsmith (1728–1774).

Goldsmith wrote a number of brief imitations of d'Argens' Chinese letters for a newspaper, the *Public Ledger*, beginning in 1760; these were collected and printed in book form in 1762 as *The Citizen of the World, or, Letters from a Chinese Philosopher, Residing in London, to His Friends in the East.* The book made Goldsmith's reputation, and he went on to write works that continue to matter today: his poem about rural depopulation, *The Deserted Village* (1770), had a great impact on the early Romantic movement; and his novel, *The Vicar of Wakefield* (1766), and his play, *She Stoops to Conquer* (1773), remain widely beloved today.

But *The Citizen of the World*, though it is an imitation of an imitation, also remains an important text. As the title announces, the book implicitly upholds the ideal of cosmopolitanism, suggesting that nation-states are not inevitable, and that geography is not destiny. Goldsmith's Chinese traveler, in the excerpts below, reflects on topics such as the cultural relativism of beauty and marital conventions; in satirizing the then-new phenomenon of Methodism, he suggests that religion must embrace rationalism and leave its roots in emotion and subjectivism behind.

The selection below, slightly modernized in spelling and punctuation, is based on the 1762 edition. There is a superb scholarly edition by Arthur Friedman (Volume II of *Collected Works of Oliver Goldsmith*, Oxford University Press, 1966), which provides detailed notes on exactly which segments are original with Goldsmith and which are borrowed from d'Argens and other sources—including Lyttelton's *Letters from a Persian in England.*

Letter 3

From Lien Chi Altangi, to the care of Fipsihi, resident in Moscow; to be forwarded by the Russian caravan to Fum Hoam, first president of the Ceremonial Academy at Pekin in China.

Think not, O thou guide of my youth, that absence can impair my respect, or interposing trackless deserts blot your reverend figure from my memory. The farther I travel I feel the pain of separation with stronger force, those ties that bind me to my native country and you are still unbroken. By every remove, I only drag a greater length of chain.

Could I find ought worth transmitting from so remote a region as this to which I have wandered, I should gladly send it; but instead of this, you must be contented with a renewal of my former professions, and an imperfect account of a people with whom I am as yet but superficially acquainted. The remarks of a man who has been but three days in the country can only be those obvious circumstances which force themselves upon the imagination: I consider myself here as a newly created being introduced into a new world, every object strikes with wonder and surprise. The imagination, still unsated, seems the only active principle of the mind. The most trifling occurrences give pleasure, till the gloss of novelty is worn away. When I have ceased to wonder, I may possibly grow wise; I may then call the reasoning principle to my aid, and compare those objects with each other which were before examined without reflection.

Behold me then in London gazing at the strangers, and they at me; it seems they find somewhat absurd in my figure; and had I been never from home it is possible I might find an infinite fund of ridicule in theirs; but by long traveling I am taught to laugh at folly alone, and to find nothing truly ridiculous but villainy and vice. When I had just quitted my native country, and crossed the Chinese wall, I fancied every deviation from the customs and manners of China was a departing from nature: I smiled at the blue lips and red foreheads of the Tonguese; and could hardly contain when I saw the Daures dress their heads with horns. The Ostiacs powdered with red earth, the Calmuck beauties tricked out in all the finery of sheep-skin appeared highly ridiculous; but I soon perceived that the ridicule lay not in them but in me; that I falsely condemned others of absurdity, because they happened to differ from a standard originally founded in prejudice or partiality.

I find no pleasure therefore in taxing the English with departing from nature in their external appearance, which is all I yet know of their character; it is possible they only endeavor to improve her simple plan, since every extravagance in dress proceeds from a desire of becoming more beautiful than nature made us: and this is so harmless a vanity that I not only pardon but approve it; a desire to be more excellent than others is what actually makes us so, and as thousands find a livelihood in society by such appetites, none but the ignorant inveigh against them.

You are not insensible, most reverend Fum Hoam, what numberless trades, even among the Chinese, subsist by the harmless pride of each other. Your nose-borers, feet-swathers, tooth-stainers, eyebrow pluckers, would all want bread, should their neighbors want vanity. These vanities, however, employ much fewer hands in China than in England; and a fine gentleman, or a fine lady, here dressed up to the fashion, seems scarcely to have a single limb that does not suffer some distortions from art.

[. . .]

Letter 18

*From Lien Chi Altangi to * * * merchant in Amsterdam*

The English love their wives with much passion, the Hollanders with much prudence. The English when they give their hands, frequently give their hearts; the Dutch give the hand, but keep the heart wisely in their own possession. The English love with violence, and expect violent love in return; the Dutch are satisfied with the slightest acknowledgments, for they give little away. The English expend many of the matrimonial comforts in the first year; the Dutch frugally husband out their pleasures, and are always constant because they are always indifferent.

There seems very little difference between a Dutch bridegroom and a Dutch husband. Both are equally possessed of the same cool unexpecting serenity; they can see neither Elysium nor Paradise behind the curtain; and *Yiffrow* is not more a goddess on the wedding night than after twenty years, matrimonial acquaintance. On the other hand, many of the English marry, in order to have one happy month in their lives; they seem incapable of looking beyond that period; they unite in hopes of finding rapture, and disappointed in that, disdain ever to accept of happiness. From hence we see open hatred ensue; or what is worse, concealed disgust under the appearance of fulsome endearment. Much formality, great civility, and studied compliments are exhibited in public; cross looks, sulky silence, or open recrimination, fill up their hours of private entertainment.

Hence I am taught, whenever I see a new married couple more than ordinarily fond before faces, to consider them as attempting to impose upon the company or themselves, either hating each other heartily, or consuming that stock of love in the beginning of their course which should serve them through their whole journey. Neither side should expect those instances of kindness which are inconsistent with true freedom or happiness to bestow. Love, when founded in the heart, will show itself in a thousand unpremeditated sallies of fondness; but every cool deliberate exhibition of the passion, only argues little understanding, or great insincerity.

Choang was the fondest husband, and Hansi the most endearing wife in all the kingdom of Korea: they were a pattern of conjugal bliss; the inhabitants of the country around saw, and envied their felicity; wherever Choang came, Hansi was sure to follow; and in all the pleasures of Hansi, Choang was admitted a partner. They walked hand in hand wherever they appeared; showing every mark of mutual satisfaction, embracing, kissing, their mouths were for ever joined, and to speak in the language of anatomy, it was with them one perpetual anastomosis.

Their love was so great, that it was thought nothing could interrupt their mutual peace; when an accident happened, which, in some measure, diminished the husband's assurance of his wife's fidelity; for love so refined as his, was subject to a thousand little disquietudes. Happening to go one day alone among the tombs that lay at some distance from his house, he there perceived a lady dressed in the deepest mourning (being clothed all over in white) fanning the wet clay that was raised over one of the graves with a large fan, which she held in her hand. Choang, who had early been taught wisdom in the school of Lao, was unable to assign a cause for her present employment; and coming up, civilly demanded the reason. Alas, replied the lady, her eyes bathed in tears; how is it possible to survive the loss of my husband, who lies buried in this grave, he was the best of men, the tenderest of husbands; with his dying breath he bid me never marry again till the earth over his grave should be dry; and here you see me steadily resolving to obey his will, and endeavoring to dry it with my fan. I have employed two whole days in fulfilling his commands, and am determined not to marry till they are punctually obeyed, even though his grave should take up to four days in drying.

Choang, who was struck with the widow's beauty, could not, however, avoid smiling at her haste to be married; but, concealing the cause of his mirth, civilly invited her home; adding, that he had a wife who might be capable of giving her some consolation. As soon as he and his guest were returned, he imparted to Hansi in private what he had seen, and could not avoid expressing his uneasiness, that such might be his own case if his dearest wife should one day happen to survive him. It is impossible to describe Hansi's resentment at so unkind a suspicion. As her passion for him was not only great, but extremely delicate, she employed tears, anger, frowns, and exclamations, to chide his suspicions; the widow herself was inveighed against; and Hansi declared she was resolved never to sleep under the same roof with a wretch, who, like her, could be guilty of such barefaced inconstancy. The night was cold and stormy, however, the stranger was obliged to seek another lodging, for Choang was not disposed to resist, and Hansi would have her way.

The widow had scarce been gone an hour, when an old disciple of Choang's, whom he had not seen for many years, came to pay him a visit. He was received with the utmost ceremony, placed in the most honorable seat at supper, and the wine began to circulate with great freedom. Choang and Hansi exhibited open marks of mutual tenderness, and unfeigned reconciliation: nothing could equal their apparent happiness; so fond a husband, so obedient a wife, few could behold without regretting their own infelicity. When, lo! Their happiness was at once disturbed by a most fatal accident. Choang fell lifeless in an apoplectic fit upon the floor. Every method was used, but in vain, for his recovery. Hansi was at first inconsolable for his death: after some hours, however, she found spirits to read his last will. The ensuing day she began to moralize and talk wisdom; the next day she was able to comfort the young disciple; and on the third, to shorten a long story, they both agreed to be married.

There was now no longer mourning in the apartments; the body of Choang was now thrust into an old coffin, and placed in one of the meanest rooms, there to lie unattended until the time prescribed by law for his internment. In the meantime Hansi and the young disciple were arrayed in the most magnificent habits; the bride wore in her nose a jewel of immense price, and her lover was dressed in all the finery of his former master, together with a pair of artificial whiskers that reached down to his toes. The hour of their nuptials was arrived; the whole family sympathized with their approaching happiness; the apartments were brightened up with lights that diffused the most exquisite perfume, and a luster more bright than noonday. The lady expected her youthful lover from an inner apartment with impatience; when his servant approaching with terror in his countenance, informed her, that his master was fallen into a fit, which would certainly be mortal, unless the heart of a man lately dead could be obtained, and applied to his breast. She scarce waited to hear the end of his story, when, tucking up her clothes, she ran with a mattock in her hand to the coffin where Choang lay, resolving to apply the heart of her dead husband as a cure for the living. She therefore struck the lid with the utmost violence. In a few blows the coffin flew open, and the body, which, to all appearance had been dead, began to move. Terrified at the sight, Hansi dropped the mattock, and Choang walked out, astonished at his own situation, his wife's unusual magnificence, and her more amazing surprise. He went among the apartments, unable to conceive the cause of so much splendor. He was not long in suspense before his domestics informed him of every transaction since he first became insensible. He could scarce believe what they told him, and went in pursuit of Hansi herself, in order to receive more certain information, or to reproach her infidelity. But she prevented his reproaches: he found her weltering in blood; for she had stabbed herself to the heart, being unable to survive her shame and disappointment.

Choang, being a philosopher, was too wise to make any loud lamentations; he thought it best to bear his loss with serenity: so, mending up the old coffin where he had lain himself, he placed his faithless spouse in his room; and, unwilling that so many nuptial preparations should be expended in vain, he the same night married the widow with the large fan. As they both were apprised of the foibles of each other beforehand, they knew how to excuse them after marriage. They lived together for many years in great tranquility, and not expecting rapture, made a shift to find contentment. Farewell.

Letter 19

From Lien Chi Altangi to Fum Hoam, first president of the Ceremonial Academy at Pekin in China.

The gentleman dressed in black, who was my companion thro' Westminster Abbey, came yesterday to pay me a visit; and after drinking tea, we both resolved to take a walk together, in order to enjoy the freshness of the country, which now begins to resume its verdure. Before we got out of the suburbs, however, we were stopped in one of the streets by a crowd of people gathered in a circle round a man and his wife, who seemed too loud and too angry to be understood. The people were highly pleased with the dispute, which upon enquiry we found to be between Dr. Cacafogo, an apothecary, and his wife. The doctor, it seems, coming unexpectedly into his wife's apartment, found a gentleman there in circumstances not in the least equivocal. The doctor, who was a person of nice honor, resolving to revenge the flagrant insult, immediately flew to the chimneypiece, and taking down a rusty blunderbuss, drew the trigger upon the defiler of his bed; the delinquent would certainly have been shot through the head, but that the piece had not been charged for many years. The gallant made a shift to escape through the window, but the lady still remained; and as she well knew her husband's temper, undertook to manage the quarrel without a second. He was furious, and she loud; their noise had gathered all the mob who charitably assembled on the occasion, not to prevent, but to enjoy the quarrel.

Alas, said I to my companion, what will become of this unhappy creature thus caught in adultery! Believe me, I pity her from my heart;

her husband, I suppose, will show her no mercy. Will they burn her as in India, or behead her as in Persia; will they load her with stripes as in Turkey, or keep her in perpetual imprisonment, as with us in China? Prithee, what is the wife's punishment in England for such offenses? When a lady is thus caught tripping, replied my companion, they never punish her, but the husband. You surely jest, interrupted I; I am a foreigner, and you would abuse my ignorance. I am really serious, returned he; Dr. Cacafogo has caught his wife in the act; but as he had no witnesses, his small testimony goes for nothing; the consequence therefore of his discovery will be that she may be packed off to live among her relations, and the doctor must be obliged to allow her a separate maintenance. Amazing, cried I; is it not enough that she is permitted to live separate from the object she detests, but must he give her money to keep her in spirits too? That he must, says my guide; and be called a cuckold by all his neighbors into the bargain. The men will laugh at him, the ladies will pity him; and all that his warmest friends can say in his favor, will be that the *poor good soul has never had any harm in him.* I want patience, interrupted I; what! Are there no private chastisements for the wife; no schools of penitence to show her her folly; no rods for such delinquents? Pshaw man, replied he smiling; if every delinquent among us were to be treated in your manner, one half of the kingdom would flog the other.

I must confess, my dear Fum, that if I were an English husband, of all things I would take care not to be jealous, nor busily pry into those secrets my wife was pleased to keep from me. Should I detect her infidelity, what is the consequence? If I calmly pocket the abuse, I am laughed at by her and her gallant; if I talk my griefs aloud like a tragedy hero, I am laughed at by the whole world. The course then I'd take would be, whenever I went out, to tell my wife where I was going, lest I should unexpectedly meet her abroad in company with some dear deceiver. Whenever I returned, I would use a peculiar rap at the door, and give four loud hems as I walked deliberately up the staircase. I would never inquisitively peep under her bed, or look behind the curtains. And even though I knew the captain was there, I would calmly take a dish of my wife's cool tea, and talk of the army with reverence.

Of all nations, the Russians seem to me to behave most wisely in such circumstances. The wife promises her husband never to let him see her transgressions of this nature; and he as punctually promises, whenever she is so detected, without the least anger, to beat her without mercy: so they both know what each has to expect; the lady transgresses, is beaten, taken again into favor, and all goes on as before.

When a Russian young lady therefore is be married, her father, with a cudgel in his hand, asks the bridegroom, whether he chooses this virgin for his bride? To which the other replies in the affirmative. Upon this, the father turning the lady three times round, and giving her three strokes with his cudgel on the back; *my dear, cries he, these are the last blows you are ever to receive from your tender father, I resign my authority, and my cudgel to your husband; he knows better than me the use of either.* The bridegroom knows decorum too well to accept of the cudgel abruptly, he assures the father that the lady will never want it, and that he would not for the world make any use of it. But the father, who knows what the lady may want, better than he, insists upon its acceptance. Upon this, there follows a scene of Russian politeness, while one refuses, and the other offers the cudgel. The whole, however, ends with the bridegroom's taking it, upon which the lady drops a curtsy in token of obedience, and the ceremony proceeds as usual. There is something excessively fair and open in this method of courtship. By this, both sides are prepared for all the matrimonial adventures that are to follow. Marriage has been compared to a game of skill for life; it is generous thus in both parties to declare they are sharpers at the beginning. In England, I am told both sides use every art to conceal their defects from each other before marriage, and the rest of their lives may be regarded as doing penance for their former dissimulation. Farewell.

Letter 111

From Lien Chi Altangi to Fum Hoam, first president of the Ceremonial Academy at Pekin in China.

Religious sects in England are far more numerous than in China. Every man who has interest enough to hire a conventicle here, may set up for himself and sell off a new religion. The sellers of the newest pattern[7] at present give extreme good bargains; and let their disciples have a great deal of *confidence* for very little money.

Their shops are much frequented, and their customers every day increasing, for people are naturally fond of going to Paradise at as small expense as possible.

7. The "newest pattern" satirized here is Methodism, which was often mocked in the literature of the era for being too emotionally demonstrative.

Yet you must not conceive this modern sect as differing in opinion from those of the established religion: Difference of opinion indeed formerly divided their sectaries, and sometimes drew their armies to the field. White gowns and black mantles, flapped hats and cross pocket holes were once the obvious causes of quarrel; men then had some reason for fighting, they knew what they fought about; but at present they are arrived at such refinement in religion making, that they have actually formed a new sect without a new opinion; they quarrel for opinions they both equally defend; they hate each other, and that is all the difference between them.

But though their principles are the same, their practice is somewhat different. Those of the established religion laugh, when they are pleased, and their groans are seldom extorted but by pain or danger. The new sect, on the contrary weep for their amusement, and use little music except a chorus of sighs and groans, or tunes that are made to imitate groaning. Laughter is their aversion; lovers court each other from the lamentations; the bridegroom approaches the nuptial coach in sorrowful solemnity, and the bride looks more dismal than an undertaker's shop. Dancing around the room is with them running in a direct line with the devil; and as for gaming, though but in jest, they would sooner play with a rattlesnake's tail, than finger a dice box.

By this time you perceive that I am describing a sect of Enthusiasts,[8] and you have already compared them with the Faquirs, Bramins, and Talapoins of the East. Among these you know are generations that have been never known to smile, and voluntary affliction makes up all the merit they can boast of. Enthusiasms in every country produce the same effects; stick the Faquir with pins, or confine the Bramin to a vermin hospital, spread the Talapoin on the ground, or load the Sectary's brow with contrition; those worshippers who discard the light of reason are ever gloomy; their fears increase in proportion to their ignorance, as men are continually under apprehensions who walk in darkness.

Yet there is still a stronger reason for the enthusiast's being an enemy to laughter, namely, his being himself so proper an object of ridicule. It is remarkable that the propagators of false doctrines have ever been averse to mirth, and always began by recommending gravity, when they intended to disseminate imposture. Fohi, the idol of China, is represented

8. "Enthusiast" and "enthusiasm" were pejorative terms in the period. The Greek word originally meant possession by a god, but it was used in the eighteenth century to describe any extreme in irrationality, any sort of mania, and it was primarily applied to demonstrative religious groups.

as having never laughed; Zoroaster the leader of Bramins is said to have laughed twice, upon his coming into the world and upon his leaving it; and Mahomet himself, though a lover of pleasure, was a professed opposer of gaiety. Upon a certain occasion telling his followers, that they would all appear naked at resurrection, his favorite wife represented such an assembly as immodest and unbecoming. Foolish woman, cried the grave prophet, though the whole assembly be naked, on that day they shall have forgotten to laugh. Men like him opposed ridicule, because they knew it to be a most formidable antagonist, and preached up gravity, to conceal their own want of importance.

Ridicule has ever been the most powerful enemy of enthusiasm, and probably the only antagonist that can be opposed to it with success. Persecution only serves to propagate new religions; they acquire fresh vigor beneath the executioner and the ax, and like some vivacious insects, multiply by dissection. It is also impossible to combat enthusiasm with reason, for though it makes a show of resistance, it soon eludes the pressure, refers you to distinctions not to be understood, and feelings which it cannot explain. A man who would endeavor to fix an enthusiast by argument, might as well attempt to spread quicksilver with his fingers. The only way to conquer a visionary is to despise him; the stake, the faggot, and the disputing Doctor, in some measure ennoble the opinions they are brought to oppose; they are harmless against innovating pride; contempt alone is truly dreadful. Hunters generally know the most vulnerable part of the beasts they pursue, by the care which every animal takes to defend the side which is weakest; on what side the enthusiast is most vulnerable, may be known by the care which he takes in the beginning to work his disciples into gravity, and guard them against the power of ridicule.

When Philip the Second was King of Spain, there was a contest in Salamanca between two orders of friars for superiority. The legend of one side contained more extraordinary miracles, but the legend of the other was reckoned most authentic. They reviled each other; as is usual in disputes of divinity, the people were divided into factions, and a civil war appeared unavoidable. In order to prevent such an imminent calamity, the combatants were prevailed upon to submit their legends to the fiery trial, and that which came forth untouched by the fire was to have the victory, and to be honored with a double share of reverence. Whenever the people flock to see a miracle, it is an hundred to one, but that they see a miracle; incredible therefore were the numbers that were gathered round upon this occasion; the friars on each side approached, and confidently threw their respective legends into the flames, when lo to the utter disappointment of all the assembly, instead of a miracle, both legends were consumed. Nothing but thus turning both parties into contempt could have prevented the effusion of blood. The people now laughed at their former folly, and wondered why they fell out. Adieu.

4) Maria Edgeworth, *Murad the Unlucky* (1804)

Maria Edgeworth (1767–1849) is best remembered today for her realistic novels about her native Ireland, such as *Castle Rackrent* (1800) and *The Absentee* (1812). But she also wrote widely on a number of other topics, notably education, publishing her *Practical Education* in 1798. Strongly influenced by Jean-Jacques Rousseau's view on the education of children, Edgeworth saw narratives as one of the best ways to inculcate moral lessons for children and young people. When moral topics are treated in an abstract way, she argued, they make little impact; but when embodied in stories, they come to life.

To put her theories into practice, she wrote a collection of tales for young children, *Moral Tales* (1801), and then turned to a set of stories for older children—the reading group we today call "young adult." This was a three-volume set titled *Popular Tales*, most of which are realist and Irish or English in setting. But among the stories is "Murad the Unlucky," a late example of the prose "oriental tale" that began with the first publication of *The Arabian Nights* (in the original French, *Les mille et une nuits*) by Antoine Galland in 1704, and was given a more contemporary emphasis by Montesquieu.

"Murad the Unlucky" can be contrasted to Voltaire's "Zadig" in terms of both its realism and its moral or philosophical intent. Edgeworth's world is more concrete and less exotic than Voltaire's. The incident involving the baker is an example. And while both works have a didactic aim, Edgeworth's point about the actual nature of luck is more straightforward and less ambiguous than Voltaire's.

We present only the first chapter of "Murad the Unlucky," a bit less than half of the tale. Punctuation and spelling have been modernized.

MURAD THE UNLUCKY

CHAPTER I

It is well known that the grand seignior amuses himself by going at night, in disguise, through streets of Constantinople; as the caliph Haroun al-Rashid used formerly to do in Baghdad.[9]

One moonlit night, accompanied by his grand vizier, he traversed several of the principal streets of the city without seeing anything remarkable. At length, as they were passing a rope-maker's, the sultan recollected the Arabian story of Cogia-Hassan Alhabal, the rope-maker, and his two friends, Saad and Saadi, who differed so much in their opinion concerning the influence of fortune over human affairs.[10]

"What is your opinion on this subject?" said the grand seignior to his vizier.

"I am inclined, please your majesty," replied the vizier, "to think that success in the world depends more upon prudence than upon what is called luck, or fortune."

"And I," said the sultan, "am persuaded that fortune does more for men than prudence. Do you not every day hear of persons who are said to be fortunate or unfortunate? How comes it that this opinion should prevail amongst men, if it be not justified by experience?"

"It is not for me to dispute with your majesty," replied the prudent vizier.

"Speak your mind freely; I desire and command it," said the sultan.

"Then I am of the opinion," answered the vizier, "that people are often led to believe others fortunate, or unfortunate, merely because they only know the general outline of their histories; and are ignorant of the incidents and events in which they have shown prudence or imprudence. I have heard, for instance, that there are at present, in this city, two men who are remarkable for their good and bad fortune: one is called Murad the Unlucky, and the other Saladin the Lucky. Now, I am

---

9. Haroun al-Rashid ruled as caliph in Baghdad from c. 763–809 and presided over an era of great prosperity and cultural flourishing; he was in fact said to go among the people in disguise. The "grand seignior" of this tale is unnamed, but the story is set during the eighteenth century, and he may be identified with Osman III, who reigned from 1754 to 1757; he too was said to go out into the city in disguise from time to time.

10. The story of Cogia-Hassan Alhabal occurs in *The Arabian Nights*. The two friends give the honest rope-maker gold, which he loses; later, they give him lead, and he finds a way to use the lead to make his fortune.

inclined to think, if we could hear their stories, we should find that one is a prudent and the other an imprudent character."

"Where do these men live?" interrupted the sultan. "I will hear their histories from their own lips before I sleep."

"Murad the Unlucky lives in the next square," said the vizier.

The sultan desired to go thither immediately. Scarcely had they entered the square, when they heard the cry of loud lamentations. They followed the sound till they came to a house of which the door was open, and where there was a man tearing his turban, and weeping bitterly. They asked the cause of his distress, and he pointed to the fragments of a china vase, which lay on the pavement at his door.

"This seems undoubtedly to be beautiful china," said the sultan, taking up one of the broken pieces, "but can the loss of a china vase be the cause of such violent grief and despair?"

"Ah, gentlemen," said the owner of the vase, suspending his lamentations, and looking at the dress of the pretended merchants, "I see that you are strangers: you do not know how much cause I have for grief and despair! You do not know that you are speaking to Murad the Unlucky! Were you to hear all the unfortunate accidents that have happened to me, from the time I was born till this instant, you would perhaps pity me, and acknowledge I have just cause for despair."

Curiosity was strongly expressed by the sultan; and the hope of obtaining sympathy inclined Murad to gratify it by the recital of his adventures. "Gentlemen," said he, "I scarcely dare invite you into the house of such an unlucky being as I am; but if you will venture to take a night's lodging under my roof, you shall hear at your leisure the story of my misfortunes."

The sultan and the vizier excused themselves from spending the night with Murad, saying that they were obliged to proceed to their khan,[11] where they should be expected by their companions; but they begged permission to repose themselves for half an hour in his house, and besought him to relate the history of his life, if it would not renew his grief too much to recollect his misfortunes.

Few men are so miserable as not to like to talk of their misfortunes, where they have, or where they think they have, any chance of obtaining compassion. As soon as the pretended merchants were seated, Murad began his story in the following manner:

"My father was a merchant of this city. The night before I was born he dreamed that I came into the world with the head of a dog and the

11. "Khan" is a Persian word for a house—in this case, an inn for travelers.

tail of a dragon; and that, in haste to conceal my deformity, he rolled me up in a piece of linen, which unluckily proved to be the grand seignior's turban; who, enraged at his insolence in touching his turban, commanded that his head should be struck off.

"My father awaked before he lost his head, but not before he had lost half his wits from the terror of his dream. He considered it as a warning sent from above, and consequently determined to avoid the sight of me. He would not stay to see whether I should really be born with the head of a dog and the tail of a dragon; but he set out, the next morning, on a voyage to Aleppo.

"He was absent for upwards of seven years; and during that time my education was totally neglected. One day I inquired from my mother why I had been named Murad the Unlucky. She told me that this name was given to me in consequence of my father's dream; but she added that perhaps it might be forgotten, if I proved fortunate in my future life. My nurse, a very old woman, who was present, shook her head, with a look which I shall never forget, and whispered to my mother loud enough for me to hear, 'Unlucky he was, and is, and ever will be. Those that are born to ill luck cannot help themselves; nor can any, but the great prophet, Mahomet himself, do anything for them. It is a folly for an unlucky person to strive with their fate: it is better to yield to it at once.'

"This speech made a terrible impression upon me, young as I then was; and every accident that happened to me afterwards confirmed my belief in my nurse's prognostic. I was in my eighth year when my father returned from abroad. The year after he came home my brother Saladin was born, who was named Saladin the Lucky, because the day he was born a vessel freighted with rich merchandise for my father arrived safely in port.

"I will not weary you with a relation of all the little instances of good fortune by which my brother Saladin was distinguished, even during his childhood. As he grew up, his success in everything he undertook was as remarkable as my ill luck in all that I attempted. From the time the rich vessel arrived, we lived in splendor; and the supposed prosperous state of my father's affairs was of course attributed to the influence of my brother Saladin's happy destiny.

"When Saladin was about twenty, my father was taken dangerously ill; and as he felt that he should not recover, he sent for my brother to the side of his bed, and, to his great surprise, informed him that the magnificence in which we had lived had exhausted all his wealth; that his affairs were in the greatest disorder; for, having trusted to the hope of continual success, he had embarked in projects beyond his powers.

"The sequel was, he had nothing remaining to leave to his children but two large china vases, remarkable for their beauty, but still more valuable on account of certain verses inscribed upon them in an unknown character, which were supposed to operate as a talisman or charm in favor of their possessors.

"Both these vases my father bequeathed to my brother Saladin; declaring he could not venture to leave either of them to me, because I was so unlucky that I should inevitably break it. After his death, however, my brother Saladin, who was blessed with a generous temper, gave me my choice of the two vases; and endeavored to raise my spirits by repeating frequently that he had no faith either in good fortune or ill fortune.

"I could not be of his opinion, though I felt and acknowledged his kindness in trying to persuade me out of my settled melancholy. I knew it was in vain for me to exert myself, because I was sure that, do what I would, I should still be Murad the Unlucky. My brother, on the contrary, was nowise cast down, even by the poverty in which my father left us: he said he was sure he should find some means of maintaining himself; and so he did.

"On examining our china vases, he found in them a powder of a bright scarlet color; and it occurred to him that it would make a fine dye. He tried it, and after some trouble, it succeeded to admiration.

"During my father's lifetime, my mother had been supplied with rich dresses by one of the merchants who was employed by the ladies of the grand seignior's seraglio. My brother had done this merchant some trifling favors, and, upon application to him, he readily engaged to recommend the new scarlet dye. Indeed, it was so beautiful, that, the moment it was seen, it was preferred to every other color. Saladin's shop was soon crowded with customers; and his winning manners and pleasant conversation were almost as advantageous to him as his scarlet dye. On the contrary, I observed that the first glance at my melancholy countenance was sufficient to disgust everyone who saw me. I perceived this plainly; and it only confirmed me the more in my belief in my own evil destiny.

"It happened one day that a lady, richly appareled and attended by two female slaves, came to my brother's house to make some purchases. He was out, and I alone was left to attend to the shop. After she had looked over some goods, she chanced to see my china vase, which was in the room. She took a prodigious fancy to it, and offered me any price if I would part with it; but this I declined doing, because I believed that I should draw down upon my head some dreadful calamity if I voluntarily relinquished the talisman. Irritated by my refusal, the lady, according to the custom of her sex, became more resolute in her purpose; but neither entreaties nor money could change my determination. Provoked beyond measure at my obstinacy, as she called it, she left the house.

"On my brother's return, I related to him what had happened, and expected that he would have praised me for my prudence; but, on the contrary, he blamed me for the superstitious value I set upon the verses on my vase; and observed that it would be the height of folly to lose a certain means of advancing my fortune for the uncertain hope of magical protection. I could not bring myself to be of his opinion; I had not the courage to follow the advice he gave. The next day the lady returned, and my brother sold his vase to her for ten thousand pieces of gold. This money he laid out in the most advantageous manner, by purchasing a new stock of merchandise. I repented when it was too late; but I believe it is part of the fatality attending certain persons, that they cannot decide rightly at the proper moment. When the opportunity has been lost, I have always regretted that I did not do exactly the contrary to what I had previously determined upon. Often, whilst I was hesitating, the favorable moment passed.[12] Now this is what I call being unlucky. But to proceed with my story.

"The lady who bought my brother Saladin's vase was the favorite of the sultan, and all-powerful in the seraglio. Her dislike to me, in consequence of my opposition to her wishes, was so violent, that she refused to return to my brother's house while I remained there. He was unwilling to part with me; but I could not bear to be the ruin of so good a brother. Without telling him my design, I left his house careless of what should become of me. Hunger, however, soon compelled me to think of some immediate mode of obtaining relief. I sat down upon a stone, before the door of a baker's shop: the smell of hot bread tempted me in, and with a feeble voice I demanded charity.

"The master baker gave me as much bread as I could eat, upon condition that I should change dresses with him and carry the rolls for him through the city this day. To this I readily consented; but I had soon reason to repent of my compliance. Indeed, if my ill luck had not, as usual, deprived me at this critical moment of memory and judgment, I should never have complied with the baker's treacherous proposal. For some time before, the people of Constantinople had been much dissatisfied with the weight and quality of the bread furnished by the bakers. This species of discontent has often been the sure forerunner of an

12. *"Whom the gods wish to destroy, they first deprive of understanding."* [Edgeworth's note.]

insurrection; and, in these disturbances, the master bakers frequently lose their lives. All these circumstances I knew, but they did not occur to my memory when they might have been useful.

"I changed dresses with the baker; but scarcely had I proceeded through the adjoining streets with my rolls before the mob began to gather round me with reproaches and execrations. The crowd pursued me even to the gates of the grand seignior's palace, and the grand vizier, alarmed at their violence, sent out an order to have my head struck off; the usual remedy, in such cases, being to strike off the baker's head.

"I now fell upon my knees, and protested I was not the baker for whom they took me; that I had no connection with him; and that I had never furnished the people of Constantinople with bread that was not weight. I declared I had merely changed clothes with a master baker for this day, and that I should not have done so but for the evil destiny which governs all my actions. Some of the mob exclaimed that I deserved to lose my head for my folly; but others took pity on me, and whilst the officer, who was sent to execute the vizier's order, turned to speak to some of the noisy rioters, those who were touched by my misfortune opened a passage for me through the crowd, and thus favored, I effected my escape.

"I quitted Constantinople; my vase I had left in the care of my brother. At some miles' distance from the city I overtook a party of soldiers. I joined them, and learning that they were going to embark with the rest of the grand seignior's army for Egypt, I resolved to accompany them. 'If it be,' thought I, 'the will of Mahomet that I should perish, the sooner I meet my fate the better.' The despondency into which I was sunk was attended by so great a degree of indolence, that I scarcely would take the necessary means to preserve my existence. During our passage to Egypt I sat all day long upon the deck of the vessel, smoking my pipe, and I am convinced that if a storm had risen, as I expected, I should not have taken my pipe from my mouth, nor should I have handled a rope to save myself from destruction. Such is the effect of that species of resignation, or torpor, whichever you please to call it, to which my strong belief in fatality had reduced my mind.

"We landed, however, safely, contrary to my melancholy forebodings. By a trifling accident, not worth relating, I was detained longer than any of my companions in the vessel when we disembarked, and I did not arrive at the camp till late at night. It was moonlight, and I could see the whole scene distinctly. There was a vast number of small tents scattered over a desert of white sand; a few date trees were visible at a distance; all was gloomy, and all still; no sound was to be heard but that of the camels feeding near the tents, and, as I walked on, I met with no human creature.

"My pipe was now out, and I quickened my pace a little towards a fire which I saw near one of the tents. As I proceeded, my eye was caught by something sparkling in the sand: it was a ring. I picked it up and put it on my finger, resolving to give it to the public crier the next morning, who might find out its rightful owner; but, by ill luck, I put it on my little finger, for which it was much too large, and as I hastened towards the fire to light my pipe, I dropped the ring. I stooped to search for it amongst the provender on which a mule was feeding, and the cursed animal gave me so violent a kick on the head that I could not help roaring aloud.

"My cries awakened those who slept in the tent near which the mule was feeding. Provoked at being disturbed, the soldiers were ready enough to think ill of me, and they took it for granted that I was a thief, who had stolen the ring I pretended to have just found. The ring was taken from me by force, and the next day I was bastinadoed[13] for having found it; the officer persisting in the belief that stripes would make me confess where I had concealed certain other articles of value which had lately been missed in the camp. All this was the consequence of my being in a hurry to light my pipe and of my having put the ring on a finger that was too little for it, which no one but Murad the Unlucky would have done.

"When I was able to walk again, after my wounds were healed, I went into one of the tents distinguished by a red flag, having been told that these were coffeehouses. Whilst I was drinking coffee I heard a stranger near me complaining that he had not been able to recover a valuable ring he had lost, although he had caused his loss to be published for three days by the public crier, offering a reward of two hundred sequins to whoever should restore it. I guessed that this was the very ring which I had unfortunately found. I addressed myself to the stranger, and promised to point out to him the person who had forced it from me. The stranger recovered his ring, and, being convinced that I had acted honestly, he made me a present of two hundred sequins,[14] as some amends for the punishment which I had unjustly suffered on his account.

"Now you would imagine that this purse of gold was advantageous to me. Far the contrary; it was the cause of new misfortunes.

13. To be bastinadoed is to be beaten with a cudgel or stick.

14. Sequins were gold coins. Murad's reward is very generous.

"One night, when I thought that the soldiers who were in the same tent with me were all fast asleep, I indulged myself in the pleasure of counting my treasure. The next day I was invited by my companions to drink sherbet with them. What they mixed with the sherbet which I drank I know not, but I could not resist the drowsiness it brought on. I fell into a profound slumber, and when I awoke, I found myself lying under a date tree, at some distance from the camp.

"The first thing I thought of when I came to my recollection was my purse of sequins. The purse I found still safe in my girdle; but on opening it, I perceived that it was filled with pebbles, and not a single sequin was left. I had no doubt that I had been robbed by the soldiers with whom I had drunk sherbet, and I am certain that some of them must have been awake the night I counted my money; otherwise, as I had never trusted the secret of my riches to any one, they could not have suspected me of possessing any property; for ever since I kept company with them I had appeared to be in great indigence.

"I applied in vain to the superior officers for redress: the soldiers protested they were innocent; no positive proof appeared against them, and I gained nothing by my complaint but ridicule and ill will. I called myself, in the first transport of my grief, by that name which, since my arrival in Egypt, I had avoided to pronounce: I called myself Murad the Unlucky. The name and the story ran through the camp, and I was accosted, afterwards, very frequently, by this appellation. Some, indeed, varied their wit by calling me Murad with the purse of pebbles.

"All that I had yet suffered is nothing compared to my succeeding misfortunes.

"It was the custom at this time, in the Turkish camp, for the soldiers to amuse themselves with firing at a mark. The superior officers remonstrated against this dangerous practice,[15] but ineffectually. Sometimes a party of soldiers would stop firing for a few minutes, after a message was brought them from their commanders, and then they would begin again, in defiance of all orders. Such was the want of discipline in our army, that this disobedience went unpunished. In the meantime, the frequency of the danger made most men totally regardless of it. I have seen tents pierced with bullets, in which parties were quietly seated smoking their pipes, whilst those without were preparing to take fresh aim at the red flag on the top.

---

15. *Antis' Observations on the Manners and Customs of the Egyptians.* [Edgeworth's note, referring to the book of that title by John Antes (1800).]

"This apathy proceeded, in some, from unconquerable indolence of body; in others, from the intoxication produced by the fumes of tobacco and of opium; but in most of my brother Turks it arose from the confidence which the belief in predestination inspired. When a bullet killed one of their companions, they only observed, scarcely taking the pipes from their mouths, 'Our hour is not yet come: it is not the will of Mahomet that we should fall.'[16]

"I own that this rash security appeared to me, at first, surprising, but it soon ceased to strike me with wonder, and it even tended to confirm my favorite opinion, that some were born to good and some to evil fortune. I became almost as careless as my companions, from following the same course of reasoning. 'It is not,' thought I, 'in the power of human prudence to avert the stroke of destiny. I shall perhaps die tomorrow; let me therefore enjoy today.'

"I now made it my study every day to procure as much amusement as possible. My poverty, as you will imagine, restricted me from indulgence and excess, but I soon found means to spend what did not actually belong to me. There were certain Jews who were followers of the camp, and who, calculating on the probability of victory for our troops, advanced money to the soldiers, for which they engaged to pay these usurers exorbitant interest. The Jew to whom I applied traded with me also, upon the belief that my brother Saladin, with whose character and circumstances he was acquainted, would pay my debts if I should fall. With the money I raised from the Jew I continually bought coffee and opium, of which I grew immoderately fond. In the delirium it created I forgot all my misfortunes, all fear of the future.

"One day, when I had raised my spirits by an unusual quantity of opium, I was strolling through the camp, sometimes singing, sometimes dancing, like a madman, and repeating that I was not now Murad the Unlucky. Whilst these words were on my lips, a friendly spectator, who was in possession of his sober senses, caught me by the arm, and attempted to drag me from the place where I was exposing myself. 'Do you not see,' said he, 'those soldiers, who are firing at a mark? I saw one of them, just now, deliberately taking aim at your turban; and observe, he is now reloading his piece.' My ill luck prevailed even at this instant—the only instant in my life when I defied its power. I struggled with my adviser, repeating, 'I am not the wretch you take me for; I am not Murad the Unlucky.' He fled from the danger himself; I remained,

16. Europeans tended to view Muslims, and especially Turks, as exceptionally fatalistic.

and in a few seconds afterwards a ball reached me, and I fell senseless on the sand.

"The ball was cut out of my body by an awkward surgeon, who gave me ten times more pain than was necessary. He was particularly hurried at this time, because the army had just received orders to march in a few hours, and all was confusion in the camp. My wound was excessively painful, and the fear of being left behind with those who were deemed incurable added to my torments. Perhaps, if I had kept myself quiet, I might have escaped some of the evils I afterwards endured; but, as I have repeatedly told you, gentlemen, it was my ill fortune never to be able to judge what was best to be done till the time for prudence was past.

"During the day, when my fever was at the height, and when my orders were to keep my bed, contrary to my natural habits of indolence, I rose a hundred times, and went out of my tent in the very heat of the day, to satisfy my curiosity as to the number of the tents which had not been struck, and of the soldiers who had not yet marched. The orders to march were tardily obeyed, and many hours elapsed before our encampment was raised. Had I submitted to my surgeon's orders, I might have been in a state to accompany the most dilatory of the stragglers; I could have borne, perhaps, the slow motion of a litter, on which some of the sick were transported; but in the evening, when the surgeon came to dress my wounds, he found me in such a situation that it was scarcely possible to remove me.

"He desired a party of soldiers, who were left to bring up the rear, to call for me the next morning. They did so; but they wanted to put me upon the mule which I recollected, by a white streak on its back, to be the cursed animal that had kicked me whilst I was looking for the ring. I could not be prevailed upon to go upon this unlucky animal. I tried to persuade the soldiers to carry me, and they took me a little way; but, soon growing weary of their burden, they laid me down on the sand, pretending that they were going to fill a skin with water at a spring they had discovered, and bade me lie still, and wait for their return.

"I waited and waited, longing for the water to moisten my parched lips; but no water came—no soldiers returned; and there I lay, for several hours, expecting every moment to breathe my last. I made no effort to move, for I was now convinced my hour was come, and that it was the will of Mahomet that I should perish in this miserable manner, and lie unburied like a dog: 'a death,' thought I, 'worthy of Murad the Unlucky.'

"My forebodings were not this time just; a detachment of English soldiers passed near the place where I lay: my groans were heard by them, and they humanely came to my assistance. They carried me with them, dressed my wound, and treated me with the utmost tenderness. Christians though they were, I must acknowledge that I had reason to love them better than any of the followers of Mahomet, my good brother only excepted.

"Under their care I recovered; but scarcely had I regained my strength before I fell into new disasters. It was hot weather, and my thirst was excessive. I went out with a party, in hopes of finding a spring of water. The English soldiers began to dig for a well, in a place pointed out to them by one of their men of science. I was not inclined to such hard labor, but preferred sauntering on in search of a spring. I saw at a distance something that looked like a pool of water; and I pointed it out to my companions. Their man of science warned me by his interpreter not to trust to this deceitful appearance; for that such were common in this country, and that, when I came close to the spot, I should find no water there. He added, that it was at a greater distance than I imagined; and that I should, in all probability, be lost in the desert if I attempted to follow this phantom.

"I was so unfortunate as not to attend to his advice: I set out in pursuit of this accursed delusion, which assuredly was the work of evil spirits, who clouded my reason, and allured me into their dominion. I went on, hour after hour, in expectation continually of reaching the object of my wishes; but it fled faster than I pursued, and I discovered at last that the Englishman, who had doubtless gained his information from the people of the country, was right; and that the shining appearance which I had taken for water was a mere deception.

"I was now exhausted with fatigue: I looked back in vain after the companions I had left; I could see neither men, animals, nor any trace of vegetation in the sandy desert. I had no resource but, weary as I was, to measure back my footsteps, which were imprinted in the sand.

"I slowly and sorrowfully traced them as my guides in this unknown land. Instead of yielding to my indolent inclinations, I ought, however, to have made the best of my way back, before the evening breeze sprang up. I felt the breeze rising, and, unconscious of my danger, I rejoiced, and opened my bosom to meet it; but what was my dismay when I saw that the wind swept before it all trace of my footsteps in the sand. I knew not which way to proceed; I was struck with despair, tore my garments, threw off my turban, and cried aloud; but neither human voice nor echo answered me. The silence was dreadful. I had tasted no food for many hours, and I now became sick and faint. I recollected that I had put a supply of opium into the folds of my turban; but, alas! When I took my turban up, I found that the opium had fallen out. I searched for it in vain on the sand, where I had thrown the turban.

"I stretched myself out upon the ground, and yielded without further struggle to my evil destiny. What I suffered from thirst, hunger, and heat cannot be described. At last I fell into a sort of trance, during which images of various kinds seemed to flit before my eyes. How long I remained in this state I know not: but I remember that I was brought to my senses by a loud shout, which came from persons belonging to a caravan returning from Mecca. This was a shout of joy for their safe arrival at a certain spring, well known to them in this part of the desert.

"The spring was not a hundred yards from the spot where I lay; yet, such had been the fate of Murad the Unlucky, that he missed the reality, whilst he had been hours in pursuit of the phantom. Feeble and spiritless as I was, I sent forth as loud a cry as I could, in hopes of obtaining assistance; and I endeavored to crawl to the place from which the voices appeared to come. The caravan rested for a considerable time whilst the slaves filled the skins with water, and whilst the camels took in their supply. I worked myself on towards them; yet, notwithstanding my efforts, I was persuaded that, according to my usual ill fortune, I should never be able to make them hear my voice. I saw them mount their camels! I took off my turban, unrolled it, and waved it in the air. My signal was seen! The caravan came towards me!

"I had scarcely strength to speak; a slave gave me some water, and, after I had drunk, I explained to them who I was, and how I came into this situation.

"Whilst I was speaking, one of the travelers observed the purse which hung to my girdle: it was the same the merchant for whom I recovered the ring had given to me; I had carefully preserved it, because the initials of my benefactor's name and a passage from the Koran were worked upon it. When he gave it to me, he said that perhaps we should meet again in some other part of the world, and he should recognize me by this token. The person who now took notice of the purse was his brother; and when I related to him how I had obtained it, he had the goodness to take me under his protection. He was a merchant, who was now going with the caravan to Grand Cairo: he offered to take me with him, and I willingly accepted the proposal, promising to serve him as faithfully as any of his slaves. The caravan proceeded, and I was carried with it."